NETWORKED URBANISM

Networked Urbanism
Social Capital in the City

Edited by
TALJA BLOKLAND
Delft University of Technology, The Netherlands

MIKE SAVAGE
University of Manchester, UK

ASHGATE

Published by
Ashgate Publishing Limited
Gower House
Croft Road
Aldershot
Hampshire GU11 3HR
England

Ashgate Publishing Company
Suite 420
101 Cherry Street
Burlington, VT 05401-4405
USA

www.ashgate.com

British Library Cataloguing in Publication Data
Networked urbanism : social capital in the city
  1. Sociology, Urban 2. Social capital (Sociology)
  3. Communities 4. Neighborhood 5. Social integration
  I. Blokland-Potters, Talja II. Savage, Michael, 1959-
  307.7'6

Library of Congress Cataloging-in-Publication Data
Networked urbanism: social capital in the city / [edited by] Talja Blokland and Mike Savage.
      p. cm.
    ISBN 978-0-7546-7201-2
  1. Sociology, Urban. 2. Social capital (Sociology) 3. Communities. 4. Neighborhood. 5. Social integration. I. Blokland-Potters, Talja. II. Savage, Michael, 1959-

    HT151.N477 2008
    302--dc22

                                                                        2007048812
ISBN 978 0 7546 7201 2

Printed and bound in Great Britain by
TJ International Ltd, Padstow, Cornwall

Contents

PART 3: URBAN ASSOCIATIONS AND SOCIAL CAPITAL

List of Figures

List of Tables

List of Contributors

Alberta Andreotti is economic sociologist at the University of Milan, Department of Sociology and Social Research. Her main interests are in social networks and social capital, local welfare systems and social services, poverty and social exclusion, and the middle classes.

Rowland G. Atkinson is Director of the Housing and Community Research Unit at the University of Tasmania. He is an expert on urban change and social segregation, with a particular emphasis on the neglected political and moral connections between affluence and its impact on social and spatial problems. His research has focused on gentrification, social exclusion, area effects and gated communities, while dabbling in the social effects and order of sound in urban space.

Talja Blokland is Professor at the Delft University of Technology. She is author of *Urban Bonds* (Polity 2003) and specialises in ethnographic analyses of urban inequality.

Nadia Joanne Britton is Lecturer in Applied Sociology at the University of Sheffield.

Tim Butler is Professor and Head of the Department of Geography at King's College London. He is an expert on gentrification processes and social stratification, and his recent publications include *London Calling* (Berg 2003, with Garry Robson) and *Understanding Social Inequality* (Sage 2007, with Paul Watt).

Alexandra M. Curley is a Post-doctoral researcher in the Department of Urban Renewal and Housing at TU Delft's OTB Research Institute in the Netherlands. Her research interests include urban poverty, social policy, housing mobility, and social capital.

Fiona Devine is Professor of Sociology at the University of Manchester, where she was Head of Discipline until 2007. She is an expert on social stratification and mobility using qualitative methods and her recent work includes *Class Practices* (Cambridge 2005).

Peter Halfpenny is Professor of Sociology at the University of Manchester, where he is Executive Director of the ESRC National Centre for e-Social Science (NCeSS). Until 2006 he was first Head of the School of Social Sciences. His research interests are in e-science and philanthropic giving.

Bruce D. Haynes is Associate Professor of Sociology at the University of California, Davis. He is an authority on race, ethnicity, and urban communities. His recent publications include *Red Lines, Black Spaces: The Politics of Race and Space in a Black Middle-Class Suburb* (Yale University Press 2001).

Jesus Hernandez is a PhD student at the University of California, Davis. His dissertation research links housing credit markets and residential segregation to the current subprime mortgage crisis and social reproduction.

Patrick Le Galès is Directeur de Recherche at CNRS (National Scientific Centre for Research) at CEVIPOF (Centre for political research) and Professor of Sociology and public policy at Sciences Po. He has published widely on urban sociology (*European Cities*, Blackwell 2002), the sociology of public policy and regional political economy (*Changing Governance of Local Economies in Europe*, Oxford University Press 2004).

Rosemary Mellor was a Senior Lecturer in Sociology at the University of Manchester until her untimely death in March 2001.

Floris Noordhoff was a PhD student at the Amsterdam School for Social Science Research based at the University of Amsterdam. His research interests are in poverty, social inequality and urban sociology.

Douglas Rae is Richard Ely Professor of Management and Political Science at Yale University. He is the author of *City, Urbanism and its End* (2003), and once served as Chief Administrative Officer of New Haven, Connecticut.

Mike Savage is Professor of Sociology at the University of Manchester, where he is Co-director of the ESRC Centre for Research on Socio-Cultural Change (CRESC). His recent publications include *Culture and Class after Distinction* (Routledge 2008, with Tony Bennett, Elizabeth Silva, Alan Warde, Modesto Gayo-Cal and David Wright) and *Globalisation and Belonging* (Sage 2005, with Gaynor Bagnall and Brian Longhurst).

Gindo Tampubolon is Research Fellow at the Institute for Social Change, University of Manchester.

Alan Warde is Professor of Sociology at the University of Manchester, where he was Research Director of the School of Social Sciences and co-Director of the ESRC Centre for Research in Innovation and Competition (CRIC) until 2007. He is an expert on the sociology of consumption and his recent publications include *Trust in Food: An Institutional and Comparative Analysis* (Palgrave 2007, with Unni Kjaernes and Mark Harvey) and *Culture, Class, Distinction* (Routledge 2008, with Tony Bennett, Mike Savage, Elizabeth Silva, Modesto Gayo-Cal and David Wright).

Preface

The concept of social capital has now been so much discussed that one may wonder whether there is anything to add. This collection of original commissioned papers reflect the editor's belief that there is. We have been inspired to write this book by three concerns. First, we believe that the spatiality of social capital has not received the attention that it deserves. We argue that to interrogate social capital from a position that takes space seriously redefines some of its taken-for-granted conceptions, such as the notion that specific sites contain a fixed amount of social capital. Second, we have felt that the much discussed connection of bridging and bonding social capital with weak and strong ties is at best too quick and possibly flawed – and definitely not approached enough from an empirical angle. Third, we are both concerned with changing cities and the consequences of urban change for social inequalities. Underlying all these concerns is our belief that a properly geographical and sociological account of social capital demands a more critical perspective.

From initial interests that started in 2001, this book has been in the making for a long time, for a variety of reasons. Some of the authors, such as Tim Butler, Fiona Devine and her colleagues, Bruce Haynes and Jesus Hernandez, have been extremely patient with us, and rewrote their chapters as our own thinking on the topic proceeded. We would also like to thank the others, Alberta Andreotti, Rowland Atkinson, Alexandra Curley, Patrick Le Gales, Floris Noordhoff and Douglas Rae who came on board more recently and have helped shape up this book.

During the time we have edited this book, we have benefited enormously from intellectual exchange with a variety of scholars. Researchers in the ESRC funded Centre for Research on Socio-Cultural Change (CRESC) at the University of Manchester/ Open University, have addressed issues of social cohesion in unusual and original ways, which have shaped the arguments of this book: thanks are due especially to Tony Bennett, Nick Crossley, Hannah Knox, Penny Harvey, Elizabeth Silva and Nick Thoburn for their reflections. Discussions in the newly formed Manchester Social Networks Analysis Group, and in the Department of Sociology have also been invaluable in exploring the relationships between networks and social capital. In the Netherlands, the Section of Urban Renewal and Housing at the OTB Institute for Housing, Urban and Mobility Studies at the Technical University Delft provided a platform for discussions on social capital, social cohesion and social networks in neighbourhood contexts. Thanks in particular to Reinout Kleinhans for his valuable suggestions.

We would also like to thank Jolien Veensma (Erasmus University), Martine Lansbergen and Truus Waaijer (Delft University) and, in particular, Petra Nijhuis (Erasmus University) for their support at various stages of preparing the manuscript.

We would like to thank Ashgate for having faith in this book. Ebru Soytemel, a graduate student at CRESC superbly edited some of the chapters, and Petra has done a fine job in editing other chapters and assembling the manuscript in a very short time. Finally, thanks also to Saskia Binken and Eva Bosch for their help with the proofs.

Chapter 1

Social Capital and Networked Urbanism

Talja Blokland and Mike Savage

Introduction

The concept of social capital has passed from being an interesting idea at the turn of the 21st century to being a policy 'doxa' a decade later. Any supposed 'lack' of social capital is now a matter for concern, requiring research and appropriate policy intervention. This book argues that the city, in all its complexity and grandeur, poses a major challenge to this agenda. Urban researchers have been studying social capital, though not under that name, for a long time, and have developed powerful understandings of the processes that both divide and unify urban dwellers. Contemporary urban changes associated with the decentralization of residential space, employment, and service provision has led to a new kind of urban life, where the nature of the social order is once again under discussion. Our book shows how subjecting social capital to urban critique may advance our understanding of contemporary spatial processes and inequalities.

In this introduction, we begin by arguing that the social capital debate rehearses long-standing themes in community studies, yet in a way which is 'urgent' and which cannot be shrugged off. This leads us to two specific analytical themes that frame this collection. In the second section, we explore how social network analysis can be used in urban contexts to inform our understanding of the exclusive and inclusive aspects of social capital. In the third section we examine how social capital itself needs to be seen as a spatial process. Finally, we introduce the chapters of this book, that each take on the challenges that a perspective of 'networked urbanism' poses to us.

Social Capital: In Need of Networks, in Need of Space

The concept of social capital has been the most remarkable success story of the social sciences since the 1990s. From being a relatively specialized, not widely used, concept in the work of Pierre Bourdieu (1985) and James Coleman (1990), it has been popularized, especially by the political scientist Robert Putnam, so that it came to be seen as of fundamental importance for explaining a range of individual and collective benefits, ranging from good health, personal income, democratic cultures and low crime rates.[1] Much academic and policy interest was generated by Putnam's (2000) book, *Bowling Alone*. Here Putnam argued that declining electoral turnout,

---

1 The terms of this debate and its key contributions are now rehearsed in a number of valuable publications, and we do not seek to cover this ground here. Good summaries of the

falling organizational membership, increased public cynicism and falling levels of inter-personal trust are related to a wide-ranging collapse in social capital. Putnam's work has aroused interest in the role of voluntary association membership both as a key indicator of the stock of social capital, and as an important vehicle through which individuals learn to relate to each other so that the beneficial effects of social capital are realized (Anheir and Kendall 2002; Putnam 1993; Paxton 1999; 2002; Li *et al.* 2003; Stolle and Hooghe 2003).

More recent work has seen the theoretical remit of social capital extended to include the significance of social networks, notably in Putnam's definition of social capital as 'features of social organization such as networks, norms, and social trust that facilitate coordination and cooperation for mutual benefit' (Putnam 1996, 67). Social capital has also been defined in more instrumental forms, where it equips people to either get by or get ahead through mobilizing resources by virtue of their memberships of groups and networks (Portes 1998; Briggs 2005; Lin, Cook and Burt 2001). Both meanings can be invoked simultaneously, apparently allowing individual and collective interests to be reconciled. Through this extension, social capital comes to be identified as part of the social fabric itself.

Some critics argue that the popularity of social capital to the wider social science and policy community is due to the way it provides a 'neo-liberal' account of the social, which packages the social as a beneficial, bounded, form of capital which can then be evaluated alongside other kinds of capital in measuring and accounting processes (see most stridently Fine 2001). Yet the story is a little more complex than this. Looking at this process of popularization metaphorically, we might see that social capital acts as a kind of Greek Horse which has entered the city of Troy – the stronghold of economists, policy makers, and political scientists who have excluded sociological concerns from their thinking. From the outside, the horse itself seems to offer the attractive possibility of bringing the social, in the form of 'social capital', into the economists' city: yet inside the belly of the horse, all kinds of diverse, nefarious, and unruly 'social processes' hide, ready to spring out.

And certainly, in keeping with this metaphor, as the concept of social capital has become popular, so its meaning has been broadened, and become more diffuse, permitting the prospects of a more fully sociological account which cannot so easily be bundled and reified as 'capital'. Bourdieu's (1985) conception of social capital as the exclusive networks of the elite had the advantage of defining the term in a clear and focused, even if reductive, way. Robert Putnam's early work (Putnam 1993), with its neo-Tocquevillian concern with the benefits of voluntary associations, had the even greater advantage of allowing measures of social capital to be readily derived from standard survey questions. However, increasingly, social capital has lost this clear specificity. Putnam's definition, which referred to social capital as networks and norms, always hinted towards a much broader, diffuse, understanding of the social ties that might produce co-operation and trust. At the time of our writing, there has been a minor research industry concerned with unpacking the different 'dimensions', or 'aspects' of social capital (see for instance Li *et al.* 2005; Halpern

---

concept are available in Field (2003); reviews of the empirical importance of social capital can be found in Halpern (2005).

2005). A particular growth of interest here is in the way that informal social networks of friendship, neighbouring, and more generally what Putnam calls 'schmoozing' might be important for generating trust and involvement (see further, Warde *et al.* 2005). Increasingly, a wider range of methodological approaches have been used, including an interest in qualitative research (Stolle and Hooghe 2003). With this broadening, the idea of social capital has begun to merge into the broader, and all too familiar, ideas of 'social cohesion' or 'community'.

Those concerned about social capital, then, seem to have returned to similar concerns to the classical sociologists like Weber and Durkheim, rephrasing old question of how social norms, bonds and reciprocities can be enhanced (Nisbet 1980, 46; Mazlish 1989). The same problems of definition which undermined community studies in the 1970s, rear their heads again (cf. Bell and Newby 1974, xlii).

We might, following Boltanski and Chapello (2005) see the appeal of social capital within policy domains as linked to the rise of the 'projective city' which they see as part of the 'new spirit of capitalism'. Drawing on a longitudinal study of management texts, Boltanski and Chapello show how between the 1960s and 1990s there was a remarkable growth of reference to networks as intrinsically valued aspects of organization. They argue that this indicates the rise of new principles of justification. 'This city is founded on the *mediating* activity in the creation of networks, making it valuable in its own right, independently of the goals pursued or the substantive properties of the entities between which the meditation is conducted' (Boltanski and Chiapello 2005, 107). So it is that policy makers of all kinds have found social capital a seductive concept, not only through the benefits it is supposed to convey, but also as a good in itself (see more generally Riles 2000; Knox *et al.* 2005). It has thus become subsumed with other terms such as 'sustainable communities', 'integration' or 'cohesion.' Survey analyses and policy research on public space and public safety (Oppelaar and Wittebrood 2006; Bellair 1997; Body-Gendrot 2001; Holland *et al.* 2007), on interethnic relations (Blokland 2003a; RMO 2006; SCP 2007) and on support for democracy (RMO 2007) show that worries about community or cohesion are not simply laments that we can dismiss as nostalgic, but are invocations to act. It may indeed be a selective reading of the past that cities used to be better places in previous times, but social scientists have long accepted the idea that reflecting on the past and comparing it with contemporary times is an active reconstructive process that serves to tell us just as much, if not more, about understandings of the social today as it teaches us about a past (see Halbwachs 1994; Vansina 1985; Leijdesdorff 1987; Passerini 1987; Fentress and Wickham 1992; Blokland 2001) So, however difficult it may be to hammer this down empirically, urban residents have a real sense that *something* about the social deserves attention and needs to be 'fixed'. Urban policy seems to have found that 'fix' in social capital. So inner city neighbourhoods that are not doing well on a number of statistical indicators need 'social capital', and new immigrants, that are not upwardly mobile, need 'weak ties' to get ahead. Youth problems in urban areas are being seen as a problem of having bonds that are too strong. Social capital hence serves as an urban policy 'fix', one that seeks to abstract a 'magic bullet' from the complex nature of the lived urban relations.[2]

This perspective takes little notice of the long history of urban research (on which, see, for example, Abu-Lughod 1991; Hubbard, Kitchin and Valentine 2004; Savage, Warde and Ward 2003; Parker 2003) which has shown how the city has always been a vortex of contestation and dispute as much as a site of solidarity and cohesion. We need to bring this tradition of scholarship to bear.

The thesis of declining social capital articulates, as did earlier social science theories of disintegration and mass society, with 'folk wisdom and political rhetoric alike' (Tilly 1984, 50–3). We argue for a perspective which respects and acknowledges people's everyday concerns, but avoids romanticism. This recognizes the contested and fraught nature of social relations, and links the idea of social capital to a wider ranging analysis of social ties. One way of rendering this point, albeit tongue-in-cheek, is that the social capital literature has caught up with Durkheim and Weber, but not with Marx or Simmel. More Marxist analyses demand more attention to power and structural inequalities. Attention to Simmel's ideas would raise more awareness of the countless minor 'sociations' and the *inter*actions that determine society as we play it (Simmel 1950, 48–51).

The chapters in this book are inspired by both the need to relate social capital to matrices of power and inequality, and by the need to explore more fully, how the actual ties and relationships which bring social capital about are spatially and socially organized. Situated case studies show how social capital is bound up with the relationality of social life (see Tilly 1998). We explore how trust, bonds, and connections are relationally constructed in ways which problematize the idea that any specific parts can be 'bounded' as a discrete 'social capital' variable (for a powerful account along these lines, see Latour 2006). We seek to elaborate these relational dimensions through focusing specifically on the network dimensions of social capital. Here, we deliberately invoke, and seek to deepen, two kinds of network thinking. One of these, originating from concerns of social network analysis, explores the specific kinds of inter-personal ties which facilitate mobilization, and hence allows more specific understanding of the dynamics of communication and socialization underlying social action. The other, for which we deploy the term 'networked urbanism', emphasizes the need to understand contemporary 'sociation' not in terms of bounded, small-scale, communities with an intense public realm, but in terms of

---

2 See Kearns 2004 for an overview of how this applies to British public policy programs. See Mayer 2003 for the approach of social capital as a 'quick fix'. For a full overview of social capital in relation to urban neighbourhoods, see Kleinhans 2004. See for concrete examples of such approaches in urban policy several national advisory boards to the Dutch government, like WRR (2005) and VROM-raad (2006), who have both advised in this direction, as well as RMO 2005 and 2006 for linking neighbourhoods and integration, and the connection of neighbourhoods and integration into one Ministry in the current Dutch cabinet. Earlier, the cabinet made explicit reference to social capital as a vehicle to reduce urban problems (see Blokland 2001 for a Dutch overview). Media coverage of the Paris riots of 2005 as well as of several incidences in the Netherlands make strong reference to the idea that youngsters, as do urban gangs in the US in the public opinion, are too attached to each other, a point also developed in some of the urban public health discussions and in De Souza Briggs 1998.

their decentralized, diffuse, and sprawling character which depend on multiple and myriad technological, informational, personal and organizational networks that link locations in complex ways (Castells 1996/97; Amin and Thrift 2002; Graham and Marvin 2001; Savage *et al.* 2005). Pursuing these network concerns in tandem, both through deploying aspects of social network analysis, and through reflecting on the character of 'network urbanism', allows us to develop insights into how new forms of inequality are created. In itself, this may help advance the research agenda of social capital. A more attuned understanding of the spatiality of social capital helps us to avoid simplistic and reductive notions. We elaborate on these points below.

Social Networks, Social Capital, and Exclusionary Mechanisms

There is a tension between the way networks are understood by researchers on social capital, and within the longer tradition of social network analysis. For Putnam, networks are means of securing ties and hence forging connections, whether of a 'bonding', or 'bridging' type. Within social network analysis, by contrast, the analytical focus is on distinguishing cliques and factions (for instance Scott 1990; Wasserman and Faust 1988), and on charting gaps, or what Burt famously calls 'structural holes' within networks (Burt, 1992). When we bring together the simultaneous capacities of networks to link and separate, we can fully address how social capital is embedded in webs of power and inequality. This also requires us to look at networks without abstracting them from their context.

Coming to social capital from a formal network approach, we may measure the existence of ties of certain types and *then* assume that these ties qualitatively produce social capital in consistent matters for everyone, independent of class, race, ethnicity and gender as categorical inequalities. To establish that certain networks exist and that there is a statistical likelihood that such networks produce social capital is useful, but does not reveal *how* this likelihood comes about. If we are to at least explore the potentials of social capital for making cities better places for those who live in them, we will need to know exactly how such workings come about, in their contexts. This is one of the arguments of Savage, Tampubolon's and Warde's chapter which shows how two different voluntary associations in Manchester have very different potentials for encouraging activism, and trust, and that this is in part related to their urban context. Attention to power (as Haynes and Hernandez will ague in their contribution to this book), a detailed understanding of people's structurally embedded agency in their social ties (as Blokland and Noordhoff show in their chapter), a focus on the normativity as part of all interactions including weak ties (as demonstrated in Blokland's chapter) and an eye for alternative uses of social ties as shown in Butler's, Curley's and Devine and Halfpenny's chapters, all contribute to our understandings of the actual workings of social capital.

Most of our work is critical of Putnam's often quoted distinction between bonding and bridging social capital, which is adopted from the network theorist Granovetter's distinction between strong and weak ties (Granovetter 1973). This allows Putnam to claim weak, bridging social capital as beneficial in allowing connections to be forged between different kinds of people, and to reserve the exclusionary aspects of social ties only to some aspects of bonding social capital, where ties cement internal solidarities. He develops this distinction using metaphors such as 'machers' and 'schmoozers', rather than through elaborations of social ties in particular contexts. Others have applied network theory more concisely (Lin, Cook and Burt 2001; Flap and Völker 2003), although they have often focussed on ego-centred networks rather than on the study of whole networks (see Freeman 2005; Scott 1991; Wasserman and Fasut 1994 for more discussion). In this volume Andreotti and Le Galès use such ego centred analysis to show how bonding social capital can be amongst middle class residents of Paris and Milan. However, the analysis of whole networks would theoretically fit better with the overall concern of social capital as how to access resources *not* existing in one's own circuit (such as developed by Burt's notion of structural holes) and would permit it to be related systematically to neighbourhoods, cities or even states, but is only occasionally used in studies of social capital. Here, the tradition of network analysis which studies community relations using 'whole neighbourhoods' (following in the long tradition of Wellman 1979, and Fischer 1982) offers a powerful corrective. As a method, these analyses allow empirical assessment of how far people's ties are locally organized, rather than assuming a priori that they would be forged in local settings and that if they are not, community has ceased to exist. This, in turn, enables us to study people's access to resources, rather than assuming that their places – and for example the extent to which such places are segregated – will reveal this to us. The chapter by Blokland and Noordhoff is illustrative of this point: although their interviewees, long term poor residents of three disadvantaged neighbourhoods in Rotterdam and Amsterdam, do live in deprived urban areas, Blokland and Noordhoff argue that it is not place, but agents taking positions as independent under conditions of structural dependency that is of main importance to understand the nature of their social ties.

Yet even though network theorists have been crucial in developing insights about contemporary urban attachments, their methods depend on abstracting ties from given locations so that their formal properties can be delineated. Such methods privilege the formal characteristics of networks which any network, in any location or through any media, can share. These abstractions then do not necessarily examine the everyday workings of social networks, and do not address how networks operate in practice. The mere existence of weak ties, for example, does not necessitate access to resources, even though statistically this may be predicted. The absence of social ties, in particular when 'draining', as Curley puts forward in her chapter here, can also enhance social positions of stability in people's lives. Savage, Tampubolon and Warde show that engagement and trust is generated where networks are more organized around cliques and factions, compared to where there are uncontested 'leaders'.

Contextualization of, and in-depth approaches to, social networks are of particular relevance when we discuss features of 'sociation' such as trust, reciprocity, honour, status or reputation and cooperation, core elements in the social capital literature. Trust, for example, is often measured through the survey question; 'do you think other people can be trusted or you cannot be too careful in dealing with them' or some variation of this. However, as Sztompka in his study on trust has shown (Sztompka 1999 see also Khodyakov 2007; Tilly 2005, 12) trust is not a stable characteristic or attitude of individuals, but a contextual, relational process. Moreover, ethnographic work can show that expressing trust in others is not at all the same as 'doing' trust in practice. For example, crack cocaine dealers in inner city neighbourhoods may express a general attitude of distrust ('you can't trust nobody in this game') and *at the same time* depend for their work entirely on a precious trust in particular others: in suppliers who have to sell them decent dope, in customers who need to be reliable and will not snitch, and on others who are instrumental to their business, providing them with space to bag and store drugs, or hide money (Blokland, forthcoming, Venkatesh 1999; Williams 1989; Bourgeois 1995.).

Survey results on attitudes to trust, therefore, whilst interesting as constructs in their own right, should not be treated as a proxy for the analysis of how trust is, or is not, generated in situated urban case studies. If social capital is to be fostered to resolve all sorts of social ills in an increasingly individualized, retreating welfare state regime, then the question becomes essential whether networks of certain formal types and measures work as support mechanisms in their own right independently of their association with the inequalities of race, class, and gender within with agents in such networks are positioned. The assumption that they *do* inspired public policy makers to stimulate social network formation. The analysis of the ills that such policies aim to challenge is deceivingly simple: social problems are expressions of social exclusion, social exclusion results from an imbalance between integration and differentiation, and more social capital will better integrate excluded individuals into 'society' and strengthen the social fabric overall. Several chapters in this book will show the complexity of social networks and their value; a better understanding of such networks and the actual workings of social capital in such networks may eventually also contribute to a more nuanced policy approach.

The Spatiality of Social Capital

Our second focus concerns elaborating the connection between social capital and space. Most academics have not focussed explicitly on the spatiality of social capital, yet urban policy makers *are* implicitly working with assumptions about social capital and space, in ways actually quite similar to the earlier concerns about community. Here, according to Wellman's account of 'community lost', it was assumed that if one could not find a vibrant face to face neighbourhood community, then community itself was lost (Wellman 1979, 1201–31; Abu-Lughod 1991, 310-1; also Blokland 2003: ch 3). Social capital seems to travel down a similar road: if within a spatially bounded area people seem to be deprived, and where little support among neighbours can be measured, the 'neighbourhood' is said to lack social capital.

That is not good enough. We need to better understand the spatial contexts of social capital formation. In part because of its provenance in policy circles, measures of social capital are all too easily abstracted from place, where they become decontextualized and construed as abstract 'measures' and 'indicators'. But we cannot understand how social capital is changing and what we may want to do about it, if we *only* look at social capital as if it were unrelated to *where* the agents are engaged in the social relations that are held to produce social capital. This is the point developed by Atkinson who shows how far reaching the contemporary concern of the middle classes is to segregate themselves from the urban fabric. The study of social capital cannot be separated from this politics of inequality and territoriality.

In reflecting on how best to explore these spatial aspects of social capital, we need to avoid seeing space in terms of it being a 'container' that can be filled with 'more' or 'less' social capital. This is the danger with many of the attempts to formally measure social capital using survey measures. Putnam, most famously, examined aggregated trends in social capital first in Italy (Putnam 1993) and then in America (Putnam 2000) as if the boundaries of Italy, its Northern and Southern part, and the United States, as a whole and as states within the federation, are 'natural' boundaries for such considerations. In contrast to social capital research as conducted by (among others) Portes (1998), who discusses migration in relation to social capital and thus makes it an inherent part of their approach that social capital can travel across continents within networks of geographically dispersed people, Putnam's concerns tend to be confined to whether or not, or to what extent, such social capital is found within nation, state or city or neighbourhood borders.[3] Subsequent work has mostly shared this assumption that it is possible to determine 'stocks' of social capital in various kinds of spatial containers,[4] and stimulated seeking 'local solutions to local problems', through fostering local engagement and participation (see Williams 2005).   *k*

Theoretically, however, urban sociologists and geographers have thoroughly discredited this way of seeing space as just a container of smaller spaces, set off by boundaries within which social processes operate. Lefebvre's (1990) arguments that social relations are produced in and through the organization of space are now familiar within social theory, for instance in the work of Giddens (1985) or Harvey (1987). More specifically, the claims of globalization theorists that social relationships are stretched over space and that national boundaries are not necessarily of overriding cultural or social importance is mostly neglected within the social capital literature. An exception is debates about the role of the internet (on which see Putnam 2000, Chapter 9; Wellman *et al.* 2001; Urry 2002). But actually, even in analyses of the internet, space itself plays little role because *all* global space appears to become one container, with the instantaneous transmission of information through electronic communication (for a critique, see Allen 2003).

Alternatively, authors like Neil Brenner have argued for the need to carefully unpack the 'scaling' of state and social relations (see Brenner and Theordore 2002; also Smart and Lin 2007). When, however, rescaling is seen primarily (if not only) as coming from above (see Smart and Lin for a powerful, empirically grounded critique), localities in turn become – conceptually – bound regions (Olds and Yeung 1999, 535 quoted in Smart and Lin 2007, 283). Such critical views on space and relations have not informed social capital debates substantially, where the notion of space remains undertheorized Even if they had, one may wonder whether they

---

3 A comparable problem can be found in Florida's work on 'creative capital' in regions and cities, where these, too, are seen as discrete entities with clear borders (Florida, 2003).

4 There is now a burgeoning debate about the extent of variation between nations in their social capital (see for instance Putnam (ed.) 2003, Stolle and Hooghe 2003; Hall 1999; Paxton 1999; 2001).

would have contributed to a more relational understanding of space (see Blokland and Savage 2001).

Of course, for research reasons, it is obvious that borders need to be drawn, even if only pragmatically. These will still reflect, as we will see in the second chapter of this volume, material changes in the nature of urban relations (Rae 2003; Harding 2007: 443–4). But it is still necessary to reflect on how such pragmatic borders are aligned, or not, with those of multiple social agents (Swyngedouw 1997 quoted in Harding 2007). However, that cultural borders cannot be a priori geographical and coincide with state, regional or nation state borders, raises questions especially once we aim to understand social capital and space: after all, social capital presumes overcoming distances of diversity, while spatially such diversity may have become closer. In the words of Gupta and Ferguson:

> We need to account sociologically for the fact that the distance between the rich in Bombay and those in London may be much shorter than that between different classes in the same city. Physical location and physical territory seemed for a long time the only grid on which cultural differences could be mapped. It is now time to reconceptualize this, and look for new angles from which to study cultural difference (1997: 5).

This critique of methodological nationalism is well established in the social sciences (Glick Schiller 2001; Beck 2002; Urry 2003), and there is a burgeoning interest in diasporas and cosmopolitanism. We do not have to go across assumed borders to observe that social capital invites comparisons other than between states and regions, comparisons that may contribute to a better understanding of the actual mechanisms through which social capital operates and the role of space in such mechanisms. It is abundantly clear that different social groups vary considerably in how much social capital they have access to, with more affluent groups nearly always having higher 'stocks' (Li *et al.* 2003; 2004). It thus may make more sense to compare the social capital of different social groups, rather than nations, regions or cities. Cities, as well as nation states, need to be relationally defined. Active processes of 'boundary work' can then be seen as central to the formation of social capital itself.

Spatial conceptions, especially the small town and village versus the large city, do feature to a certain extent in the social capital literature. This draws on long standing images about the way that 'community' has long been perceived and studied. Indeed, Putnam acknowledges that social capital is 'to some extent merely new language for a very old debate in American intellectual circles' (Putnam 2000, 24). However, as numerous commentators have indicated (see Edwards 2004), Putnam's account of the virtues of settled family and community life paints a rather selective past – not that 'nothing has changed', but the connection between changes in spatial structures, mobilities and time and space are easily being confused with changes in the moral character of people.

There is, for example, the idea that community finds its most fertile soil in small towns or in neighbourhoods that function as urban villages. Putnam sees 'sprawl' as an important factor in the decline of social capital. His evidence suggests that 'residents of small towns and rural areas are more altruistic, honest and trusting than other Americans. In fact, even among suburbs, smaller is better from a social capital point of view' (Putnam 2000, 205). But, Putnam continues, 'as suburbanization continued, however, the suburbs themselves fragmented into a sociological mosaic – collectively heterogeneous but individually homogeneous, as people fleeing the city sorted themselves into more and more finely distinguished "lifestyle enclaves" segregated by race, class, education, life stage and so on' (but see Lewis 2004). He endorses Jacobs' arguments that 'regular contact with the local grocer, the families on the front stoop, and the priest walking the blocks of his parish, as well as the presence of street fairs and conveniently traversed parks, developed a sense of continuity and responsibility in local residents'. Here Putnam's interpretation meshes with the mass society thesis, as in Robert Bellah *et al.* (1985), *Habits of the Heart.* Bellah and his colleagues argued that old style American community life based on knowledge and tolerance of local residents was giving way to more individualized forms of attachment to lifestyle enclaves where one would seek out people like oneself to associate and mix with. Likewise, Putnam's pleas for neighbourhoods as the places where community ties could blossom and where diversity hampers this (as in Putnam 2007) assume a rather simple relation between community and a bounded space. These arguments are variations of the social psychological contact hypotheses (see Homans 1951; Niekerk *et al.* 1989) that to know each other will automatically result in caring for each other, combined with the idea that physical proximity will necessarily entail meeting others. Putnam's approach here contradicts the arguments developed by urban sociologists such as Claude Fischer (1982) who argues that cities allow increasing sociability. People chose their social contacts in an environment where a greater concentration of population gives them a wider choice of people who they share common interests with. This indicates that the very terms in which such debates are framed, with their assumptions about space and community, need to be questioned, and that a priori division between small places and community and large cities and disintegration, each with their own ways of life, is not the most fruitful way to think about community (see also Wellman and Leighton 1979), especially not under globalization (Eade 1997; Savage *et al.* 2005) but also historically (Scherzer 1992). Physical proximity provides local relationships with a specific context, but proximity only does not guarantee that relationships will be formed, as Bulmer (1986, 18-9) and Gans (1967, 154) have argued. Physical proximity may offer public familiarity, and, as we will see in the next chapter, centralized industrial cities of the past may have had better opportunities to develop such familiarity. But public familiarity should not be confused with having a dense network of *personal* ties that one may access to acquire resources. While some familiarity, and a context in which one repetitively sees the same people and can thus casually learn who they are without ever having direct dealings with them, may be instrumental to the eventual development of social ties (Blokland 2003) this is *not* the same as equating public familiarity with social networks, let alone a nice and warm community. In Fischer's words:

> Public familiarity is often taken (…) for private intimacy and public impersonality for private estrangement (…) But such public familiarity has nothing to do with people's

private lives. The friendly greeter on the streets may have few friends, while the reserved subway rider may have a thriving social life (Fischer 1982, 61–2).

In other words, public familiarity, or knowing about others in one's neighbourhood or town by sharing the same space for daily routines, *is not* the same as and will not necessarily result in communities rich in social capital, as such familiarity is a context for but not the content of interactions and social relationships. On the contrary; such public familiarity, as was common in, for example, Rotterdam's working class neighbourhoods in the first half of the 20th century can be just as much a context for exclusion and division among residents, through negative gossip and other mechanisms, as a context for community, trust and the like (see Blokland 2003 and the next chapter). As Blokland and Noordhoff show in their chapter here, mechanisms such as gossip, that presuppose at least public familiarity, may even be detrimental to the development of social capital. As noted, Curley shows how local ties can also be draining rather than supporting. Devine and Halfpenny demonstrate how such familiarity can be strongly excluding. In short, we need to base our understanding of social capital, not on a notion of what community used to be like (or of what we, for whatever reasons, selectively remember it to have been) but on an elaborated understanding of *contemporary* urban forms, which we call 'networked urbanism'. As we show in the next chapter by Blokland and Rae, historical accounts do not serve the purpose of showing better times and finding ways to return to those, but help us understand what historical developments have brought this networked urbanism about.

This insistence on the spatiality of social capital leads us to insist on the politics of territoriality. Social capital involves contestation over space, means by which people make claims on territory and seek to define themselves and outsiders, an array of 'others'. This is hardly an original point. The literature on the dynamics of voluntary association membership within community studies (nearly entirely neglected within the social capital literature) argues precisely such associations as intrinsically bound up with disputes over local belonging, a point further developed by Devine and her co-authors in this volume. In the UK, the tradition of community studies associated with Ronald Frankenberg (1957), Margaret Stacey (1960), Marilyn Strathern (1981), Jeanette Edwards (2000) and Ray Pahl (1965; 1970) has argued that local associations are far from 'neutral' associations which people might or might not join, but are means of establishing different kinds of 'insider' status in various local contexts (see also Elias and Scotson 1965). Similar arguments have been made in the USA, where notions of neighbourhoods as 'communities of limited liability' have attempted to move away from the idea that, localities need to be sites of convergence of likeness of social interests, and moral values (Janowitz 1974). Residents' involvement to and attachment with their residential communities vary greatly, and cannot be measured on a one-dimensional scale of 'more' or 'less'. In this book, Savage, Tampubolon and Warde bring out the implications of the way that a neighbourhood-based association generates different kinds of engagement compared to a group of city-wide enthusiasts. Moreover, where meanings of neighbourhoods are contested in place-making processes, we may not find 'one' community, but certainly social capital is being used, although analyses do not necessarily use the concept (see for example Berrey 2005; Pendall 1999; Walsh and Warland 1983).

Such spatial sensitivity may enable a more careful approach to the distinction between bridging and bonding social capital, by exploring the connection between spatial and social segregation. Put crudely, for Putnam, bridging social capital is good by establishing diverse links between different kinds of people, whilst bonding social capital is bad through establishing exclusive communities. Implicit within this formulation is, again, the idea of linking otherwise empty containers, with bridging social capital straddling these. However, as anthropologists of community have demonstrated, community ties do not form within isolated, bounded spaces. Rather, boundaries are drawn through dis-identifying with other locales (Cohen 1985). To this extent, the ties of social capital simultaneously create boundaries which distinguish 'others'. 'Insiders' and 'outsiders' are mutually constituted in the same process. If this point is granted, then we need to understand social capital as implicated in processes of boundary maintenance and division, which are simultaneously social and spatial formations.

When it comes to 'bridging' social capital, the theories of social capital that most strongly rely on networks too evoke an image of bridges between spatially separate sites. One does not have to support theories of meeting chance logics and contact hypotheses to see that bridging social capital needs encounters between people with diverse resources to happen. Practices of creating, maintaining and crossing borders make no spatial reference and they will often consist of interactions that take place in sites that are not without identities, and thus they are not empty spaces to be filled by social capital, but influence the very mechanisms through which social capital works. We cannot talk about such mechanisms other than within social spaces – and within processes of border formation, including those imaginary borders and actual borders (with Mexicans or other outsiders jumping over the American border). Social capital is both a way to establish borders and a way to establish relationships across borders and communicate understandings of the other's identity and social positioning. Meanwhile social capital can only be reproduced relationally.

Segregation, in residence, as well as in appropriation of other sites, is an organization of space that both results from social capital, and as we have argued above, that affects further capital formation precisely because spatial arrangements can affect network formations. For instance, space can be appropriated and given specific meanings, as when gentrifiers appropriate a park in a neighbourhood through setting the standards of what is and what is not acceptable (their drinking white wine at a neighbourhood picnic is, while the beer wrapped in a brown bag of a homeless man is not). Social capital in used here in very different ways. In turn, the appropriation of space serves as an exclusionary practice to maintain their local networks, and thus further affects the distribution of social capital among a *subsection* of neighbourhood residents. Without attention for such processes of place making and the practices of in- and exclusion and social capital formation they relate to, social network theories of social capital are unable to address the question of how precisely social capital does its work on the ground, in everyday life situations – and yet such a question is crucial for understanding especially the unequal distributions of social capital.

The spatial determinism that problematic neighbourhoods, cities or city-regions lack the sort of cohesion or community that is needed to be a place rich in social capital and thus to be a successful place is dominant in much urban policy, including regeneration strategies where the demographic make-up of areas is being changed. It also informs wide-ranging attempts to stimulate participation in all sorts of voluntary associations, community action and organization and other forms of civil society, as such participation is hold to create cohesion in a geographical unit as well as to enhance individual's engagement in 'society' and thus *by definition* their social capital.

The Aims and Structure of This Book

We argue that first, social capital research needs a wider acknowledgement that social capital is border-creating and maintaining, hence exclusionary and laden with power, and that its negative sides are thus not some contingent feature, but actually quite central to it. This, of course, is a point that Bourdieu has always argued, though he focuses on elite social capital, and in the development of the social capital debate with all its 'feel-good' flavour has thoroughly been positioned as a critical aside. Acknowledging this requires us to contextualize the study of social capital in terms of an understanding of the dynamics of contemporary urban relations. This leads us to our second concern, to challenge the lack of spatiality in the social capital concept as it is commonly used, that keeps from sight important dynamics of the workings of social capital.

As part of our concern to relocate social capital, we recognize that both voluntary associations *and* networks are crucial to social capital, and associations can often (but not always) be seen as special forms of networks. We seek to draw on the tradition of social network analysis, yet also to refuse its tendency to abstract social ties from their spatial context. The formal aspect of network research is important, and several chapters in this book such as by Savage, Tampubolon and Warde deploy it, but we also need to explore how resources are actually organized and deployed within networks. Drawing on Bourdieu and Tilly, we see social capital as assets in webs of relations of persons or sets of persons in which interaction might create a greater advantage for one than for the other.

We argue against the popular, but in our view poorly defined, distinction between bonding and bridging social capital. Bridging social capital can simultaneously create bonding social capital as it defines those 'insiders' in comparison to 'outsiders' with whom bridges are made. Bridging and bonding social capital become two aspects of one and the same process. This leaves too little analytical room for defining *how* these forms develop, other than differentiating between weak and strong ties. As several of our chapters show, weak ties do not guarantee bridges, and strong ties do not guarantee bonding. On a more practical level, we thus also criticize two assumptions common in all sorts of urban policy programs, (e.g.) that simply stimulating networks will bring about social capital, especially in deprived areas, and that stimulating all sorts of participation, especially on the local level, will do the same trick.

In emphasizing the contextuality of social networks, our starting point, elaborated in the next chapter, is to recognize how fundamental changes in the urban social fabric, described as the 'end of urbanism' by Douglas Rae (2003), or what we refer to as 'networked urbanism' relate to changing forms of social capital in the city. The 'urbanist' decades of the beginning of the twentieth century included among other things centralized manufacturing, mixed neighbourhood use, thick layers of locally embedded social organizations and networks, and congruence between economic, social and political citizenship when elites not only had their economic interests firmly located in one place, but also contributed to its civic texture trough actual residence within that city. Various processes – technological, economic and social – have changed this urbanism through decentralizing energies towards more peripheral locations. Efforts of local governments to alleviate poverty and poor housing conditions in cities have over the years brought improvements in other respects, but have not forestalled the end of urbanism. Most cities are, after all 'sitting ducks, unable to move out of the way when change come soaring at them' (Rae 2003, xvi). This has led to the emergence of what we call, 'networked urbanism'. As geographers such as Ash Amin and Nigel Thrift, or Stephen Graham and Simon Marvin (2001) argue, we are seeing the elaboration of a post-urban environment, where the core organizing role of the central urban public space is eclipsed, and we see the rise of decentred neighbourhoods and zones of activity, loosely and multiply connected to each other through road, telecommunications, and organizational circuits that have no clear centres or foci. But we need here, to avoid either demonizing or glamorizing these contemporary patterns: we do not argue that *life* was better, or that people as individual persons with their own peculiarities, tastes and desires were better, more solidary or whatever. There is neither logic nor an empirical base to justify the image that individual people were morally superior in other times or, similarly, in other places like the villages of Vermont.

Our objective, then, is to investigate 'making' social capital rather than 'having' social capital, recognizing that *where* we do this is a central aspects of our analysis. Although each of the authors have their own interpretation of social capital – and we have thought it necessary to give them their room to outline this – they all share the stress on the need to understand the *specific mechanisms* through which social capital operates through people and groups crossing borders, forming borders and maintaining borders. All chapters thus also show that social capital does not simply have a 'dark' side that complicates the story, but that its very workings are inherently bound up with unequal results for involved parties, as relationships are rarely so balanced that no inequalities are created or reinforced.

The first section sets the context by exploring the changing character of urbanism, and the extent to which changes in the urban form require us to see social capital as increasingly concerned with segregation. Chapter 2 elaborates the notion of 'the end of urbanism' and discusses the consequences for our understanding of networked urbanism. Blokland and Rae lay out the historical parameters which need to inform our current analysis. They show that to hark back to a social capital dependent on a dense civic infrastructure and public realm is fundamentally flawed because we no longer live in the kind of urban environment which allows this. We need, instead, to grapple with the contemporary dynamics of networked urbanism.

This theme is taken up in Chapter 3, where Rowland Atkinson further elaborates on the nature of contemporary segregation and isolation in new urban spaces. He explores the urban world of the affluent middle classes, as they flee central urban locations and mark out their exclusiveness. Refusing simple ideas of their being a 'creative class', he focuses on their concern to demarcate themselves from the wider urban population. He shows how powerful psycho-social forms of segregation are, and how they affect not only the increasing numbers of gated communities, but also more hybrid and apparently less segregated urban forms. He presents a powerful and evocative account of the difficulty of appealing to old communal identities in new forms of networked urbanism.

Chapter 4 by Bruce Haynes and Jesus Hernandez is an historical exemplification of these arguments. It zooms in on a core processes of the end of urbanism, namely suburbanization, and shows how new forms of social capital emerge in these new spaces. Using a case study of a middle class black neighbourhood in Yonkers in New York State, they forcefully show how power and exclusion are inherent to suburban development and how ignoring the matrix of inequality produced by race in much of the theories of social capital enables one to remain blind to power and structural inequalities and racisms.

The second section of the book focuses specifically on urban social networks, examining how far they can really address issues of social exclusion. This section reports a series of case studies with both poor, and affluent, urban dwellers, and the contrasts are instructive. In Chapter 5, Alexandra Curley takes issue with the underdeveloped notion of spatiality in social capital literature, as she questions whether geographical relocation has consequences for social capital formation of poor people, and if so, how. In her study of poor women who found new residences as part of the HOPE VI program, she found that the women had *more* weak, leverage ties in the concentrated areas where they had lived before, and also that strong ties could both be supportive *and* draining.

The distinction between strong and weak ties in the networks of poor people is further explored by Talja Blokland and Floris Noordhoff in Chapter 6, where they analyse through a qualitative study of poor residents of three neighbourhoods in Amsterdam and Rotterdam how interviewees reflect on their social ties, and what challenges they face to make these ties productive. Chapter 7, then, is the last chapter that challenges the policy suggestion that all one needs to do is, help people getting better networks, as Andrea Andreotti and Patrick Le Galès here show the exclusionary practices of network formation across spaces of successful middle class residents in Paris and Milan. They criticize the idea that affluent professionals and managers are withdrawing from their urban environment, and emphasize the density of their local ties, yet also point out how exclusive these are.

The final section of the book explores how voluntary associations and more generally the urban public realm allows the potential for significant interaction between different kinds of urban resident. Talja Blokland in Chapter 8 offers a further discussion of the argument that weak ties across categorical boundaries of race and class, especially to be achieved through local participation, will result in social capital for the disadvantaged. Through a case study of a gardening project in an American low-income housing development adjacent to a gentrified area she discusses social capital within participatory, mixed networks.

In Chapter 9, Mike Savage, Gindo Tampubolon and Alan Warde use case studies of the social networks of political activists in Manchester to show that not all kinds of membership create active engagement. Counter-intuitively, they show that an organization with more internal feuding is better able to generate activity from its members than in some which appears more efficiently organized. Similarly, the organization which is more closely related to the institutional organization of urban governance is better able to rouse its members than that which acts in more responsive mode.

This vision is explored through specific empirical reference in Chapter 10. Fiona Devine and her colleagues explore the urban politics of two affluent suburbs near Manchester. They point to the concern of leading local activists to define their locales as exclusive, yet at the same time they show how commercial development pressures and the wish to attract a wide clientele to restaurants, shops and bars can conflict with such pressures. They therefore emphasize the open and contested nature of urban politics in the contemporary British suburb.

The book closes, in Chapter 11, with Tim Butler's article which ties together many of the themes of this book. Discussing both Putnam's and Bourdieu's concepts of social capital, Butler explores how different gentrified areas of inner London create very different 'mini-habituses' which are linked to radically divergent amounts of social involvement. Rather than a simple model of middle class 'isolation', it is necessary to distinguish between alternative kinds of middle class relationship to the city. Butler's insistence that London, a leading global city, is characterized by such important spatial variation, is a final and ringing endorsement of our book's key message, that urban space cannot be abstracted out of the study of social capital, and that we need to recognize the complex interplay between social capital and urban space in further research.

Our case studies are drawn from different urban settings and can be read independently of each other, yet also provide a powerful demonstration of how we need to understand social capital in its intimate surrounds. This is an argument that has wider resonance to all those interested in contemporary social change.

References

Abu-Lughod, J. (1991), *Changing Cities: Urban Sociology* (New York: Harper Collins).

Amin, A. and Thrift, N.J. (2002), *Cities: Reimagining the Urban* (Cambridge: Polity Press).

Anheier, H. and Kendall, J. (2002), 'Interpersonal Trust and Voluntary Associations: Examining Three Approaches', *British Journal of Sociology* 53: 3, 343–362.

Beck, U. (2002), *Globalisation* (Cambridge: Polity Press).

Bellah, R. (1985), *Habits of the Heart* (Berkeley, University of California Press).

Bellair, P.E. (1997), 'Social interaction and community crime: examining the importance of neighbour networks', *Criminology* 35: 677–703.

Bell, C. and Newby, H. (1974), Introduction. In Bell, C. and Newby, H. (eds) *The Sociology of Community* (London: Frank Cass, pp. xliv–li).

Berrey, E.C. (2005), 'Divided Over Diversity: Political Discourse in a Chicago Neighbourhood', *City & Community*, 4 :2,143–170.

Blokland, T. (2001), 'Bricks, mortar, memories: Neighbourhood and networks in collective acts of remembering', *International Journal of Urban and Regional Research*.

—— (2003), *Urban Bonds* (Cambridge: Polity Press).

—— (forthcoming), 'Facing Violence: Everyday Risks in an American Housing Project', *Sociology*.

Blokland, T. and Savage, M. (2001), *International Journal of Urban and Regional Research*.

Body-Gendrot, S. (2001), *The Social Control of Cities* (Oxford: Blackwells).

Boltanaski, L. and Chiapello, E. (2005), *The New Spirit of Capitalism* (London: Verso).

Bott, E. (1957), *Family and Social Networks* (London: Tavistock).

Bourdieu, P. (1985), *Distinction* (London, Routledge).

Bourgois, Ph. (1995), *In Search of Respect: Selling Crack in El Barrio* (Cambridge: Cambridge University Press).

Bulmer, M. (1986), *Neighbours: The Work of Philip Abrams* (Cambridge: Cambridge University Press).

Brenner, N. and Theodore, N. (eds) (2002), *Spaces of Neoliberalism: Urban Restructuring in North America and Western Europe* (London: Blackwell).

Briggs, X. de Souza (2005), *The Geography of Opportunity: Race and Housing Choice in Metropolitan America* (Washington: Brookings Institute).

Burt, R. (1992), *Structural Holes: The Social Structure of Competition* (Cambridge MA: Harvard University Press).

Castells, M. (1996/97), *The Network Society*, 3 volumes (Oxford: Blackwells).

Cohen, A.P. (ed.) (1985), *Symbolising Boundaries: Identity and Diversity in British Cultures* (Manchester: Manchester University Press).

Coleman, J.S. (1990), *The Foundations of Social Theory* (Cambridge MA: Harvard University Press).

Eade, J. *et al.* (1997), *Living the Global City* (London: Routledge).

Edwards, J. (2000), *Born and Bred* (Oxford: Clarendon).

Edwards, R. (2004), 'Present and absent in troubling ways: women and families in social capital debates', *Sociological Review*, 52, 1, pp. 1–21.

Elias, N. and Scotson, J.L. (1965), *The Established and the Outsiders* (London: Frank Cass & Co).

Fentress, J. and Wickham, C. (1992), *Social Memory: New Perspectives on the Past* (Oxford: Blackwells).

Fine, B. (2001), *Social Capital versus Social Theory: Political Economy and Social Science at the Turn of the Millennium* (London: Routledge).

Fischer, C.S. (1982), *To Dwell among Friends* (Chicago: University of Chicago Press).

Frankenberg, R. (1957), *Village on the Border* (London: Cohen & West).

Freeman, L. (2004), *The Development of Social Network Analysis: A Study in the Sociology of Science* (Vancouver: Empirical Press).

Gans, H. (1967), *The Levittowners* (New York: Columbia University Press).

Graham, S. and Marvin, S. (2001), *Splintering Urbanism: Networked Infrastructures, Technological Mobilities and the Urban Condition* (London: Routledge).

Granovetter, M.S. (1973), 'The strength of weak ties', *American Journal of Sociology* 78: 1360–80.

Gupta, A. and Ferguson, J. (1997), 'Culture, Power, Place: ethnography and the end of an era', in: Gupta, A. and Ferguson, J. (eds) (1997), *Culture, Power, Place: Explorations in Critical Anthropology* (Durham: Duke University Press, 1–29).

Halbwachs, M. (1994), *Les cadres sociaux de la memoire* (Paris: Albin Michel).

Halpern, D. (2005), *Social Capital* (Cambridge: Polity Press).

Harding, A. (2007), 'Taking City Regions Seriously?', *International Journal of Urban and Regional Research*, 31: 2, 443–58.

Harvey, D. (1987), *The Condition of Post-modernity* (Oxford: Blackwells).

Holland, C., Clark, A., Katz, J. and Peace, S. (2007), *Social Interactions in Urban Public Places* (London: The Policy Press).

Homans, G. (1951), *The Human Group* (London: Routledge and Kegan Paul).

Hubbard, P., Kitchin, R. and Valentine, G. (eds) (2004), *Key Thinkers on Space and Place* (London: Sage).

Janowitz, M. (1974), Foreword In: A. Hunter (1974), *Symbolic Communities: The Persistence and Change of Chicago's Local Communitie*s (Chicago: Chicago University Press).

Khodyakov, S. (2007), 'Trust as a Process: A Three-Dimensional Approach', *Sociology*, Vol. 41, No. 1, 115–132 (2007).

Knox, H., Savage, M., Harvey, P. (2006), 'Social networks and the study of relations: networks as method, metaphor and form', *Economy and Society* 35:1, 113–140.

Latour, B. (2006), *Reassembling the Social* (Oxford: Clarendon).

Lefebvre, H. (1990), *The Production of Space* (Oxford: Blackwells).

Leijdesdorff, S. (1987), *Wij hebben als mensen geleefd* (Amsterdam: Meulenhoff).

Lewis, R. (ed.) (2004), *Manufacturing Suburbs* (Philadelphia: Temple University Press).

Li, Y., Savage, M. and Pickles, A. (2003), 'Social Capital and Social Exclusion in England and Wales (1972–1999)', *British Journal of Sociology*, 54: 4, 497–526.

Li, Y., Pickles, A. and Savage, M. (2005), 'Social Capital and Social Trust in Britain', *European Sociological Review*, 21: 2, 105–123.

Lin, N., Cook, K. and Burt, R.S. (2001), *Social Capital: Theory and Research* (New York: Aldine de Gruyter).

Mazlish, B. (1989), *A New Science: The Breakdown of Connections and the Birth of Sociology* (Oxford: Oxford University Press).

Niekerk, M. Van, Sunier, T. and Vermeulen, H. (1989), *Bekende vreemden: Surinamers, Turken en Nederlanders in een naoorlogse wijk* (Amsterdam: Het Spinhuis).

Nisbet, R. (1980), *The Sociological Tradition* (London: Heinemann).

Oppelaar, J. and Wittebrood, K. (2006), *Angstige burgers? De determinanten van onveiligheidsgevoelens* (Den Haag: SCP).

Pahl, R. (1965), *Urbs in Rure* (London: Weidenfeld & Nicolson).

—— (1970), *Patterns of Urban Life* (London: Longman).

Parker, S. (2003), *Urban Theory and Urban Experience: Encountering the City*, (London: Routledge).

Passerini, L. (1987), *Facism in Popular Memory* (Cambridge: Cambridge University Press).

Paxton, P. (1999), 'Is Social Capital Declining in the United States? A Multiple Indicator Assessment', *American Journal of Sociology* 105, 88–127.

—— (2002), 'Social Capital and Democracy', *American Sociological Review* 67, 254–277.

Pendall, R. (1999), 'Opposition to Housing: NIMBY and Beyond', *Urban Affairs Review*, 35(1): 112–136.

Portes, A. (1998), 'Social Capital: Its Origins and Applications in Modern Sociology', *Annual Review of Sociology*, 24, 1–24.

Putnam, R.D. (1993), *Making Democracy Work: Civic Traditions in Modern Italy* (Princeton, N.J.: Princeton University Press).

—— (1996), 'The Strange Disappearance of Civic America', *American Prospect*, 24, 34–48.

—— (2000), *Bowling Alone. The Collapse and Revival of American Community* (New York: Simon & Schuster).

—— (2007), '*E Pluribus Unum*: Diversity and Community in the Twenty-first Century. The 2006 Johan Skytte Prize Lecture', *Scandinavian Political Studies*, 30 (2), 137–174.

Rae, D.W. (2003), *City: Urbanism and its End* (New Haven, Yale University Press).

Riles, A. (2000), *The Network Inside Out* (Ann Arbor: University of Michigan Press).

RMO (2005), *Binding, Eenheid, Verscheidenheid* (Den Haag: SDU).

—— (2006), *Niet langer met de ruggen naar elkaar* (Den Haag: SDU).

—— (2007), *Vormen van democratie: een advies over democratische gezindheid* (Amsterdam: SWP).

Savage, M., Bagnall, G. and Longhurst, B. (2005), *Globalisation and Belonging* (London: Sage).

Scott, J. (1991), *Social Network Analysis* (London: Sage).

SCP (2007), *Interventies voor integratie. Het tegengaan van etnische concentratie en bevorderen van interetnisch contact* (Den Haag: SCP).

Scherzer, K.M. (1992), *The Unbounded Community: Neighbourhood Life and Social Structure in New York City 1830–1875* (Durham: Duke University Press).

Simmel, G. (1950), *The Sociology of Georg Simmel* (New York: Free Press).

Smart, A. and Lin, G.C.S. (2007), 'Local Capitalism, Local Citizenship and Translocality: Rescaling from Below in the Pearl River Delta Region', *China International Journal of Urban and Regional Research*, 31 (2), 280–302.

Stacey, M. (1960), *Tradition and Change: A Study of Banbury* (London: Oxford University Press).

Strathern, M. (1981), *Community at the Core* (Cambridge: Cambridge University Press).

Stolle, D. and Hooghe, M. (eds) (2003), *Generating Social Capital: Civil Society and Institutions in Comparative Perspective* (Basingstoke: Palgrave).

Sztompka, P. (1999), *Trust: A Sociological Theory* (Oxford: Oxford University Press).

Tilly, C. (1984), *Big Structures, Large Processes, Huge Comparisons* (New York: Russell Sage Foundation).

—— (1998), *Durable Inequality* (Berkeley: University of California Press).

—— (1995), *Trust and Rule* (Cambridge: Cambridge University Press).

Urry, J. (2002), *Sociology Beyond Societies* (London: Routledge).

Vansina, J. (1985), *Oral Tradition as History* (London: James Currey).

Venkatesh, S.A. (1999), *American Project: The Rise and Fall of a Modern Ghetto* (Harvard: Harvard University Press).

Völker, B. and Flap, H. (2003), 'The Strength of Weak Ties Revisited. The Case of East Germany', in Uslaner, E.M. and Badescu, G. (eds), *Social Capital and the Transition to Democracy* (London: Routledge) pp. 28–45.

Walsh, E.J. and Warland, R.H. (1983), 'Social movement involvement in the wake of a nuclear accident: Activists and free riders in the TMI Area', *American Sociological Review*, 48 (December), 764–780.

Warde, A., Tampubolon, G. and Savage, M. (2005), 'Recreation, informal social networks and social capital', *Journal of Leisure Research*, 37, 4, 402–425.

Wasserman and Faust (1994), *Social Network Analysis: Methods and Applications* (Cambridge: Cambridge University Press).

Wellman, B. (1979), 'The community question: the intimate networks of East Yorkers', *American Journal of Sociology*, 84: 1201–231.

Wellman, B. and Leighton, B. (1979), 'Networks, neighbourhoods and communities: approaches to the study of the community question', *Urban Affairs Quarterly*, 14 (13): 363–90.

Wellman *et al.* (2001), 'Physical Place and Cyber Place: The Rise of Networked Individualism', *International Journal of Urban and Regional Research* 25, 2 (June, 2001): 227–52.

Williams, T. (1989), *The Cocaine Kids* (New York: Addison-Wesley).

Williams, C. (2005), 'Cultivating Community Self-Help in Deprived Urban Neighborhoods', *City & Community*, 4 (2), 171–188.

PART 1
Social Capital
and the End of Urbanism

Chapter 2

The End to Urbanism: How the Changing Spatial Structure of Cities Affected its Social Capital Potentials[1]

Talja Blokland and Douglas Rae

Introduction

In Chapter 1, Blokland and Savage argued that the concept of social capital needs to properly confront the urban. This encounter, we argue, involves a greater attention to networks, and to the exclusionary character of social capital. In this chapter, we initiate this encounter through an examination of how urban relations are changing, and how this affects the nature of social capital. We draw here on our two recent books on urban change, showing how what Rae (2003) has identified as 'the end or urbanism' and Blokland (2003) as 'the privatisation of community' form a key, inter-related, framework for interrogating social capital. Our two studies developed independently, are based on different regions in the Western world, and use different research methods, yet we will show that they are complimentary in their analyses of change. Whilst neither one focuses explicitly on social capital, the empirical data and theoretical arguments in both, especially when combined, have implications for social capital theory.

It is clear that there is a dominant sense of urban malaise. Cities have changed in their capacities to generate what we may call 'effective personal encounters', and there

---

1 We refer to the two main sources of most or our arguments only more precisely when functional for the text here, and where we feel the reader may need more empirical detail than we can here offer. For methods and general framing of the thesis of end of urbanism, in particular to the debate on government and governance in political science, that we here omit but did form the context for Rae's original publication, see Rae (2003: Chapters 1 and 2). The second source that inspired this chapter is Blokland (2003) which consists of a study of change in community and place attachment in Rotterdam, the Netherlands and contains the methodology used. We draw some empirical examples from this study where useful, and the thesis of the relevance of public familiarity is further developed there. Incidentally, we also draw on a New Haven study by Blokland, and refer to Blokland 2008 for the methodology used in that study. We deliberately do not discuss the position of African Americans and the role of race in the city of New Haven since the 1950s. To do so duly would require too much space, and would not add substantially to the discussion of the very dark sides of social coital that racism constitutes discussed in the next chapter by Bruce Haynes. This issue is however extensively discussed in Rae 2003, see especially Chapter 8.

is increasing concern to generate policy intervention to remedy what is seen as the breakdown of urban social cohesion. The first 'path of repair' consists of interventions to stimulate network formation, especially among residents of disadvantaged neighbourhoods within their administratively confined 'spaces'. The second 'path of repair' is to enhance participation in all sorts of institutions, assuming that such memberships will eventually and automatically result in increased level of social cohesion – and, by consequence, social capital. We see here a politics characterised by the imperative to connect, seeking to recover a lost world of urban encounters, quite ignorant of urban changes or of a thorough understanding of social ties.

We might read this kind of imagery as a familiar, nostalgic, communitarian refrain, the kind which dates back to the romantic movement of the late 18th century. Yet we insist that we do indeed need to recognize that cities as spatial structures have changed, and that we cannot meaningfully seek to recreate some kind of 'lost urban community'. We need to place our understanding of the capacity of cities to generate social capital in the context of contemporary urbanism, not in terms of 'imagined community'. We want to show how what has been called the 'Golden Age' of social capital in the late nineteenth and early twentieth century rested upon a particular urban fabric which no longer exists. Only by recognizing that we now live in a situation of 'networked urbanism' can we understand the contemporary prospects for social capital. We propose here that social capital increasingly has become a feature of privatized communities; in contrast to Putnam's account, we are not 'bowling alone', but we are bowling in social circles of our own choosing, where social divides come to play an even more important role when they are expressed through spatial boundaries. This is a theme which is taken up empirically in many of the chapters to follow.

We show how the changing spatiality of social capital affects its character as a *public* or *collective* asset, and by consequence, its value for effective urban governance. In the first part of our chapter, we selectively summarize the thesis of the end of urbanism, as in Rae's *The City: Urbanism and Its Ends* (2003). Urbanists certainly have drawn attention to patterns of change in networks and space, for example in the work of Barry Wellman (Wellman and Leighton 1979, Wellman 1979) or Claude Fisher (1982) and many authors who have followed into their footsteps (for example Oliver 1988; Guest and Wierzbicki 1999; Smith 2000; Hennig 2006; Völker, Flap and Lindenberg 2007). Whereas their perspective has consequences mainly for our understanding of social capital as the roads of individuals to access resources, students of suburbia (for example Gans 1967; Jackson 1985; Oliver 1988; Murphy 2007) have discussed whether the spatial form of suburbia affect the possibilities of social capital in its more collective form (albeit not always in social capital terminology). These bodies of literature have not, however, provided the detailed historical analyses of the consequences of changing urbanism for social capital of the city – in contrast to social capital in the city or in society at large. This is precisely the approach that we take based on *The City*.

In the second part of the chapter, we use parts of Blokland's *Urban Bonds* (2003) to maintain that the changes in urbanism as we knew it have not diminished social capital in its collective forms. Instead, what we will describe as the thesis of the 'privatization of community' has resulted in networked urbanism, where collectivities rich in social capital are still being formed, but have taken on forms that do not limit their bounded spatiality to specific cities, and which allow exclusive social groups to emerge with even greater force. This, we argue, then has profound effects on the potentials of social capital for urban governance. Methodologically, we draw on historical and sociological empirical research conduced in New Haven and Rotterdam, covering the 20th century.

Urbanism at its Height: Social Capital of the City

We need to avoid nostalgia at the outset. The local level of the city never was a bounded site for social capital to develop in some unspecified past. There never was a golden age of entirely autonomous grass root voluntary associations. Skocpol (2000 and 2003, see also Skocpol and Fiorina 1999) has shown that the conventional wisdom has since become that voluntary groups were tiny and local, and that, as Joyce and Schrambra (1996 quoted in Skocpol 2003) put it, 'spontaneous grass roots creations devoted to things apart from politics and governments' determined the rich civic texture of the Western world, in particular of the United States. Skocpol challenges this view. She argues that classic American voluntary groups never had predominantly local activities, and that most of these groups did not operate apart from politics and government. Organizations with a local presence in the USA were part of translocal networks as early as the days of the Revolution, and most belonged to federations by the late 19th century. Just like Scherzer (1992) argued on the basis of his study of New York City that people's personal social networks extended beyond neighbourhood and city in the 19th century, no matter the imagery now as if life was only local then, Skocpol shows that social capital vehicles like voluntary associations extended well beyond a locality.

In Europe, Savage (1996) has similarly argued that working class militancy in the 19th and early 20th century did not rely on the dense networks of occupational communities, so much as the ability of trade unions, Friendly Societies, and other mutual organizations to transcend specific locations through networked structures of affiliated branches. Such analyses offer critical perspectives to how space and spatial distances affect the potentials for social capital. After all, if associational life never was purely local, then the approach that face to face contacts create trust, and that trust makes democracy work better, and that the absence or decrease in face to face contacts thus accounts for a whole lot of the concerns with democracy and social cohesion, may be inaccurate.

A better starting point than the lament for local urban community is to focus on the city's intersection with political institutions. We define urbanism, then, as the pattern of private conduct and decision-making that by and large make the successful governance of cities possible even when City Hall is a fairly weak institution. Rae's study is an account of how New Haven has moved from a 'centred urbanism', when even with a weak City Hall (as between 1910–1917) rich urban interactions flourished to the post-war period when, even in the existence of strong local government, urban networks declined. In the earlier decades, 'collective' social capital did not demand formal policy intervention, but was generated as by-product of numerous urban processes. In the more recent period, however, this no longer happens, and collective social capital produces sectionalised, and privatised bonds and solidarities (and see also, Atkinson's chapter in this volume).

Processes contributing to urbanism

We can identify four key features of the days of New Haven's classic urbanism in the early twentieth century. Firstly, these were the days of booming industrial capitalism. The industrial convergence created large flows of products out of the city of New Haven and its region. This formed the basis for a powerful stream of investment in capital to energize the city. The wages earned in this growing industrial sector were the juice that nurtured a richly variegated community of retail businesses, a robust housing market and a textured city life. Most of all, industrial convergence meant a bountiful supply of relatively attractive jobs. This lured workers and their families into the city and kept them there.

Secondly, many hundreds of tiny grocery stores, saloons, bakeries and so on carpeted the city's neighbourhoods. This provided a potent source of social networks (and streams of income to proprietors). We should not romanticize this image as if to run into each other all the time would automatically create networks that were nice and friendly. But to run into each other within a locality on a regular basis creates public familiarity. Public familiarity, a term we adapt form Fisher (1982, 61–2), can be understood as where we position ourselves in relation to others on a continuum of privacy (how much do I reveal about who I am?) versus a continuum of access (is a space accessible to all or restricted to a private party?) (Blokland 2003). When we regularly meet the same others, we develop familiarity with them, even when we never speak with them but overhear their conversations with others, and such familiarity in the public space of a neighbourhood then provides a frame for social identifications – it enables us to accumulate the necessary knowledge about others to socially connect or keep our distance form others whom we can socially place. Even when friendships and love-affairs do not develop, we at least have a context to differentiate between who we consider to be us, and who we do not on the basis of more than basic stereotypes. We can thus develop a place attachment in ways we cannot with the same quality in spaces where such familiarity is lacking. Role differentiation (Hannerz 1980) has made, as we will argue below, such familiarity less likely. Public familiarity, not romantic close-knitted, nice communities provided the basis for social identifications and community. Exclusion was as much part of it as inclusion, but the local neighbourhood provided the stage.

The neighbourhood stores also mattered in another way: the resident-owners of these businesses had a vested interest in the locality, where they strongly depended on a local clientele and where the small scale of their businesses made, different from current chain stores, relocating less of an option. A decaying neighbourhood would thus mean less business. A vibrant community with a positive role of themselves as engaged business owners who cared about the place and its people would bring about business. Such dedicated shop owners could have a sense of betrayal when customers felt little loyalty to the local businesses as soon as cheaper chain stores came in (see Blokland 2003). Public familiarity, in turn, had potentials for social capital in ways that anonymous interactions with continuously changing others in suburban large shopping malls and their parking lots do not (cf. Jacobs 1961).[2]

Thirdly, centralised clustering of housing concentrated families of all social classes, races and ethnicities in a relatively compact city (although the African American population of New Haven remained numerically small until the 1950s, and European cities like Rotterdam saw large influxes of immigrants from abroad only after the 1960s). This was not so much a matter of taste. Cities at the turn of the twentieth century need not be seen as better places to live – in that sense, the rhetoric of a middle class flight is slightly mistaken: to vote with your feet becomes an option only if there are suitable alternatives. That middle classes and whites lived in the cities in greater numbers should be understood as driven by economic and technological forces, not choice: one simply had to live relatively close to one's job. Limited options for quick and reliable transportations kept the geographical lines of production and supportive services of all kinds, including banking, legal advice and so on, geographically compact. Whereas distinctive working class neighbourhoods did emerge, all groups lived in close proximity to others of very different economic strata. Combined with the public familiarity that developed through the density of mixed use of the city spaces, dealing with diversity was part and parcel of everyday life. That is not to say that all sorts of bridging networks across boundaries of race and class came simply into being. But the *potential* through repeated casual interactions in such a 'sidewalk republic' with limited options to opt-out was there. It is therefore *likely* that social capital of the bridging type was easier available, to the benefit of individual residents seeking for a housecleaning lady or a house to clean and certainly for the civic texture of the city, and thus for the smoothing of everyday life small scale endeavours (like running a local school or organizing a children's summer camp or soccer club). As we will see in the second part of our chapter, the current voluntary character of 'doing community' (cf. Jenkins 1996) has reduced the relevance of locality to such a civic texture.

---

2   Indeed, research addressing the current role of shop owners in social control shows that arbitrary accidental choices of locations of businesses in which attachment to the area plays hardly a role have changed the loyalties of small businesses to specific places as well as reduced their expectations of the loyalties of their clients (Blokland 2008, forthcoming). Historically, place created a context for local business people to connect identity with the neighbourhood and the city in ways that they currently do not. Grand Avenue in New Haven, for example, dotted with all sorts of business in 1910–1917, in 2003 was a decayed shopping street where none of the businesses interviewed reported to feel particularly attached to the area or feel they had a local role to play, none of the business-owners interviewed, with one exception, lived in the neighbourhood. All reported the access to the highway (sick!) as the major asset of their current location. This included a bakery dating back to the beginning of the twentieth century, where the person interviewed reported to find the Italian-American heritage of the neighbourhood of commercial value but 'not really more than that.' Similarly, in four shopping areas in Rotterdam, the Netherlands, two in post-war neighourhoods and two in prewar traditional European mixed-use areas, retailers felt little to no commitment to the area, were motivated only by economic reasons in their choice of location, and reported little to no social identification with their local clients.

Fourthly, New Haven had a dense civic fauna of organizations outside the business sector that provided another layer of social cohesion and governance, be it fraternities, mutual benefit societies or religious congregations. Often they were part of a state or nation wide web of organizations rather than spontaneous and grass roots. Yet they still had a specific role for social capital of the city. For example, the typically locally rooted but hierarchically imposed system of Catholic parishes counted 16 in New Haven, seven of which were founded after 1900, totalling over 60.000 parishioners. Of course, such figures do not say much. Indeed, the Italians of the St Michael's parish were far less likely to make it to Easter Mass than were the residents of Polish descent (see Rae 2003, 151–2 for details). But St. Michael's parish was intertwined with three mutual benefit societies, knitting the social fabric of the surrounding neighbourhood closely together, as the activities of these societies, in particular of St. Andrews, were again supported by local Italian-American businesses of various sorts. Whereas St Andrews Society and the St Michael parish continue to exist, its members have generally moved out of the city. Although some members continue to refer to the neighbourhood as 'theirs', their current involvement is mostly one of consumers. Most of this civic fauna was not just for the benefit of the city residents, but also run *by* those residents. Detailed analyses (see Rae 2003, chapter 5, in particular 164–5) show that organizations' leaders were not just drawn from elites, but also came from lower tiers of the economy and from working class neighbourhoods, ranging from railroad conductors to bricklayers and a saloonkeeper and cigar packer as organizational presidents. In such organizations substantial rationality of a shared common goal helped overcome other social distinctions and they were organized in a manner that was based on face-to-face contact with some regularity over time. This strengthened urbanism and meant social capital for the city, independently of whether or not they were local or just the local chapters of national, politically connected organizations. They may have derived their power to be effective in their aims from such wide networks. They were, however, also providing a layer of cohesion to the city.

Finally, then, locally constituted elites did have a specific role. A pattern of political integration was made possible by the concentration of leaders from business and civic organizations inside the city on a more or less full time basis. Absentee management of local banks, manufacturing plants, schools, civic clubs and congregations was exceptional. Thus economic citizenship, expressed as the ownership and active management of enterprise, generally coincided with political citizenship, expressed as local political participation and organizational membership, and, although to a lesser extent, social citizenship of both forming networks with others in the city to socialize and spend free time and of engaging in the social and cultural activities and facilities that the city offered. In New Haven between 1910 and 1917, then, city government was weak. But city government could be weak precisely because there was leadership in all sorts of other ways. The social capital for the city that came with this triple citizenship attributed to urbanism. A community of stakeholders was close to a community of residence. That made the city and its neighbourhoods sustainable in ways that policy-makers now often hold as their ideal.

Our point, then, is that the classic period of the industrial city did generate an institutional, social and economic environment in which local social capital could flourish, and which at least provided a suitable context to facilitate forms of support and identity It is not incidental that numerous historical studies have demonstrated how social and political movements both drew on, and in turn helped to constitute, this rich urban domain (e.g. on the rise of the labour movement in the United Kingdom, see Savage 1987).

The end of urbanism and the separation of economic, social and political citizenship

These features did not mean a golden age in all respects – intense poverty, racism and social distances, lack of sanitary facilities and clogging traffic were all part of daily life. One need not be sentimental, however, to observe that the patterns of social life then, within the spatial context of the city and under the conditions of economy and technology of that time, provided a social capital for the city that was inherently different from what it later became, and now is. This is not to take a view about whether there has been a decline in social capital as such, but we do argue that *for cities as entities to be somehow 'governed'* the heights of urbanism provided a different social capital than contemporary cities do, one in which a weak City Hall mattered less to the changes that mattered most to people. And not for long.

Electricity, mass transportation and suburbanization

Urbanism was not altogether popular, not even in its heydays. Many Americans had since Jefferson's days mistrusted cities, and just as elsewhere associated cities with fear (cf. Body-Gendrot 2001). The suburban ideal contrasted with the city as evil, and many became urbanites by default rather than choice. The American suburban way of life also acquired cultural meanings in America's national identity (cf. Beauregard 2006). Two developments, the advent of the AC electric grid and of automotive transport, set the stage for major changes: they created the possibility of mass mobility, and especially of mobility outside the grids of fixed transportation lines or other resources. These technological changes had large social impacts. AC electricity made the distribution of energy to almost anywhere possible. This enabled new ways of production other than on-site steam manufacturing, *and* real estate development farther away – and thus suburbanization (see also Lewis 2004 who argued that suburbanization of manufacturing and people dates back to the second half of the 19th century already). Open spaces once useful only to farming became accessible with the arrival of cheap automobiles. And they could be reached by the AC grid, and thus invited manufacturing, commerce and residence as never before.

All this set in motion an avalanche of spatial reorganization that determined the fate of American cities intensely, affecting all factors noted above. Whereas such developments also influenced these factors within European cities, the smaller size of European countries, especially small countries like the Netherlands, mediated the processes. A steam tram, for example, would connect New Haven to its outskirts, but in Rotterdam, where cars arrived much later than the T-Ford in the US. This tram had much more of a pull effect of people from the already existing villages and towns in the country side to the new opportunities of industrial developments in the larger urban cores. For example, the tramcar that connected Rotterdam with the South West Holland's islands connected cities and hinterland well from the 19th century onwards and provided opportunities to migrate to the city from rural areas and towns, rather than pulling away form them (similarly it was the implosion and greater crowding with cars that was the initial concern in New Haven, Rae 2003, 226–8). But the cheap labour that these migrants provided for the shipbuilding industries and harbours of Rotterdam also gave rise to its segregation by social class, with entire neighbourhoods developed in the Southern part of the city solely aimed at housing workers. Eventually suburbanization would set in here, too. Historical processes hence differed and followed different patterns in scale and time, but all affected the social capital in the city. Albeit such developments differed throughout the West, they share that they were far beyond the control of the city. Such developments took place on a scale that, as far as anyone 'steered' them at all, hardly took the specific interests of any city as such into account. The increasing mobility of capital and people, noted by so many geographers (for example and notably Castells 1989 and 2000, see also Urry 2000), and most recently incorporated in theories of 'rescaling' (for example Brenner and Theodore 2002), meant a rescaling of governance at that time already. The cheap automobiles that Ford produced affected government, but *also* governance of the city, because the city had to stick to its initial territory, while almost everything and everybody else can move – and increasingly so. And so they did.

Industrial Production and the Decline of Local Attachment

Industrial production, with the major firms around which the city had grown and expanded and around which its civic texture was formed, would disappear or change from the 1920s onwards. Again for contextualized reasons, such patterns of deindustrialization of specific types of manufacturing had also characterised a number of European cities (Rotterdam, with its harbour and shipbuilding, being one of them) In New Haven, they were being reorganized as part of larger corporations with headquarters far away, boards of directors and stakeholders with eyes for efficiency and quality of production but no heart for New Haven – and why would they – all led to a process of detachment between the needs of corporate management and those of the community that happened to have grown around the plants owned by that firm. Or they would go out of business, as did most of the ship building industry of Rotterdam later on (on such processes in British shipbuilding oriented cities, see also Roberts 1993). Such changes impacted the civic texture of the city and the commitments of elites, but also affected the congruence of political, social and economic citizenship in working class neighbourhoods like Hillesluis, a neighbourhood in Rotterdam South. Where this working class neighbourhood had been the site for making class, also in its political sense, it gradually became the site for unmaking class (cf. Savage 1996, 65; Blokland 2005, 124–5). It became the site where other salient divisions of categorical nature, such as ethnicity, became more pronounced markers of division and the demographic make-up of the areas change.

In New Haven, the cheap U.S. automobiles made suburbanization possible, and the flexible transport with trucks enabled the coming of chain grocery stores, as did the national emergence of new and more aggressive strategies for food distribution, organizing itself in ways that by definition would push neighbourhood grocery stores out of business. And as (affluent) people moved away from the central city, chain stores followed. Central corporate management would then determine that large economies of scale could be won by shutting down smaller, older outlets in favour of superstores, and even they would engage in deadly competition. This process was certainly more pronounced in American cities than in Europe, due to size, a much more interventionist state and other contextual factors, but took a similar course. And as people moved, societies and associations dwindled, and everyday social interactions within the city changed. That is not to say that people stopped using the city, as we will see in more detail below, but their everyday interactions no longer produced that type of public familiarity that it used to bring about in the early decades of the century, when most people lived most of their daily routines quite locally. Although they may still have travelled to a Cape Cod summer house, have had friends and families in far-away places and networks far beyond the neighbourhood even in other times (Scherzer 1992) it is everyday routines that we mean to point to.

What resulted, then, were indications of the end of urbanism. No longer did centred capitalism provide city government with great economic leverage over firms that need opportunities for land use. No longer was a central location superior to a peripheral one for a new factory, warehouse, or (especially in the US) retail store. In the US and Europe alike, middle class workers were no longer compelled to live near their places of work, and no longer were nearly all those places of employment located within the central city. No longer did civic institutions and neighbourhood retailing hence provide such a thick a web of social connectedness within city neighbourhoods. And no longer could city government afford to remain passive or rigid and unresponsive to its changing environment – and still succeed in governance of the city.

There is an interesting example of this in the case of New Haven. With the arrival of Mayor Lee, elected in 1953, New Haven entered a period of heroic governance, yet one which ultimately could not turn the tide of the 'end of urbanism' and indeed, indirectly, contributed to it. Lee's passion for slum clearance and regeneration was not that peculiar, as it fitted the trend of modernism of the time, including its extravagant physical determinism that good buildings in and of itself will make good places. Peculiar was his intensive and passionate management of government. Yet despite this he finally was unsuccessful in his aim to restore the urbanism that the city was losing, mainly because the underlying problems, some of which we have laid out above, that Lee's New Haven faced were so deeply rooted in history, so powerful and so complex, that no mayor could possibly had overcome them. By setting out to re-create a region in which firms ad families pressed inward to the central city, seeking out opportunities to produce, sell, and live in the middle of New Haven, Lee had set himself against history. With structures, as Community Progress Inc (CPI, see Rae 2003, chapter 11 for details) to expertly repair a tattered social fabric, Lee had taken on a project of social engineering that no government of any scale has successfully managed. Change continued, and urban regeneration only accelerated these processes: highways did, even when they cut right through the city, bring nothing to the city but only furthered decentralized. The demolishing of neighbourhoods meant the end to what was left of small retailers, and as they were so engaged and connected to locality starting anew some place else under changed conditions was hardly a viable option – a trend of changes in city businesses that was irreversibly underway due to increasing competition with larger firms anyway.

For our purpose here, it is important to note that the changes in residential location, location of labour, commitment of elites to the local scale and the increasing geographical mobility overall meant that to be a citizen was taking on quite a different meaning than it had in 1910–1917. In that period economic citizenship, political citizenship and social citizenship all tended to converge in the city. Hence the public familiarity, the social networks and the civic fauna that residents brought about together created social capital of the city, and thus opened up possibilities of governance. We need to recognise that this kind of urban structure is now lost, and we cannot usefully seek to recover it through policy initiatives, however well meant. The capacity of urban governance has consequently diminished.

Privatization of Community, or How *Schmoozing* Stopped Producing a Sidewalk Republic

Let us now consider in this second part of the chapter how patterns of private conduct and decision making that contribute to the successful governance of cities (urbanism) were affected by the changes we noted, and stress in particular the disappearance of a *self evident* relation between place and participation in patterns of conduct and decision making.

Individualization and bureaucratization

Firstly, cities have witnessed changing organizations and other forms of what we have called civic fauna. Organizations were crowded out by alternative uses of leisure time, including the rise of television (compare of course also Putnam 2000). Organizations of mutual insurance professionalised and became part of government and market programs including their bureaucratization (cf. H. Blokland 2007). Generic welfare state provisions on the bases of abstracted solidarity as well as individualised provisions by the market can both be seen as trends of individualization. Such bureaucratization and individualization also changed the civic fauna of the city, especially when connected with geographical mobility. To begin with, with the exception of religious organizations, participation became more and more a middle-class affair. Moreover, as noted by many others and mentioned above, organizations changed in kind: they moved from members to clients, and participation became more of a check book affair. There has been quite a debate about whether or not this negatively affects the social capital of society, whether it is a bad or a good thing or simply fits the post-modern times (Field 2003; Fukuyama 1995). For our purpose of discussing social capital of the city, the effects of these changing profiles of organization included the potentials of such organization for social capital of the city (or even the ward or neighbourhood): check book participation and virtual networks may thus clearly affect the social capital of the city – in type, that is. Skocpol's observation that local organizations had close ties to government and were more often than not chapters of national organizations does not change the fact that the localness of their on the ground activities was of a different nature.

For example, Rotterdam Catholic parishes and Protestant congregations run local community houses where children of the neighbourhood were lured in by giving them oranges if they sat through a Bible club or inviting them to come and play games if they first attended Mass. Up to the 1950s, to both civilize the urban crowds of the working classes (cf. Elias 1939; De Regt 1984) by offering them housing, health care, schools and social clubs as well as to emancipate them through social democratic and several Christian movements were forms of national or even transnational movements translated to a spatial site of neighbourhoods and blocks. Professionalization and bureaucratization of the social sector reduced the role of faith-based organizations in neighbourhoods, in, as was the case in the Netherlands, in a quickly secularising society with a growing welfare state. The increase of state involvement thus reduced the extent to which patterns of private conduct contributed to the welfare of citizens and, at times, to the governance of cities. The ideological basis of such locally embedded organizations that typically connected people of different backgrounds through a shared substantial rationality was exclusionary to outsiders and often paternalistic, but also included strong commitment to a place – be it a neighbourhood or a city. Firstly, the geographical mobility of those committed to social change based on political or faith-based ideologies was limited enough to make them 'do good' there where they lived. Secondly, the congruence of economic, social and political citizenship also may have implied an attachment to one place with an intensity that elites currently no longer display or practice. Thirdly, the engagement with local clubs and organizations that made up the civic fauna of the city came, so to say, naturally as part of urban life. There were no separated geographical arena's for different roles, so that whether or not one was going to be part of the Committee that would organize Christmas baskets for the poor was not a matter of weighting obligations as a social citizen and obligations as, for example, economic citizenship as a retailer, but part of the same social life. That is no longer the case.

The telephone and the internet

The possibilities of forms of citizenship detached from place were further enlarged recently by technological developments and their dissemination, such as the telephone since the late 19th century and the internet most recently. Social scientists have been discussing their impacts on ties, especially on face to face relationships and community (for example Fischer 1993, see also Katz *et al.* 2001, 406–7). The telephone, indeed, enabled residents of changing neighbourhoods like Hillesluis, where commonalities of class related life styles disappeared as the area became more and more heterogeneous, to continue patterns of family oriented community life. To have a daily chat, to point each other to good deals at the (now chain) stores, and for gossip about mutual acquaintances, an older resident would just as easily call her daughter living two hours away as she would step into her house before her daughter moved. What *did* change, though, was the use of public space of the neighbourhood for such casual interactions and the degree to which knowing about each other was a by-product of daily routines that one could hardly opt out of.

In their overview of the debates, Katz and colleagues show that the role of technologies for community is not univocal. Some, Katz *et al.* (2001) summarize, have argued that the internet destroys voluntarism needed for social capital. Others, in contrast, have stated that such technologies produce different communities, although not the traditional local ones. Whether or not the internet produces meaningful interactions has also been subjected to debate. Research on the role of internet and email communication is said to strengthen rather than to demolish local networks of governance and participation, or simply neighbouring. As Quan-Haase *et al.* (2004) have argued, online social contact supplements the frequency of face-to-face and telephone contact, as well as participation in voluntary and political associations. There is no a priori reason to assume that for a vivid civic fauna people actually need to only meet face to face, and there is compelling evidence that new ways of communication merely add more to already existing communication patterns. Stern and Dillman (2006) provide an overview of the body of research that addresses specifically whether or not internet usage pulls people's interests away from their local area or instead strengthens their 'participatory capital' on a local level (Wellman *et al.* 2001, 437 quoted in Stern & Dillman 2006, 411). They find that the role of modern communication technologies is supportive to the governance that is already in place. It does not seem to contribute much to new locally organized forms of participation, and not to enlarge the proportion of groups so far unlikely to participate. Applied to our framework, this means that the telephone and then the internet have further detached schmoozing from place and to an extent even from face to face relationships, although we admit that on the latter the jury is still out. Forms of social citizenship and political citizenship thus remain disconnected and fragmented, with the internet strengthening the geographical differentiation set in by other processes. It was precisely this multilayered commitment and attachment to one place that provided social capital of a not better or more, but thicker kind than do contemporary societies, organizations and networks.

Differentiation of role repertoires

So *something* changed when it comes to social capital of the city. Views diverge on the extent of change, its evaluation and whether the change can be expressed as more or less, social capital of the dense city with its vivid daily traffic that created public familiarity as the simple side-effect of going about one's daily routines is, in many cities and neighbourhoods in the West, no longer self-evident. Let us thus consider in more detail how the spatial differentiation of social, political and economic citizenship influenced social capital of the city. Two general patterns emerged.

First, roles, as defined by Hannerz (1980), have changed. To Hannerz, people assume the same role when they exhibit identical and somewhat standardized behaviour in a particular situation (1980, 101): an individual's role repertoire (a woman may be a mother, a wife, an employee, a teacher, member of a choir of a church and a neighbour, taking on these roles at different moments and in various domains) tends to stretch out over domains that are spatially further apart than they used to be a century ago. The children in the classroom are no longer by definition the children next door. The choice for a choir that sings well may be more important than the congregation with which it is affiliated. One may drive every Sunday to another town because the preacher there is closer to one's own interpretation of religious beliefs. The role of a brother who sends money oversees to his siblings in Morocco or India is interconnected and yet geographically dislocated from his role as a labourer, a neighbour or a member of the board of directors of a local mosque (built, as was the case in Hillesluis, with funds raised mostly abroad and not among the local Muslim population). Role repertoires have become more diverse and include more roles, especially for women who entered the labour market in larger numbers and in different types of jobs than they previously did – a pattern probably slower and with more pronounced effects in Europe than in the US. When factories left neighbourhoods and work changed in nature, the relation between class and culture changed (for overviews see Crompton 1998; Devine 1997), but we also see a change in the differentiation of role repertoires. Neighbours ceased to be colleagues. Leisure time possibilities have grown. Life styles have diversified. So, the role repertoires of individuals differentiated and became spatially more stretched out. Neighbourhood use and even city use, or the extent to which an individual or group fulfils roles in situations within the neighbourhood or city's geographical confines, thus changed over time and differentiated between sections of the population. Formulated a little more abstractly, we argue that social ties no longer have that multiplexity that they had in the heydays of urbanism, and have also and in connection to this become geographically more dispersed (see also Eade *et al.* 1997).

Whereas interpersonal networks have thus been fragmented as a result of increasing role repertoires and their spatial differentiation, and this is our second point, the extend to which a geographically confined area can be said to be one's home may continue to be of great symbolical value, while the daily life practices of doing community extend to wider geographical areas. Community, Jenkins argued (1996, 106) is processual and interactional:

> Saying this or that, participating in rituals, mounting political protest, fishing together, or whatever. It is in and out of what people *do* that a shared sense of things and a shared symbolic universe emerge. It is in talking together about "community" – which is, after all, a public *doing* – that its symbolic value is produced and reproduced.

We do not suggest that when one shared a place of work and a place of residence, these provided a set meaning to an experience of community. As Cousins and Brown have argued (1975, 55–6) religious groups or work gangs in 'traditional' communities competed: rivalry, not homogeneity characterized the working class neighbourhoods of the first half of the century. But the visibility of others in repeated casual encounters in public space and local institutions, resulting in public and institutional familiarity with others, diminished. Religion and class no longer determine community experience. And where they do attribute to it, they are no longer confined to the neighbourhood and no longer cover as much domains of our role repertoires as they did.

These processes, then, amount to a privatization of community: increasingly, people's imagined communities (Anderson 1990) have become private affairs of *bonds* (ties based on affinity) or self-chosen *attachments* (ties informed by substantial rationality) outside public and institutional spaces. Public and institutional spaces become sites where networks are developed with some, but not everybody. Plural lifestyles and systems of meanings and a differentiated and spatially dispersed role repertoire supply few compulsory frameworks for imagined communities. What we hence see is not that people stopped *schmoozing* or are all glued to their TV-sets and forgot what it is like to speak to another human being. They have continued schmoozing, and doing all sorts of other forms of socializing, supporting, helping out, providing social capital and cashing in on previous capital investments. But they no longer *have* to do so within the confines of their neighbourhood or city, and in this sense, the communities of social capital have changed indeed. Whereas the possibilities to choose one's attachments and one's distances were limited in times of high visibility of daily life, strong organizational levels or ethnic and religious group affiliations, and limited geographical mobility, such possibilities have greatly advanced since the 1910–1917 period. Our options have been enlarged to choose where to belong to and in choosing how strongly we want to relate to the localities where we live, and whether or not we would *want* out political, economic and social citizenship to coincide – and research in Rotterdam by Van de Land (2003) suggests that middle class professionals may have their voluntarism and professional connections to the city but keep these removed from where they live, so that organizations for the residents no longer are of the residents indeed. His analyses help us understand what the change sin role repertoires mean to social, political and economic citizenship. Based on an extensive study of the urban ties of middle classes in Rotterdam (see also Van der Land 2003 and 2005), he argued that contemporary connections of middle class residents to the city are diverse:

> … nowadays it is optional rather than inevitable to identify with local culture […] Many people who live in Rotterdam but do not live there […] have strong emotional ties with Rotterdam, which are similar to those of he actual inhabitants. It seems that feeling home in Rotterdam for the new middle class is not only related to their own house, but also to a past place of residence and, perhaps more surprisingly, to a habitus which centers around the place of work and the routines that go with that habitus […] ties based on proximity [do not] [..] so much manifest themselves in a literal sense, but more on a mental level. (Van der Land 2007, 488)

Participatory ties hence are geographically dispersed, and people may still identify with a city, but such place attachment may be one of a selective set of frames that one uses for social identifications. Consumption and expression through consumption which we tend to do with whom we know, not in order to meet new people, has increasingly become important. As a result, the communities to which we sense we belong have become privatized to a large extent and have lost their public and much of their institutional dimensions, at least to the extent to which such institutions implied or were based on automatic group affiliations that were given and could, at the time, not be fundamentally contested or simply escaped. By privatization we do not mean that they have become a matter of closed doors of the personal home, but that there are few compulsory frameworks left for whom we define we belong to; it is hence much more up to the individual to determine our conduct in daily practice (Elias 1991). That does not make us into atomized lonely urbanites, but into members of communities that we spatially define in more socially exclusive ways. We have not stopped schmoozing, but where we schmooze and with whom we do so is no longer determined by spatial opportunities and restrictions.

The individual freedom that privatized communities provide have consequences for social capital of the city: we have lost need, force and priority for creating such social capital in and for the city. As far as there is, then, still governance trough social capital, this is conceptually seen networked rather than spatial, and has lost is connection to one city as a site: in this sense, urbanism has truly come to an end. Patterns of private conduct and decision making continue to exist, but can contribute to governance on many levels, of which the city and its neighbourhood are only one. Doing all the things that added up to community still happen – but these are not communities as they were a century ago, and the changing nature of what people understand to be their 'communities' hence affects the potentials of governance.

Conclusion: Implications of the End of Urbanism and Privatization of Community for Social Capital of the City

To summarize, then, the 'urbanist' decade of the beginning of the twentieth century included among other things central manufacturing, mixed neighbourhood use, thick layers of locally embedded organizations and networks, and a congruence between economic, social and political citizenship when elites not only had their economic interests firmly grounded in the city, but also contributed strongly to its civic texture through their actual residence within the city borders. Various processes – technological, economic and social – have changed this urbanism. Efforts of local governments to alleviate poverty and poor housing in cities have over the years brought improvements in other regards, but have not forestall the end of urbanism: cities are 'sitting ducks, unable to move out of the way when change comes roaring at them' (Rae 2003, ixv).

The dense city of the early twentieth century provided plenty of possibilities for *schmoozing* in much more self-evident, less deliberately chosen settings than does contemporary urban life. That is definitely not to say that we are now disintegrated and move around in anonymous circles. In some respects the amount of local schmoozing remains strong, and we continue to schmooze without a need to do so locally *by definition*, but social ties have lost their multiplexity that characterised networks of earlier industrial cities, as role repertoires diversified. The degree of self-evidence in forming local attachments, through the civic fauna and through the coincidence of our various forms of citizenship, have affected not *our* potentials for social capital but have affected the potentials of social capital of *cities* and their neighbourhoods.

The end of urbanism thesis means, after all, that the local civic fauna and the local forms of citizenship, as well as the role of localism in all our everyday routines, have diminished. And that changing role of the local means, in turn, that both the city-based networks available to individual residents that are potentially useful to their advantage (Putnam's *Bowling Alone* interpretation of social capital) and the by-products of other interactions and transactions in the city that may create the trust that supports the institutional forms of governance (Putnam's *Making Democracy Work* interpretation of social capital) have changed. So a century after the period that we addressed here as a decade of high urbanism (1910–1917), cities have fundamentally changed in their social fabric, and new urban constellations have emerged that might provide social capital to some, but do so in more exclusionary ways, thereby confirming rather than challenging inequalities within cities and the various enclaves that can be found there – ranging from gated communities and gentrified neighbourhoods on the one hand to ghettos and poor enclaves on the other – and between central cities and their suburbs. All these spatial structures will be the sites of study in chapters to come.

References

Anderson, B. (1990), *Imagined Communities: Reflections on the Origin and Spread of Nationalism* (London: Verso).

Beauregard, R. (2006), *When American became Suburban* (Minnesota: University of Minnesota Press).

Blokland, T. (2003), *Urban Bonds: Social Relations in the Inner City* (Oxford: Polity Press).

—— (2008), Ogen op straat: sociale controle, veiligheid en publieke familiariteit (Amsterdam: Amsterdam University Press).

Body-Gendrot, S. (2001), *The Social Control of Cities* (Oxford: Blackwell).

Brenner, N. and Theodore, N. (eds) (2002), *Spaces of Neoliberalism: Urban Restructuring in North America and Western Europe* (Oxford: Blackwells).

Castells, M. (1989), *The Informational City: Information Technology, Economic Restructuring and the Urban-Regional Process* (Oxford: Blackwell).

Cousins, J. and Brown, R. (1975), 'Patterns of paradox: shipbuilding workers' images of society', in: M. Bulmer (ed.) *Working-Class Images of Society* (London: Routledge & Kegan Paul) SSRC, pp. 55–82.

Crompton, R. (1998), *Class and Stratification. An Introduction to Current Debates* (Cambridge: Polity Press).

Devine, F. (1997), *Social Class in America and Britain* (Edinburgh: Edinburgh University Press).

Fischer, C. (1982), *To Dwell Among Friends: Personal Networks in Town and City* (Chicago: University of Chicago Press).

Fischer, C.L. (1993), *America Calling: A Social History of the Telephone to 1940* (Berkeley: University of California Press).

Fukuyama, F. (1995), *Trust: The Social Virtues and the Creation of Prosperity* (New York: Free Press).

Gans, H. (1967), *The Levittowners* (New York: The Free Press).

Guest, A.M. and Wierzbicki, S.K. (1999), 'Social ties at the neighbourhood level: Two decades of GSS evidence', *Urban Affairs Review*, 35 (1): 92–111.

Jackson, K. (1985), *Crabgrass Frontier: The Suburbanization of the United States* (New York: Oxford University Press).

Jacobs, J. (1961), *The Death and Life of the Great American Cities* (New York: Random House).

Jenkins, R. (1996), *Social Identity* (London: Routledge).

Katz, J., Rice, R.E. and Aspden, P. (2001), 'The internet, 1995–2000: Access, civic involvement and social interaction', *American Behavioral Scientist* 45 (3): 405–19.

Lewis, R. (ed.) (2004), *Manufacturing Suburbs* (Philadelphia: Temple University Press).

Murphy, A.K. (2007), 'The suburban ghetto: The legacy of Herbert Gans in understanding the experience of poverty in recently impoverished American suburbs', *City & Community*, 6 (1): pp. 21–37.

Putnam, R., Leonardi, R. and Nanetti, R. (1993), *Making Democracy Work. Civic Traditions in Modern Italy* (New York: Princeton University Press).

Putnam, R. (2000), *Bowling Alone: The Collapse and Revival of American Community* (New York: Simon & Schuster, Inc).

Quan-Haase, A. and Wellman, B. (2004), 'Local Virtuality in a High-Tech Networked Organization', *Analyse and Kritik* 26 (Special Issue 1): 241-57.

Rae, D. (2003), *City: Urbanism and its End* (New Haven: Yale University Press).

Scherzer, K. (1992), *The Unbounded Community: Neighborhood Life and Social Structure in New York City 1830–1875* (Durham: Duke University Press).

Skocpol, T. and Fiorina, M.P. (eds) (1999), *Civic Engagement in American Democracy* (Washington, DC: Brookings Institute/Russell Sage Foundation).

Skocpol, T., Ganz, M. and Munson, S. (2000), 'A nation of organizers: the institutional origins of civic voluntarism in the United States', *American Political Science Review*, 94 (3): 527–46.

Skocpol, T. (2003), *Diminished Democracy: From Membership to Management in American Civic Life* (Norman, OK: University of Oklahama Press).

Stern, J. and Dillman, M. (2006), 'Community participation, social ties and the use of the internet', *City and Community* 5 (4): 409–24.

Urry, J. (2000), *Sociology Beyond Societies: Mobilities for the Twenty-first Century* (London: Routledge).

Van der Land, M. (2003), *Vluchtige verbondenheid: Stedelijke bindingen van de Rotterdamse middenklasse* (Amsterdam: Amsterdam University Press).

—— (2005), 'Urban consumption and feelings of attachment of Rotterdam's new middle class', *Sociological Research Online* 10 (2), <http://www.socresonline. org.uk/10/2/van_der_land.html>.

—— (2007), 'Cursory connections: Urban ties of the new middle class in Rotterdam', *Urban Studies*, 44 (3): 477–499.

Chapter 3

The Flowing Enclave and the Misanthropy of Networked Affluence

Rowland G. Atkinson

The extent to which people can learn to pursue aggressively their interests in society is the extent to which they learn to act impersonally. The city ought to be the teacher of that action, the forum in which it becomes meaningful to join with other persons without the compulsion to know them as persons (Sennett 1974, 340).

Introduction

The image of the ghetto has long been a focal point in urban sociological and spatial analyses. Our continued impressions of disconnected and concentrated poverty now contrast ever more sharply with the characterization of contemporary urban systems as dynamic and networked (Castells 1989; 2000). Spaces of urban poverty condensation persist not least because they are locked out, or bypassed, by this wider economic and social life of the city. A key feature of life in deprived areas has been the implied containment in place for residents, locked in by the 'weight' of their world (Bourdieu 1999) and the centripetal social forces of the local area, reinforced by discriminating media and social repertoires outside such neighbourhoods.

Built around these islands of urban poverty is a complex, exclusive and nodal world of affluence, constructed to support the needs for privacy, safety and status. Robert Park's description of 'a mosaic of little worlds that touch but do not interpenetrate' expressed the proximity and yet simultaneous isolation of groups locked into the orbits of their neighbourhoods (Park 1925, 40). This theme of social disconnection in cities has then a long and distinguished heritage but these features of urban life have also become more entrenched and complex not least in the way that our attention has increasingly sought to grasp the patterns of sociability and residence of the affluent. Such neighbourhoods are now more often understood as points on a circulatory pathway for high-income households, both superimposed on, and embedded in, the social and physical constitution of the city – simultaneously separated from and yet also integrated in selective ways.

In *Flesh and Stone* Sennett argues that it was a fear of touching, between Venetians and the city's Jewish population that led to the creation of the ghetto (Sennett 2003). Such examples are by no means unique; what he calls the 'urban prophylactic', the spatial ghettoization of groups to avoid social contact, can be seen today not only in areas of concentrated poverty but also the retreat and physical boundedness of affluent neighbourhoods. Gated communities, affluent enclaves, common interest communities and many new suburbs reveal not only concentration and spatial separation but also a broader set of social fears, desires for status, common values and identities. Neither are these attributes 'left at home'; they also form the basis of a portable lifestyle that supplements insulated residential spaces (Atkinson, 2006). Interlocking and advanced technologies with high price barriers confer the ability of the affluent enclave to flow around the city, a pattern of motion and transmission that has important implications for the nature of urban political systems and their ability to function as public and democratic spaces.

As writers like Butler and Robson (2003) have shown, this kind of flocking together in communities of social similarity appears to be predicated on a need for feelings of safety and status. The affluent enclave is the result of a search for sanctuary amongst a common identity-group based on relative wealth; in this sense it is the result of searches for social affiliation (Abrahamson 2006; Low 2003), yet at the same time its corollary, disaffiliation from other social groups (Fogelson 2005; Fishman 1989). For the affluent the neighbourhood is almost a defensive mode of social life, enacted in ways that might minimise the risk to the twin projects of social life – the home and work. The character of these enclaves as spaces of both withdrawal and selective social engagement is also supported, indeed made possible, by a complex network of telecommunications and travel that enable separation and concealment. Like the lifestyles of the elite Medici of Florence's sixteenth century, today's cities are being adapted to facilitate the withdrawal and protection of wealth (Boddy 1992).

In this chapter I seek to work Castells' ideas about the space of flows to aid the conceptualization of what might be understood as flowing places wherein circuits of affluence have created mobile enclaves and social exclusivity. I also turn to the work of Bauman in working his complementary ideas about physical mobility to social class which appears to add depth to an understanding of the degrees to which rich and poor are locked into place or disencumbered by it. Finally, in the light of recent contributions on the fortification and capsularization of the built environment and the development of mobile information and transportation technologies I develop the idea of the flowing enclave, a space which flows and is created by the affluent in ways that aid the management of risk and engagement with social difference in the city.

The affluent enclave has then become more than the sum of its concrete presence as 'neighbourhood'; the requirement that place extends such defensive properties now sees these fortifications and insulation coating the ebb and flow of social elites around the urban system, supported by the extension of various 'tubes', pipes, wires and capsules – roads, cars, malls, offices and so on. Like the 'splintering' city described by Graham and Marvin (2001), the world of the affluent is maintained and concealed in mutual ignorance from the micro-worlds of the poor and it is this particular lack of social connection and empathy between these extremities of the income/residence scales that concerns me in this chapter. These concerns are addressed in the final part of the chapter in which the disembedded lives of social elites are played out across the subtly split political arenas of many cities today.

Alone is the New together: Lives of Affluence in the City

It is important to remember that segregation is seen as a problem because it has been taken as a measure, not only of the apartness of social groups, but also its suggestion of discrimination and diminished resources for lower income and particular ethnic groups (Massey 1996). As social and political elites have withdrawn from the civic public realm of cities (Lasch 1996) a stronger mutual exclusivity between affluent and poorer groups has emerged focused on circuits of consumption and private life. In fact this spatial separation and social polarization has continued to deepen in Western cities (Massey and Denton 1998; Massey 1996; Dorling and Reese 2003: Meen *et al.*, 2006). If suburbanization marked a dominant shift in urban form and the social life of cities in the post-war period, the latest phase in these changes has been a re-sorting of people and places across the urban system in which identity, social class, income and education have formed the basis of today's urban social mosaic which has produced processes of gentrification and the 'forting-up' of central city spaces.

An apparent paradox of residential life for urban elites is the way in which social and spatial seclusion in the neighbourhood persists alongside the advantages of these spaces due to their position as nodes in broader urban systems of information, economic opportunity and leisure. The loneliness of affluence in the spheres of professional life (Sennett 1999; 2006) and residential settings (Baumgartner 1991) is compensated by a range of connecting networks and technologies. The privilege of residential positions of affluence is their ability to selectively shield domestic life. Gated communities provide the central example of spaces that mediate between positions offering social refuge yet enabling social contact via gates, electronic ports and transportation appendages that enable seamless connectivity with other social and economic contexts and resources. In line with contemporary debates about shifts and a decline in levels of social capital (Putnam 2001) the apparent isolation of social elites from the urban setting suggests a need to revise how we look at the interaction between place and the stores of social resources inhering in social relationships.

While the affluent seal up their neighbourhoods, the places of concentrated poverty create generate spatial isolation, but with little of the connecting infrastructure or resources that allow these contexts to be escaped (Atkinson and Kintrea 2001). Restrictive social networks, fatalistic world views, constrained opportunity structures and overloaded or deficient neighbourhood services have all been well covered by a now extensive literature. These phenomena, known as 'area effects', suggest that the social composition of neighbourhoods may impact on residents in ways that go beyond personal or household characteristics – the neighbourhood thereby becomes a key variable that may facilitate or constrain the lives of residents. The work of Savage *et al.* (2005) is also important in setting our understanding of these forces within a broader context, as they argue:

> Residential space is crucial also in allowing people access to other fields, such as that of education, employment, and various cultural fields. One's residence is a crucial, possibly *the* crucial, identifier of who you are (Savage *et al.* 2005, p. 207).

Neighbourhoods are clearly acknowledged as important ingredients of identity, life-chances and as social worlds and fields in their own right. What is particularly disheartening about the growing segregation and enclavism of middle-class and high-income groups is the amplification of negative effects on low income people in low income neighbourhoods (Wilson 1996). Suburbanization, zoning ordinances, gated communities, and other forms of socio-spatial and legal closure may be seen as attempts to escape these nightmares (Fogelson 2005). In countries like the UK these processes have been supplemented by the spatial concentration of public housing stock which has become stigmatised as a place of last resort, and buttressed by social-legal measures against disorder (Flint 2006), poverty and other income-based 'traps' which both maintain and contain deprived populations. Fishman (1989) has, for example, indicated that the new suburbs of Manchester in the nineteenth century generated spaces of affluence, privatism and domesticity, with high walls and streets designed to prohibit access to non-residents. This development occurred as part of a wider attempt to lower contact with the working classes of the city.

If suburbia and the 'virtuous' area-based effects of concentrated affluence represent the fleeing of nightmares and embracing of new utopias, so such shifts now produce new nightmares. The discussion that follows ponders the implications of this elite withdrawal on the future of urbanism. While writers like Davis (1998) see a bleak future for cities based on extreme social polarization and a resulting militarization of civic life, others, like Douglas Rae (2005), see a delocalization of elites and economic shifts producing a death of urbanism predicated on a decline in civic life and commercial vitality. Massey has sought to describe this in arguing that the separation of rich and poor creates:

> New cultural forms rooted in the ecological order of concentrated affluence and poverty... the affluent will experience the personal benefits of high income; in addition, they will profit increasingly from the fact that most of their neighbours possess these advantages as well (Massey 1996, 407).

This spatial form of wealth condensation (the process by which newly created wealth is further concentrated in those who already have high levels of wealth) has generated a tendency for what can be described as forms of social insulation (Atkinson 2006) in which the affluent seek to shield themselves from scenes of social distress, difference and envisaged risks. Commentators on gated communities, for example, have argued that residents of these places are both metaphorically and actually incarcerated by their fears (Low 2003). Similarly, there is growing evidence that this 'capsularization' of social life (De Cauter 2003) also confers status, privacy and safety on those able to access what may be social or price-based mechanisms of exclusion.

As Sennett (1999) has demonstrated in the workforce, and as Butler and Robson (2003) have for the neighbourhood, work and social life are increasingly precarious in ways that raise the value of neighbourhood in terms of its role as a space of comfort and refuge. For Lasch (1996), the US middle class was marked less by its rapidly rising income than by its lifestyle in which clusters of Reichian symbolic analysts gathered in 'specialized geographical pockets' (such as Silicon Valley) where networking was made possible. For writers like Lasch this spatial withdrawal was deemed problematic because of its contribution to the withdrawal, or 'revolt', of social elites from civic life.

The social capital of the affluent now lies in extended networks and the latent resources inhering in relationships that can be mobilised when local contacts prove insufficient. Suburbia continues to 'work' for the affluent even without proximate friends, family and associates because these contractual and reciprocal relationships can be invoked when they need to be. Similarly the physical changes witnessed in the fortification of local neighbourhoods, such as gated communities, wraps physical and defensive exoskeletons around household units that are no less disadvantaged by these arrangements in an age of electronic communication.

Gates, forts and the flowing enclave

In considering the structure of opportunities and constraints in the emerging globalised world, Zygmunt Bauman (1998) has discussed a typology of social class based around mobility that supplements notions of economic position. In referring to 'nomads' and 'vagabonds' he is able to contrast the time-rich but spatially delimited lives of the poor with a time-poor, yet spatially unencumbered, class. The impression that Bauman manages to convey in this treatment and that on community (2001) is of an interdependency between two broad classes, one emerging in a kind of stratospheric space that is capable of excluding those less fortunate, the other marginalised and servicing the needs of these mobile nomads. Such images can be usefully connected to Castells' treatise on the information age; in particular his discussion of the rise of a space of flows and its contrast with a space of places (Castells 2000). Castells seeks to articulate the way in which urban design and space supports interaction without physical proximity, through new communication technologies. Edge cities, gentrified neighbourhoods and traditional enclaves are cited by him as examples of the physical signifiers of the presence of this new set of social and technological constellations.

The space of flows, and its secured spaces of affluence, is contrasted by Castells with the space of places, much resembling the spaces inhabited by Bauman's vagabond class, and requiring physical proximity for interaction over the kind of distanciated communication and travel flows of the affluent. Through the work of these theorists we can usefully interrogate the specific fortification and mobility strategies of the affluent and social elites in contemporary cities and consider the ways in which social resources inter-relate with these re-makings of physical space and the re-positioning of the urban poor within these scenarios. In this section I consider the growth of gated communities and their connections with other privileged nodes in today's urban systems. Not only are such 'communities' a deepening in the degree to which neighbourhoods have become enclaves, they are also indicative of a new unimpeded and privileged circuit of affluence.

Gated communities consist of clusters of housing around which common spaces and services are provided by private subscription; they are also surrounded by walls and gates which prevent public access. The precise number of such communities is hard to gauge but recent research in the UK (Atkinson and Flint 2004) showed that there were around a thousand gated communities, while in the US survey evidence suggests that around 3.4 per cent of Americans live in 'access-controlled' developments (just over 4 million households), this figure rose to 5.9 per cent if walls and fences was included (or just over 7 million households). In parts of the US, particularly the south-east and western states, gating is the dominant form of new housing development in many city-regions. In countries like Argentina, Brazil and South Africa such 'communities' have been common for the past two to three decades, either as systemic responses to risk, as with South Africa, or as a response to growing levels of crime, in countries like Brazil, which have been destabilised by economic downturns. In emerging economies, like Russia, which have produced significant numbers of wealthy in-migrants and indigenous wealth, the scale of new developments of this kind are extraordinary (Lentz 2006). This can be witnessed in the scale of developments like the 'millionaires town' of Rublyovo-Arkhangelskoye where 30,000 residents live three kilometres to the west of Moscow.[1]

Such entrenched patterns are not distinctly a Western phenomenon. While the West has produced many examples of gated communities we can find whole gated cities in China and Taiwan (Webster *et al.*, 2002). Gated compounds also provide some of the fastest growing property markets in the international, and sometimes dangerous zones, of cities like Lebanon into which property capitalists, like Ivana Trump who has recently constructed a new 'Trump' tower, invest surplus liquidity to create secured neighbourhoods. Fiction has run apace of these shifts and none more so than the author J.G. Ballard who has written a series of novels exploring the retreat of the affluent and the kind of dystopia that may emerge. For Ballard:

> The notion of the community as a voluntary association of enlightened citizens has died for ever ... Today we scarcely know our neighbours, shun most forms of civic involvement and happily leave the running of society to a caste of political technicians. People find all the togetherness they need in the airport boarding lounge and the department-store lift. They pay lip service to community values but prefer to live alone (Ballard 2000, 263).

This vision is remarkably cognisant of the kind of networked (Castells, 2000) and nodal (Graham and Marvin 2001) forms of urbanism being generated by the residential choices of the affluent and the provisions of developers responding to and seeking to generate need for this kind of development. These forms of linked and concentrated spaces of affluence can be interpreted as a kind of end to city life, if we conceive of urbanism as an open, public and diverse space of accountability and encounter in the way that writers like Rae (2005) have suggested.

These changes appear to be occurring because the 'secession of the successful' (Reich 1991) threatens cities with the withdrawal from civic life of its traditional patrons and philanthropists (Lasch 1996). Under new models of gated and common interest enclaves the affluent seek to provide for themselves, thereby threatening models of redistributive and universal provision. It is within this model that Galbraith's (1958) prophetic words about the infringement on private affluence of public squalor are made apparent. However, my key contention in this chapter is that these changes enable broader networks of social circulation to be attached to these primary residential spaces so that the qualities of the enclave can be made

---

1 President Vladimir Putin is also reported to have a dacha outside Moscow from which a private highway can be closed to enable his swift and safe arrival at the Kremlin.

portable. Thus capsular modes of transport, the defensive aspect to architectures of home, work and education, to say nothing of gated and walled communities allows a sanitised and domesticated impression of the social life of the city in which various social dangers and spaces of poverty are concealed or skirted. These socio-technical shifts now make it possible to split from the public spaces of the city in ways that Galbraith had not anticipated. In the context of neoliberal and revanchist attacks on support for the poor and the aggressive cutting of welfare programmes and fiscal privileging of the affluent the 'negative externalities' of poverty (health costs, crime and disorder and other socio-economic shifts) do not fully impinge on the daily lived realities of life within the privileged spaces and modes of the flowing spaces of affluence.

The growth of gated communities appears to indicate the internationalization and entrenchment of these trajectories of segregation, implying not only the containment of the poor (both in compounded poverty neighbourhoods and the incarcerative infrastructure of the penal system) but also a growing readiness of higher income households to seek an escape from the social distress and visible signs of danger that they find in cities. Over the period of perhaps the last two to three decades commentators have observed signs of these shifts in the growing corporate and elite delocalization (Heying 1997), reduced civic participation, philanthropy and leadership (Lasch 1996; Rae 2005), and the declining social capital and associational behaviour (Putnam, 2001) of social elites and high-income groups more generally. The lonely authorship of personal and work lives (Sennett 1999) is now supplemented by isolated patterns of movement, from home to work, to school and to leisure:

> Our daily life can be exactly described as a movement from one enclave or capsule (home for instance) to another (campus, office, airport, all-in hotel, mall and so on) … neoliberal individualism plus suburbanization of daily life equals capsularization. (De Cauter 2003, 96)

Among the key changes in the social and spatial structure of cities lies a fundamental shift in what neighbourhood means. As the affluent withdraw into their neighbourhoods they have taken on the objective of defending their privileges still further. The enclave has become not only a static site of residence but also a strategic imperative that can be applied to an understanding of how the affluent circulate around the city. Far from being restricted to fortified nodes, the affluent are at liberty and autonomy in their control of public encounters and risks. The qualities of the neighbourhood as a defensive space are made portable by the technologies and processes of capsularization that De Cauter (2003) describes – SUVs, private highways, taxis and so on.

These shifts promote both the mutual invisibility of the affluent and those they seek to avoid. The enclave, as a flowing and networked space of privilege and insulation, can be used to help us conceptualise the character of changes in today's cities and the mutating character of sociability within and between social elites and other segments of the city. The space of flows has become, in large part, the place of the affluent in the city, and such places are neither restricted to the exchanges of the new economies but also to neighbourhoods and the places in between them. To take one example, when Setha Low interviewed a colleague in Caracas they spoke of such patterns in this way:

> You can walk in my neighbourhood, or on patrolled streets, but basically you must go from one secured location to another, and not stray into other parts of the city (Low 2003, 112)

As the desire for safety has combined with escalating real incomes and lower tax burdens this has had the effect of simultaneously releasing and containing social elites in compound spaces. These 'bunkers with a view' (Ballard 1997) offer a place to sally forth like the 'berserker' of Norse mythology, sent out to destroy as many foes as possible before trying to get back into the castle. However, in our case here the dangerous others of street homeless, 'aggressive beggars' and other diverse criminals are skirted before returning to a place resembling a strategic base, rather than a place of domesticity (Atkinson and Blandy 2007).

The Nightmare of Bourgeois Utopias

In this section I want to focus on what I see as some of the key issues raised for the analysis of cities in which these shifts in residential and network flows are taking place. The first of these is what we might think of as a series of social skill effects. Here I want to focus on these skills at the upper end of the social spectrum and to propose that the move to 'exit' civic society, by being transported, contained and insulated within flowing enclaves, may have the broader effect of creating less accomplished social actors. Similar arguments have already been advanced in relation to citizenship skills by Sennett (1970) who argues that diverse communities are important in socializing people as a precursor to empathy and compassion. However, my concern here is with the very real possibility that these outcomes will further continue to wedge apart the spatial and social disconnection between rich and poor and diminish the possibility of a social politics capable of challenging the spatial and social inequalities around us.

Writers like Wilson (1999) have suggested that role models are important in the neighbourhood context in order to generate aspirational examples for young black residents. Local social composition would therefore appear to be important to a set of skills relating to our engagement with public life and, by extension, a broader sense of the constitution and aims of political life. While writers like Whyte (1957) have similarly argued that families in the past chose to live in the city because it brought them closer to the kinds of issues that helped them develop into adults capable of coping with difference these values seem more challenging to sustain in today's socially toxic cities. The extent of segregation, social inequality and both real and perceived risks associated with crime make these decisions more difficult. Whyte considered that the great drift to the American suburb represented a shift to antiseptic 'anti-cities', a shift which would reproduce itself in time:

The middle class identification with suburbia will be made more compelling yet … here they are breeding a whole generation that will have never known the city at all. (Whyte 1957, 10)

Now the ability of suburbanites and the inhabitants of inner-urban compounds may be more or less urban, yet they are similarly divorced from the diversity of contact and social complexity and difference in the city. An enclave logic extends these capacities for insulation and the inter-generational reproduction of similar preferences appears almost locked in place. Evidence for this can be seen in accounts like that of Low (2003). As well as describing the continued fears of the withdrawn inhabitants of gated communities, Low comes into contact with children who, in a brief exchange, talk about their ideal neighbourhood in terms of further security ('I'd like a higher wall and more security' says one of her young contacts). American cities are by no means the only examples of such transitions or concerns. Concern has also been expressed for the socialization of the children of the super-rich in Russia where life in gated enclaves and chaperoning by minders has led analysts to suggest they lack the ability for 'self-evaluation' in the wider social context (Parfitt 2005).

What might be the implications of such combinations of risk-averseness and social incapacitation for urban inequalities in the longer term? To turn back to Low (2003) we can find useful analyses of these broader effects by considering Kleinian views of child development in which 'splitting' between good and bad takes place at an early stage. For Low, gates represent a boundary that demarcates not only those inside from outside but also those are conceived as good and bad, safe and dangerous. Critically these effects seem to be more potent for younger people who are being socialised in secured environments. These spaces often contain a very limited cross-section of social contact and identity largely as a result of house prices limiting entry to low income and, thereby, 'dangerous' and different groups. Under these circumstances:

> security has developed into a consumer activity involving suburbanization, technology, self-segregation, and the partitioning of neighbourhoods and schools in homogeneous, and often-private micro-societies … that lead not so much to surveillance and other controlling mechanisms, but to a freeing of wills and choices that lead to residential isolation and school segregation. (Cassella 2003, 129)

At this point a personal anecdote may be worth repeating. In conversation with a friend I talked about research we had carried out on the emergence of gated communities in the UK and how privatised and segregated were the inhabitants of these relatively new neighbourhoods. In response my friend observed that an acquaintance, who worked in the City of London, had described feeling intimidated in going into a shop to buy a hoover. So outside of his daily experience was this environment that he did not have the required 'recipe for action' to deal with the common courtesies and expectations of such an encounter. The anomic sensibility generated by the blur of continual international travel, the de-linking of community and responsibility via hyper-mobility and the drive towards status and privacy within spaces of social homogeneity may perhaps tend to produce subjects, if not entirely deskilled, skilled in asymmetrical ways in relation to the skewed range of social contexts they explore on a daily basis.

Of course to remark on the absence of social elites from social and civic life is not new. Lasch's (1996) commentary on the isolation of political and cultural elites was used to indicate how a reduction in civic participation has impoverished society more generally. Lasch, for example, comments on the 'wonderment' of George Bush Senior at seeing a scanning device in a supermarket as evidence of how out of touch this political elite were. Such stories suggest the social detachment and lack of social *savoir faire* by the affluent in ordinary social situations but also an absence of the foundations for empathic and common understandings of citizenship in social skill inventories. The isolation of the affluent from the grittier and mundane elements of urban social experience, particularly of those excluded from flowing places, appears to have become a significant strategy of high income groups. As Todd Gitlin remarked in the foreword to Slater's *The Pursuit of Loneliness*:

> The wide open spaces of suburbia were *meant* to be escapes from urban congestion. They had the effect of rendering the poor "invisible" to the middle classes (Slater 1990, xiii, italics added).

These concerns mirror more recent developments in cities like London where a near totalizing gentrification, particularly in the inner city, has created a new kind of social geography built around the tectonic relationships that create proximity generally without social contact. As Butler and Robson observe, these new entrants are:

> the cosmopolitans living in a metropolitan environment. "Locals", to whom they largely counterpose themselves, live elsewhere: either *hidden* away in social housing, or indeed anywhere else in the United Kingdom (2003: 8, italics added).

These points lead me to discuss a second bundle of effects relating to the political impacts of the secession of the affluent. Bauman's notion of extra-territoriality (2006) suggests that the location of new elites and high income groups has had the effect of moving them 'out of political space'. The neighbourhood is now a key space of identity formation, pride and defence – for the affluent as much as the poor. A key effect of these changes has been to secede the political control of local space to neighbourhood and homeowner associations both within gated communities and other affluent enclaves without gated, but commonly provided, spaces and maintenance contracts.

The first comment we might make on these changes is that the form of the built environment itself is now interrelated with concerns about social capital and civic engagement. For writers like Putnam there is a certain civic 'sluggishness' to suburbia. Putnam sees the rise of suburbia linked to lower rates of civic participation but his research suggests that this is not because of increased mobility (this has stayed roughly the same for the last fifty years) but because of the hostility of these new non-places to civic engagement itself. Moves to these locations are seen as the result of choices to improve schooling, safety and amenity but result in declining connectedness yet these perverse outcomes suggest a public cost to these private choices when considered en masse.

For Lasch (1996) and Putnam (2001), among others, these shifts produced a philanthropic disengagement with localities by social elites that is the major casualty of delocalization stemming from the re-scaling of corporate life over state boundaries. The growing insularity of elites has also meant they lose touch with the concerns of ordinary citizens. This theme has recently been picked up by Frank Furedi (2005) who argues that the obsession with focus groups under the Blair government has been a sign of desperation in trying to reconnect distant political elite. For Furedi, today's cultural and political elites (very much like Lasch's) have an absence of purpose, no strong convictions or engagement in public life. For this elite:

> The problem of legitimacy is experienced through the feeling of being disconnected and detached from the rest of society. The sensation of being out of touch is a dominant theme in the deliberation of the political classes ... a thousand other varieties of consultation exercises represent a desperate attempt to put an otherwise disconnected elite in touch with popular opinion. (Furedi 2005: 107)

Of course it is also true that the politics of fear now 'pushed' by this elite is not only the lifeblood of political capital and legitimacy but also the source of a diffuse anxiety that feeds residential choices for armament and withdrawal. The distinct downside of the meshing of suburban withdrawal with political life is the way in which it leads to a sense of superciliousness by the affluent. As Slater (1990) has commented, the affluent are actually comfortable with violence, as long as it is played out in poor areas. The contrast is between well-maintained neighbourhood atolls in a broader sea of decay and deprivation, itself seen as further confirmation of the need to make these choices. In this, there is a reinforcing circularity as:

> exclusion leads to crime and crime leads to exclusion. This might end up changing the world into an archipelago of insular entities, fortresses, gated communities, enclosed complexes (like hotels and malls), enclaves, envelopes, cocoons, in short capsules in a sea of chaos. (De Cauter 2003, 96)

In Fishman's work the utopia of suburbia was predicated, in part, on the reduction of contact with working-class life, the bare minimum required to sustain economic life. The political life resulting from early waves of suburban development was clearly distasteful:

> In the context of the industrial city turned into an escape and an evasion. Because middle-class women and their families were safely placed behind the walls of Victoria Park, the rest of Manchester could indeed be turned into a "furnace ground"... human beings a short distance away could be left to sink (Fishman 1989, 102)

Being left to sink is a familiar theme for analysts of contemporary social policy systems, yet it is the way in which social withdrawal might further diminish the political imperatives for reform that have barely been considered. The clustering of the excluded in ghettoised and socially residualised public housing, clearance from public streets (Mitchell 1997), complex surveillance and categorization through meagre welfare systems (Flint 2006) and displacement through housing market pressures (Atkinson 2000) has revealed a virulent lack of compassion that may be the result of the spatial sorting of cities as well as existing political ideologies. Since many social problems are managed into being out of sight and out of mind the impact of such problems, in terms of spurring public intervention, has become much more limited.

A New Urban Medici? Life Above the Streets

In this chapter I have tried to argue that urbanism, as a public and interdependent form of human life, appears to find its end in the kind of sealing and partitioning practices of high income groups in new neighbourhoods and through the way in which the qualities of protected enclaves now flow more freely through urban systems. Here I want to turn back to my opening comment relating these practices to those of the Florentine Medici who built elaborate systems of conveyance out of the view of a potentially dangerous public. It was the early Giovanni Medici who advised his son, Cosimo, to keep out of the public gaze, knowing that envious political rivals or criminals might prey on their conspicuous wealth. Perhaps one of the most remarkable achievements to come from this was the creation of cloisters above the streets of Florence, the Percorso del Principe. These halls and passages connected the Palazzo Vecchio to Palazzo Pitti and the Boboli gardens, through the Ponte Vecchio and the Uffizi, so that movement could be achieved without the risks of the street below. Over time these connecting spaces became a gallery as the Medici and other patrons began to enjoy spending social time here.

Bringing ourselves back to matters at hand we may remember that, in the early 1990s, there was a proposal to construct a travelling walkway connecting London's Waterloo station with the South Bank work and leisure quarter. This proposal was made on the basis that it was now 'uncomfortable' to walk past so many homeless people, some of whom were described as aggressively begging. In the end the 'solution' was the bricking-up of interstitial spaces and the building of an IMAX cinema in an underpass where many homeless people often found refuge. This interdictory urbanism (Flusty 2001) has squeezed out those who, with least resources, apparently threatened those passing by. Of course, those homeless people are still there, somewhere, but the effect has been to displace their public visibility. A visitor to the South Bank today would know nothing of this past history or the existence of this desperation since it is possible to circulate through the city in ways which deny the presence or existence of these problem people. If the South Bank, and many places like it, is in some sense a 'better' place it is not because we have managed to solve these problems in our society, yet we are effective in removing the traces of their existence.

Graham and Marvin's (2001) splintered urbanism is perhaps the central lens through which to view these changes, as private and protected nodes are linked by secured pathways and networks with premiums attached to access. In shopping districts this is often visible in which:

> Movement in the streets is just a short transaction period for us to go to different enclosed and controlled areas. In new towns such as Tai Po or commercial centres such as the north part of Wanchai in Hong Kong, people can walk through all of the shopping centres,

hotels, office towers, exhibition centres, and residential buildings without even stepping on the streets for a second (Siu 1999, 679).

The value of nodal points, residential or otherwise, has become a selective engagement and fortified withdrawal. Yet this is a form of withdrawal that presents advantages, both in co-locating with others of resources as well as being sites of connectivity to information and travel networks. The flowing enclaves of social elites have created a pattern of interaction and drift that is like an invisible fluid running through the veins of urban systems. Virillio has described the impact of these changes in stark terms:

> A regression of the City in which the *cosmopolis*, the open city of the past, gives way to this *claustropolis* where foreclosure is intensified by exclusion of that stray, the outsider, what we might call a SOCIOCRUISER, who is threatening the metropolitan inhabitant's peace of mind … to require us to erect an EXOSPHERICAL fence to fend off the dangers of the void (Virilio 2005, 68).

The exospherical fence can be interpreted both as the physical walls of gated communities and the invisible lines of social segregation, but it may also refer to the strategic engagement with urban life exhibited by high income groups. These comments lead us back to my preceding comments about the misanthropic quality of the resources and social capital articulated between urban enclaves and other nodes in a networked urbanism. It appears plausible that the search to live among 'people like us', to confer feelings of safety and common identity (Butler with Robson 2003), generates the very threat to a diverse and open urban system in which we find the identification of those who are outside or dangerous to this personal project.

We know that the key drivers behind gated communities lie in aspirations to safety, status and privacy. Such drivers are suggestive of what we might think of as a misanthropic form of social capital. These spaces appear to offer residents a release from their fears of open spaces, social difference and incalculable social dangers. Like the titular character of Moliere's play *The Misanthrope*, the retreat into sealed enclaves suggests that there is a mistrust of 'mankind' in its generalised understanding, yet like true misanthropes this lack of trust is not matched by a dislike for immediate neighbours. This quality of misanthropy may appear to diminish social capital and, to the extent that diversity *within* networks is reduced, this is partially true. However, it is within the relative confines of trust, reciprocity and the selective bridges built to contacts, who are socially alike or needed for exchange, that a striking resilience and strength can be found.

Successive waves of public expenditure cutbacks have combined with the seepage of economic rationalism into areas of social life that have left the city sparkling yet highly hostile to social need and to those outcasted by contemporary welfare and work regimes. Social capital has been located in senses of connection and the resources implied by these connections (Putnam 2001). In the conception of a misanthropic form of such networks and resources we might usefully locate a desire for selectivity over the range of relationships attached to us. In other words the ability to invite, include and exclude is essential in constructing a resilient and socially homogenous network. Those outside these networks are reviled or feared and campaigns articulated through political systems capable of removing or destroying these vagabonds (Mitchell 1997).

It is not only, then, that a resident's own social milieu and contacts shape life chances; the neighbourhood extends these complex webs of social causation by, for example, sheltering residents from certain forms of crime as well as operating as private status goods which confer privileged status in other social contexts. As neighbourhood becomes articulated as a part of broader strategies of social and spatial insulation (Atkinson 2006) and identity (Savage *et al.* 2005) by those with the means to do so, social resources which help us to deal with shocks and challenges are bolstered or impaired by these residential locations, in addition to those stocks of capital we carry with us as individuals.

Class hierarchies based around occupation, wealth and so on, are now perhaps supplanted by their interaction with, and production by, residence within a broader hierarchy of neighbourhoods that connect in complex ways with our life chances. If where we live is one of a bundle of variables that influence our capacities and achievements in life then attention to the social composition and quality of neighbourhoods becomes a critical point of debate for public policy, yet one which has barely been dealt with. Private household choices in an unequal society have the public consequences of creating neighbourhood hierarchies and mosaics of segregation that few are generally brave enough to defend, even if some political representatives are prepared to condemn those shabby and unprepared people they produce. In this way the production of a premium space of flows and flowing enclaves serves to reinforce the vagabond (Bauman 2006) and place-bound (Castells 2000) status of the poor while leaving little room for hope of reform and counteraction.

Conclusion

Secure high-income neighbourhoods have created the nodes that form part of a broader network, a buried social circuit, largely out of the view of, or contact with, those who are perceived to be socially different or 'dangerous'. With rising real incomes, a growth of the social 'middle' and cheapening of technologies of security and personal defence, these social shifts have had spatial impacts, impacts which are now being brought into sharper relief by the greater fortification and hardening of affluent enclaves. A flowing form and extension of these enclaves is created by a networked urbanism that has generated the ability of circuits of affluence to go beyond the relatively static containers of residential neighbourhoods. In addition portable versions of the insulation and selective social connectivity found in their neighbourhood counterparts have been produced that have made it more possible for the affluent to steer clear of the perceived dangers of the city. As I have tried to indicate in this chapter, the consequences of these new socio-spatial forms may have important implications for how we might think about social capital, that it may act as both a resource as well as expression of disconnection and hostility as well as alliances and pro-social values.

The desire to secede and occupy defended neighbourhood positions now appears to threaten the vitality and empathic capacities of urban spaces described in earlier accounts of cities and their public realms. Heightened segregation of different identity and income groups also threatens to reproduce itself in more emphatic ways. As I have argued here, the reason for this lies in the kind of social resources and capital that inhere among high income groups, what I have termed a misanthropic form of social capital which embraces social similarity and shuns contact with social difference. Most importantly, these desires have been more fully realized under conditions in which gated communities and enclaves have been able to position themselves as spaces of insulation from the decline in public amenity and safety that have occurred under conditions of neoliberal urban governance.

In this context private neighbourhood governance and policing come to act as strategies that further 'pad' and spatially separate the affluent in their bunkers. The worrying logic is that the democratization of fortification, as it becomes cheaper, holds out the prospect that partitioning becomes a banal strategy that sets the new baseline from which assessments of social risk are estimated. As Low's (2003) gated community residents so often stated, life beyond the gates is unthinkable after life behind them.

I have tried to suggest that the longer-term impacts of residential isolation and segregation of this flowing kind may be a range of social skill deficits among high income groups. It seems that these challenges of social identity formation and the splitting between good and bad invoked by neighbourhood boundaries may form a necessary condition for the development of an urban politics which is less likely to be empathic (at its most extreme) or able to engage with and understand diversity (in its weaker forms). The repertoire of social techniques and abilities generated by socialization and daily life in the city as a place of difference and social challenges appears to be being replaced by the city negotiated along axes of social similarity, bubbles of safety and insulated neighbourhoods that make it possible to strategically avoid 'dangerous' contact.

The misanthropy suggested by the social networks of the affluent in many of today's urban systems appears capable of helping us to understand how the end of an urbanism comprising diversity, difference and a shared public realm may arise as a result of the secession of the successful and fragmentation of local state authority into petty fiefdoms of private governance. A re- and de-skilling of high income groups is producing social actors accomplished in the interaction of the workplace, and other spaces governed by market principles and personal connections, yet far less able to engage with nurturing roles and the social needs of those unable to access the networked spaces of the well-off. For those now able to live socially 'outside' the city, yet remain inside its physical boundaries, the end of urbanism (Rae 2005) may appear less as the death of a civic public realm and post-industrial decline and more as the hideous spectacle of circuits of privilege continuing to flow unchecked by knowledge of, or empathy with, social destitution.

References

Abrahamson, M. (2006), *Urban Enclaves: Identity and Place in the World*, 2nd Edition (New York: Worth).

Atkinson, R. (2006), 'Padding the bunker: Strategies of middle class disaffiliation and colonisation in the city', *Urban Studies*, 43, 4, pp. 819–832.

Atkinson, R. and Blandy, S. (2005), International perspectives on the New Enclavism and the Rise of Gated Communities (eds) (Special Issue), *Housing Studies*, 20, 2, pp. 177–186.

—— (2007), 'Panic Rooms: The Rise of Defensive Homeownership', *Housing Studies*, 22, 4, pp. 443–458.

Atkinson, R. and Flint, J. (2004), 'Fortress UK? Gated Communities, the Spatial Revolt of the Elites and Time Space Trajectories of Segregation', *Housing Studies*, 19, 6, pp. 875–892.

Atkinson, R. and Kintrea, K. (2001), 'Disentangling Area Effects: Evidence from Deprived and Non-Deprived Neighbourhoods', *Urban Studies*, 38, 12, pp. 2277–2298.

Auge, M. (1995), *Nonplaces: Introduction to Anthropology of Supermodernity* (London: Verso).

Ballard, J.G. (1997), *Cocaine Nights* (London: HarperCollins).

—— (2000), *Super Cannes* (London: HarperCollins).

Bauman, Z. (1998), *Globalization: The Human Consequences* (New York: Columbia University Press).

—— (2001), *Community: Seeking Safety in an Insecure World* (Cambridge: Polity Press).

—— (2006), *Liquid Fear* (Cambridge: Polity Press).

Baumgartner, M. (1991), *The Moral Order of a Suburb* (Oxford: Oxford University Press).

Boddy, T. (1992), Underground and Overhead: Building the Analogous City, chapter in Sorkin, M. (ed.), *Variations on a Theme Park: The New American City and the End of Public Space* (New York: Hill and Wang), pp. 123–153.

Bourdieu, P. (1999), *The Weight of the World: Social Suffering in Contemporary Society* (Cambridge, Polity Press).

Boyle, T.C. (1995), *Tortilla Curtain* (London: Penguin).

Butler, T. with Robson, G. (2003), *London Calling: The Middle Classes and the Remaking of Inner London* (Oxford: Berg).

Cassella, R. (2003), 'Security, Schooling, and the Consumer's Choice to Segregate', *The Urban Review*, 35: 2, pp. 129–148.

Castells, M. (1989), *The Informational City: Information Technology, Economic Restructuring, and the Urban-Regional Process* (Oxford: Blackwell).

Castells, M. (ed.) (2000), *The Rise of the Network Society*, 2nd Edition (Oxford: Blackwell).

Davis, M. (1998) *Ecology of Fear: Los Angeles and the Imagination of Disaster* (London: Picador).

De Cauter, L. (2003), 'The Capsule and the Network: Notes Toward a General Theory', chapter in: Graham, S. (ed.) *The Cybercities Reader* (London: Routledge), pp. 94–97.

Dorling, D. and Rees, P. (2003), 'A Nation Still Dividing: The British Census and Social Polarisation 1971–2001', *Environment and Planning A*, 35, pp. 1287–1313.

Fishman, R. (1989) *Bourgeois Utopias: The Rise and Fall of Suburbia* (New York: Basic Books).

Flint, J. (eds) (2006), *Housing, Urban Governance and Anti-Social Behaviour* (Bristol: Policy Press).

Flusty, S. (2001), 'The Banality of Interdiction: Surveillance, Control and the Displacement of Diversity', *International Journal of Urban and Regional Research*, 25, 3, pp. 658–664.

Fogelson, R.M. (2005), *Bourgeois Nightmares: Suburbia, 1870–1930* (New Haven: Yale University Press).

Furedi, F. (2005), *Politics of Fear* (London: Continuum).

Galbraith, J.K. (1958), *The Affluent Society* (Harmondsworth: Pelican).

Graham, S. and Marvin, S. (2001), *Splintering Urbanism: Networked Infrastructures, Technological Mobilities and the Urban Condition* (London: Routledge).

Heying, C.H. (1997), Civic Elites and Corporate Delocalization: An Alternative Explanation for Declining Civic Engagement, *The American Behavioural Scientist*, 40, 5, pp. 657–668.

Lasch, C. (1996), *The Revolt of the Elites and the Betrayal of Democracy* (London: Norton).

Lentz, S. (2006), 'More Gates, Less Community? Guarded Housing in Russia', in Glasze, G., Webster, C. and Frantz, K., *Private Cities: Global and Local Perspectives* (London: Routledge).

Low, S. (2003), *Behind the Gates: Life, Security, and the Pursuit of Happiness in Fortress America* (London: Routledge).

Massey, D. (1996), 'The Age of Extremes: Concentrated Affluence and Poverty in the Twenty-First Century', *Demography*, 33: 4, pp. 395–412.

Massey, D. and Denton, N. (1998), *American Apartheid: Segregation and the Making of the Underclass* (Boston: Harvard University Press).

Meen, G., Gibb, K., Goody, J., McGrath, T. and Mackinnon, J. (2006), *Economic Segregation in England: Causes, Consequences and Policy* (Bristol: Policy Press).

Mitchell, D. (1997), 'The Annihilation of Space by Law: The Roots and Implications of Anti-Homeless Laws in the United States', *Antipode*, 29: 3, pp. 303–335.

Parfitt, T. (2005), 'Golden Curtain Divides Old and New in Russia: Moscow's Rich Keep their Children under Lock and Key as Social Unrest Grows', *The Guardian*, 10 October.

Park, R.E. (1925), 'The City: Suggestions for the Investigation of Human Behavior in the Urban Environment', in Park, R.E. and Burgess, E.W. (eds), *The City: Suggestions for the Investigation of Human Behavior in the Urban Environment*, pp. 1–46 (Chicago: University of Chicago Press).

Putnam, R. (2001), *Bowling Alone: The Collapse and Revival of American Community* (New York: Simon & Schuster).

Rae, D.W. (2005), *City: Urbanism and its End* (New Haven: Yale University Press).

Reich, R. (1991), 'Secession of the Successful', *New York Times Magazine*, 20 January.

Savage, M., Bagnall, G. and Longhurst, B. (2005), *Globalization and Belonging* (London: Sage).

Sennett, R. (1970), *The Uses of Disorder: Personal Identity and City Life* (New York: Knopf).

—— (1974), *The Fall of Public Man* (New York: Norton).

—— (1999), *The Corrosion of Character: The Personal Consequences of Work in the New Capitalism* (London: W.W. Norton).

—— (2003), *Flesh and Stone* (London: Penguin).

—— (2006), *The Culture of the New Capitalism* (New Haven: Yale University Press).

Siu, K.W.M. (1999), 'The Escalator: A Conveyor of Hong Kong's Culture', *Human Relations*, 52: 5, pp. 665–681.

Slater, P. (1990), *The Pursuit of Loneliness: American Culture at the Breaking Point*, 3rd Edition, (Boston: Beacon Press).

Virilio, P. (2005), *City of Panic* (Oxford: Berg).

Webster, C., Glasze, G. and Frantz, K. (2002), 'The global spread of gated communities', *Environment and Planning B: Planning and Design*, 29: 3, pp. 315–320.

Wilson, W.J. (1996), *When Work Disappears: The World of the New Urban Poor* (New York: Vintage).

Whyte, W.H. (1957) (ed.), *The Exploding Metropolis* (Berkeley: University of California Press).

Chapter 4

Place, Space and Race: Monopolistic Group Closure and the Dark Side of Social Capital

Bruce D. Haynes and Jesus Hernandez

Introduction

Since the early twentieth century, suburban developments made up of detached single-family dwellings surrounded by grass and tree-lined streets have held the utopian promise of refuge from the disorganized, congested, crime-ridden city for the most prosperous of the American working and middle classes (Fishman 1987). The community of Runyon Heights[1] is no exception. Situated in the northeast section of Yonkers, New York, Runyon Heights looks like many middle-class suburban settlements. Amid private homes dotted by picket fences and prize-winning flower gardens live more than 1378 residents that comprise some 352 middle-class families. In 1990, median family income in the area was $43,500, slightly above that of the City of Yonkers and well above the national figure of $35,353.[2] In stark contrast, only 56 percent of the homes in Runyon Heights were owner-occupied, a figure significantly below the national average.

Runyon Heights stands out among American suburban communities for another important reason: the majority of its nearly 1400 residents are black.[3] While three small black middle-class residential enclaves also developed in Yonkers in the first half of the twentieth century, only the residents of Runyon Heights were able to establish a stable home-owning enclave that was not overwhelmed by the forces of ghettoizaton. The stories of these middle class residents reveal the link between race and class inequality in the organization of American suburban communities and sheds light on the role of social capital in the lives of the suburban middle class. Social capital was critical to their success. But Runyon Heights also reveals the dark side of social capital by drawing attention to its unequal distribution and its contradictory role within a historically segregated context. Our case demonstrates that

---

1 This chapter is based on fieldwork collected by the first author between 1991 and 1993. A portion of this data has appeared in *Red Lines Black Space: The Politics of Race a Space in a Black Middle-Class Suburb*, New Haven: Yale University Press, 2001.

2 U.S. Census of the Population, 1990.

3 Sigelman and Welch (1991) report that 'Blacks' prefer the term black over African American 66 percent to 22 percent; Runyon Heights' residents also preferred the tem black in self-describing themselves and their community.

even middle-class blacks had to bridge their marginalized networks to resource-rich white-dominated networks in mainstream institutions before they could effectively defend their collective interests.

Bourdieu's understanding of the concepts of social capital enables us to see how racial and class distinctions are reproduced in a suburban setting. Drawing from Bourdieu, we will follow the definition of social capital that others have also used in this book: social capital consists of the socially imbedded resources that actors draw upon through their social ties for instrumental purposes (Frank and Yasumoto 1998, Coleman 1994; Lin 1999, 2001; Burt 1992, 1997, 2000; Portes 1998; Fernandez-Kelly 1995). Specifically, we focus on the role of social capital as a resource for constructive civic engagement and the assertion of collective interests.

While some scholars have identified a need to explore the less desirable consequences of social capital (Portes 1998, 15; Lin 2001, 95; Arneil 2006), most have focused on its positive effects. Scholars like Robert Putnam view civic engagement as a panacea for the complex web of social problems plaguing poor urban neighborhoods – but 'understate the importance of race and ethnicity in their conceptualization and analysis' (Hero 2003, 120). To call for civic engagement through associations and social networks misses the point that these institutions and informal networks have long-existed in black communities like Runyon Heights, but they did not insure prosperity among residents, nor were they sufficient to protect community interests. Indeed, implicit in Putnam's call for a revival of civic unity and virtue is the transcendence of difference (Arneil 2006, 7). According to Putnam, transcending difference allowed for the creation of a common civic culture. But the civic unity forged during the Progressive era and idealized by Putnam was imbedded within a racialized framework that designated black Americans as racially outside of mainstream social life. Thus Putnam misstates the problem when he links growing American diversity to declining levels of social capital, or when he frames the American dilemma as the tension between fraternity and equality (Putnam 2000, 354). Rather than looking to explain urban politics by looking at how government policy and the shape of the urban infrastructure shapes civic participation, Putnam suggests that liberty itself is at odds with fraternity and that immigration and desegregation have threatened civil society because people who are different simply cannot get along.[4]

At a basic level, the inequality inherent to segregation meant residents had limited social capital resources from which to mobilize and promote community interests. As Loury (2002) observes, '… access to developmental resources is mediated through race-segregated social networks … (103).' In Yonkers, local white citizens, representatives of city government, school officials, and private employers used race to bound public institutions and social networks, a process that created social closure around whiteness and fostered black social and political disenfranchisement from white dominated institutions, while also encouraging civic trust and race solidarity among blacks. In the post-World War Two era, key individuals served as brokers

---

4 See The Johan Skytte Prize Lecture given in 2006 by Robert Putnam, and published in *Scandinavian Political Studies* in 2007 under the title '*E Pluribus Unum*: Diversity and Community in the Twenty First Century,' in *Scandinavian Political Studies* Vol. 30, No 2.

between black social capital networks (black social capital)[5] and resource-rich white networks. Green, Tigges, and Browne (1995) note that bridging ties outside of segregated contexts are necessary for residents of the black community to find employment, and DeFilippis (2001) notes that 'bridging capital' is needed when a community's residents are poor (790). We assert that bridging capital, the establishing of 'weak ties' that expand the opportunities of closed social networks, is necessary for the black middle class community of Runyon Heights as well (Granovetter, 1973, Burt 2000).

The ability of the Runyon Heights community to access resource-rich white-dominated networks and institutions in Yonkers has been constrained by a complex set of historical and contextual factors. The residents of Runyon Heights have always been concerned with maintaining good schools, property values, and safe, clean streets. Like other members of the suburban middle class, they have staked a claim on the American Dream by actively engaging in their local community. In fact, community institutions and organizations have been prominent in Runyon Heights for well over seventy years; when community interests were undermined by outside forces, voluntary associations centered and coalesced residents. Collective solidarity was bolstered by the community's repeated confrontations with local government, school officials, local industry, and neighboring white residents. Relegated by race to the margins of the respectable bourgeoisie, the black residents in Runyon Heights used their social and human capital[6] resources to fight for schools, jobs, political participation, and the general interests of community residents.

Community access to resource-rich white-dominated networks and institutions accelerated significantly following the formal dismantling of state-imposed segregation after World War II. Residents who attended the locally integrated elementary school, School 1, during the twenties and thirties were, by the nineteen fifties, serving as brokers between the black community and white networks that dominated mainstream institutions. Interracial friendships that had developed during the early decades at School 1 were constrained by strict norms that encouraged racial endogamy, but once state support of race waned, these personal connections and friendships could function publicly to bridge group networks. By linking the thick social networks of the black residents of Runyon Heights, these brokers created bridges that proved critical to community influence in the local civic arena and crucial to defending community interests. In fact, Runyon Heights reveals the importance of context and history in determining the ability of residents to activate both strong and weak ties in mobilizing resources for community defense.

---

5 Marion Orr makes a distinction between Black social capital and inter-group social capital. Black social capital refers to its interpersonal and institution forms within the African-American community. Inter-group social capital refers to cross-sector formations of mutual trust and networks of cooperation that bridge the black-white divide, especially at the elite level of sociopolitical organization. Orr's definition closely resembles the use of Granovetter's (1973) weak ties concept and the brokerage functions described by Burt (2000).

6 Coleman, Bourdieu, and Lin all suggest that social capital can produce human capital and vice versa.

These networks, rich in human capital, were a necessary but not sufficient condition for black civic empowerment and what Putnam calls 'effective government'. Types of capital differ in their 'liquidity and convertibility', and 'by comparison to [to economic capital] the convertibility of social capital into economic capital is costlier and more contingent; social capital is less liquid, "stickier", and subject to attrition' (Anheirer et. al. 1995, 862). The ability to exchange or transfer social capital for political influence was dependent upon the state institutional environment and not merely on the vibrancy of residents' social networks or the amount of human capital imbedded in the group. Changes in federal policy in the post-war era encouraged black mobilization, participation, and inclusion in the civic arena. Similarly, both whites and blacks increased their acceptance of friendships across the color line, especially instrumental relationships, which partially opened political access to white networks. This shift in racial policy is best symbolized by the landmark 1954 Brown decision, which signaled the incorporation of blacks into the nation's political institutional framework. In Runyon Heights, Brown encouraged a shift in organizational strategy from the inward focus of church and social clubs to the outward focus of local voluntary associations, like the Runyon Heights Improvement Association (R.H.I.A). Civic engagement in voluntary associations like the R.H.I.A. is paradoxically rooted in resident's reactions to the forces of exclusion from white civic organization. Thus social capital among the black middle class residents of Runyon Heights is both encouraged and limited by the racialized character of civil society and the role of state institutions[7] in maintaining racial segregation.

Social Capital

Social capital is a popular metaphor for social advantage, but the social processes encompassed by the concept are not new and have deep roots in American social science (Burt 2000, 2; Portes 1998, 5). Many contemporary scholars commonly define social capital as some combination of resources embedded in social networks that are activated by trust.[8]

Scholars have been consistent in recognizing that social capital is a characteristic created by and held within the group (Burt 1997, 339). James Coleman, who was the

---

7 Arneil (2006) argues that social capital alone may not be sufficient to overcome the forces of exclusion and discrimination, and further discusses the role of the state and/or the courts in unleashing certain forms of social capital (57).

8 Today, even the World Bank has linked social capital to its understanding of global poverty, stating on it's website that 'Increasing evidence shows that social cohesion – social capital – is critical for poverty alleviation and sustainable human and economic development.' Scholars have used the concept to talk about trust and the organization of urban spaces, and to analyze civil society and social networks. The concept has been used in the study of intergovernmental relations (Orr 1999); parent-child-school interaction and dropout rates (Teachman, Paasch, Carver 1996, 1997); the effects of parental involvement on truancy (McNeal, 1999); the reproduction of inequality and information networks (Stanton-Salazar and Dornbusch, 1995); confidence in political institutions (Brehm and Rahn, 1997); and the management of work environments by organizations (Cohen and Prusak, 2001).

first to popularize the concept within the social science community in the late nineteen eighties (DeFillipis 2001, 784; Portes 1998, 6) defines social capital in broad terms by its function (1994: 302); it consists of some aspect of social structure that facilitates the productive actions of trusting individuals within that structure. In asserting that '… social organization constitutes social capital' (304), he echoes the ecological models of an earlier generation of Chicago school scholars. For Coleman, social capital is simply social organization based on trust; it is, by definition, productive. While many of the definitions used by social scientists overlap in their emphasis on either the individual actor or the social structure, Portes (1998) concludes that a growing consensus is emerging among sociologists. Focusing on the individual level, he suggests that '… social capital stands for the ability of actors to secure benefits by virtue of membership in social networks or other social structures' (6).

While Putnam has recently re-ignited the social capital debate and provides the focal point for our discussion, it is Bourdieu who provides the first systematic analysis of the concept (Portes 1998, 3) and the foundation for the theoretical approach deployed here. Bourdieu defines social capital as 'the aggregate of the actual or potential resources that are linked to possession of a durable network of more or less institutionalized relationships of mutual acquaintance and recognition – or in other words, to membership in a group – which provides each of its members with the backing of the collectively-owned capital' (1997). The amount of social capital depends on both the size of the network of connections one can mobilize and on the volume of the capital (economic, cultural) possessed by each of those to whom he is connected. In Bourdieu's view, social capital remains a collective asset shared by members of a defined group; access to social capital is dependent upon being a member of a closed network.

Bourdieu's concept of social capital has strong implications for understanding the reproduction of class and race among the black residents of Runyon Heights. Unlike either Coleman or, as we shall see, Putnam, Bourdieu draws attention to unequal group-based power relations. His notion suggests that both race-based and class-based groups comprise sets of social relationships that regulate the distribution of power and status. Institutionalized racial boundaries in Runyon Heights in the pre-Brown era limited access to resource rich white social networks, and consequently, to Capital in all of its forms.

Monopolistic Group Closure and the Racial Dimensions of Social Capital

While Bourdieu's model has been traditionally interpreted as one that underscores the reproduction of class boundaries, our focus is on the consequences of the racalization and segregation of black social networks. Prior to Brown, black institutional exclusion encouraged white racial endogamy[9] and guaranteed that the

---

9 Opposition to interracial marriage was vehement throughout the first half of the twentieth century. In 1952, more than thirty states still enforced miscegenation laws that prohibited interracial unions between Blacks and whites. In states that banned interracial unions, the courts routinely refused to recognize marriages from states where unions were legal. The 1967 Supreme Court decision, ironically titled Loving v. Commonwealth of Virginia, struck

social capital of blacks held less relative value than that of whites. Glenn Loury (1977) was one of the first scholars to re-emphasize the social origins of social capital, asserting that an individual's social origin 'has an obvious and important effect on the amount of resources that is ultimately invested in his or her development'. More recently, Fernandez Kelly (1995) has argued that social capital is toponomical, that is, dependent on physical and social location. She contends that because people derive their knowledge from the social and physical spaces in which they live, the environment constrains social possibilities. Lin (1999; 2001) contends that social capital is contingent on both the initial structural positions in the social hierarchy and the extent of social ties. We draw from Bourdieu's model and focus on the importance of the diminished value of black social capital networks. Due to the unequal distribution of power imbedded in social institutions, individuals and groups have differential access to social capital networks and not all networks wield equal power. While group membership for residents of Runyon Heights was defined by a combination of race- and class-based boundaries, repeated exchanges (investment) among group members, what Coleman calls obligations (Coleman 1994 , 300–324), both reinforced recognition of the group and dictated the boundaries of inclusion, which reinforced racial solidarity within the community.

Long before Bourdieu, Max Weber made similar observations concerning groups and status differentiation in his famous essay 'Ethnic Groups,' where he argued that the social goods of nobility and honor are tied to race in American society (Weber 1968, 386), and that racial group boundaries were solidified in the post-Emancipation era as a way for whites to monopolize social power and honor. He posited that the incorporation of African-American slaves into the status hierarchy of the late nineteenth century led to a curtailment of the patriarchal discretion previously exercised by white slave masters, and that a rigid color line was necessary to redraw group distinctions following Emancipation. In Weber's words, 'the smallest admixture of Negro blood disqualifies a person unconditionally' from the white group (1968).

Referring to the post-Reconstruction South, Weber concluded that 'the social honor of 'poor whites' was dependent upon the social declassement of the Negroes' (Weber 1968, 391.) Weber identified this kind of group honor as 'ethnic honor', a process closely related to status honor (Weber 1968, 390); by the 1920s, the one-drop rule had reclassified people of mixed African and European ancestry as black (Davis 1991). In short, in the post-Emancipation era, racial categories were used as a basis for white racial endogamy. Those defined as "white" drew closure, limited identification with their racial kin, and formed a monopoly on power that was constituted in their segregated social networks; whites experienced an inclusive structure and social entitlement that reinforced group networks.

Historically in the Unites States, race may be even more significant than class in the distribution of social resources. 'Race' has been used to imply a breeding lineage that embodies inbred and innate human differences (Smedley 1993, 39). By the early

---

down as unconstitutional anti-miscegenation laws that prohibited marriage between people of European and African descent. By 1970 only 65,000 black/white interracial marriages were recorded nation-wide (Daniel 2002; 98).

twentieth century, blacks were widely regarded as an inferior and distinct biological group; racial endogamy and the adoption of the one-drop rule helped to produce the illusion of distinct bounded racial groups and set the stage for the racialization of suburban residential and civic life. Until the post-War era, race was used to solidify a social hierarchy that kept blacks on the bottom and permitted economic mobility for whites (Smedley 1993, 206). Weber's insight into the process of monopolistic group closure is consistent with Bourdieu's; both scholars suggest that social capital is something more than 'connections'. The power and influence of a community's social capital and its ability to protect civic life are not merely dependent upon the volume of resources or the size of the group membership, as scholars have suggested. They also depend on the status (nobility) of the group that holds the social capital. As such, the black category symbolizes the absence of power, regardless of the presence or absence of networks. Total social exclusion was the norm for Blacks across north-eastern suburban communities before World War II.

As Michael Omi and Howard Winant point out, prior to the war, state institutions were racial institutions that enforced the racial politics of everyday life (Omi and Winant 1994, 83). The Federal Housing Authority's (FHA) policies, widely known as redlining, directly contributed to the widespread use of restrictive covenants by white property owners. Both the FHA and the Home Owners Loan Corporation (HOLC) issued residential security maps to define desirable and undesirable areas for investment by the banking industry. black residential areas (marked in red) and racially mixed areas were deemed undesirable investments. Public policy throughout the first half of the twentieth century supported racial homogenization of residential areas, thus contributing to the devaluation of black-owned property (Jackson 1985, 199–218; Oliver and Shapiro 1995, 40; Palen 1995, 121). State policies were directly responsible for encouraging the development of residentially-based racial networks.

Omi and Winant argue that state institutions set the 'rules of the game' and 'the limits for political legitimacy in general' (83). Prior to the Second World War, racial rule restricted the growing urbanized black population from entry into the political sphere and set the limits for their mobilization within civil society (Winant 2001, 112). It denied commonalities between otherwise similar whites and idealized racial categories as all-embracing social differences. Barred from participation in the broader civil society, the residents of Runyon Heights were engaged in what Omi and Winant describe, and what Antonio Gramsci call, a *war of maneuver*. Under the oppressive conditions of the racial state, subordinate groups sought to extend their territory, ward off violent assault, and develop an internal society (Omi and Winant 1994). The nineteen forties marked the beginning of the democratization of state institutions and a concomitant shift in the strategy of residents from a *war of maneuver* to a *war of position*. This second strategy, predicated on local political struggle, was encouraged by the evolving post-war institutional environment; community organizational efforts shifted from religious and social activities to political activities and community defense. Consistent with the classic description of a war of position, having a voice in the political system was a precondition for open confrontation in Runyon Heights (Winant 2001, 113).

Recent scholars have mischaracterized social capital as a cultural phenomenon that reflects enduring group norms that cannot be explained in terms of rational values or social structure (Jackman and Miller 1998). In his early work, which seeks to explain differences in the development of regional government in Italy, Putnam argued that the lack of 'civic culture' of particular regions has condemned them to stunted citizenship, meager social and cultural associations, fear of lawlessness, and the demand for sterner discipline (Putnam 2002). These 'uncivic' regions lack voter-turnout, newspaper readership, membership in choral societies, literary circles, and social and sports clubs (Putnam 1993).

In *Bowling Alone* (2000), Putnam turns his focus to the United States and again emphasizes the importance of trust in establishing norms and networks that encourage civic engagement and serve as preconditions for economic development and effective government. He contrasts romantic images of the good society circa 1950 with selective contemporary evidence to argue that people are no longer producing social capital by 'schmoozing' in bowling leagues, but now spend their time isolated and engaged in spectator activities like 'bowling alone'. This, he argues, accounts for the decline in political participation of the past decades, a claim that has been critically discussed by others (for example Lin 2001).

Important for our purpose here is that Putnam maintains that culturally grounded connections between individuals are by definition a public good and lead to good government. While citing voluntary associations and bowling leagues as preconditions for the good society, he discounts the significance of the dark side of social capital, such as youth gangs and organized crime. While Putnam acknowledges in Bowling Alone (2000), 'some kinds of bonding social capital may discourage some kinds of bridging capital and vice versa,' we emphasize the role of the state in shaping segregation racial endogamy, and the formation of closed social networks around whiteness that also serve the role of restricting access to social goods (362).

Putnam's view of social capital as a public good is consistent with Coleman's position that '… despite the public-good aspect of social capital, the more extensive persons call on one another for aid, the greater will be the quantity of social capital generated' (Coleman 1990, 321). Putnam's conception of social capital as predicated upon a common cultural orientation echoes that of Coleman, who views social capital as tantamount to social organization. But while Coleman emphasizes structural constraints and the rational responses of actors in explaining the development of social capital, Putnam privileges culture as the driving force. Lowry and Fernandez-Kelley side with Coleman, recognizing that social groups are segregated by race as well as by class and that different social capital networks have unequal value and power. Weber reminds us that social capital is more than a way to measure the social networks of Bourdieu's model and the civic engagement of Putnam's model; it is also a mechanism for closure and the reproduction of unequal group status along racial lines. This unequal distribution is significant when assessing the value of the segregated networks that developed in Runyon Heights, and it informs our understanding of both Putnam and Bourdieu's conception of social capital as 'schmoozing' and having 'connections'. As Lin (2000) observes, scholarship widely supports the notion that social capital is unevenly distributed across social groups

(787). The unequal capital distribution between the black and white middle classes in all of its forms had dire consequences for the residents of Runyon Heights.

A summary of recent literature reveals four central functions of social capital: 1) as a source of social control for parents, teachers and communities (Zhou and Bankston 1996; McNeal 1999; Coleman 1988, 1997); 2) as a source of support for families and communities (Coleman 1988; MacGillivray 2002); 3) as a source of employment and mobility (Loury 1977, 2002; Granovetter 1973), 4) as a basis for civic engagement and governmental performance (Brehm and Rahn 1997; Putnam 1995). We will turn to an examination of three of the four functions of social capital identified above: as a source of support for families and communities, as a source of control for parents and teachers, and as a basis for civic engagement and governmental performance.

Community Institutions and the Development of Social Capital

Interviews and archival sources revealed that Newcomers to the Runyon Heights community since the 1920s have experienced racial steering and racially-biased mortgage practices that directed them specifically to the area. These practices were part of an inhospitable social climate based on the stigma[10] of race that encouraged both the development of an all-black residential area and the formation of local institutions and social networks along racial lines (Haynes 2001). According to Goffman (1963), stigmatization hinders the development of social networks between normals and the stigmatized because of the tendency for a stigma to spread from the stigmatized to their close connections (30). One result of racial stigmatization was that neighboring areas were developed using racially restrictive covenants that barred blacks. Although restrictive covenants would be deemed unconstitutional by the Supreme Court in the Shelley v. Kraemer (1948) decision, black residents in Westchester County region have continued to experience racial steering practices and resistance from white homeowners into the 1990s.

The south, east, and west sides of Runyon Heights are bounded by major boulevards, and the north is bordered by a four-foot-wide strip of land adjacent to a nearly all-white community named Homefield. In 1924, the 'reserve strip' was created by the Homeland Company, the developer that subdivided the estate that was to be called Homefield, with the clear purpose of marking a physical boundary between Black-dominated Runyon Heights and the new predominantly-white

---

10 Erving Goffman (1963) outlined the concept of stigma in his classic work, *Stigma: Notes on the Management of Spoiled Identity* (1963). A stigma is a stereotyped physical attribute or sign that discredits the moral character of the possessor. It is an undesired difference that reduces a person to something less than human (3–6). Goffman identified three types of stigmas: abominations of the body; blemishes of individual character; and the tribal stigma of race, nation and religion. He argued that stigma is part of a system of honor; it is a relationship between status groups: the normals and the stigmatized (7). The central feature of the stigmatized individual's situation is 'acceptance' by the normals and normals tend to avoid association with the stigmatized, except for a minority, who are called 'the wise' (30). One might argue that bridging networks constitutes a type of 'wise' individual.

community. The exclusionary motivation behind the creation of the reserve strip was made clear by the Homefield Association's purchase and maintenance of the strip in 1947. Additionally, Homefield properties used restrictive covenants to bar Negro homeowners. A deed dated 1935 from Curtis Lane, near the Homefield-Runyon border, contained a typical restrictive covenant: 'The granted premises shall be sold only to and occupied by members of the Caucasian race.' Not only did the reserve strip result in dead-end streets in Runyon Heights, but it also served as a symbolic reminder of white racial exclusivity and black rejection (Haynes 2001). Spatial demarcations provided an important context for the reproduction of racial endogamy and the formation and solidification of segregated social institutions and networks. Homefield remained virtually all white into the 1940s and 92 percent white as late as 1990 (Haynes 2001). While the strip created dead-end streets between Homefield and Runyon Heights that helped to isolate the neighborhood from outsiders and provide a protective environment for local children, it reinforced the symbolic link between race and place; since Runyon Heights was known across the region as a place where blacks lived, race made place, and, in doing so, place symbolically reproduced race.

During the early years, four categories of community institutions were significant sites for the development of social capital resources for the families and the community of Runyon Heights: the family, the church, voluntary social and political organizations, and the local elementary school. Multigenerational ties between families developed early on in Runyon Heights; marrying the gal or guy next door and moving back to the neighborhood was not uncommon among the first generations of residents. After the family, the church has long been recognized as the second most important institution in the black community (Frazier 1948, 333); Runyon Heights is no different. Early generations of blacks in the city of Yonkers were unwelcome at established 'white' churches. By the 1870s several all-Negro churches had begun to develop (Haynes 2001). Finding an inhospitable climate at the all-white churches in their area, newcomers to Runyon Heights formed a small prayer group. The group continued to recruit members as new folks, and by 1931, when the group dedicated a church building, membership had grown considerably. The group now joined the African Methodist Episcopal Church, naming their new church Metropolitan. By this time, the church had established itself as a central community institution and many of the most prestigious families in the area were members.

The cultural and religious orientations of the original Runyon Heights residents varied greatly from unskilled rural Baptists and Methodists to skilled Catholics from the Caribbean. Nevertheless, racial segregation encouraged cooperative community activities from the outset. Black and white adults remained socially segregated from one another; a largely Italian-born Catholic minority that lived in the neighborhood largely kept to itself, while other whites shunned black participation in local social and religious life. Social isolation and marginality encouraged blacks to create their own social world. They established a church, social clubs, sports leagues, and civic and political associations. Barely fifty years after the end of Reconstruction, a thriving black suburb was making its bid for inclusion in the American Dream.

The church provided the key institutional anchor for these developing social networks. It welcomed new members into the community, provided them with a sense of place and group identity, and fostered strong communal solidarity and trust between group members. The church represents a source of ethnic/racial solidarity and a form of bonding capital within the group, rather than a source of bridging capital linking Runyon residents to resource-rich white networks (Arneil 2006, 170). While never a direct source of political mobilization, the church in Runyon Heights nevertheless remained the hub for strong inter-generational family networks and served to extend these networks deep into community life. A number of civic-minded groups like the Men's Club and the Women's Civic Club were a direct outgrowth of Metropolitan A.M.E.

Numerous collective associations took the form of social clubs that held overlapping membership and provided a rich network of 'connections' that could be invoked for specific community-oriented goals. Over the next two decades, Runyon Heights evolved into a community of hyper-organized social networks and effective ties. One long-time resident explained about growing up in Runyon Heights in terms that echo Putnam and the idyllic American community:

> And it has a link I think through our morals and our values again because you know it was kind of a place – where everybody knows everybody else as a child, everybody else, at least back when I was growing up, is your supervisor or guardian and you were a little more restrained about doing things because you always kind of had eyes on you all the time. And I'd like to feel that in other communities that might not have been the case. You know, in other communities where maybe the first, some of the first and strongest links are made through you know schools and things like that, and being next door neighbors and belonging to school organizations, a lot of the initial links, I mean even as a child is family links. I mean people who I met later on through school or through participating in sports together, that was because again, my mother's sister-in-law, her cousin or sister-in-law, her kids, it's just family. Basically it kind of started as this large extended family, it kind of, you know, gets down to your core family, but I think you meet first that way too. There's always a family kind of thing. People out here identify themselves as being a part of such and such family. They identify somebody's house, that's the so and so house, and that's the way you do normally with, let's say a town or a larger area, but people out there still say that. They'll say well the car is parked out in front of the so and so house. That family could have been out of that [house] seventy years ago, but this person is going to say the so and so house ... That's how we identify things. And we identify a lot of things here by people. I am Joe Jones' son. I am Carol Jones' son. Until I get to a certain point, and maybe when my generation dominates a little bit then and my kids will be, that's Pete Jones' son.

The third most important source for the development of social capital was the local voluntary association, the Runyon Heights Improvement Association (R.H.I.A). Founded in the 1920s, it has remained the principal civic organization throughout the community's history. Originally, the R.H.I.A. was oriented towards fostering neighborliness, social activities, and children's recreation, and scholars have noted that dense social networks and residential stability fosters strong social organizations and safe neighborhood environments (Patillo 1999). Women members proved to be a critical resource by publishing a newsletter called the *Nepperhan*[11] *Civic Recorder*, which was an important source linking resources and information. A number of clubs and associations listed in the *Recorder* in 1933, such as the Women's Civic Club, The Men's Club, and the Mother's Club, have maintained intergenerational membership and still exist today. Other groups, like the local all-Negro baseball team the 'Runyon AC's,' survived little more than a generation.

Soon after it's founding, the R.H.I A. built a small community center, which locals called the Community House. Complete with ping pong and pool tables and adult supervision, it provided a meeting place for community youths. The Community House was soon destroyed by a fire in the late 1930s, and the R.H.I.A. declined in importance over the next twenty years. In 1956, a city-proposed public housing complex prompted the reactivation of the R.H.I.A., and a second community house was dedicated in 1963. The R.H.I.A. has moved beyond its original function as a recreational facility for children. Not only has it been a place to hold community meetings, throw holiday parties for local children, and provide recreation, but it has increasingly come to serve as a political instrument that represents and protects community interests. We will revisit this topic in the next section.

The fourth institution that proved critical for the development of social capital in Runyon Heights was the local elementary school, School 1. Because the population in the region was generally dispersed, School 1 served both black and white children from the surrounding area. As a result, the school was integrated for nearly two decades. Not only did the school provide its first black pupils with unprecedented access to quality elementary education; it also served an important role in the organization of civic life. School 1 was a place where multiple generations attended; teachers, students, and the community were intertwined. The building itself provided a central meeting place for Runyon Heights parents. Even the local Boy Scout troop held meetings there. School volunteering, local PTA's, and informal ties to educators have shown to increase the amount of information about schooling available to parents and even intensify ties among parents in the local community (Lareau 1989). While black residents in Runyon Heights formed their own collective associations, like the local Parent Teachers Association and the Men's Club, and joined national Christian-based associations like the Prince Hall Masons and the Order of the Eastern Stars, what should not be overlooked is that all of these groups held much less power relative to white Protestant and white voluntary associations (Arneil 2006, 23).

While black and white adults in the area were generally cordial to one another, they socialized little. Occasionally, black and white children established lasting friendships, some of which would later serve as bridges to white social capital networks. Old timers from the area often reminisced about Sunday afternoons lost to games of sandlot baseball and football among white and black neighborhood children. More importantly, 'connections' made with the children of the largely immigrant minority that lived in the neighborhood later proved to be instrumental to the success of local battles in the Runyon Height community.

---

11 Nepperhan and Runyon Heights were used interchangeably as names for the area. See Haynes (2001).

Early residents were active in party politics and often split their party affiliation, much like middle-class suburban blacks do today. By the time the Runyon Heights Democratic Club was formed in June 1933, both the Republican Club of Nepperhan and the Phyllis Wheatley Republican Club had already been established. While early voter participation rates were not available, residents recalled being active participants and the percentage of active registered voters has remained high (Haynes 2001). Residents reported that trips to the local barber or hairdresser might also double as an opportunity to engage in political discussions with fellow residents. Women frequented two locally-owned beauty salons along Saw Mill River and Tuckahoe Roads; men often frequented a small barbershop known as Trent's in the basement of a local resident's home. These establishments did more than provide an important personal service; they served as a place where information was exchanged and local opinions shaped. One resident stated it simply, 'Trent's, it was a very political atmosphere. You know, when you went in, they talked about what was going on in the community.'

One 31-year-old resident explained how the community uses multiple networks to tap the resource-rich networks within mainstream political institutions, and how National civil rights organizations like the N.A.A.C.P. provided an important extra-communal legal framework for local challenges to discrimination:

> What happens is, politicians count every vote, no matter which one it is, and fortunately for us, because of the education of the folks in the neighborhood, this is something that's been there way before my time. So people are smart enough to be on both sides of the playing field. We have a Republican leader of the Tenth Ward ... and he has a lot of networks. And a lot of the folks that live in Runyon Heights either work for the city as employees ... so they have a lot of political savvy. They know that you have to show up at the fund raisers, and all that other kind of stuff, and that's how that works, that people are able to make phone calls and do that ... And now it hits them twice, because is this going to be a problem with people of color, is this going to be a problem for the N.A.A.C.P. ... or is this a problem in the neighborhood, is this a problem for Runyon Heights? And we know how to use our leverage appropriately to get the things done.

In the early period of Runyon Heights, the church provided the basis for a rich network of community organizations; later it served as a basis for high levels of political involvement. Putnam (2000) argues that 'faith-based organizations' are particularly central to building social capital and civic engagement in African American communities (68). But Putnam fails to account for the changing institutional environment in which black social networks emerged in the late Progressive era. The early period of community life was dominated by the kind of institution and culture building characteristic of Gramsci's *war of maneuver* leading to the development of rich social networks that served as a source of social control and support for families and community. But as residents found themselves unable to wield influence in the formal social and political arenas, they soon tested a more confrontational civic strategy that resembles Gramsci's *war of position*. As we detail below, a conflict over public education in 1928 provided just the context for shifting strategies. The community's success in this conflict foreshadowed more open political struggles that would become characteristic of the post-War community. The next section explores how residents used their social capital as a basis for a new, more confrontational style of civic engagement as they shifted to a strategy of war of position.

The Limits of Social Capital as a Basis for Civic Engagement

Although World War II marks the beginning of the democratization of state institutions, which further encouraged minority political engagement and protest. Residents had already made a subtle shift, however, testing a strategy of a *war of position* in the late 1920s; As the first generation of Runyon Heights children reached their teens, efforts were made by the local school board to segregate them in inferior schools, thus limiting the development of human capital across generations.

In 1925, Runyon Heights was 53 percent black and comprised only 369 residents; by 1940 it was more than 72 percent black and was home to some 1,015 people.[12] The growth in population in the general area led to the building of a new high school, Roosevelt High School. While the school was located just one-half mile away from the Runyon Heights community, the Yonkers School Board had planned to bus Runyon children to schools across town. Parents questioned the standards at these alternative schools, which were widely considered less academically oriented, and believed that the all-white policy threatened their children's future mobility. Mothers quickly responded by organizing community residents to petition the Yonkers School Board. Their challenge was based on the grounds that taxes from the Nepperhan Valley region, which included the Runyon Heights area, were used in the construction of Roosevelt. Residents understood that their tax obligations entitled them to access to public services. Threatened with legal action, the school board reluctantly withdrew their segregationist plan and permitted local black teens to attend the new high school. As the spouse of one activist-mother recounted, 'The black mothers fought and got their children in the school'.

The Roosevelt affair was the first outside event to trigger a collective political response on the part of community residents; from that point forward, race shaped their collectively defined interests. Emboldened by their successes, residents began shifting to more open and direct challenges to local race subordination. Encouraged by a new anti-discrimination policy in federal contracts during World War Two, residents shifted attention to discrimination in local industry.

Using a strategy not too different from Jesse Jackson's Operation Push, a group of concerned black citizens went to local industries as representatives of their local Yonkers' communities and petitioned for better hiring practices. Middle-class and working-class blacks organized, taking their message directly to employers. One long-time resident explained:

Not only community people, but they were people from out of the community who were interested in it. But they decided that the community should get busy, because in all of these plants and things people were going to work for defense. And they weren't hiring black people here, you know. So they decided that they would make a survey and a visit to all of these plants. And Mr McRae and Dr Rivera, I think it was, and me, the three of

---

12 1925 New York State Census Manuscripts, U.S. Census of the Population 1940.

us went to these various places like Alexander Smith down here. That was a big going factory then. And we went to Phelps Dodge, and we went to Anaconda Wire and Cable, and asked them why they didn't hire blacks … I didn't go to Otis, but I think they went. I think they went, but I think Otis had one or two black people anyway … And there was money around, and black people weren't getting any. And so that's why they went into it. We were being called to go fight, well not really to go fight, but to go serve those fighters.

The Depression years had a detrimental impact on the demographic makeup of School 1. In 1938, school district lines were redrawn and School 1 was made into the smallest school zone in Yonkers, destroying the integrated character of the school. Over the next fifteen years, Runyon children were increasingly isolated at School 1, where the quality of education significantly dropped, and white students were relocated to the already predominantly-white Schools #5 and 22 (80 CIV. 6761 LBS Cited in Haynes 2001). Runyon Heights' residents firmly believed that education was the ticket to future middle-class prosperity for their children; after the war, their attention returned to the schools. By 1950, School 1 had become 91 percent black. First and second grades and third and fourth grades were combined into single grades, and the school enrolled a mere 100 students in a facility designed for 240 (80 CIV. 6761 LBS.: 274 Cited in Haynes 2001). Once again, residents' experiences with the Yonkers Board of Education helped to reinforce collective solidarity around race, and their collective interests in the financial future of their children prompted their civic engagement. Race subordination linked residents together in a community of common fate.

The community petitioned the Yonkers Board of Education to re-expand the School 1 district lines, effectively reintegrating the school. Integration with whites, while socially desirable for some middle-class blacks, was never the primary goal of Runyon Heights' residents. For them, integration was a method of achieving equal educational opportunity for their children. One woman who was a part of the protest committee reported:

Number 1 had become a nothing. Number 1 had become just a place to put black children. Number 1 had become totally an all-black school. I think they had white teachers there that were pulling in a salary who really had no interest in our children. And they could draw and they could sing, you know, but don't ask them to add anything.

The response of the Yonkers Board of Education to the May 1954 Brown decision by the Supreme Court marks the turning point in the development of social capital resources in the Runyon community. Residents began to use national organizations to fight local battles; the N.A.A.C.P. joined the petitioners in both the Brown case and the Roosevelt High School conflict. Following the precedent of the Brown case, the Board decided to close School 1 and desegregate Schools 5 and 22 by reassigning Runyon Heights' children to them. The era of School 1 as both community resource and substitute Community House had come to an end; Runyon children would henceforth be bussed to other areas. Social capital resources, in the form of ties between children, ties between children and parents, and ties between parents were weakened as children were dispersed across the city.

In 1956, another issue confronted the collective interests of Runyon residents. The Yonkers City Council proposed building 335 units of low-income public housing in the Runyon Heights, not far from the Homefield border. This was the first in a series of public housing proposals the community would confront over the next forty years. This first project , which called for the building of 335 low-income units in the area, would have transformed the economic character of the community and undermined local efforts to maintain property values, low crime rates, and a sense of community. One former president of the R.H.I.A. summed it up, 'This is the reason why you see a Community House. This is the reason why you see us organized now, because we had to get organized. That was it.'

The battle over public housing brought the black residents of Runyon Heights into allegiance with the neighboring Homefield community. Both groups objected to the city government's low-income housing plan as they sought to protect their own class interests. The local N.A.A.C.P. was once again called upon to advocate for Runyon Heights residents, although it was also advocating for low-income housing in Yonkers. Not only had the organization been supported by community residents, many of whom were dues-paying members, but Runyon Heights had also been home to many former and current N.A.A.C.P. leaders. The battle against low-income housing in Runyon Heights placed Homefield residents in indirect alliance with the N.A.A.C.P. What is striking is that after having created and maintained the four-foot reserve strip as an artificial border separating Runyon Heights, the Homefield community now made common cause with their black neighbours. New coalition aside, one crucial difference remained between the motivations of Runyon Heights and Homefield residents: residents of Runyon Heights were not troubled by the fact that most of the low-income residents would be black and Latino. Their motivation for resistance was based on protecting the class composition of the community.

The rejuvenated R.H.I.A. had learned how to broker external resources and community interests by creating a bridge between both local and national organizational networks. Tapping into the resources of the N.A.A.C.P. and mobilizing local dissent around common class interests, residents of Runyon Heights united with the predominantly white Homefield community to defeat the proposal. But city demands for housing led to a compromise, and a smaller 48-unit public housing complex, called Hall Court, was subsequently approved for construction in Runyon Heights and completed in 1962. Insult was added to injury when the old School 1 site was designated as the location for the new project.

Focused on community defense, residents saw the need for another Community House. A number of residents participated in fundraising efforts and the new center was finally dedicated in 1963.[13] Born in an era of increased government spending on community service programs, the Community House expanded its programs and services under the auspices of the Runyon Heights Improvement Association. Active participation in the R. H. I. A. helped to maintain community cohesion in an era in which residents faced both the destruction of School 1 and a gradual decline in church attendance by newer residents.

---

13 Penny socials and tea parties were held to raise funds for the construction and operation of the center.

As residents became knowledgeable of the institutional environment and the multiple resource networks necessary to defend their collective interests, local ward politics and bridging networks grew in importance. Social clubs and community voluntary associations could not alone defend community interests in the current era, thus residents shifted their focus from service to political advocacy. One young male resident explained how local concerns encouraged residents to split party loyalties and get involved:

> The community would survive without the different organizational levels, but they wouldn't survive if they did not participate politically. If they didn't participate politically they would get left out, as everyone does when you don't participate politically. That's been the general problem for our folks is that they vote and they vote one line. They vote Democratic, but they don't look at issues. I try to educate people, you don't have to vote Democratic. You vote for the person that does, that handles your issues best – that supports the things you're looking to support. And if that person is from the New Zimbabwe Party, then you vote for them … Political support doesn't mean you voted for somebody. It meant who you worked for. Because they need foot soldiers, and all that stuff, going out there, priming the pump, talking to people, delivering whatever percentage of votes, because one vote, Nicholas Wascizco can tell you, he won by twelve votes.

Informal channels were equally important in addressing community concerns. By linking the social networks of local residents to individuals who held positions of power, brokers provided an important access to local resources. As one resident explained, 'You network, you work for the city, you know the right people, you talk to the right people. And if you do that properly, you'll get things done, because you'll be able to pick up the phone and talk to the right person. You see the appropriate person is not always the one that's in charge. The one that's appropriate may be the one that's sitting on the truck.' Personal ties and residential life in the City of Yonkers was closely linked to a political patronage system that was built into local ward politics. Fortunately for the community, many residents had attended the integrated School 1 and developed friendships with whites whose families were often positioned in local government and city administration. Those ties have proven critical to acquiring public services.

One individual played an especially instrumental role in galvanizing community resources: long-time resident Mr. Milton Holst. Sometimes called the 'mayor' by local officials and community residents, Holst is a man who takes pride in knowing his neighborhood and neighbors. He is a man who appears to know everyone when he drives through his neighborhood. Building on the networks he developed at School 1, Holst has since established relationships with individuals throughout the entire city. Following the example set by his parents, Holst became involved in community affairs as a young man. When he was only 25 and still living at home, he volunteered to become Scout Master of local Boy Scout Troop 34. After World War II, he became a city employee. He first became involved in local politics during the early sixties when the R.H.I.A. came into prominence; Holst became a critical link between the local community and public resources. As an adult with his own children, Holst began participating in club house and party politics, attending city hall meetings and escorting local political candidates door to door. He described local district leaders as the 'first line of offence' in local political battles. By 1990, Holst had become the president of the Tenth Ward Republican Club. He was also a major force in the local R.H.I.A., where he took on a number of responsibilities, including president (five occasions) and Action Chairman under at least four presidents. An outgoing and personable individual, 'Milty,' as those close to him sometimes call him, helped to build numerous social networks that tapped resources for the community. Currently retired, Milton Holst still takes his responsibility to the community seriously and most days can be found busy at the Community House. One sixty-year-old second generation mother details the importance of the Community House as place of safety for children during the 1960s:

> When they were young the parents with young kids used to take turns going over. With Mr. Wilson (former President of R.H.I.A.) they used to have, on weekends, little socials. As long as the parents, someone could be there to supervise … Before that they were in the day camps and things over there. They played on the basketball teams. That was very instrumental in their development too. The center over there, that was sort of a focal point for them and their activities.

Bruce: Did most of the kids in the neighborhood participate?

> Yeah, quite a few participated in some way over there. That was one thing that was good for them. They got a chance to be with their own, you know, their own peers and things, right in their own community. They didn't have to go to another area. So from that community center they were able to make a lot of friends, you know. A lot of them are still friends now, after all these years.

Mothers tended to organize the household around their children, and banded together to balance family and career responsibilities. Employed mothers organized day care when their children were young, often sharing duties or employing a local relative. Some stay-at-home moms formally structured their relationships with groups like the Idlers Club, while others relied on the general resources of the local community. One resident, born in 1925, had lived in Runyon Heights since the age of five and attended School 1. After marriage, she lived for a brief time in a housing project on the west side of the city with her husband and six children. In 1961, she moved the family back to Runyon Heights. Following the sudden death of her husband in 1964, she became trained as a dental assistant and returned to the workforce, with the assurance that her children were safe in the neighborhood:

> I found that when my husband died and my baby was about two, and my children were all in grammar school or starting to go into junior high school, and I found that here I never worried. I had to go to work then, but I didn't worry. When I went out of here I never worried that they'd get in to gangs or fighting, because everybody was a community. A community that I knew, you worried about my kids like I worried about hers. Everybody around would look, and if something went wrong they would tell me … Oh, yeah! We were all right here for each other.

Despite our respondent's rich social networks, her college credentials, and the safety of the community, her children enjoyed far less success; all of her children had attended at least two years of college, but only one had actually graduated. The inability to pass down social status and capital to the next generation remains a major challenge for the black middle class. Small (2004) discusses the importance of generational status[14] in explaining varying levels of civic participation (157, 179).

Throughout the nineteen seventies, eighties, and nineties, the suburban character of the community continued to come under assault from outside forces, and Runyon Heights increasingly took on the characteristics of the defended community (Suttles 1972). Businesses sought development in the area and the city repeatedly proposed building additional low-income housing in the community's backyard. The R.H.I.A. continued to grow both in membership and importance as older residents successfully mobilized newcomers and developed strategies for defending local interests.

Discussion

The case of Runyon Heights provides strong empirical evidence to refute Putnam's view that communities need only trust-based social networks to create sufficient amounts of social capital for the good society. Active civic engagement, strong voter turnout, and high levels of social organization did not lead to the prosperous society and good government for the residents of Runyon Heights. While the community displayed all of the essential qualities of the ideal civic-mined community, segregation and institutional exclusion limited the operational value of their social capital networks. DeFilippis (2001) argues that Putnam's position fails to account for differences in power and economic capital in the production of communities. Using levels of "schmoozing" as the foundation for a conception of social capital is limiting because the central issue facing a segregated community is access to power. Prior to Brown, schmoozing with "Coloreds" brought few rewards to white Americans. One local business woman detailed how she hired a white man to negotiate particular issues with clients in her real estate business; she even reported that she purchased a home in Homefield because the seller, seeking vengeance against his neighbor, purposefully sought out a black realtor. Bourdieu suggests that race is a set of social relationships that regulates the distribution of power and status. In Runyon Heights, institutionalized racial boundaries reinforced black isolation while providing differential access to Capital in all of its forms. Emerson (1962) posits that power resides implicitly in the dependency of others. The very nature of segregation instills dependency in the segregated since access to social institutions, such as housing, education, employment, and government, is controlled by the segregator. Putnam's analysis of community development fails to consider concepts of power-dependent relationships and the differing values of social capital in alienated communities. Despite strong familial and civic ties, residents could not manage the inequities imposed by segregation. Rendered ineffective, as alienation prohibited access to critical social institutions, the social capital of the segregated

---

14 We define generational status as a resident's position in the life course, as well the timing of their cohort's settlement in the area. Small (2004), however, uses the term 'generational status' to refer to resident's 'generation of migration' as discussed by Portes and Rumbaut (2001) (157).

was devalued. The strong ties among Runyon Heights residents were consequently ineffective in negotiating resource-rich white networks; thus their material wealth was always threatened by racial subordination.

While the number and strength of locally-based social clubs and voluntary associations have declined since the first decades, Runyon Heights witnessed a high level of civic engagement during the decades following World War II. And contrary to the expectations of Putnam, one of the more active groups in Runyon Heights during the 1990's was Senior Group 8, a bowling league made up of long-time community residents. Although we did not find competitive bowling leagues for children in Runyon Heights, older residents have continued to be engaged in spirited bowling competition against other senior teams representing other Yonkers communities. The growth in importance of the R.H.I.A demonstrates that social capital (community networks) have changed, rather than simply declined, in the post-Brown era. Residents have shifted network membership from local clubs to more formal political institutions like the R.H.I.A. and supra-community associations like the N.A.A.C.P., which channel social capital towards community defense.

Conclusion

The story of Runyon Heights details how racial endogamy shaped the creation of racially defined suburban residential space. Race provided the basis for determining moral value, as well as the unequal distribution of power and resources that were reflected in segregated social and civic institutions. By implementing racially biased policies prior to the Brown decision, federal and local agencies created a unique set of dilemmas for the black middle class. State institutions helped to structure the physical boundaries of community around race and strongly influenced the value of the social capital that developed among black residents. The limited value of residents' social capital is evidenced by their institutional marginality and lack of political influence prior to the Brown decision.

Civic engagement was indeed a precondition for manifesting social capital in Runyon Heights, but it was changes in the post-Brown institutional environment that prompted residents towards a strategy of *war of position*, redirecting organizational efforts towards formal politics and agitation through the Runyon Heights Improvement Association. What occurred was not an absolute decline in social capital, as Putnam would surmise, but a shift in collective focus towards more formal methods of civic engagement. Neighborhood conditions and external threats redirected the thrust of social organization towards instrumental ends. The Brown ruling had a direct impact on the decision to close School 1 in 1956. The court's recognition of institutional discrimination gave blacks political power and transformed Runyon Heights into a defended community, as residents were able to draw upon the increased value of their social capital and claim a place in the civic arena (Suttles 1972; Haynes 2001). The value of their social capital changed because institutional inclusion reduced the level of social stigma attached to race. Whites recognized this symbolic breakdown in the color bar, and as a result, felt an increased freedom to socialize and network with blacks.

Contrary to the classic description of the defended community (Janowitz 1967; Suttles 1972), Runyon Heights had already experienced high levels of social organization, yet neighborhood conditions and external threats redirected the thrust of social organization towards instrumental ends. The issue of equal rights took on a local dimension as black residents organized, protested and eventually aligned with their white neighbors to protect community interests. As the community united for defense, political alliances based on prior bridge relationships, could be nurtured with whites who had once excluded them. The development of light industry in the area and repeated proposals for low-income housing led residents to organize their resource networks more strongly than ever.

Segregation throughout America is characterized by physical, social and psychological boundaries of exclusion. Runyon Heights residents demonstrate, through the use of extensive social networks, how social capital is utilized to transcend group boundaries. These race-based boundaries act to limit black residents' access to social goods. Despite a high degree of civic engagement, Runyon Heights residents became dependent on relationships with dominant groups and their ties to local government. Theoretically, we challenge Putnam's culturalist orientation that social networks carry intrinsic value and provide a case that demonstrates the importance of state institutions in determining the value of a group's social capital. Contrary to Putnam's notion that civic engagement leads to good government, Runyon Heights reveals the 'dark side of social capital' and the importance of state institutions in creating and maintaining race and class inequities.

References

Anheier, H.K., Gerhards, J. and Romo, F.P. (January, 1995), 'Forms of Capital and Social Structure in Cultural Fields: Examining Bourdieu's Social Topography', *The American Journal of Sociology*, Vol. 100, No. 4, 859–903.

Bourdieu, P. (1997), 'The Forms of Capital,' in Halsey, A.H., Lauder, H., Brown, H.P. and Wells, A.S. (eds), *Education: Culture, Economy, Society* (Oxford: Oxford University Press).

Brehm, J. and Rahn, W. (1997), 'Individual-Level Evidence for the Causes and Consequences of Social Capital', *American Journal of Political Science* 41 (3), 999–1023.

Burt, R. 'The Contingent Value of Social Capital', *Administrative Science Review* 42 (2), 339–365.

—— (2000), 'The Network Structure of Social Capital', *Research in Organizational Behavior*, Vol 22. Robert Sutton and Barry Staw (eds) (Greenwich: JAI Press).

—— (1992), *Structural Holes: The Social Structure of Competition* (Cambridge: Harvard University Press).

Cohen, D. and Prusak, L. (2001), *In Good Company* (Boston: Harvard Business School Press).

Coleman, J. 'Social Capital in the Creation of Human Capital', *American Journal of Sociology*, 1988 (94), s95–s120.

—— (1994) *Foundations of Social Theory* (Cambridge: Harvard University Press).

Daniel, G. and Reginald, G. (2002), *More Than Black: Multiracial Identity and the New Racial Order* (Philadelphia: Temple University Press).

Davis, J. (1991), *Who is Black? One Nation's Definition*, State College (Pa: Pennsylvania State University Press).

DeFilippis, J. (2001), 'The Myth of Social Capital in Community Development', *Housing Policy Debate*, vol. 12, No. 4, 781–806.

Emerson, R. (1962), 'Power-Dependence Relations', *American Sociological Review*, 27 (1), 31–41.

Falk, I. (2001), 'Human and Social Capital: A Case Study of Conceptual Colonisation', *Centre for Research and Learning in Regional Australia*, CRLRA Discussion Paper Series ISSN 1440–480x, Discussion Paper D8/2001, University of Tasmania.

Fernandez-Kelly, M.P. (1995), 'Social and Cultural Capital in the Urban Ghetto: Implications for the Economic Sociology of Immigration,' in *The Economic Sociology of Immigration: Essays on Networks, Ethnicity and Entrepreneurship*, Alejandro Portes (ed.) (New York: Russell Sage Foundation).

Fishman, R. (1987), *Bourgeois Utopias: The Rise and Fall of Suburbia* (New York: Basic Books).

Frank, K. and Yasumoto, J. (November 1998), 'Linking Action to Social Structure Within a System: Social Capital Within and Between Subgroups', *American Journal of Sociology*, 104 (3), 642–686.

Granovetter, M. (1973), 'The Strength of Weak Ties', *American Journal of Sociology*, 78 (6) 1360–1380.

Green, G.P., Tigges, L.M. and Brown, I. (1995), 'Social Resources, Job Search and Poverty in Atlanta', *Research in Community Sociology*, vol. 5, pp. 161–182.

Haynes, B. (2001), *Red Lines, Black Spaces* (New Haven: Yale University Press).

Hero, R.E. (2003), 'Social Capital and Racial Inequality in America', *Perspectives on Politics*, Vol. 1, No. 1, 113–122.

Jackman, R.W. and Miller, R.A. (1998), 'Social Capital and Politics', *Annual Review of Political Science*, vol. 1, pp. 47–73.

Jackson, K. (1985), *Crabgrass Frontier* (New York: Oxford University Press).

Janowitz, M. (1967), *The Community Press in an Urban Setting* (Chicago: University of Chicago Press).

Johnson, C. (2003), 'A Model of Social Capital Formation', *SDRC working paper series 03-01*, Social Research and Demonstration Corporation.

Lareau, A. (1993), *Home Advantage: Social Class and Parental Intervention in Elementary Education* (New York: The Falmer Press).

Lin, N. (2001), *Social Capital: A Theory of Social Structure and Action.* (Cambridge: Cambridge University Press).

—— (2000), 'Inequality in Social Capital', *Contemporary Sociology*, vol. 29, no. 6, 785–795.

—— (1999), 'Social Networks and Status Attainment', *American Review of Sociology* (25), 467–487.

Loury, G. (2002), *Anatomy of Racial Inequality* (Cambridge: Harvard University Press).

—— (1977), 'A Dynamic Theory of Racial Income Differences', in *Women, Minorities, and Employment Discrimination*, Phyllis Wallace and Annette LaMond (eds) (Lexington: Lexington Books).

MacGillivray, A. (2002), 'The Glue Factory – Social Capital, Business Innovation and Trust', New Economics Foundation, cited in *Social Capital: A Discussion Paper*, Aldridge, S., Halpern, D. and Fitzpatrick, S.. The Prime Minister's Strategy Unit, London.

McNeal, R. Jr. (1999), 'Parental Involvement as Social Capital: Differential Effectiveness on Science Achievement, Truancy, and Dropping Out', *Social Forces*, 78 (1), 117–144.

Oliver, M. and Shapiro, T. (1995), *Black Wealth, White Wealth: A New Perspective on Racial Inequality* (New York: Routledge).

Omi, M. and Winant, H. (1994), *Racial Formation in the United States: From the 1960s to the 1990s*, 2nd Edn. (New York: Routledge).

Orr, M. (1999), *Black Social Capital: The Politics of School Reform in Baltimore, 1986–1998* (Lawrence: University Press of Kansas).

Palen, J.J. (1995), *The Suburbs* (New York: McGraw-Hill).

Pattillo, M.E. (March 1998), 'Sweet Mothers and Gangbangers: Managing Crime in a Black Middle-Class Neighborhood', *Social Forces*, vol. 76, No. 3. 747–774.

Portes, A. (1988), 'Social Capital: Its Origins and Applications in Modern Sociology,' *Annual Review of Sociology* (24), 1–24.

Putnam, R.D. (2000), *Bowling Alone: The Collapse and Revival of American Community* (New York: Touchstone).

—— (2002), 'The Prosperous Community: Social Capital and Public Life', *American Prospect*.

—— (1993), 'The Prosperous Community', *American Prospect*, vol. 4 (13) http://www.prospect.org/ppprint/V4/13/putnam-r.html.

—— (1995), 'Bowling Alone: America's Declining Social Capital', *Journal of Democracy* 6:65–78.

—— '*E Pluribus Unum*: Diversity and Community in the Twenty-first Century. The 2006 Johan Skytte Prize Lecture.' *Scandinavian Political Studies*, Vol. 30 – No. 2, 2007.

Siegelman, L. and Welch, S. (1994), *Black American's Views of Racial Inequality: The Dream Deferred* (Cambridge: Cambridge University Press).

Sirianni, C.J., and Friedland, L.A (2001), *Civic Innovation in America: Community Empowerment, Public Policy, and the Movement for Civic Renewal* (Berkeley and Los Angeles: University of California Press).

Small, M.L. (2004), *Villa Victoria: The Transformation of Social Capital in a Boston Barrio* (Chicago: The University of Chicago Press).

Smedley, A. (1993), *Race in North America: Origins and Evolution of a World View* (Boulder Colorado: Westview Press).

Stanton-Salazar, R. and Dornbusch, S. (April 1995), 'Social Capital and the Reproduction of Inequality: Informational Networks Among Mexican-Origin High School Students', *Sociology of Education*, 68 (2), 116–135.

Suttles, G. (1972), *The Social Construction of Communities* (Chicago: University of Chicago Press).

Teachman, J., Paasch. K. and Carver, K. (August 1996), 'Social Capital and Dropping Out of School Early', *Journal of Marriage and the Family*, 58 (3), 773–783.

Teachman, J., Paasch. K. and Carver, K. (June 1997), 'Social Capital and the Generation of Human Capital', *Social Forces*, 75 (4), 1343–1359.

Weber, M. (1968), *Economy and Society*, Roth, G. and Wittich, C. (1968) (eds) (Berkeley: University of California Press).

Zhou, M. and Bankston, C. (1998), III. *Growing Up American: How Vietnamese Children Adapt to Life in the United States* (New York: Russell Sage Foundation).

PART 2
Networks and Urban Social Capital

Chapter 5

A New Place, a New Network? Social Capital Effects of Residential Relocation for Poor Women

Alexandra M. Curley

Introduction

Social capital and social networks have become popular topics of interest among poverty scholars as more and more studies suggest that people who live in concentrated poverty neighborhoods have fewer 'life chances'. Research to date, however, does not provide a clear story of what social capital means for poor people. For example, some maintain that 'concentrated' neighborhoods reduce the social capital of the poor by limiting their social networks, and therefore, their ability to access resources and information necessary for social mobility (Briggs 1998; Wilson 1987). This stance suggests that people living in concentrated communities have little opportunity to connect and form social ties with well-educated and steadily employed families – the types of 'bridging' relationships through which one might access new opportunities. On the other hand, ethnographic studies of low-income communities have documented how poor people often rely on their social networks to make ends meet and cope with the hardships of poverty (Edin and Lein 1997; Stack 1974). These studies suggest that low-income communities can be rich in social capital, as they have well-functioning support systems that provide an important safety net for residents (Edin and Lein 1997; Stack 1974; Vale 2002). Still, others have found that being part of such support systems can be draining for some who provide more assistance than they receive in return (Belle 1982; Cohler and Lieberman 1980). Overall, this research leaves us with many questions about the status of social capital among low-income people living in concentrated poverty. For example, are the social networks of the poor supportive, resourceful, limited, draining, or some combination?

An additional question is whether where one lives affects social capital to the extent that simply moving some place else would improve one's chances to build social capital. Opportunities to further study the social networks of low-income people and to assess whether networks change for better or worse when families are relocated out of poor communities have arisen with the creation of new housing programs aimed to deconcentrate poverty. Such programs are currently underway in the United States, as well as in Europe. HOPE VI, for example, is one program that has been redeveloping 'severely distressed' public housing developments in the United States into new mixed-income communities since 1993. Targeted communities are those that suffer from physical deterioration as well as extreme concentrations of poverty, female-headed households, unemployment, crime, and a lack of social services. Residents typically have three options for relocation while their communities are redeveloped: move to another public housing development, use a portable Section 8 voucher,[1] or relocate on-site during construction.[2] By altering the communities in which residents live, the program is thought to have an impact on residents' social capital and opportunity structure. Yet, research and theory offer contending perspectives on the effects of initiatives that disperse poverty and relocate poor people.

On the one hand, some maintain that the social networks of poor people living in poverty-concentrated communities are limited in that they consist only of other disadvantaged people (Briggs 1998; Wilson 1987), suggesting that relocation out of concentrated developments will improve residents' social capital by diversifying their social networks. If residents' networks were rooted in their neighborhood prior to relocation, as William Julius Wilson's (1987) social isolation theory suggests, then relocation to other communities (some different, some similar) will likely affect their access to social capital, and subsequently their access to jobs and opportunities. On the other hand, others suggest that rather than improve residents' prospects for mobility, relocation out of their communities may impose additional barriers by breaking up well-organized systems of exchange that help many single mothers survive (Edin and Lein 1997; Stack 1974; Vale 2002).

This chapter reports the results from a qualitative study that examined the dynamic changes in low-income women's social networks as they relocated from one HOPE VI site and settled into different types of housing and communities. The goal of the research was to explore the following questions: How does relocation out of a poverty-concentrated public housing project impact female residents' stock of social capital? That is, does relocation dismantle inferior social networks or break apart well-functioning support systems? Does relocation expand or promote social capital-building opportunities for low-income women, and if so, does the impact differ by relocation group (i.e. Section 8 vs. public housing)?

Through repeated semi-structured interviews, the study captured the essence of women's social networks prior to relocation and the changes that occurred in their networks after relocation. The study focused on women in particular due to the high percentage of female-headed households in public housing.[3] This chapter presents findings from three waves of in-depth interviews conducted with a sample of women during their first and second year of relocation (2004–2005). The women in the

---

1 Section 8 (also known as the Housing Choice Voucher Program) is a subsidized portable voucher program that enables families to rent in the private market rather than in a public housing development.

2 Projects are often conducted in phases, enabling some families to relocate to older vacant units on-site while the rest of the community is demolished and rebuilt.

3 Means-tested programs in the U.S. (including public housing), historically have discouraged women from marrying because a husband's earnings would decrease or cut the public benefits the woman received.

study had all relocated during the first phase of the HOPE VI program at Maverick Gardens, a public housing development located in Boston, Massachusetts.[4] Women were chosen from the three main relocation groups (on-site, off-site public housing, and Section 8) and contacted in-person to participate in the study. Responses to the study were generally positive, as many women reported that they enjoyed the interviews and appreciated that someone was interested in hearing about their lives and experiences during this transition period. The sample consisted of 28 women, including 11 on-site movers (39 per cent), 9 Section 8 movers (32 per cent), and 8 public housing movers (29 per cent). The participants in the study were comparable to the larger population of Maverick residents. The women were mostly Hispanic and African-American, but some were White and Asian. Half of the women spoke primary languages other than English.[5] The women in the sample had lived at Maverick Gardens an average of 13 years, and the majority had children living in their households.

The Neighborhoods

Selected for HOPE VI redevelopment in 2002, Maverick Gardens was originally constructed in 1941 and was typical of the 'barracks' style public housing built in the US in the post-World War II era: twelve brick buildings (413 units) with flat roofs surrounded by paved interior walkways. The development was located on an eight acre site on a dead-end street and had no streets running through it. One side of the development abutted a run-down park with remarkable views of Boston Harbor and the city beyond. Maverick is physically isolated from the larger Boston community due to its location across the harbor in East Boston. In order to get to downtown Boston and most other Boston neighborhoods, one must drive over a toll bridge or through a tunnel under the harbor (both requiring a $3 U.S. toll), or take the train under the harbor ($1.25 one way). While its physical location contributed to some feelings of isolation, Maverick was actually much less isolated than many other public housing developments in Boston. Unlike many other housing developments, Maverick Gardens was about two blocks from Maverick Square, a bustling block that houses the Maverick subway station and numerous restaurants and shops catering to the large local Hispanic population. The neighborhood poverty level of Maverick Gardens was 43 per cent according to the 2000 U.S. Census tract data.

During the demolition and construction of the new Maverick HOPE VI community, some residents moved from their buildings, which were scheduled to be demolished and rebuilt during the early phases of the program, into vacant units that would be demolished two to three years later. The goal of redeveloping the neighborhood in phases was to allow some families to move directly from their old buildings into the newly constructed buildings without ever having to move

---

4 Of the 116 phase one households that relocated in 2003, 41 per cent relocated on-site (into vacant older units scheduled for demolition in the next phase), 39 per cent relocated to other public housing, 18 per cent relocated with Section 8 vouchers, and 2 per cent moved out of subsidized housing altogether.

5 Eight of the interviews were conducted in Spanish.

off-site. Those 'on-site movers' were scattered into any available units in buildings on the other side of the development. On-site movers in the study slowly watched the rest of their community being demolished and rebuilt while living there during the redevelopment. The atmosphere during this time was one mixed of sorrow and gloom and transformation and hope.

Ironically, Maverick HOPE VI families that chose to relocate to other public housing developments could not relocate to completed HOPE VI developments in the area. For example, although Boston has two previously redeveloped HOPE VI projects, these developments were not among the choices provided to Maverick residents due to changes in ownership and management typical of completed HOPE VI projects.[6] Therefore, Maverick families that chose public housing as their relocation option moved to other housing projects that were similar to the one they were forced to leave: communities of concentrated poverty that were physically, socially, and economically distressed. The neighborhoods of public housing movers had poverty levels that were lower on average than Maverick (28 per cent vs. 43 per cent), but they are still considered high poverty communities.[7] Although the projects varied in sizes and locations, most public housing projects to which the women relocated were made up of numerous squat brick buildings built over several city blocks. As with Maverick, this type of construction ensures that tenants are cut off from the surrounding neighborhood. Most projects, constructed in the 1940s, stand out because of the unusual density and block pattern, as well as the use of architectural materials and styles that do not blend in with the surrounding homes. With few streets running through the developments, interior spaces typically consist of paved areas with dumpsters in the middle. Due to depleted resources and mismanagement, many developments have long suffered disrepair. Many buildings have shabby metal doors that are scratched, dented, and often hanging from their hinges. Stairwells are cold and damp, often smelling of urine; and the cement stairs chipped and filthy. The interior of the units are often dark and boxy, and most buildings suffer from severe cockroach infestation.

In contrast to public housing developments, Section 8 vouchers enabled people to rent apartments in the private market. However, not all landlords accept these vouchers and there are some areas that voucher holders are priced out of. Still, Section 8 vouchers led the women in this study to neighborhoods of two or three story clapboard homes. Their new neighborhoods had poverty levels ranging from 4–33 per cent, with an average of 17 per cent. Overall, neighborhood poverty levels for Section 8 movers (17 per cent) were substantially lower than Maverick (43 per cent) and public housing movers (28 per cent). Rather than twenty families sharing

---

6 For example, once public housing developments are redeveloped into HOPE VI communities, they are no longer solely owned or run by the Public Housing Authority. Therefore, these developments are no longer included in the public housing waiting list; they have their own site-based waiting lists run by a new management company.

7 Poverty rates are from the 2000 census tract data. Average poverty levels for the public housing and Section 8 sample neighborhoods were identical to the poverty rates of the larger mover population neighborhoods. Note that while all residents living in public housing developments are poor, census tracts often include the surrounding areas, which can decrease the overall poverty level.

a front entrance, two or three families may share an entrance in these homes, and some have separate entrances altogether. Many of these multifamily homes include a small front porch and some have front and backyards. Although Section 8 housing can vary and some of the movers in this study did end up in higher poverty areas suffering from crime and disrepair, others moved to working-class and middle-income neighborhoods where rundown homes were the exception, not the norm. Visually, these communities are much more welcoming than public housing projects. Sidewalks line the streets, trees are planted in backyards, corner stores are often located throughout, and streets and businesses make the neighborhoods accessible to residents and non-residents alike.

Did, then, the moves of women to these different types of neighborhoods have an impact on their social networks, and did the type of relocation matter? While living at the old Maverick women talked about ties that we may classify as supportive ties, leveraging ties, and draining ties. The nature of these ties and how they were altered by relocation are discussed below, followed by a discussion of how the women struggled to make new ties in their new communities.

Supportive ties

Given that the women in this study had lived at Maverick an average of 13 years, it was not surprising that the majority had established extensive social support networks where they exchanged child care, loans of food and money, and emotional support. Supportive ties were most often ties to neighbors, friends, family, boyfriends, and services. For example, all of the women with young children in this study (17) relied on their social ties for child care. Some would only ask others to babysit in times of emergency, while others had ties they relied on for childcare on a regular basis. Overall, the women selectively drew on their social networks according to their needs. For example, Sheila had one neighbor to talk to about personal troubles and get rides from; her brother from whom she could borrow small amounts of money; and another friend who was good for advice.[8]

As expected, relocation impacted residents' social networks by changing their proximity to people that provided them social support. Almost half (46 per cent) of the women experienced negative changes in their social networks due to moving further away from supportive ties. Many women were caught off guard by the losses in social support. Only two women were able to move closer to family, which led to an increase in support.

Rita, a Hispanic single mother of three young children who moved with a Section 8 voucher, talked about the loss of informal child care as a key disadvantage to moving away from Maverick. Like many working women at Maverick, she held a low-paying job that lacked a predictable schedule, stability, and health benefits. She said: 'The days I didn't work during the day, and I had to work at night, I had my neighbor taking care of my children. And it was close for me to go to work.' Although she moved to Chelsea, a neighborhood that is less poor than Maverick (28

---

8 All names are pseudonyms to protect the identity of participants.

per cent vs. 43 per cent), she complained that her new neighborhood was 'horrible' and she found no one she could trust to watch her children.

Lisa's experience similarly illustrates how involuntary relocation can lead to unanticipated problems as extensive support systems are broken up. Lisa too was a single mother who relied heavily on her Maverick neighbor Cynthia for child care, which allowed her to work nights at the airport. Cynthia had a key to her apartment and would make sure her children had dinner, finished their homework, and went to bed on time. She would also check on the children again after they had gone to bed. After relocating to another public housing development on the other side of Boston, Lisa found she just could not care for her children and keep her job without the support she received at Maverick. Because she was unable to find anyone in her new community to provide this type of support, she lost her job of five years and her health declined. Lisa was unable to find a job until her adult son moved back in with her (one and a half years later) and could be there at night for her younger children. Both women's experiences suggest that these types of supportive arrangements are not established overnight – they develop over time among families who live in close quarters to each other and who learn to trust and rely on one another.

Rita and Lisa's childcare arrangements were informal in the sense that the women paid their neighbors for childcare in cash when they could, and other times offered food, cigarettes, or other loans and favors in exchange. At Maverick, both women were living among mostly other poor women, yet they established ties with neighbors that were unique because each party was flexible enough to do without immediate payment (in cash or non-cash form) for favors like childcare. After moving, both women were unsuccessful in forming ties with neighbors where goods and favors were exchanged in times of need, even when living next door to other poor women 'in the same boat.' These relationships may take longer to develop and may involve not just close proximity, but also a distinct period of trial and error before people trust each other to the point where they feel confident investing their time or money by loaning things and providing services without immediate repayment.

Many of the women in the study experienced increased isolation in their new communities. Nilda talked about the loss she experienced: 'We supported each other; we also consulted each other on things that happened to us in Maverick. We helped each other a lot. Here, I don't have anybody else to talk about my happiness, and my sorrows. Right now, I don't have anybody to talk to... to tell my personal problems to.' Another typical example of increased isolation was illustrated by Gianna.

> Well, it changed my life because over there [at Maverick] ... I had like close friendships with people. When I moved here, I lost contact with all the people from Maverick. ... For some people that I used to see over there, they think I moved so much further away. I don't know why. ... My nieces and them, they used to get off at the train and just walk down. But nobody likes getting off [here] and walking up. Even the ones that drive, they feel like I am living in the dungeons.

Gianna's experience suggests that neighborhood spatial arrangement can affect one's social network, including the frequency and likelihood of receiving visits. Gianna moved to another public housing development that her family and friends described as "the dungeons." The project is a bleak looking community located atop a hill; quite isolated from stores and other conveniences. The community was built 'barracks style' in the 1950s and has an ominous feel inside and out. Although Maverick was similar in its brick superblock structure, Gianna's family and friends were willing to visit because it was near the train – not isolated on top of a hill.

Clearly, many women regretted losing contact with close friends from Maverick. While some were able to remain connected with their former ties through the telephone, others lost contact altogether. Contact was difficult to maintain because they and/or their friends frequently lost their phone service (due to non-payment); other times the distance itself and the lack of face-to-face interaction contributed to the loss of ties over time.

In addition to disrupting ties to supportive friends and neighbors, relocation also affected ties to supportive services, such as food pantries, local shops, and other programs for families and children. One woman explained: 'If one day I didn't have money for breakfast, one can go and have breakfast with the children and lunches in the housing office area [at Maverick]. Here is completely different.' Others relied on the local 'bodegas' (the convenience stores around the neighborhood) at Maverick to loan them food in times of need: 'When I find myself tight with money … and I need bread, my bodegas help me out.' Other women missed the information they received monthly from the Maverick tenant's organization on local activities and resources for families. 'They sent you a little pamphlet to tell you this is what is happening. But over here, it's not the same. There's nothing over here'; 'I've been here two years and I haven't heard of anything that's going on within this little community. I mean, nothing has been sent out to residents about anything that's going on or any of the programs they may have right here.'

While the majority of women experienced a loss of supportive social ties by moving further away, two women, both of whom relocated with Section 8 vouchers, were able to move closer to their families and support systems. Living closer to family translated into concrete benefits, such as free child care and more material assistance and emotional support. Nilda, for example, was a 26-year-old single mother who remained determined to escape poverty and who got a boost from relocation. HOPE VI relocation prompted Nilda to move closer to her mother, which has helped her continue her education while working full-time. In addition to caring for her three young children before and after school while Nilda works, three nights per week her mother watches the children, feeds them dinner and puts them to bed while Nilda takes classes after work.

Draining Ties

While many strong ties were important because they helped low-income families 'get by,' other strong ties were 'draining' and had a negative impact on people's lives. Though not popular in the social capital literature, some studies have revealed that participating in exchange networks can sometimes exacerbate the hardships of poverty when one provides more assistance than one receives in return (Belle 1982; Cohler and Lieberman 1980).

Over a third of the women (39 per cent) in this study reported they had ties to people at Maverick that were draining. Some draining social ties brought women down emotionally, while others drained their households of resources. Stephanie was a mother of three young children who spent nearly all of her time in the development (she had not worked in over a decade). She had an extremely draining social network, and she talked about how her participation in exchange networks became burdensome because she ended up providing her neighbors more support than she received in return.

> Well, especially, when you know it's true, you know. I feel embarrassed to say to you, "Hey, remember, I gave you such and such, and I need such and such myself." I don't know, it kind of put me in a bad situation over there in a way. Like it was nice because I knew people, and you could come and have coffee or whatever. But … the next thing I know, like they kept coming all the time. … It was Grand Central Station, we used to call it! … they dog you for everything. "Could you give me a ride? Could you this, could you that, could you this, could you that?" … The favors become deeper and deeper and you don't know how to get out.

The spatial arrangements of public housing in the U.S. create an environment that encourages frequent contact among residents. While this can lead to supportive systems of exchange, it can also lead to draining relationships that are difficult to break. Having 'severely disadvantaged' families all around is likely to increase the frequency that one will be asked to loan food or money. Even just one person in a network making repeated requests without paying them back can quickly drain one's budget and household resources. Avoiding people who 'need' too much was a common theme that arose when women talked about draining social ties. One elderly woman complained that her ties had prevented her from getting ahead: 'If I had all the money that I loaned people, I could buy a house.'

Several women purposefully stay to themselves to avoid relationships they perceive as bringing them trouble. Jessica, a white woman in her 50s who raised three children at Maverick, explained why she chose to isolate herself.

> I stay to myself. Ever since I've lived here [Maverick] – I don't get too chummy with people. Because when I first moved in [22 years ago], I did and the individuals was too – they get too involved in your life. So I just stay to myself. I just find that some – some of the people that live in the development, they just like to go in and find out your business. So I said no, I don't need that problem.

Wilson's theory of concentrated poverty and social isolation implies that relocation from poverty-concentrated public housing communities may improve residents' mobility prospects by breaking up 'inferior' social networks and diversifying job networks (Wilson 1987). Nine of the women in this study (32 per cent) did experience positive changes in their social networks by moving away from draining social ties. Yet, several women indicated that although some of their old Maverick neighbors were often draining, at times these same people could be relied on for friendship and loans of food or money. Some women felt obliged to provide repeated favors to neighbors because they might need their help some day. Thus, while moving away from such ties can reduce stress, it can also reduce social support. Therefore, many ties do not fit neatly into one category or the other, and perceptions of ties may change depending on the moment in time. For example, Stephanie may see a neighbor as a stressful tie when that neighbor is having a difficult month and requests a lot of support. But this same neighbor may be seen as a 'life saver' when Stephanie has a crisis and can go to the neighbor for help.

Women talked about the benefits of moving away from people that brought them down emotionally and/or financially. For example, Gianna, a public housing mover, no longer loans friends money on a weekly basis like she used to at Maverick. 'Because now if somebody wants to borrow some money, I'll tell them to come and get it. But they can't get here. They want me to come and drop it off, but I'm like "no – come and get it."' Moving to another public housing development helped Stephanie realize that she was 'in too deep with people at Maverick'. She gave too much, did not know how to say no, and in this respect saw moving to a different housing development as a new beginning.

> I don't know, I kind of made a new start and I kind of thought, you know, I don't want any of that nonsense. So when I moved here, I kind of did that. The neighbors [at Maverick] … they were very nice and friendly, but they needed *a lot.*

Stephanie planned to be very picky about letting new people into her life because she did not want to end up with an overly demanding network again. She used several strategies to avoid new draining relationships, including not being friendly with neighbors and not disclosing that she is fluent in Spanish. She was even nervous about her children making friends because this could lead to her own burdensome relationships with their parents. Although Stephanie was cautious about forming new ties in her new community, it was not always easy. During the second interview in the study, Stephanie complained that her neighbor downstairs 'unfortunately introduced herself', and already she was providing more help to her neighbors than she received in return.

While some people benefited from leaving draining neighbors behind when they moved to other communities, others gained from moving away from draining *household members*. HOPE VI relocation prompted some larger families to split up because multigenerational families were given the option to form two separate households (each receiving its own housing subsidy). Three women in the study did just that, and all reported benefits to splitting up their families, including reduced stress and improved health. For example, Sherry, a petite African-American woman in her late 70s, reported improvements in emotional and physical well-being due to moving on her own. Like many other multigenerational families, she had raised all her children at Maverick and two of her adult children never moved out – they continued living with her and eventually raised their own children in the same apartment. At Maverick, she lived with her son, her daughter, and three grandchildren. Although she never wanted to leave the community, relocation gave Sherry the opportunity to get out and live on her own, which she felt she deserved at her age. Relocation also gave her adult children the push to move out and become more independent. Sherry reported that her asthma and blood pressure improved, both of which she attributed to the reduction in stress from moving away from a noisy, busy environment where she constantly picked up after everyone. Thalia is a younger Hispanic mother in her

40s who was similarly relieved to have her older children out of the house. Her stress level decreased significantly and she was much more at ease with her three adult children no longer living with her.

In addition to the reported benefits of moving away from draining ties, several Section 8 movers talked about how moving away from 'the projects' reduced the hassle of neighbors constantly being involved in each others' business and led to an increase in privacy. Katherine explained:

> For me – it's good [Section 8]. ... I don't like bothering with other people; I don't like other people knowing my business – I like it. When you live in the projects, it's like – don't get me wrong, I'm not putting it down – that's where I grew up. But you got like all these different smells from all these different foods; everybody who blares their stereo, who's slamming their door; who's yelling at their kids; or who's knocking on your door to use your phone or borrow something; or who's looking out the door to see when you bought something or when you're having company – I don't miss that *at all*. It's a total different way of living [here], you know – it's not my own house but I have my own space. It's bright, it's private, my landlord – he doesn't bother me.

Clearly, the physical structure of public housing is unique in that so many families live in such tight quarters, making it inevitable that residents will know each others' business. Vanessa, an African-American woman who moved with Section 8, tries to keep to herself in her new community in order to avoid problems. 'I am antisocial. ... I don't really want to make friends; when you make friends that is when you bring problems. That is how we brought problems in the projects. Making friends and friends telling their business.' Relocating out of Maverick provided some the opportunity to step back and regain their privacy and sense of anonymity.

Leveraging ties

In addition to supportive and draining ties, the women also had leveraging or 'bridging' social ties. These ties are thought to be particularly helpful for 'getting ahead' in life because they provide social leverage to access new opportunities and information (Briggs 1998). It is thought that people living in concentrated poverty are isolated from people who are well-educated and steadily employed – those in positions to provide social leverage – and therefore isolated from an important source of social capital. That is, the social networks of people living in such neighborhoods are thought to be particularly homogeneous and include only ties to other disadvantaged people. One way to assess people's leveraging ties and their access to resourceful people is to ask them how they went about finding their current job, who they would use in a future job search, and how they find out about other opportunities and resources.

Analyzing the ties that helped the women in this study 'get ahead' in life revealed that both strong and weak ties were important and used as leverage. Overall, the women most often received job information through their close, more intimate social ties, and learned about other opportunities, including education and training through weaker, more distant ties. Job searches typically entailed asking friends, relatives, and neighbors about job openings at their workplaces. A typical example was Jennifer, a 30-year-old Puerto Rican mother of four, who got her job working in a factory through her brother-in-law, who informed her of the job opening and put in a good word for her. While most women had at least one tie to someone who was steadily employed in a higher level position (i.e. at a hospital or college), and most tried using their ties to such people in job searches, all but one found their jobs through their close ties to people who were in lower level positions – not the people they knew who were highly educated or better connected. These findings are consistent with others who found that low-income people most often got jobs through their close, not weak, ties (Elliot 1999; Kleit 2001).

The low-income women in the study were not entirely lacking in social capital since they had people in their networks who were employed and/or had access to job information. Yet, the jobs the women had access to were often limited in quality, supporting Wilson's (1987) theory of poverty concentration and social isolation. Most of the 10–14 women who were working at some point during the study held low-wage jobs in the service industry (i.e. food service, hospitality, healthcare) – jobs that lacked benefits and stability.

Since it was through their strong – not weak – ties that woman found work, the findings from this study do not support Granovetter's (1974) 'strength of weak ties' thesis. Why is it that the overwhelming majority had found their jobs through close ties rather than weak ties? Many had successful people in their networks that could, presumably, help them get better jobs. But the existence of successful or well-connected people in a network did not necessarily translate into successful job contacts. The findings suggests that even when low-income people have access to educated and steadily employed people, without a strong sense of obligation and trust, it is unlikely that they will benefit from the true potential of these ties. Smith (2003) notes: 'one's connections to well-placed others does not guarantee resources. What promotes the transmission of valued resources are obligations of exchange, shared expectations, and mutual trust, the key ingredients of collective efficacy' (see Smith 2003, 1033). Also, as Blokland and Noordhoff argue in their chapter in this volume, other factors, such as a concern to prove one's position of independence, may prevent people from accessing weak ties. Further, the insecurities people might face in becoming dependent on close ties may be even greater in ties that are weak. Close ties, such as very good friends and family members, after all, may be directed more by principles than the rules of reciprocity and exchange, which may make them more accessible than weak ties. Another important and often overlooked factor is that even with ties to well-connected people, many low-income people lack the skills and work histories necessary for better jobs to which these ties may be able to connect them.

The findings of this study support Wilson's (1987) argument that the poor have limited access to decent job opportunities. But the findings suggest that relocation and deconcentrating poverty may not improve their job networks. Relocation to different types of housing and neighborhoods did not improve access to job networks or jobs for women in this study, at least in the short-term (in the two years following relocation). Both women who moved to public housing and those who moved to other neighborhoods with Section 8 vouchers reported little interaction with people in their new communities, and none had used a new neighborhood tie for job information. Similar to Kleit's (2001) findings on public housing movers' job networks, women in the current study continued to use their close social contacts for job leads rather than their new neighbors (some of whom were higher income). Further, since many of the women relied on their close ties for job information, and many reported losing contact with some of these ties after relocation, moving may have a negative effect on some job networks.

While close supportive ties typically connected the women to employment opportunities, weaker, more extended social ties tended to link them to other resources, including education and training, housing, and services. For example, Stephanie learned about an early childhood education program through her counselor; Josie was being encouraged to go to college by an acquaintance at work; Gianna learned about a homeownership program for low-income people through a loan officer at a bank; and Jocelyn reduced her utility payments after connecting with a service recommended by her landlord. Several of the older women in the sample also reported using their weaker connections to obtain a public housing unit at Maverick (prior to redevelopment).

The fact that most women learned about education and training and other opportunities through their weaker, more distant, social ties supports the notion that weaker, bridging ties *are* important because they can provide access to information and opportunities not available among close social ties and can lead to social mobility. However, the findings do not support the idea that relocation to different neighborhood environments is necessary for residents to have such weak ties in their social networks. In fact, none of their weak or leveraging ties were formed in women's new communities; they had all *existed* in their networks when living in Maverick – a poverty-concentrated public housing development. The findings suggest that low-income people living in concentrated communities may not be as isolated from social networks as some suggest, and that moving does not simply increase access to weak or bridging ties.

Rather than having more well-educated and employed ties, the missing links for social mobility appear to be the lack of skill-building opportunities, the lack of services that enable single mothers to engage in education, training, and work (i.e. affordable childcare for non-traditional hours, free skill-building programs, etc.), and the limited availability of stable low-skilled jobs that pay a living wage and provide career ladders (see for example, Fitzgerald 2006).

Further, while leveraging ties were important because they provided information on opportunities, it was often the social support the women received that enabled them to take advantage of such opportunities. Several women talked extensively about how social support was crucial to their ability to obtain resources for their households, to get or to keep their jobs, or to enroll in education programs. Without their ties to people who provide emotional support, childcare, transportation, and food and money loans, many of these women would not be able to hold jobs or take other steps toward self-sufficiency. The focus on bridging vs. bonding or weak vs. strong ties as dichotomous, unrelated forms of social capital disregards the importance of the intersection of these ties and that jointly they can be important for social mobility and stability.

Making new ties

This study revealed the changing dynamics of women's social ties after relocation, including their prospects for making new ties. While a few women were successful in forming new supportive ties, the majority reported making no new ties in their new neighborhoods. Besides five women who had formed some sort of relationship with at least one person in their neighborhood two years after relocation, the majority of women in all relocation groups had formed no ties in their new communities. Why were most unsuccessful in forming new ties? *Collective efficacy* and neighborhood spatial arrangements were key factors that influenced movers' willingness and ability to get to know their neighbors and get involved in their communities. Collective efficacy has been defined in the literature as the social cohesion and shared expectations among residents and has been measured by the willingness of residents to intervene for the public good (i.e. supervise neighborhood children) and the density of residents' social networks (Sampson, Raudenbush and Earls 1997). Research suggests that collective efficacy is important for communities and can help control crime even in high-poverty neighborhoods (Sampson, Raudenbush and Earls 1997). Women in this study were asked questions about neighborhood safety, how well they knew their neighbors, whether neighbors looked out for one another and for neighborhood children, and whether residents helped each other out – all factors that provide a picture of the level of collective efficacy in their communities.

While several women gave examples of experiences that indicated signs of collective efficacy, many gave vivid examples of low collective efficacy, including 36 per cent of on-site, 88 per cent of public housing, and 33 per cent of Section 8 movers. Signs of low collective efficacy included having an extreme mistrust of neighbors; an unwillingness to report crime for fear of retribution; and a lack of commitment to the community in terms of safety and cleanliness. The findings are organized by relocation group in order to account for important housing and neighborhood differences.

First, what was the level of collective efficacy at Maverick – the community the women were leaving? The story painted by residents (both on and off-site) about the Maverick community prior to redevelopment was mixed. Some gave examples of mutual trust and exchange among neighbors at Maverick, while others experienced hostility and retribution by neighbors. Looking out for one another; keeping an eye on neighbors' apartments; monitoring each others' children were typical comments shared by those who painted a cohesive community with collective efficacy. In contrast, others talked about keeping to themselves; not reporting criminal activity for fear of reprisal; and mistrust and disrespect among neighbors. Some residents respected and trusted a small number of neighbors at Maverick, at the same time they feared and mistrusted everyone else. Age, ethnicity, and length of residence at Maverick did not appear to account for differences in perception of collective efficacy. Overall, the findings suggest different residents can experience the same community differently, and that pockets of collective efficacy may exist in public housing communities that otherwise appear to be severely lacking in collective efficacy.

Women who relocated to off-site public housing developments were more likely than other movers to complain about signs of social disorder and a lack of common norms, indicating low collective efficacy in these communities. Over three quarters of the public housing movers (88 per cent) had problems with their neighbors and/or safety concerns with the neighborhood. Themes around safety, mistrust, and lack of respect for neighbors and the neighborhood were common. Some had personal items stolen or broken; some were wary of persistent violence and crime in the neighborhood; and others felt personally threatened by their neighbors. For example, one woman had her car windows broken in the new development; another had her laundry stolen from the hallway; and another had several packages stolen from the entryway of her building. Another woman was still shaken up about a recent murder in her community. She said:

> The other day, like two months ago, a man got killed behind the building. The mailman saw everything, dropped the mail and ran away. Then the mailman didn't want to deliver the mail here. And it was during the day. ... I don't like it here. ... I am afraid because of my daughters – you always have to be watching them when they downstairs. One cannot be peacefully ...

Another woman also feared for her family's safety in her new development because she recently awoke to gunshots at three in the morning. She rearranged her children's bedroom so their beds are away from the windows, but she continues to fear such violence.

Fear of retribution from neighbors was a recurring theme for public housing movers. For example, Bianca had problems in her building, and she did not report them for fear of retribution. 'Sometimes they urinate in the hallways. Teenagers hang out in the stairs with their girlfriends. They put the music very loud almost every day, especially Sunday mornings when one wants to rest. But I cannot say anything... one has to be silent.' Bianca was very cautious of her neighbors: 'You have to have four eyes – you have to be careful with whom you hang out and with whom you talk.' Norma also had conflicts with one of her new neighbors. 'She would play the music very loud and her teenage son was smoking marijuana in my front door. They would put the garbage outside my door so that I would be blamed for that. And she was threatening me that if I complained about her she would take me to court.'

Lisa, an African-American mother, reported that when she first relocated to her new housing development she experienced racial discrimination from her neighbors and the management.

> You know, every time my two kids go out to play with the whole neighborhood, everything is "Jacob and Jared". I have been to the office for so many little things, and I'm getting tired of it. They look out the window and the only thing they see is these two black kids and they blame us, when everybody is white and Spanish. But they only pick on my two little ones, do you know what I mean? The residents, management – they don't want to complain I guess about everybody else. We are here, so they "let's get rid of them", you know. I hate it.

Lisa also complained about the filth in her community, and she eventually did something about it. 'This is the worst thing about this whole project. They just started cleaning up here because I went to the office and complained. Because it was a mess out there before. It was nasty ... But yesterday, I helped the guy pick up all the cups and stuff, because the kids are throwing stuff out there. It's never clean.'

Given the problems with safety and disrespectful neighbors, it was not surprising that few public housing movers had made new social ties in their communities. Several women spoke of the difficulty involved in making new friends. One commented: 'I get the paper work from the office. I mean, I come in, I say "good morning". They don't even speak to me. They don't even say hi, the residents – the older ones, you know.' She was disappointed because she liked how the neighborhood looked when she first moved in, but found the people were not at all welcoming.

While some women wanted to connect with their new neighbors, others were clearly put off by their neighbors altogether. Several public housing movers talked about keeping to themselves, a tactic many on-site movers used to cope with the crime and disorder at Maverick. A typical comment came from Sherry: 'The best thing – just stay away. Keep your mouth closed.' From the beginning, Stephanie knew her new neighbors were not the type of people with whom she wanted to associate. When asked if her children had made any friends in the new neighborhood, Stephanie confessed:

> I just don't want them to, because you know what? Then I've got to meet his mother, and the next thing you know she's over. ... And it's just better not to. Because most of the time it just ends up into something that I didn't want it to be. So this is kind of a fresh start where I don't even – I know that sounds really bad, but – I don't even *want* to interact. And the impressions I'm having, the first impression I'm having at these parks and around here are *not* pretty. ... I'm sure there are other nice people here that I haven't met, and they don't know me, and I don't know them, and hey, maybe we could help each other. But, the ones that make themselves available are not giving a good first impression that I would want to take it to another level.

While the majority of those who relocated to public housing developments described communities low in collective efficacy, which contributed to their lack of interest and ability to form new social ties, a few were able to connect with some of their new neighbors in a healthy, supportive way. Although in the first year after she relocated, Bianca did not know anyone in her new housing development, six-months later she had become very friendly with one of her neighbors. They now visit each other almost every day and she trusts her with her daughter. Two other women also reported having contact with a neighbor; however it was to a lesser extent. For example, toward the end of the study Lisa had gotten to know three neighbors through her children, but she said: 'I still don't try going in their houses and sit down with them and have a drink or whatever. It's just hi, bye, borrow some sugar, whatever.'

Section 8 movers were much less likely than public housing movers to experience problems in their new communities that impeded their ability and interest in forming new ties and indicated low collective efficacy (33 per cent vs. 88 per cent). Still, however, one third of the Section 8 women reported safety problems and low collective efficacy in their new communities. Josie, for example, complained about gangs in her neighborhood 'tagging' homes and local businesses with graffiti and people stealing packages from front steps. Josie was also frustrated because she felt her neighbors were unfriendly because she does not speak Spanish. 'It seems that just everybody – it's just one culture – they are all Hispanic. And that's sort of nerve-racking. Because how come you can speak no English. …They speak perfect English! They just don't want to speak it to you.' These experiences have made her cautious of people in the community and pessimistic about making new ties.

Rita complained about problems on her street – a main avenue in a commercial district where few people are seen after business hours. She condemned the public drunkenness and disorder in the neighborhood.

> Over there, next to the apartment at the corner, some of them hang out there all drunk and they are very fresh. … And two weeks ago there was an incident across the street. Some drunks had an accident and I heard it, and I say, "they kill themselves". I heard a noise and when I saw at the window, I saw they destroyed two cars and they just left laughing. And people were watching.

Rita had no interest in getting to know her neighbors. 'The neighbors bother me, and it bothers me that on the weekends I cannot rest because they make noises. One works during the week and we want to rest during the weekend. And there is a man that drinks outside and they smoke in the hallways.'

While the crime and disturbances these Section 8 movers experienced were similar to some of the problems public housing and on-site movers had in their communities, there was one theme unique to the Section 8 group. Three Section 8 residents talked about how the structure of their neighborhoods does not facilitate interaction the way public housing communities sometimes do. That is, they believe the spatial arrangements of their neighborhoods matter. In public housing developments, a dozen or more families may share an entryway and hundreds may share a common mail room. Some recognized the increased opportunities for interaction in public housing compared to their Section 8 units. They pointed out that because most people in their new neighborhoods have their own their homes and/or their own yards, they do not congregate in public spaces. Josie explained: 'since everybody [here] has a house, they tend to stay on their own property and do what they want to do.' Shakira similarly said 'you don't see a lot of people just hanging out. Everybody's like stays to themselves. They don't bother nobody. … I guess when you're living in the projects, you see a lot of people coming out.' Nilda explained that there were more opportunities to connect with neighbors at Maverick than in her current Section 8 housing:

> The neighbors here are quiet; they are always inside their apartments. They don't share. I don't like that. Maybe it's because we don't have any park around here where we can sit and talk. At Maverick, we used to sit down at the park; all the neighbors gathered and had conversations; or go to the office and talk to the staff. This way we shared, supported each other. … We were all one family. And we used to get along well. Here – I don't know my neighbors. … Life is very sad here. But people don't let me get close to them. When I go out I say "hi" and that is it.

Clearly, spatial arrangement of neighborhoods can influence the likelihood and frequency of contact among neighbors. Traditional public housing developments house many families in close quarters, which inevitably leads to more opportunities for interacting and forming ties with neighbors. Voucher holders recognized the different interaction patterns among neighbors in their new communities and attributed these to the spatial differences. While Section 8 movers appreciated the newfound privacy that came with the structure of their new neighborhoods, many struggled as they tried to make ties in these communities.

Discussion

This investigation into low-income women's social capital and the impact of relocation revealed that social networks are often complex. Women's social networks were not fully captured by existing categories of analysis, such as 'strong versus weak' ties or 'bonding versus bridging' ties. Some strong ties provided rich social support, while other strong ties drained households of resources. And some strong ties were supportive and draining at different times. Therefore, many ties cannot fit neatly into one category or the other, and perceptions of ties may change depending on the moment in time. In addition, weak ties did not always provide social leverage, nor were they always 'bridging'. Likewise, the impact of relocation was not uniform.

As anticipated, relocation did break up many existing networks. For some, this translated into a loss in supportive social capital; for others this meant fewer draining ties; and for others a combination. What relocation did not appear to do, however, is improve access to leveraging or bridging social ties – an outcome expected by many policymakers and researchers. That is, the women typically did not expand or diversify their networks to include residents of their new communities, at least in the short-term.

While the findings challenge traditional categorizations of social capital, there were some consistencies with prior research. For example, that many of the women were enmeshed in exchange networks where they provided and received social support while living in a poverty-concentrated community is consistent with other research (Belle 1983; Edin and Lein 1997; Fernandez-Kelly 1995; Stack 1974). The losses in support the women experienced as a result of networks fragmenting as residents were dispersed to different locations is also consistent with other recent studies (Greenbaum 2002; Clampet-Lundquist 2004; Popkin *et al.* 2004; Saegert and Winkel 1998).

While strong ties were important sources of support for the low-income women in the study, they were sometimes sources of stress. In other words, having strong social networks had both advantages *and* disadvantages. For some, engaging with an exchange network meant they could tap into neighbors' resources when needed, but it also sometimes translated into an overload of responsibility when neighbors were in need and drained their households of resources. While understudied, this important 'downside' of social capital has been recognized before (Belle 1982; Portes and Sensenbrenner 1993). The findings from the current study are also consistent with Stack's (1974) finding that strong social ties sometimes constrained savings and social mobility for low-income women. Future social capital research should pay close attention to this often overlooked dynamic of low-income people's social networks.

The findings on social leverage were interesting in that weak ties were important, but not for providing job information to the women in this study, as Granovetter's (1974) 'strength of weak ties' thesis might predict. Job links came primarily through their close ties, suggesting that trust and obligations of exchange are necessary components for sharing job information, and these components are likely to be much stronger among close ties (Smith 2003). On the other hand, the current study found weaker ties to be useful for linking women to other resources, including education and training opportunities. Interestingly, many women had these weak leveraging ties in their networks while living in Maverick, a poverty-concentrated community. Perhaps more important is that none had formed a new leveraging social tie in their new neighborhoods two years after relocating. That few were able to form new social ties in their new communities is consistent with two other HOPE VI studies (Clampet-Lundquist 2004; Georing and Feins 2003). The findings indicate that connecting with neighbors in new communities is particularly difficult when collective efficacy is low and shared common space is absent. Neighborhood spatial arrangements must be taken into account when assessing the formation of new ties.

Overall, the research suggests that relocation out of high-poverty public housing developments can lead to a combination of positive and negative changes in social networks, and not always in the directions one might expect. Therefore, housing dispersal programs may be short-sighted if they expect that simply relocating the poor will lead to positive changes in social capital. Relocation is a complex process that can lead to a variety of complex outcomes for low-income women and their families. Further research is greatly needed to assess the impact of relocation on networks and social capital-building opportunities in the long run. While some families will end up moving back to the redeveloped HOPE VI communities, others will remain permanently relocated in other communities. Future longitudinal studies are needed to assess changes in social networks and other long-term outcomes in order to evaluate the unique impacts of relocation and income-mixing initiatives on low-income women and their families.

References

Belle, D. (1982), The stress of caring: Women providers as providers of social support. In Goldberg, L. and Breznitz, S. (eds), *Handbook of Stress* (1982), pp. 496–505 (New York: The Free Press).

—— (1983), 'The impact of poverty on social networks and support', *Marriage and Family Review*, 5, 89–103.

Briggs, X. (1998), 'Brown kids in white suburbs: Housing mobility and the many faces of social capital', *Housing Policy Debate*, 9:1, 177–213.

Clampet-Lundquist, S. (2004), 'HOPE VI relocation: Moving to new neighborhoods and building new ties', *Housing Policy Debate*, 15:2, 415–447.

Cohler, B. and Lieberman, M. (1980), 'Social relations and mental health among three European ethnic groups, *Research on Aging*, 2:4, 445–496.

Edin, K. and Lein, L. (1997), *Making Ends Meet* (New York: Russell Sage Foundation).

Elliott, J.R. (1999), 'Social isolation and labor market insulation: network and neighborhood effects on less-educated urban workers', *Sociological Quarterly* 40:2, 199–216.

Fernandez-Kelly, P. (1995), Social and cultural capital in the urban ghetto: Implications for the economic sociology of immigration, 213–47. In Portes, A. (ed.), *The Economic Sociology of Immigration* (New York: Russell Sage Foundation).

Fitzgerald, J. (2006), *Moving up in the New Economy: Career Ladders for US Workers* (New York: Cornell University Press).

Granovetter, M. (1974), *Getting a Job: A Study of Contacts and Careers* (Cambridge MA: Harvard University Press).

Greenbaum, S. (2002), *Social capital and deconcentration: Theoretical and policy paradoxes of the HOPE VI program*. Paper presented at the Conference on Social Justice, Windsor, Canada, 5 May 2002.

Kleit, R.G. (2001), 'The role of neighborhood social networks in scattered-site public housing residents' search for jobs', *Housing Policy Debate*, 12:3, 541–573.

Popkin, S.J. *et al.* (2004), 'The HOPE VI program: What about the residents?', *Housing Policy Debate* 15:2, 385–414.

Portes, A. and Sensenbrenner, J. (1993), 'Embeddedness and Immigration: Notes on the social determinants of economic action', *American Journal of Sociology*, 98, 1320–1350.

Saegert, S. and Winkel, G. (1998), 'Social capital and the revitalization of New York City's distressed inner-city housing', *Housing Policy Debate*, 9:1, 17–60.

Sampson, R.J. *et al.* (1997), 'Neighborhoods and violent crime: A multilevel study of collective efficacy', *Science*, 227, 918–24.

Smith, S. (2003), 'Exploring the efficacy of African-Americans' job referral networks: A study of the obligations of exchange around job information and influence', *Ethnic and Racial Studies*, 26:6, 1029–1045.

Stack, C. (1974), *All our Kin: Strategies for Survival in a Black Community* (New York: Harper and Row).

Vale, L.J. (2002), *Reclaiming Public Housing* (Cambridge MA: Harvard University Press).

Wilson, W.J. (1987), *The Truly Disadvantaged* (Chicago: The University of Chicago Press).

Chapter 6

The Weakness of Weak Ties: Social Capital to Get Ahead Among the Urban Poor in Rotterdam and Amsterdam

Talja Blokland and Floris Noordhoff[1]

Introduction

The policy relevance of social capital relates directly to the difficulties that welfare states face in preserving social security arrangements and general welfare provisions. Public policy aims to harness community self-help as a means to compliment formal provision 'by filling the "welfare gap" left by the public and the private sphere' (Williams 2005, 173, see also Briggs 2001, 5 and Giddens 2000, 2002). Indeed, commentators have pleaded for 'building social capital' to create a welfare system based on the principles of mutual support, through active public support for self-help and mutual aid groups (cf. Wann 1995, quoted in Field 2003, 118). To Putnam (2000, 318), public policy should be aimed at increasing social capital of the poor 'precisely because poor people (by definition) have little economic capital and face formidable obstacles in acquiring human capital (that is, education), [so] social capital is disproportionately important to their welfare.'

As poverty concentrates in urban areas, neighbourhood revitalization is becoming a popular tool for creating environments that will help people help themselves or each other. Creating a more diversified housing stock is in the Netherlands currently one of the dominant policy approaches to create more liveable neighbourhoods but also, and explicitly so, to enhance the possibilities to enjoy the city's 'escalator functions' of residents currently 'locked' in disadvantaged positions. Public policy thus connects space and social capital, albeit in slightly different words, though by adopting physical determinism: if the poor would only live closer to the more affluent, they would build the ties to get ahead.

There are also programs for community development. To expect people to profit from the presence of the better situated assumes an exchange of resources – information about jobs, babysitting for taking an evening class, and so on (Williams

---

1 We express our thanks to Mike Savage and Godfried Engbersen on drafts of this chapter in their various forms, as well as to the initial team of the Landscapes of Poverty Project that collected the data. We thank the Amsterdam School for Social Science Research for facilitating the PhD-trajectory for Floris Noordhoff. We thank Jolien Veensma and Petra Nijhove for their support in preparing the manuscript.

2005). Community development approaches often assume that community participation brings about associational networks that then, in and of themselves, provide poor residents with social capital to get ahead. We see here the confusion of social capital to foster coordinated collective action and social capital as access roads to resources by virtue of memberships of social networks that individuals may use to get ahead, a distinction also discussed elsewhere in this book. The assumptions about the potential for neighbourhood revitalization sits rather uncomfortable with the historical developments sketched in chapter two, that urban environments themselves have undergone tremendous changes as sites of social capital. The expectation that *neighbourhood social capital* can bring social leverage about, if only neighbourhoods would be more mixed, may thus need a little more careful consideration.

This chapter sheds light on the workings of social capital of residents of three impoverished urban neighbourhoods in the Netherlands, to see how far their networks help them to 'get ahead'. As these three neighbourhoods are so-called poverty 'concentration areas', these can be expected to be the type of places – if such places exist – that keep people down. Places, in other words, where residents lack the weak ties with people beyond their own circle to get ahead, and who may even have too much bonding or draining social capital that keeps them where they are. The long-term poor in such neighbourhoods, then, would be missing out most in social capital. We focus in this chapter on residents who have been living below the official poverty line for a number of years, using secondary analysis from the data of the Landscapes of Poverty Study to discuss their social ties. Specifically we are interested in whether having weak ties does not appear to elevate people out of poverty. After all, if living in the 'right' networks with the right resources would be all that it takes to get ahead, that is what we should expect.

The Landscapes of Poverty Study: Research Methods and Locations

The Landscapes of Poverty project, conducted between 1997 and 1999 (Engbersen 1997; Staring *et al.* 2002; Ypeij *et al.* 2002; Ypeij and Snel 2002), aimed to describe a wide variety of everyday life aspects of the long-term poor in the Netherlands at the turn of the century. Dutch people with low incomes more often live in cities, especially Rotterdam and Amsterdam, than elsewhere (Engbersen and Snel 1996, 129). The Landscapes of Poverty project collected data in two neighbourhoods in Amsterdam (Bijlmermeer and Amsterdam-Noord), and one in Rotterdam (Delfshaven), then examples of the most deprived urban areas in the Netherlands. Coming to the topic of everyday life of long-term poor residents from a quite open research question, 216 face-to-face interviews were conducted and audio taped (88 in Amsterdam-Noord, 66 in Delfshaven and 80 in Bijlmermeer) by a team of 11 sociologists and anthropologists. Respondents were found via a wide variety of entrances including schools, community organizations, migrant organizations, social services and social service employees and through simply ringing doorbells and approaching people in the street. The average interview took slightly over four hours, with a maximum of twelve hours and a minimum of one hour often in multiple sessions.

The researchers used a semi-structured questionnaire with open questions and topics and questions with fixed answers. The questionnaire contained two hundred questions on neighborhood, labor, income, social support and leverage, relationship with public services, social networks, and social participation. The wide orientation of the project and the size of the interview team allowed for quite some liberty of the researchers to pursue personal agendas. As a result, the interviews provide a wealth of information, but the methods do not allow us to do much calculations or statistics with the information. Instead, our secondary analysis of the material treats the transcript as qualitative. The answers were retrospectively categorized and entered into SPSS by the interviewers.

After reading and rereading the transcripts, Floris Noordhoff coded the data (cf. Corbin and Strauss 1990, 12), assigning 213 codes in Atlast-I. These codes referred to the respondents' situations, interactions, attitudes, perspectives, opinions, feelings and life-strategies for each of the themes of the interviews.

Social Capital Theory and the Strength of Weak Ties

Research on social capital and poverty has incorporated the now familiar distinction between social capital to get by and social capital to get ahead (Beggs *et al.* 1996; Wacquant 1998; Putnam 2000, 23; Leonard and Onyx 2003, see also Curley, this volume). In summary, social capital to get by is social support that helps individuals to meet with daily needs. It is most often associated with strong ties with kin, close neighbors and intimate friends (Dominguez and Watkins 2003, 112–3). Social capital to get ahead is social leverage trough ties that help individuals' upward mobility by providing access to information, education and employment, and weak ties are typically expected to fulfil his role (Boissevain 1974; Campbell *et al.* 1986; Granovetter 1974). Weak ties are relationships characterized by infrequent interaction or low intimacy. They are wide ranging and are likely to serve as bridges across social boundaries (cf. Bian 1997, 366).

In theory, weak ties are thus empowering. People in poverty who manage to build weak ties can escape into a world of new opportunities. So, scholars, following Granovetter (1973), speak of the 'strength of weak ties.' But whereas it is one thing to note that people who find jobs do so thanks to their weak ties, it is quite another thing to assume that the causality works as beautifully into the other direction. Does the fact that people do *not* escape from poverty mean that they simply have a shortage of weak ties? How, precisely, do weak ties of the urban poor in Rotterdam and Amsterdam operate?

Strong ties are not so often critically discussed when they are the ties of elite cliques and hardly so when they concern the ties of the mainstream middle class.[2] But when it comes to people in poverty, the common argument is that strong ties offer resources to get by, but that they make it difficult to change one's social position,

---

2 There have, of course, been studies of power elites and networks among corporations through individual linkages (Useem 1984; Scott 1997; Scott and Griff 1984) but these do not relate social networks to questions of cohesion and integration as does the literature on networks of the poor.

and may even prevent social mobility, especially in poverty concentration areas. Wacquant writes: 'Affiliative ties and bonds of obligation with friends and associates in the ghetto constitute a resource for survival, but they create impediments and obstacles when attempting to move up and into the official labour market – ties that bind and keep you down' (Wacquant 1998, 27; see also Monroe and Goldman 1998; McLeod 1994). Similarly, Rumbaut (1997, 39) states that 'family ties bind, but sometimes these bonds constrain rather than facilitate particular outcomes'. Conflicts may arise from efforts to advance above others in one's social support network (Dominguez and Watson 2003, 131). In her chapter here, Curley also shows how strong ties can be 'draining' in a neighbourhood of concentrated poverty.

If strong ties obstruct people to get out of poverty indeed, the necessary condition for economic advancement entails a shift to other, looser networks. This is a shift, hence, from bonding to bridging social networks (Leonard and Onyx 2003, 189) or from 'strong' to 'weak' ties. And if the neighbourhood is the most relevant context for the development of social ties of poor people (but see Blokland 2003) then a shift to more mixed neighbourhoods makes perfect sense. If networked urbanism has not yet reached such areas, often continuingly depicted as some sort of urban villages, then such 'places' should become, indeed, more 'networked beyond spatial boundaries'.

The question, however, still is whether the claim that strong ties fail to provide access to resources for personal advancement implies that weak ties will. When, as is the case in Rotterdam and Amsterdam, demolition of physically sound, rent-controlled housing is justified by variations of this social capital argument, this question becomes a rather urgent one. Whether or not such demolition will result in *places* that will provide the old-style urbanism that will help the disadvantaged to get ahead trough local ties is, after all, questionable, exactly because of the end of urbanism, discussed in chapter one and two here. More specifically, Granovetter investigated how people used networks to get new jobs. Most jobs were found through 'weak' acquaintances. The hypothesis of the strength of weak ties is that weaker ties form bridges that link individuals to other social circles for information not available in one's own circle, information that they can use to access resources (Lin 1999, 469; see also Burt 2000 on 'brokers', Richard and Roberts 1998, 3; Marsden and Hurlbert 1988 in Mouw 2003, 869).

Everyday survival in poor urban communities frequently depends on close interaction with kin and friends in similar situations (cf. Stack 1974; Edin and Lein 1997; Vale 2002; Curley, this volume). Henley, Danziger and Offer (2005) confirm that informal aid is important to the everyday survival of low-income families, but that members of such families are doing less well in assisting each other with economic mobility. Beggs, Haines and Hurlbert (1996, 217) also found support for the thesis that strong, homophilious ties and dense homogeneous networks were more effective channels for support in routine and crisis situations than were weak, heterophilus ties and wide-ranging networks. Fernandez Kelly (1995, 218) wrote that people in poverty largely depends on relations of mutuality for survival. Networks made up of such ties indeed lacked bridges to other social networks that control access to a larger set of opportunities and meanings (ibid, 242). Briggs argued that in groups of long-term poor people within-group solidarity is typically a generator of 'getting by' support rather than leverage, a finding that underscores the relevance of effective and durable social bridges (Briggs 2001, 8). Putnam (in Putnam and Feldstein 2003) has also acknowledged the relevance of weak ties. Weak ties, in all these instances, seem to take on remarkable properties. These bridges seem to be located outside power and exploitation, and outside values and norms, as if all that it takes for these ties to do their magical work of leverage is to be 'weak'. But *how* do people in poverty use weak ties, *if and when* they have them?

Other scholars have, however, cast doubt on the theory of bridging and bonding. First, some have disputed that the general notion of bonding coincides with strong ties and bridging simply with weak ties. For instance, Leonard and Onyx (2003) suggest that these are not synonyms, and that ties differ in degree rather than in kind. Moreover, they maintain that people *prefer* to bridge through their strong ties. It is only by absence of sufficient brokers to the powerful or of sufficient resource-rich individuals within one's personal network that the need for weak ties develops. Elites may marry each other *and* help each other to get ahead, so the sharp distinction between weak and strong ties as the equivalent to bonds and bridges needs revision. Second, Granovetter's study is often quoted as an exemplar of how weak ties operate but he investigated networks of people who *had* jobs. Although many studies have shown that social capital theory can help to explain how labour markets operate, such studies generally exclude the unemployed and underemployed from their investigations (Aguilera 2002, 871).

So, the current literature does not examine in detail what features determine 'bridging', making it a slippery concept, and does not address how, exactly, bridging works and under which conditions (cf. Leonard and Onyx 2003, 191). Policy interventions assume that weak, especially heterogeneous ties across boundaries of ethnicity, race and class not only are 'weak' by definition, but also will automatically be bridges, just like the rather uncritical use of 'weak ties' and 'bridges' in Putnam's study (Putnam, 2000; 23–24, 413). This assumes that the only issue poor people face is the lack of the right type of ties to get ahead – independent of how such ties operate. But *is* it sufficient for a tie to be weak? What social principles and mechanisms guide their use of ties?

Do Poor People have Weak Ties? Some Numbers

Poverty may have many dimensions, but we consider income as the major dimension in market-oriented, industrialized societies like the Netherlands.[3] Work, put simply, guarantees income, although increasingly less so an income considered sufficient to elevate people above the poverty level. The Landscapes of Poverty Study still aimed to include people with diverse sources of income, including those receiving welfare benefits with an obligation to seek formal employment, such as singles and couples without children, couples with children and single parents with children over the age of five, all of whom may face different challenges in escaping poverty

---

3 For discussions on the definitional question of poverty in a late-modern welfare state, see Van Loo 1992 or Engbersen and van der Veen 1987.

through employment. For these groups not applying for jobs could result in cuts of their benefits. The study also included people receiving a disability benefit, the Dutch equivalent of SSI, who may never be able to return to the labour market, and those who had reached the age of 65 and thus were considered retired. Single parents with children under the age of five were, under the welfare regulations at the time of study, not obliged to look for a job. The relevance of weak ties to get ahead, here understood as improving one's economic and / or cultural capital, hence varies for different groups of people interviewed.

We distinguish seven groups of respondents on the basis of the source of their low income and their relation to the formal labour market. Those who are retired were no longer expected to become self sufficient. The argument of the need of weak ties for social leverage trough labour market entry, thus no longer applies to them. Similarly, those on SSI benefits who are medically unfit to work may be poor and outside the formal labour market, but weak ties will not change their position in the labour market, even *if* such ties exist and provide the needed resources.

The interviewers in the Landscapes of Poverty project collected, among many other things, names of respondents' friends, families and acquaintances, on the lines of Fisher (1982). We are bound to quite rough estimates of the nature of people's networks made by the investigators at the time, as the Landscapes of Poverty Project did not contain entirely systematic collection on network data as commonly used in network surveys (for example Fisher 1982; Völker 1999). However, as respondents talked generally spontaneously about the social ties that mattered to them in diverse forms of social support, we consider the type of tie they mention most often or most extensively (e.g. family members, friends and acquaintances[4]), to be an adequate criteria to classify whether they perceive themselves to have only supportive strong family ties, to have only supportive weaker ties, or to perceive their personal networks as containing both these types of ties. The original research team coded the interviews, classified the network types, and entered these classifications into SPSS (see Noordhoff 2008 for more details).

---

4 Acquaintances are commonly referred to as *kennis* in Dutch, a wording used much more often than *vriend*, which, especially when used in the singular, commonly implies a stronger bond; however, as in the interviews friends were often referred to in plural sense, we assume that the category of friends includes friends *and* acquaintances, and not, as did the original research team, that these should all be considered one-on-one friendship bonds. Based on more systematic survey research of social networks (Blokland and Van Eijk 2008) we extrapolate from other cases that to take the category of 'friends' in the interviews to contain a mixture of friendship and acquaintance ties of various intensity. Generally, the categories of weak and strong ties form a continuum rather than a bipolar model of fixed categories.

Table 6.1   Typology of social networks for respondents grouped by labour market position

	Obliged to work				Not obliged to work			
	Couple and singles	Single parent, kids over five	Subsidized workers	Working poor	Medically unfit	Single parent, kids under five	Elderly	**Total**
Family	8	5	5	6	12	3	5	44
(strong ties)	25%	29%	25%	32%	24%	20%	22%	25%
Acquaintances	13	5	5	4	19	6	8	60
(weak ties)	41%	29%	25%	21%	37%	40%	35%	34%
Mixed (both	11	7	10	9	20	6	10	73
strong / weak)	34%	41%	50%	47%	39%	40%	43%	41%
Total	32	17	20	19	51	15	23	177
P>0.05	100%	100%	100%	100%	100%	100%	100%	100%

Source: The Landscapes of Poverty-project.

Whereas the thesis of the strength of weak ties would imply that distance to the labour market shows correlation with a lack of friends and acquaintances, we find no significant correlation between the interviewees of labour market positions and the type of social network as classified here. Over 70 per cent of the interviewees had some sort of relatively weak ties. So, as we know that the data collection method used may have brought the focus more on strong than on weak ties, it is fair to say that the people in the Landscapes of Poverty study *did* very often have weak ties. This, however, only tells us that weak ties existed. What, then, happens *within* these ties? We turn to qualitative analysis to explore this. As weak ties were used only to a limited extent, interviewers often asked one question about friends and family without differentiating between the two, and much of the coping strategies investigated in the project were about social support, not social leverage, we include stories about strong as well as weak ties, and about ties where we can hardly say whether they should be considered strong or weak, and truly explore what these findings *imply* when we would apply them to weak ties.

Bonding ties consist of people who often feel responsible for each other's welfare, and have a communal character (cf. Clark and Mills 1979). Exchange plays a significant role: people expect other persons to be responsive to their needs and to demonstrate concern for their welfare. However, solidarity, empathy and other substantial rational orientations may often outweigh exchange dimensions. Substantial rationality, either through affection of affinity (cf. Blokland 2003), is ingrained in such relationships. These ties are never based on a simple one-dimensional understanding of tit-for-tat, as especially family ties serve more purposes than the exchange of support and resources. Values and mores may need to be negotiated on a permanent basis and may be interactionally constructed, but 'social man is not only a successor but also a heir' (Simmel 1950, 12), most strongly so in those ties that continue inheritance and traditions on a micro-level. This, then, makes family ties not necessarily the most supportive or the most emotionally rewarding, or even the warmest. But they are certainly the most elastic: in absence of functional rational exchange, they continue to have a high degree of continuity. This is by no means a privilege of family ties only. But where this substantial rational dimension is weaker developed as guidance to the actions between agents in their relationships (cf. Blokland 2003, chapter 5), processes of social support will be more readily characterized as 'social exchange' rather than as one-way provisions of care or assistance: 'social exchange emphasizes that support involves costs as well as benefits to actors who engage in it and that supporters make choices about resource strategies in the context of scarcity' (Uehara 1990, 522). Social exchange of resources is thus at least partly predicated on the expectation of return of 'reciprocity' (ibid. 523, cf. also Gouldner 1960; Simmel 1950). In the following paragraphs, we will discuss interviewees' accounts of their weak ties through the lens of social exchange, or, where needed, the principles guiding their ideas about ties and exchanges that, or so we argue, affect their weak ties in certain ways.

Before we do so we need to make a qualification. The easiness with which weak ties are sweepingly made into the equivalent of resource-rich ties is, we believe, incorrect. That a tie is weak indeed indicates that ego is somewhere engaged in networks outside his or her regular bonds. But there is no a priori reason to assume that such weak ties by definition are rich in resources. Someone with whom one has a weak tie may be part of a network that lacks resources significantly different from the resources to which ego already has access in his or her own closer network. For a socially excluded individual to have weak ties with others who are socially excluded, nothing may change. Weak ties thus are *not* the equivalent of bridges. Bridges may often be weak ties, but there is no guarantee that any weak tie can function as a bridge, as is also shown in the chapters by Bruce Haynes and Jesus Hernandez, Alexandra Curley and Talja Blokland in this volume. That said, let us imagine that *some* weak ties do provide opportunities for social leverage, would that, then, be a sufficient precondition for the transfer of resources?

Blocking the Road to Access Weak Ties: Five Patterns of Maintaining Independence

Through content analyses and open coding of interview transcripts by the second author, we have looked for mechanisms that block the roads to access resources that weak ties may entail in theory. Our interviewees were located in positions of structural dependency: they depended on bureaucracies, and their rules and regulations, that curtained their possibilities to live their lives differently (Noordhoff 2008, chapter 4; Engbersen 1990). We find five empirical patterns of maintaining independency in a structural position of dependency. These patterns all amount to the contradiction that one needs social ties to build social capital of leverage, but that to build social ties is to become interdependent. It may imply the need to ask for favours in the very realm of life where one can still assert independence. Those who struggle above all to remain independent (and hence do not ask) may then not develop the weak ties needed for social leverage.

Maintaining independence: do for others, but do not receive

There is more to life than getting ahead. Securing status and honour is one of those things (cf. Baxter and Margavio 2000, 412; Polanyi 1957, 46). Honour may matter more once one has less of other things (Bourgeois, 1995). And honour may indeed keep people from making use of their weak ties.

Kees, 54, a native Dutch man, had been living in poverty for less than three years. Talking about doing things for others, he strongly expressed his dislike for getting paid. He did chores for people he knew once in a while, and some offered him money for it. He needed money badly, but he generally refused to accept it:

> I helped moving a friend, and then you get some money, and I don't like that at all. I gave it to my wife, and she puts it away and buys groceries from it. I think you ought to support your friends, you don't have to get paid for doing that. But as a matter of fact, you got to accept it. Last week, I fixed a lamp, and then [this guy gave me] some money to buy a beer. And then you get into an argument, like "you fool, take the money" and then I say, "no I won't, you don't have to pay me for everything", whereas I do need the money. But I won't take it! [*ironically*] That's pathetic.

Similarly, Kees did not want to borrow things: 'I can't, because I can't give it back. Many times they give it to you [instead of lending it]. I detest that.' In Kees' account, the social meaning of money (Zelizer, 1994) was understood as a means that belonged in the marketplace, not in his loose network of 'friends'. The position of poverty made it hard for Kees to establish and maintain friendships as he saw fit – to support but do not pay each other. Honour meant to be able to give. But getting paid 'all the time' reduced his possibilities to give. Honour also meant to not depend on other people's help. Paying him for chores that friends should, in his view, do for each other for free trespassed a radius of respect (cf. Simmel 1950, 321). And every time that he got paid, the mutuality of social care that strong friendships or bonds may acquire was aborted, as accounts were settled right there and then. Kees could thus not steer these ties into the direction of stronger bonds through gifts, nor could he access these ties later to cash in on an earlier investment. The payments he received meant money that he badly needed, but also blocked the roads to resources of different kinds that these friends might have provided him with.

Gendered independence or avoiding debt: accept and pay back or never accept

Ashley, a single mother of 21 with a small child, originally from Suriname, had been on welfare for 3 to 5 years. She would borrow from her father or mother and was never expected to pay them back, and found that perfectly acceptable. But when she borrowed money once from a male friend she insisted on paying back. But her friend refused to take the money:

> He was mad … one of my best friends, he just got so mad at me: "Are you out of your mind, paying me back." I replied, "well, it isn't called borrowing for no reason, right" and then he said "but you know borrowing from me is for free". That makes me mad. When I come and pay them back, like I am supposed to, they'll get mad.

Ashley preferred to repay in order to maintain her independency, possible even her honour. But the lender appeared to want gratitude, not money. As Simmel (1950, 387) noted, many social relations are guided by giving and returning an equivalent, and where the return of an equivalent is out of the question, gratitude is a supplement. Gratitude, Simmel argues, 'emerges as a motive which (…) effects the return of a benefit where there is no external necessity for it' (ibid, 389). That type of gratitude would put Ashley precisely in an interdependency that she wanted to avoid. She wanted to get over with it. Marianne, a 41-year-old native Dutch single parent with children under the age of five, had friends and acquaintances who were willing to help her ever since she had become poor less than three years ago, but only on their terms. Marianne therefore preferred to not go out or to pay a babysitter over depending on her friends because 'then I have control over the situation'. Here, too, refusing help was a strategy to maintain independency and keep agency over a social life otherwise controlled by state bureaucracies and other constraints. Similarly, Rebecca, originally from Cape Verdia, now 50 and on a social security income since she became unfit to work over 10 years ago, felt that acceptance of gifts from 'just a friend or an acquaintance' would compromise the honour and freedom of independence and would not even accept it from siblings:

> I can get something extra from my brother, but I don't want that. He did offer me that. He came up to me, and he was like, "if you need anything, just give me a call". And then I said, "well, for now I don't need anything". And my daughter is used to do the same. She would never asks no one for money, she'd only come to me. I have taught her to stand on her own feet. I have told her "try to ask only me, and no-one else". So you don't have to be grateful to someone else later on, you did it own your own. You have to live, but you don't need to live a wealthy life. You may help each other, but you should never take advantage of each other.

Such clearly gendered notions of independence brought these women to refuse help from male friends, and even siblings, whereas labour market studies have suggested that men have better access to opportunities for social mobility than do women (cf. Mandel and Semyonov, 2006). The honour of being a strong woman thus comes with the risk of 'being too proud' to use potential roads to resources. This pride, however, is historically locked in the intersecting marginalized positions of the women in race, class, and gender, and is not simply an outcome of individual preferences.

Masculinity and gender featured in a different way in Kees' account – his wife would put the money away that he 'earned' through doing errands for. Misztal (1996, 129) correctly observes that the role of honour is decreasing in the contemporary Western world. Honour, and respect or disrespect closely related to honour, may not be crucial control mechanisms in wider social settings. But in these cases here honour continues to guide everyday interactions.

Within this context, Kees, Ashley, Rebecca and Marianne thus sustained their honour through managing those qualities of their social ties that might affect. Their striving for or protection of independency in doing so may well limit the resources that their weak ties could provide. Self-sufficiency taking personally when self-sufficiency in the broader social structure is out of reach thus confirms to the dominant cultural paradigm, which all these interviewees confirmed – you should not depend on others – but this can come with costs.

Self-sufficiency as a dominant policy ideology and as a general concern of people who worry about appearing too dependent on others has been noted by other scholars (cf. Pahl 1984, 25; Nelson 2000, 297). Uehara (1990, 544) showed in her study how women were indeed reluctant to mobilize their associates and preferred to rely on their own, limited resources and 'suffer through it': one should stand on one's own feet. This may even extend to both weak and strong ties, as was the case for Nebahat, a 32-year-old woman of Turkish descent who raised her small children by herself. Nebahat talked about the absence of the social support in her network:

> I have a big family and many acquaintances, but they are down to chilli and beans [just like me] and they cannot offer me support. I do not have to help them, and I do not want them to help me.

Maintaining agency: do for others and expect returns

Another pattern in social exchanges occurred where people invested in doing things for others and, different from in the examples discussed above, assumed that such investments would eventually bring returns. Social exchange then is reciprocal, but a return does not need to come right then and there, and there are no given rules that guide the process of exchange. Yet because of the absence of such rules and the gap in time, participants have to rely on trust (see a.o. Simmel 1950; Misztal 1996; Eriksen 1995; Blau 1986; Bourdieu 1977; Coleman 1990). Transactions that are not monetary need trust for them to occur; or, as in Kees' example discussed above, money can abort aims to build or renew friendships beyond the realm of transactions. One may derive a sense of agency from investing in doing things for others. One is in control of the potentials of support, as one has favours in the bank, to be cashed in at later times. The gift is of lesser value than the response, or 'a present is a hen and the response is a camel' (Bourdieu 1977, 198, n 7), so one can return one's independence through supporting others before having to *ask* support, as shows Gülten, a 40-year-old woman of Turkish descent:

> I: Do you ask financial help from family or friends?

> G: No, but I do some chores for friends, so I can earn a little money. You do not get anything for free these days. You know, when you'd ask for a nickel, they'd ask two nickels back.

In the case of Gülten, the immediate repay meant she acquired a bit of money that she needed, but as accounts were then closed, she could not draw on these investments for other resources. Nor could she ask, as the price for asking would always be higher than the resource received, or the debt permanent and thus violating independence.

Accounts were not always settled right away. Our data provide many examples of people who changed their perspective on their social ties because their trust had been violated when they supported others and expected returns that they then did not receive – if only gratitude. For example, Courtney, 57 and in poverty for less than three years, gave shelter to fellow Cape Verdians without residence permits, but she stopped 'having strangers in [her] house'. Her guests disappeared as soon as they did not need her any longer:

> I used to help a lot of people, illegal immigrants without food. I took them to my place and gave them food and a place to sleep (…) but I don't do that anymore. At the very moment that you're helping others, that's good, but now they don't care about me. Well, I don't need to be repaid, but they pay you no mind, they don't even say hello. They've got an attitude.

Courtney invested in ties with people whom she hardly knew and her expectations of what she would receive in return – nothing but gratitude, may be – were not met. To act ahead of needs for support may provide actors with a sense being in charge, as they build credit that they can later use. But Courtney's words demonstrate that maintaining such agency for latter needs, however small or vague these may be, is not guaranteed. Koos and Marga, a recently married couple of Dutch descent in their thirties, had clearer expectations of how investments in social ties could be reciprocated later. Marga came from a trailer park where she grew up in what she described as a 'criminal environment'. She had had a rough life and worked all sorts of jobs until she was diagnosed with AIDS 2 years ago. Koos worked in construction for more than a decade, but off the books. When he broke his foot he was not eligible for sick payments. Now he was home to care for Marga and Marga's child. Over the last few years, they had gone through a downward spiral. They received welfare benefits for a year at the time of the interview. Marga and Koos found it difficult to accept support since they had become poor less than three years ago – as this violated independence – but their earlier support to others had not created the *inter*dependence that they had expected:

> M: I think it's always difficult to accept something [from others]. We never really had to.

> K: To put it stronger, everybody came up to us, like "can you lend me something". It's hard to imagine. Our door was always open. The entire neighbourhood came here, when they were in trouble. So, that's the situation we were used to. And then we had to [find support because our income declined] and that is terrible.

> M: Well, it's the other way around now.

> K: Yeah, well, but actually we experienced the exact opposite. Our neighbour upstairs, I tell you, she borrowed money from us twice a month. She paid everything back on time nicely. And at some point, we were broke, we didn't have a nickel. And she came over, [she was] proud, she just won a thousand [guilders] in a bingo game. So, we looked at each other, and said, "see, can you lend us a hundred?" And no, she couldn't. So, we said to each other, that's it. Never, never again! She will never receive a nickel from us. Let's face it: don't say you just won the bingo. Go upstairs, and don't say anything, or lend me the hundred. But no, that wasn't possible.

> M: We did so much for her, year after year. You're not expecting that when you're having a hard time yourself, that she won't lend you something. That's bull. After [such an

experience], there is even more of a barrier to ask her anything down the line. You bump your head again … you make yourself vulnerable, and then, yeah.

Ashley explained why exchange was difficult even with people whom she considered her 'friends'. She watched her friend's children, but her friend did not return the favour:

> I always took care of her kids. And she was supposed to take care of mine when I had to go somewhere. So at some point, I had to go to a funeral. And she was my babysitter. She called me up the day before, and asked "at what time do you bring the child over?" I said, "at 2pm". So when I got to her house, she was not home. I really didn't like that at all. Like, sometimes I am stuck with her kids, for three, four days. Her two children and my child, in my house, at my expenses. You'd never hear me complain about it. And then only once do I ask her to take care of my child, and she walks out on me. I didn't hear from her since, so I think she already felt trouble. …That it was not the right thing to do.

As many scholars have noted (Mauss 1966; Sahlins 1965; Gouldner 1960), in the time lag between giving and reciprocating, obligation, trust and cooperation are being created. As Eriksen wrote (1995, 182), 'people keep relationships by remembering their obligations to give to another'. But the time lag can, in contrast, also deteriorate a social tie. Ashley, Courtney and Koos and Marga all presented us with examples of returns that they expected but that they did not receive. As Sykes (2005, 114) has argued, reflections on exchanges alter the way people create relationships with others. Megan, a 48-year-old single mother of Dutch descent, once also lend money to a neighbour, who then took a long time to pay her back. This affected Megan's approach to exchange relations:

> I am too honest, they take advantage of you. If you give something that's a good thing, if you don't, you can drop dead. I have gone through that. I withdrew from everybody.

The strategy of maintaining agency to invest in social capital now in order to draw upon it in the future failed, and, as most explicitly expressed in the account of Koos and Marga, this comes with insecurity and a sense of dependency and, as expressed by Megan and Courtney, with a sense of betrayal. To be independent, then, means to not ask for support from others, and to not give too much support too easily. Especially (but, as Ashley showed, not only), when ties are weak, there is no guaranteed return. Precisely because weak ties are established and maintained through social exchange, refraining from exchange limits people's potential to develop weak ties, and hence to access resources through the weak ties that they do have.

Being seen as … : independence and gossip

A position of independence is, of course, not just a matter of one's own sense of self, but certainly a position one seeks to represent in wider social circles. Giving implies the obligation to reciprocate, and community sanctions may enforce such obligations (Nelson 2000, 291). If members of a community who are seen as capable of providing support fail to come forward or fail to reciprocate support given to them, 'words spread rapidly through the community' (Uehara 1990, 540). The communities, however limited in scope, that our interviewees belonged to may thus sanction actions in a web of group affiliations (cf. Simmel, 1908, such a web need not consist of strong ties only!). When such webs have a local character, information can easily flow. Gossip, conversations about other people, can effectively exclude members of a community (Elias and Scotson 1994, 94), especially when these concern vague acquaintances rather than very close friends and families. Gossip may help to ensure a community's cohesion, but fear for gossip may also hinder people in the use they make of their ties. Maika, a woman from Cape Verdia who lived in the Netherlands as an illegal immigrant for approximately seven years, no longer wanted to rely on ties with other Cape Verdian immigrants:

> Sometimes you see things that are not right. For example, after they've given you a glass of water, everybody must know that you were given a glass of water. And I don't like that at all. I learned a lot from that. So, I don't [turn to others for help] anymore.

Shelli, 32, of Surinamese descent, who worked part-time but had an income below the poverty line for the last 3 to 5 years, disliked gossip intensely. Gossip kept her from exchanging resources, from sharing her worries and from lending or borrowing money – and she kept her independence:

> It's not in my nature to borrow money from people. I try to live without bothering others. I have always been independent. I've never been blessed with a lot of friends. It's always the he say-she say shit. Therefore, I always keep people at a distance, and I never talk about anything.

Katrien, 35, a single parent with small children and of Dutch origin, also refused to use her weaker ties for resources:

> I only borrow stuff from very close friends. You know, I live in a neighbourhood where there is a lot of gossip. I prefer to borrow from people whom I fully trust. I hate to borrow stuff, because I would really hate it if it's known in the community that I can't give it back. Suppose that people would talk behind my back, and they say that I can't pay it back.

Knowing that one is being watched thus resulted in keeping one's distance from people whose support could be instrumental. Katrien, Shelli and Maika all recognized that gossip constrained their actions (cf. Davis 1969, 74; Misztal 1996, 129). Mechanisms affecting reputations, such as conformity to norms of exchange, and social control like gossip, are mechanisms of respecting and disrespecting honour. These may matter more in situations of close-knit bonds. But experiences of respect and disrespect for honour also influenced the expectations and attitudes in weaker ties. They may thus hinder poor people in making use of their weak ties, as well as limit their possibilities to develop new weak ties. After all, to talk about concerns – including concerns that would be eased by social capital – may result in gossip. Accepting support without being able to reciprocate may result in gossip. And not being independent may result in being talked about. But avoiding gossip by keeping to oneself makes *using* bridges to other social networks difficult.

Weak ties break where strong ties stretch

Finally, then, our data showed a pattern of differentiation between strong and weak ties, where reliance on strong ties was facilitated by the multiple layers of substantial rationality that actions between people in a bond contained. Violations of expectations of reciprocity may occur here as well, but their loose definitions are less problematic. Achmed, a 32-year-old man from Turkish descent, would never accept money from his friends, but would borrow from his family. Just like Mustafa, 31 and also Turkish, he could pay his family back whenever it suited him:

> If I need to borrow a large amount of money, I ask my family and nobody else. Because my family I can pay back later. With friends, it's different. If at some point they want their money back, they want it right away. So I won't ask them.

If one had to borrow, asking, or receiving favours from weak ties was seen as a threat to independence. Family ties thus were of a different nature. As we argued above, bonds have a stronger dimension of affection, or imply the substantial rationality of how things 'ought to be' that creates affinity (Blokland 2003) that weaker ties with their transactional nature do not possess to the same extent, or that require more work in weak ties. Failure to reciprocate may strain a bond. But as bonds are ruled more strongly than weak ties by other norms than reciprocity only, they do not necessarily disintegrate as a result. Weaker ties, as we have seen in the case of Ashley whose friend was no longer her friend because she violated an expectation of a return of a favour, may disintegrate indeed. The fact that Ashley considered her friend a friend and that yet all that it took for her to break with her friend was to not return a favour indicates that rather than two polar types, weak ties and strong bonds are a continuum, and many of people's ties may move back and forth on it.

Weak ties, then, tend to break where strong ties stretch once expectations are being violated, honour is being disrespected or independence is being threatened. Strong ties, too, include carefully managed honour and reputation, and are subject to the constraints of gossip – honour and independence are always at the risk of being violated. But weak ties tend to be at least as risky, and the costs of failed transactions in such ties much higher. This, then, implies that people in poverty in our study, in addition to the strategies discussed so far, used strong, not weak ties to have their needs met. However, limited investment in and flow of resources through weak ties meant also that potential uses of such weak ties for leverage remained restricted, as such ties were clearly differentiated from and felt to be of less value to one's everyday life than strong family bonds.

Conclusion: How to be Strong *and* Use your Ties?

In this chapter we join those scholars who have criticized the idea of solving social problems through social capital (Portes 1998, 19; Portes and Landolt 2000, 535; Boggs 2001, 282–290; De Fillipis 2001). DeFillipis (2001, 800) argued that social capital has become divorced from other forms of capital, stripped of power relations (see also Haynes and Hernandez, this volume), and imbued with assumptions that social networks are win-win relationships and that individual gains, interests and profits are synonymous with group gains, interests and profits. As we noted in the beginning of our chapter, commentators have argued for public policies to focus on strengthening poor people's social networks in order to help them help themselves in times of a retreating welfare state. Such arguments reflect a strong belief in an individual's potential to change their own fates. We know too little of how poor people's current social relations are roads for exchanges of resources to make strong claims about the value of weak ties as such.

We asked, first, whether poor people interviewed for the Landscapes of Poverty Study in two neighbourhoods in Amsterdam and one in Rotterdam had weak ties at all, and if so, what sort of processes and mechanisms governed their social ties. We showed that one of the challenges they faced was to keep their independence, if not to protect their honour, and that they avoided becoming interdependent or even dependent on others in several ways. First, we saw that some aimed to do well for others without getting anything in return. They thus attempted to build durable social ties governed by principles of substantial rationality, like Kees, but faced immediate payments that closed accounts whilst they would rather create a credit. More successfully and along similar lines, we have seen how some did well to others in order to get direct returns, such as money, so that when they would *need* something, they would not need to ask. We have argued that such patterns hamper the development of weak ties, because either accounts are settled right away and thus no durable weak tie develops, or when it did, someone like Kees could only call on such ties again through creating a debt – and that would violate his sense of independence, an independence already severely challenged by the position of being a welfare recipient.

Second, we have shown how typically gendered threats to independence occurred when a woman accepted a loan from a male friend who then refused to be paid back. Similarly, we have presented examples of women who for the very risk of becoming indebted without a chance to repay would refrain from accepting support. Here, too, we have argued that seeking independence in a structurally dependent context means refraining from the development and maintenance of social ties that may provide access to resources currently unavailable. For access to resources a need needs to be known: one may learn about a need of someone else *casually* – as in Putnam's example of the donor and the recipient of a kidney, where the donor casually learnt about his bowling league partner's need – or directly when one approaches someone else for a favour. But the more people keep to themselves in order to be seen and to see themselves as 'strong', the slimmer their chances of resourceful weak ties.

Third, we have looked at ways in which people attempted to do well for others in order to build up credit for later, and how such attempts failed as the return on their investment did not materialize. As experiences of social ties are carried over to new or other ties, interviewees tended to draw conclusions that helping others would not mean a return where they would expect one so that, indeed, they were less likely to invest in future or other relationships – weak or strong. We have also shown how gossip may further hamper people's reliance on others as to establish a position as strong and independent was not just a matter of personal sense of self, but also was affected by how one's wider social circle responded or was believed to respond.

Strong family ties may suffer from all these mechanisms, but in contrast to many weak(er) ties, they have abundant dimensions to them that do not depend on notions of social exchange: the more transactional the relationships we have – and weak ties almost by definition tend to be of a more the transactional nature – the higher the risk that unmet expectations or threats to independence and honour will cause the tie to break or will cause the traffic over the bridge to remain limited in scope and content.

The dilemma, then, *if* weak ties can do the magic that is generally expected from them even in the structural positions that our interviewees faced, is: how to be strong, e.g. to maintain one's independence in those spheres of life where at least some agency is possible *and* use ties, as far as they are available or can be developed, for social leverage?

Let us then, finally, turn to the specific urban context of the neighbourhoods where our interviewees resided. The spatial organization of diverse types of citizenship, where economic, social and political citizenship no longer coincide and where everyday life for many, especially those with most access to resources that the poor do not have, is multi-sited, makes this question even more pronounced.

The neighbourhood, after all, will *not* be the place to be developing weak ties that result in social leverage. The risk one runs in all weak ties, that not meeting expectations or violation of independence will break the tie, is a risk with more consequences in a neighbourhood than in any other social context. Breaking a tie with the neighbour next door is simply harder to do, because the distinctive characteristics of neighbourhood relationships is that they live physically close by: 'living near others', Abrams writes (in Bulmer 1986, 18–9), 'is a distinctive context of relationships – nothing more. And the most obvious special feature of nearness as a setting for relationships is the exceptional cheapness with which it can permit good relationships and the exceptional costs it can attach to bad ones.' Thus, the cheapness of good neighbouring ties can facilitate the exchange of very small favours and small forms of support, such as keeping an eye on each other's house when one is absent, or lending and borrowing up to an egg or a cup of sugar. But respecting each other's privacy is at least of as much value among good neighbors as is social support (cf. Bulmer 1986, 96). The type of support needed for social leverage requires more than such casual exchanges. Especially for people in poverty such support is hard to achieve without having one's independence affected. Yet the larger the distance and the respect for each other's privacy, the more privatized communities and the less connected communities are to a bounded geographical space (Blokland 2003), the less associational life in the city is becoming and the larger the changes are that affect what Blokland and Rae called in chapter two 'the sidewalk republic', the more difficult it becomes to learn casually about someone else's needs – and thus to provide access to resources through weak ties *and do so* through a tie that contains more than only a helping relationship in an unequal dyad.

References

Aguilera, M. (2002), 'The Impact of Social Capital on Labor Force Participation: Evidence from the 2000 Social Capital Benchmark Survey', *Social Science Quarterly*, 83, 853, 3.

Baxter, V. and Margavio, A. (2000), 'Honor, status, and aggression in economic exchange', *Sociological Theory*, 18, 3, 399–416.

Beggs, J., Haines, V. and Hurlbert, J. (1996), 'Situational Contingencies Surrounding the Receipt of Informal Support', *Social Forces*, 75, 1, 201–222.

Bian, Y. (1997), Bringing Strong Ties Back In: Indirect Ties, Network Bridges, and Job Searches in China, *American Sociological Review*, 62, 3, 366–385.

Blau, P. (1986), *Exchange and Power in Social Life* (New Brunswick: Transaction Books).

Blokland, T. (2003), *Urban Bonds: Social Relations in the Inner City* (Oxford: Polity Press).

Blokland, T. and Van Eijk (2008), 'Do people with a taste for diversity practice diversity in everyday life?' (Forthcoming in: *Journal of Ethnic and Migration Studies*).

Boggs, C. (2001), 'Social capital and political fantasy: Robert Putnam's *Bowling Alone*', *Theory and Society*, 30, 2, 287–297.

Boissevain, J. (1974), *Friends of Friends: Networks, Manipulators and Coalitions* (New York: St. Martin's Press).

Bourdieu, P. (1977), *Outline of a Theory of Practice* (Cambridge: Cambridge UP).

Bourgois, P. (1995), *In Search of Respect: Selling Crack in El Barrio* (Cambridge: Cambridge University Press).

Briggs, X. (2001), 'Ties that bind, bridge, and constrain: social capital and segregation in American Metropolis', *Trabalho apresentado no International Seminar on Segregation*.

Bulmer, M. (1986), *Neighbors: The Work of Philip Abrams* (Cambridge: Cambridge University Press).

Burt, R. (2000), 'The network structure of social capital', in: Staw, B. and Sutton, R. (eds), *Research in Organizational Behavior*, pp. 345–423 (New York: JAI Press).

Clark, M. and Mills, J. (1979), 'Interpersonal attraction in exchange and communal relationships', *Journal of Personality and Social Psychology*, 37, 1, 12–24.

Coleman, J. (1990), *Foundations of Social Theory* (Cambridge: Belknap Press of Harvard University Press).

Corbin, J. and Strauss, A. (1990), 'Grounded theory research: Procedures, canons, and evaluative criteria', *Qualitative Sociology*, 13, 1, 3–21.

Davis, J. (1969), '*Honour and Politics in Pisticci*. Proceedings of the Royal Anthropological', *Institute of Great Britain and Ireland*, 69–81.

DeFilippis, J. (2001), 'The myth of social capital in community development', *Housing Policy Debate*, 12, 4, 781–806.

Domínguez, S. and Watkins, C. (2003), 'Creating Networks for Survival and Mobility: Social Capital Among African-American and Latin-American Low-Income Mothers', *Social Problems*, 50, 1, 111–135.

Edin, K. and Lein, L. (1997), *Making Ends Meet: How Single Mothers Survive Welfare and Low-Wage Work* (New York: Russell Sage Foundation).

Elias, N. and Scotson, J. (1994), *The Established and the Outsiders: A Sociological Enquiry into Community Problems* (London: Sage).

Engbersen, G. (1990), *Publieke bijstandsgeheimen. Het ontstaan van een onderklasse in Nederland* (Leiden: Stenfert Kroese).

—— (1997), *In de schaduw van morgen. Stedelijke marginaliteit in Nederland* (Meppel: Boom).

Engbersen, G. and van der Veen, R. (1987), *Moderne armoede* (Leiden: Stenfert Kroese).

Engbersen, G. and Snel, E. (1996), 'Achterstandswijken in Nederland', in G. Engbersen, J. Vrooman and E. Snel (eds) *Arm Nederland. Het eerste jaarrapport armoede en sociale uitsluiting*, 121–145. (Den Haag: Vuga).

Eriksen, T. (1995), *Small Places, Large issues. An Introduction to Social and Cultural Anthropology* (London: Pluto Press).

Fernandez-Kelly, M. (1995), 'Social and Cultural Capital in the Urban Ghetto: Implications for the Economic Sociology of Immigration', in A. Portes (ed.) *The Economic Sociology of Immigration: Essays on Networks, Ethnicity, and Entrepreneurship*, 213–247 (New York: Russell Sage Foundation).

Field, J. (2003), *Social Capital* (London: Routledge).

Fischer, C. (1982), *To Dwell among Friends: Personal Networks in Town and City* (Chicago: University of Chicago Press).

Giddens, A. (2000), *The Third Way and its Critics* (Cambridge: Polity).

—— (2002), *Runaway World: How Globalisation is Reshaping Our Lives* (London: Profile).

Gouldner, A. (1960), 'The Norm of Reciprocity: A Preliminary Statement', *American Sociological Review*, 25, 2, 161–178.

Granovetter, M. (1973), 'The Strength of Weak Ties', *American Journal of Sociology*, 78, 6, 1360–1380.

Granovetter, M. (1974), *Getting a Job: A Study of Contacts and Careers* (Chicago: University of Chicago Press).

Henly, J., Danziger, S. and Offer, S. (2005), 'The contribution of social support to the material well-being of low-income families', *Journal of Marriage and Family*, 67, 122, 140.

Leonard, R. and Onyx, J. (2003), 'Networking Through Loose and Strong Ties: An Australian Qualitative Study', *International Journal of Voluntary and Nonprofit Organizations*, 14, 2, 189–203.

Lin, N. (1999), 'Social Networks and Status Attainment', *Annual Review of Sociology*, 25, 467–487.

Lofland, J. and Lofland, L. (1995), *Analyzing Social Settings: A Guide to Qualitative Observation and Analysis* (Belmont: Wadsworth).

MacLeod, J. (1994), *Ain't no Makin' it: Leveled Aspirations in a Low-Income Neighborhood* (Boulder: Westview Press).

Mandel, H. and Semyonov, M. (2006), 'A Welfare State Paradox: State Interventions and Women's Employment Opportunities in 22 Countries', *American Journal of Sociology*, 111, 6, 1910–1949.

Marsden, P. and Hurlbert, J. (1988), 'Social Resources and Mobility Outcomes: A Replication and Extension', *Social Forces*, 66, 4, 1038–1059.

Mauss, M. (1966), *The Gift: Forms and Functions of Exchange in Archaic Societies* (London: Cohen-West).

Misztal, B. (1996), *Trust in Modern Societies: The Search for the Bases of Social Order* (Cambridge: Polity Press).

Monroe, S. and Goldman, P. (1988), *Brothers – Black and Poor: A True Story of Courage and Survival* (New York: William Morrow).

Mouw, T. (2003), 'Social Capital and Finding a Job: Do Contacts Matter?', *American Sociological Review*, 68, 6, 868–898.

Nelson, M. (2000), 'Single Mothers and Social Support: The Commitment to, and Retreat from, Reciprocity', *Qualitative Sociology*, 23, 3, 291–317.

Noordhoff, F. (2008), *Persistent Poverty in the Netherlands* (Amsterdam: Amsterdam University Press).

Pahl, R. (1984), *Divisions of Labour* (Basil: Blackwell).

Polanyi, K. (1944), *The Great Transformation: Economic and Political Origins of Our Time* (Boston: Beacon Press).

Portes, A. and Landolt, P. (2000), 'Social Capital: Promise and Pitfalls of its Role in Development', *Journal of Latin American Studies*, 32, 2, 529–547.

Portes, A. (1998), 'Social Capital: Its Origins and Applications in Modern Sociology', *Annual Review of Sociology*, 24, 1–24.

Putnam, R. and Feldstein, L. (2003), *Better Together. Restoring the American Community* (New York: Simon & Schuster).

Putnam, R. (2000), *Bowling Alone: The Collapse and Revival of American Community* (New York: Simon & Schuster).

Richards, P. and Roberts, B. (1998), 'Social Networks, Social Capital, Popular Organizations and Urban Poverty', paper presented at the Seminar on Urban Poverty, Rio de Janeiro.

Rumbaut, R. (1977), *Life Events, Change, Migration and Depression: Phenomenology and Treatment of Depression* (New York: Spectrum).

Sahlins, M. (1965), 'On the sociology of primitive exchange', in M. Blanton (ed.), *The Relevance of Models for Social Anthropology*, 139–236 (New York: Praeger).

Scott, J. (1997), *Corporate Business and Capital Classes* (Oxford: Oxford University Press).

Scott, J. and Griff, C. (1984), *Directors of Industry: The British Corporate Network 1994–1976* (Cambridge: Polity Press).

Simmel, G. (1950), *The Sociology of Georg Simmel* (Glencoe: The Free Press).

Stack, C. (1974), *All Our Kin: Strategies for Survival in a Black Community* (New York: Harper and Row).

Staring, R., Engbersen, G. and Ypeij, A. (2002), *Armoede, migranten en informaliteit in Rotterdam-Delfshaven: tweede deelstudie van project 'Landschappen van armoede'* (Rotterdam: RISBO).

Sykes, K. (2005), *Arguing With Anthropology: An Introduction to Critical Theories of the Gift* (London: Routledge).

Uehara, E. (1990), 'Dual Exchange Theory, Social Networks, and Informal Social Support', *The American Journal of Sociology*, 96, 3, 521–557.

Useem, M. (1984), *The Inner Circle: Large Corporations and the Rise of Business Political Activity in the US and the UK* (New York: Oxford University Press).

Vale, L. (2002), *Reclaiming Public Housing: A Half Century of Struggle in Three Public Neighborhoods* (Cambridge: Harvard University Press).

Van Loo, L.F. (1992), *Arm in Nederland 1985–1990* (Meppel: Boom).

Völker, B. (1999), *Buren en buurten: Nederlands onderzoek op het snijvlak van sociologie en sociale geografie* (Amsterdam: SISWO).

Wacquant, L. (1998), 'Negative social capital: State breakdown and social destitution in America's urban core', *Journal of Housing and the Built Environment*, 13, 1, 25–40.

Wann, M. (1995), *Building Social Capital: Self Help in a Twenty-First Century Welfare State* (Institute for Public Policy Research).

Williams, C. (2005), 'Cultivating Community Self-Help in Deprived Urban Neighbourhoods', *City & Community*, 4 (2), 171–188.

Ypeij, A. and Snel, E. (2002), *Armoede en bestaansstrategieën: formele en informele sociale zekerheid in Amsterdam-Zuidoost; derde deelstudie van project 'Landschappen van armoede'* (Rotterdam: RISBO).

Ypeij, A., Snel, E. and Engbersen, G. (2002), *Armoede in Amsterdam-Noord. Eerste deelstudie van project 'Landschappen van armoede'* (Rotterdam: RISBO).

Zelizer, V. (1994), *The Social Meaning of Money* (New York: BasicBooks).

Chapter 7

Middle Class Neighbourhood Attachment in Paris and Milan: Partial Exit and Profound Rootedness

Alberta Andreotti and Patrick Le Galès

Introduction

In recent years, there has been a growing recognition that the nature of urban social capital is affected not only by the problems of the urban poor, but also by the strategies of the affluent middle classes. European cities have historically been characterised by greater social integration than found in the US (Legales, 2002). However, contemporary urban trends in Europe, for instance associated with gentrification (Butler and Robson, 2003; Preteceille, 2006), segregation (see Atkinson in this volume), and more generally 'the end of urbanism' (Rae, 2003), may entail significant shifts in the social fabric of European cities. This chapter, based on an exploratory comparative empirical research in France and Italy, examines whether we can detect the partial 'exit' of upper middle class both from their national society and from the cities in which they live. We tackle this question from a micro perspective, looking at the experience of the individuals, their narratives and focusing on a specific angle: the social networks of managers and engineers in Paris and Milan.[1]

This chapter is organized in five parts. Firstly, we will discuss the partial exit hypothesis, framing it in the globalization literature. Secondly, we will define what we mean by the upper middle classes and explain how we operationalise it in our research. The third to fifth sections report our empirical research on thirty one interviews with managers and engineers carried out in the city of Milan and fifty five in the city of Paris. Section three examines the mobility profiles of our respondents,

1 This chapter is based on the results of a comparative research coordinated by Patrick Le Galès and Alberta Andreotti financed by the PUCA, Ministère de l'Equipement and the the RTN-UrbEurope project (http://www.urban-europe.net). The research aims at analysing some of the dynamics of inequalities from two different angles : mobility and spatial segregation. It looks mainly at managers/professionals as one example of the differentiation within the middle classes, ie the upper strata of the middle classes. The research project is carried out in several European cities: Paris, Lyon, Madrid, Milan and tackles various issues. In this chapter we make reference only to one part of the research findings.

Other researchers include Francisco Javier Moreno Fuentes, François Bonnet, Brigitte Fouilland, Julie Pollard, Charlotte Halpern, Barbara Da Roit, Stefania Sabatinelli, Chiara Respi that we thank.

where we show that many of them are highly mobile. Section four shows that despite this mobility, the social networks of our respondents, especially in Milan, are rather localised. The final section reports the relatively limited involvement of our respondents in voluntary associations, but indicates that they are highly politically engaged. We conclude by disputing the 'partial exit' hypothesis.

All *Barbarians*? Upper Middle Classes Taking Advantage of Globalization Trends

In the *New Barbarian Manifesto*, author R. Angel offers a few tricks to young and aspiring middle class high-tech professionals. One key lesson to survive the information age is to take advantage of collective goods and services where they are, but to avoid investing in any long term resources, and go private and temporary for as many services as possible. Those new Barbarians of the 'new times' should avoid any collective interdependence, maximise their self-interest and pillage collective resources from public authorities or networks without contributing to these. This brutal painting of the 'world to come' bears some resemblance, we are told, with the behaviour of young professionals in London or New York.[2] This view echoes the lengthy description in magazines of rich nomads, whose social networks goes from paradise pacific islands to trendy bars in Los Angeles and business colleagues in Tokyo, the social networks of global cities and liquid societies. It suggests that it is the actions of the new rich and affluent who are shaping the social capital of contemporary societies.

In this world, the issue of social capital and social networks is starkly opposed to the classical view of the local community, organized around family relations, dense interactions of friends, and attachment to the rich world of voluntary associations. Urry, in his manifesto 'Sociology beyond societies' (2000), argues that flux is making 'society' an obsolete category. From his perspective, mobility, strictly related to processes of globalization, destroys classic sociological categories of class, social structure, nation state, reproduction and locality. On the same line Giddens, in his essays on the consequences of modernity (1990), explains that traditional institutions of the nation-state have been disembedded, and have been replaced by institutions that adapt to globalized communication and outcomes.

Undoubtedly, one of the key issues for contemporary sociology is to articulate the nested scales where social actors interact and take into account two series of processes – scale articulation and mobilities – which seriously confuse classic views of societies organized within frontiers. Mobilities (in the form of migration, for instance) undermines the Weberian process of national society making – that is, the dual movement, in which borders are strengthened; inside is differentiated from outside, while an internal order is organized and a national society gradually homogenizes despite international relations and international commerce. Globalization, however, according to some authors, leads to the emergence of a new social class, a mobile global urban bourgeoisie, who can act and interact at a

---

2　We are grateful to Adrian Favell for this reference.

global level, can change country and thus avoid the constraints of national societies (e.g. Bauman, 2002). Sklair defines it as 'an international bourgeoisie: a socially comprehensive category, encompassing the entrepreneurial elite, managers of firms, senior state functionaries, leading politicians, members of the learned professions … plus the media, culture, consumption' (1995: 62; 2000). This new bourgeoisie speaks English, and has learned the codes that operate within Anglo-American firms, universities, and consultancies; it is supposed to develop a common global culture and omnivorous consumption practices. Within this framework, professional networks and, increasingly more, transnational professional networks become crucial in structuring the organization of society, with norms and models of excellence driven from within the professions – by consultants, legal specialists, managers, university academics, doctors, accountants, bankers, advertising executives, that is the same profiles who are more likely to belong to the global bourgeoisie.

However, as most would argue, if cities, nations, regions, or whatever level of social structures are to disappear under the pressure of generalised mobilities, and a global bourgeoisie is under construction this is going to take quite some time, and it may be premature to announce the rise of the new global middle class at this point in time. This is for two reasons. Firstly, national social structures and their institutions continue to condense massive resources that most social actors rely on. Secondly, the more mobility there is, the more choice social actors have, the more potential there is to locate and organize their own life fluctuating from one territorial level to another one and mixing them as Harvey, Veltz, Storper or Butler and Savage have eloquently put it for firms and families alike.

This first argument is well demonstrated by A. Favell's findings. In his book *Eurostars in Eurocities*[3] (2008), Favell shows all the downsides, difficulties, illusions and excitements of middle class professionals living abroad in international European cities, far away from friends and families. As one would expect, those feelings of missing some networks and support from family and friends is vividly expressed in particular for couples with children. The vast literature on immigration has made this point clear in numerous studies. In short there continues to be a 'friction of mobility', the consequences of which continue to be felt even by the elite middle classes.

The second argument is made in research linking issues of mobility (Europeanization or globalization) to the local, spatial, urban dimension. Tim Butler's (2003) work on London or the Savage, Bagnall and Longhurst's (2005) study of 'elective belonging' – that is the differentiation and overlapping of various scales of interactions for individuals, beyond the national frontiers – in Manchester (2005) show the enduring importance of the local urban environment (the neighbourhood or the cosmopolitan environment of London) for different middle class groups. Those types of results are even more expected within a continental European environment of historically very territorialised societies (Therborn, 1985; Le Galès, 2002). Only 1.5 to 2 per cent of Europeans move each year to another country, a proportion which is relatively stable over time and one of the lowest in the world (3 per cent at the global level, ILO). Moreover, if 7.2 per cent change house every year (over 16 per cent in the US), half of them stay in the same area. To use an old song's title, if

---

3 Eurostar 2008, (Oxford: Blackwell) in the series 'Studies in Social and Urban Change'.

Americans are born to run, Europeans are born to stay. Therefore, the question of increasing mobility must be necessarily linked to the question of fixity also for those social groups who can rely on more resources as upper middle classes.

The rise of various types of mobility – which we are told are a reality for many upper class individuals – seem to open the way to new individual opportunities. These new opportunities concretely means that these individuals (who have the economic and social resources to invest) can choose their culture, consumption, friends, jobs, housing, financial investment. In other words, this increased mobility allows individuals belonging to the upper middle class to put into practice 'exit strategies' from their national society and from their own cities of residence. These 'exit strategies' from a national perspective imply, for instance, a disinvestment in national policy and disengagement from political parties or associations, an escape from taxation, or the sending of children to international schools and universities, the building of social networks and social practices at the international level, disregarding the local one. From an urban perspective, these strategies can entail the choice of living in exclusive places (e.g. gated communities) isolated from the rest of the city and not to use the public spaces and services offered at the local level.

Though this opportunity for 'exit' cannot be concretely put into practice, it can threaten to re-negotiate the position within the national social structure (to obtain more benefits). One example of this is the taxation issue: individuals of the upper middle classes can threaten to move their residence in other countries (exit strategy) or to actively campaign against high level of taxes (partial exit): it is not by chance that the income tax has on average decreased by 15 per cent in the EU 15 countries over the last decade.

A third position is possible as well, not excluding the previous one: individuals belonging to the upper middle classes can put into practise 'partial exit strategies', that is they can choose to withdraw from certain public organizations (schools in the public sector for instance, hospitals) and to retreat from those organizations. With respect to the city, this means withdrawing from the use of the local space, and from the social interaction at that level.

In this chapter we explore the 'partial exit' hypothesis through the analysis of one particular dimension: the sociability of individuals belonging to the upper middle class groups in Paris and Milan. Our intellectual concern is to link the question of mobility to the question of fixity, to study at the same time the mobility of these individuals together with the way they are rooted in neighbourhoods, cities and urban regions. To better understand whether and to what extent these individuals develop partial exit strategies, we have developed an analytical diagram with two main dimensions referring to the sociability sphere and mobility: transnational exit and urban exit/secession. The 'transnational exit' dimension entails the presence or absence of foreign people in the social network, the frequency of interactions at this level together with the degree of mobility; the 'urban exit/secession' dimension entails the fact that the interactions occur (or not) at the local level and the use of the public space and services.

Transnational exit	+	-
Urban exit/secession		
+	Nomads Retreat from the city	Immobile/retreat
-	Mobile and locally rooted	Immobile and locally rooted

The diagram gives rise to four social profiles where at one extreme we can find the *Nomads* who are very mobile, interact at the international level, do not invest on local level and adopt exit strategies (they clearly resemble to the New Barbarians of Angel). At the other extreme we find the *Immobiles* who are anchored on their local context. We will come back to this diagram at the end of the chapter after discussing our findings.

We can now move further with the analysis looking at what we mean by upper middle classes in the two contexts and how we have operationalized it, briefly presenting our two fieldwork contexts. We will then start with the empirical analysis exploring the mobility of managers and engineers interviewed in this research and their social networks.

Upper Middle Classes: Managers and Engineers belonging to 'Cadres sup' and 'Dirigenti'

Within the upper middle class different groups coexist as far as economic, financial, human and social capital are concerned, and by consequence as far as status and prestige.[4] In the French context, the upper middle class mainly includes the social (and statistical) category of 'Cadres Supérieurs'. A well-known literature exists in France on the 'cadres',[5] though much less on the 'Cadres Supérieurs'.[6] From a sociological viewpoint 'les cadres' are not defined only by their education or job content, but rather by a status: they have a separate trade union that negotiate separately wages and labour conditions, and their pension is managed by specific organizations distinct from the rest of the wage earners. From the statistical viewpoint, the INSEE (Institut National de la Statistique et des Etudes Economiques) classifies the Cadres Supérieurs in the '*Professions intellectuelles supérieures*'. In the Italian case, the profile of 'Cadres' does not have the same social meaning, and it has been officially recognized only in the 1980s. The concept of 'Cadres Supérieurs' is more similar to

---

4 For an excellent discussion on the British debate on the Middle Classes see Butler and Savage (1995) or Martin (1998). We just remind that Golthorpe brought managers and professionals together within what he coined 'service class' (1982) – even though he identifies at least two groups within the service class – while Esping-Andersen (1993) clearly contrasted them with professionals more representative of the post fordist social structures.

5 See the classic books of Guy Groux (1982) and recently, Bouffartigues (2001).

6 While it exists a literature on the very high bourgeosie (mainly Parisienne), and the most important families of Paris (see Pinçon and Pinçon-Charlot 2000).

the Italian 'Dirigenti'[7], as they have their own association, trade union organization and pension fund, exactly like the French ones.

The juridical introduction of the 'cadre' (Law 190/1985) in the Italian context makes, the two national contexts closer, at least as far as the formal definitions are concerned, yet these still remain quite different in terms of statistical definitions and weight of these categories on the total employees.

In 2005, 'Cadres and professions supérieures' accounted for the 13 per cent of the employees in France (INSEE, 2005) and 'Quadri and Dirigenti' in Italy accounted for the 7.3 per cent of the employees (Istat, Labour Force survey, 2005). Considering the international classification ISCO-88 *Legislators and managers* plus *Professionals* in 2002 accounted for the 12.6 per cent of the total employees in Italy, while in France for the 15.9 per cent (Labour Force Survey, 2002).[8] Within this framework, the cities of Paris and Milan present figures above their national averages, even though there are some differences between the two cities considering that Paris is the capital of the country and hosts more *civil servants*. In Milan, the statistical categories which include managers and engineers account for the 30 per cent of the total employment (Oecd, 2006). In Paris, the same profile account for about half of the total employment (see Preteceille, 2006).

The operationalization of the upper middle class

Given the dissimilarity of the occupational categories in the two different contexts on the one hand, and the internal fragmentation of these social categories on the other one, it is not easy to make a comparison, and from an empirical point of view to select comparable respondents in the two contexts. For the purpose of our comparative research, it was therefore necessary to find some criteria to narrow the profiles of individuals belonging to upper middle classes, that is *Cadres Supérieurs* and *Dirigenti*. Two groups were identified: engineers and managers in the public and private sectors. Three elements were further retained to make them comparable: 1) level of education – selecting individuals with at least a university degree, and most often a master degree; 2) autonomy at work – which means the capacity to manage time, and contents of work; 3) the responsibility of some people – which means coordinating a team, deciding upon their careers and salaries and 4) a level of income which put them in the top 15 per cent (in fact rather the top decile) of earnings in their respective country. All interviews carried out in Paris and Milan with managers and engineers use these criteria.

The Experience of Mobility

The empirical material returns a complex picture which does not allow us to consider the interviewees as one homogeneous social group, not even within the same city as

---

7   For a review of the historical development of the Cadres and Dirigenti in the Italian context see Ricciardi (2004).

8   To see the definitions of the International Standard Classification ISCO-88 please visit the following website: http://www.ilo.org/public/english/bureau/stat/isco/intro3.htm.

far as mobility is concerned. The following questions were asked to explore those dimensions:

- Have you lived abroad for at least six months? Where? What was your experience like?
- Would you be available to move abroad if asked?
- How many times have you taken the aeroplane in the last month?
- How many travels abroad for professional and non professional reasons have you made in the last year?

Three main groups, transversal to the two cities, can be identified: 1) the immobile; 2) the internationally mobile but locally rooted; 3) the nomads.

The immobile are the interviewees who have not lived abroad and are not available for such an experience. The reasons given to explain such decisions are disparate: from family reasons, the language gap, to the fact that they have already reached high hierarchical levels. These interviewees do not travel very much and several of them have never taken the aeroplane for months before the interview. This profile is more present within the Milanese context where it comprises one third of the interviewees.

The locally rooted mobiles are potentially available to move if asked, under two conditions: a limited period abroad and a favourable country, which means mainly Western European countries, the United States and only in very few cases China. Africa, Australia, and the Middle East are almost never mentioned. These interviewees travel rather often for professional and non professional reasons and take the aeroplane several times a month. Some interviewees belonging to this group spent a period abroad, mainly at the beginning of the career after which they decided to settle and have a more quite professional life.

The nomads, who are a minority, spent one or more years abroad, or they live in Milan or Paris but they work in another country spending the working days abroad and coming back for the week ends (a few cases in Paris and Milan) and they are still available to move. Interviewees belonging to this group make more than twenty professional journeys a year, they take the aeroplane at least once a week, and travelling is their routine.

These profiles are transversal to the hierarchical positions and life course. There are managers with high responsibility who are not likely to travel, and young interviewees not willing to move, as well as older ones available for an experience abroad. This is more relevant for Milan than for Paris, where the youngest do not appear in the immobile profile. Much depends however on the kind of work they do: engineers building infrastructures or working in the energy field, for instance, are more likely to have spent a period abroad and to be available to move, whatever their age.

Despite the fact that a relatively immobile group of managers exists, the analysis of the three profiles suggest that geographical mobility is for most of them a habit. Most of our managers are mobile in a way or another. Few of them actually leave their country but most of them, for different reasons, have some professional or personal interactions in transnational network. How this is translated in the sociability sphere?

Scales and Characteristics of the Relational Network

Dealing with social networks is a promising means of examining the idea of partial exit both from the national society and from the city. Those two dimensions are analytically different in order to avoid the simplification associated with 'ghettoes of riches' or middle classes secession. Examining the networks of friends and families, where there are located is a good proxy to analyse dynamics of de-nationalization or de-localization of our engineers and managers.

To investigate the relational network, four dimensions were considered in our questionnaire: friendship, neighbourhood relations, the hierarchical positions present in the respondents' network and families. For the first two dimensions, the name eliciting method (Fisher, 1982) was used. For each named person, all socio-economic characteristics were asked (sex, age, place of birth, place of residence, marital status, education, profession, length of the relation, where they met). Information about 130 friends and 53 neighbours were collected in the Milanese context and information about 300 friends and 70 neighbours in the Paris context.[9]

> The following questions were posed: Could you please indicate three names of your friends? Do the three friends know each other? Do you know someone (acquaintance, relative, workmate, and friends) who lives abroad and could host you for a night? How often do you contact them?
>
> In the second section, the following questions were posed: Have you asked your neighbour a service in the last month? In the last six months, has is happened that a neighbour visits you without preventing? In the last six months, have you visited one of your neighbours without preventing? In the last six months, have you invited one or more of your neighbours for a coffee, lunch, dinner? In the last six months, have you been invited for a coffee, lunch, dinner by one or more of your neighbours? For the third dimension, the position and resource generator methods were used (Lin, 2000; Van der Gaat, M.; Sneijder, T. 2004), collecting the following information for each position and resource investigated: relation with the respondent, sex, residence, length of the relation, frequency of contacts, where they met.

Before starting with the analysis, it is useful to make a brief methodological consideration. The name eliciting method favours the finding of strong and long lasting ties, while it underestimates weak ties, with the risk of having a prevalence of bonding characteristics. The presence in the questionnaire of other methods only partly mitigates this risk. Yet, in this case, we are not very much interested in bridging relations (Putnam, 2000), since our interest mainly concerns the embeddedness of relations in the different spatial and social contexts. The data we collected allows us to explore the rootedness of respondents in the local, national or international contexts, and give some hints whether the practice of friendship has become disembedded from wider social relations (Savage, Bagnall and Longhurst, 2005).

---

9 The collected information does not allow a clear profile of the respondents' social networks. Though, information about the three friends, plus the information collected with the position and resource generator methods which are not analyzed in this chapter, allows us to have a more precise idea of the sociability of the respondents.

The friendship dimension is analysed in terms of the degree of homophily (education degree; profession); closure (do the three friends know each others?); length of the relation, frequency of contacts, and the 'spatial' dimension which entails the different social circles where relations have been formed. The literature on social networks has clearly highlighted that homophily is common to all social networks (Fisher, 1982; Lin, 2000), and that this characteristic is even more accentuated for people of higher status (Kadushin, 1995). As is well known, Bourdieu saw friendship, and social capital more generally, as a means of reproducing and maintaining social hierarchical position within the social structure (1980).

Friends, Neighbours and Families: Characteristics of the Network

Our interviewees live in the central city of the urban area of Milan and Paris, both of which have concentrations of middle classes and upper middle class residents, though not exclusively. Unsurprisingly, the Milanese and Parisian interviewees confirm the strong homophily by age, sex and marital status: most respondents mention friends with similar socio-demographic characteristics.

In Milan and Paris, our managers and engineers have a large network of friends in the city and beyond the city. They physically meet on a very regular basis. They also keep close contacts with their family (very much in the same city in the Milan case), and with friends in foreign countries. By contrast, they hardly know their neighbours. Most of our interviewees see the cities of Paris and Milan as resource rich environments in terms of services and networks of friends and families allowing them to follow successful professional careers while raising a family and having a vivid social life.

In Milan, the level of homophily is very high as far as as education is concerned while major dispersion exists for professions. About four out of five of the friends mentioned by the interviewees have a university degree, in Milan mostly of the same kind of the respondents themselves even if the spectrum of professions is more complex as many friends are professionals working on their own, or with their own company, but they all belong to tertiary sector and non manual sector. The Paris' case is very similar. Most friends have been known through the education system (the elitist 'grandes écoles' or universities), or less often through two key mechanisms: at work (during training period in particular) or through their children's schools where they meet young parents who become friends, here again from a similar background. Overwhelmingly, four out of five have comparable social position and educational background. Among the engineers and managers we interviewed, couples appear very homogeneous too, with the spouse having a similar level of education even if there is some disparity in the job situation. However, in both cities where many opportunities exist for highly educated women, many couples (about half of them) have the income of two careers, which allow them to own or to rent a large flat in the city.

This homogeneity is also confirmed by the position generator analysis: high status professions are all easily accessible by respondents, while it is not always the case for the less prestigious and manual jobs. As might be expected, a very low number of Milanese interviewees declared that they knew a non skilled blue-collar. Among those that did, this was for professional reasons. In Paris however, those who know blue collars workers typically came from a more modest and provincial background and may have kept some friends (sometimes family) from the place where they grew up, who happened to be blue-collar workers. The status of Paris as the national capital and centre of the most elitist universities makes it an 'escalator urban region' (to use the metaphor used to describe the London South East). We find among our respondents an important element of geographical mobility and to a lesser extent of social mobility, the two being closely linked for those who moved to Paris.

The wide range of listed professions is partly the result of the fact that few respondents mention workmates as friends or have met friends in the workplace. In both cities, the 'Nomads' are a partial exception as they have several friends among their colleagues or former colleagues, their professional networks being central in their social life. This means that the Nomads' friendship networks are less long lasting (mainly in the Milan case) and less rooted in the local context than the other groups'. Indeed, the 'Nomads' usually mention one friendship relation formed during childhood or school while the others are formed during work-experiences, these friends often live in other cities, or countries (mainly for the Paris case). The Nomads, however – once again with more emphasis in the Milan case – mix elements of high geographical mobility, more international sociability with elements of strong rootedness such as living with their parents (even though they are 35 years old or more!).

Dense networks of friends in Milan and Paris

In all other Milanese cases, the most common way that friendships were formed was through childhood relationships, from school (high school but also primary school level) and from the *scout associations* (rather widespread among children). By contrast, cultural or political associations and neighbourhoods are never mentioned as ways to meet friends. In fact, most of the present friendship relations for the Milanese respondents have lasted for more than twenty years. Milan is a place of old social networks, deeply rooted middle class friendship with intense and regular contacts. An engineer in a high-tech firm or a manager in a bank may fly twice a week to meetings all over Europe or beyond, but he or she spends the week end with old friends and family.

In Paris, the situation is more mixed. However most respondents have good friends in Paris whom they meet on a regular basis, in particular for dinner. As mentioned above, most friends are not childhood friends but rather people they met while they were students, or more recently through work or their children. The level of interaction is also concrete and very regular. About half of our interviewees also mention family connections living in the same city or a neighbouring commune. This is no surprise as they often declare that their choice of housing was related to the proximity of family. However, by contrast to the Milanese, about half of our interviewees came from another place in France and they keep mostly family ties, and/or friends in their place of origins. Also, only a very small number of them have childhood friends in Paris.

Those conclusions contrast with the findings of Savage, Bagnall and Longhurst amongst diverse groups of the middle classes in Manchester (2005). They report that their respondents do not have many contacts with their best friends and do not share with them regular activities, as they are likely to live in other cities. By contrast, the majority of Milanese interviewees declare regular contacts, the young respondents almost once a week and the oldest ones almost once a month. Email is the privileged means of connecting, but the relation does not remain on a virtual basis, as they also meet regularly. The fact that more than half of the friends live in the city of Milan, even in the same neighbourhood where the respondents and his-her friends have grown up, makes frequent visits possible. This is also true to a lesser extent in Paris. Our respondents go out in bars and restaurants or have dinners with their best friends on a regular basis. By contrast to the Manchester case, the intensity of relations is sustained by physical contact and fostered by a limited and fixed-term geographical mobility. Savage, Bagnall and Longhurst write that 'maintaining friends require the persistence and the ability to be abstracted from time and space so it can endure over these two dimensions' (p. 242). The dimension of persistence and investment is clearly evident in our cases, as well as time and space, though in a different way than in the Manchester. While time and space need to be abstracted in the Manchester cases because friends lived in other cities, the relations reported by the Milanese respondents are very well rooted in the local physical and social space. Paris is in between, but that dimension is also central.

The difference is that in Milan, friends have grown up together, have attended university together, and have selected each other, confirming this selection over the years. In this sense, there exists, in the words of Savage and his colleagues, a sense of belonging which is both inherited, ascribed up to a point but decisively reinforced by choice.

In Paris, about a fourth of our respondents have the same deeply local and immobile background. The role of the 'grandes écoles', the elitist part of the higher education system is decisive in the socializing process and the making of best friends. Those 'grandes écoles' attract young people from all of France (with an important proportion from the Paris region) but overwhelmingly from the same social background. The sense of belonging is important but mediated by the socializing impact of Parisian 'grandes écoles'.

The analysis of the proxy of the network closure (do the three friends know each other and meet independently) further contribute to understand the sociability of our respondents. In 28 out of the 31 Milanese cases, the three friends know each other and would meet without the respondent. This information can have a twofold reading: on the one hand it points the embeddedness of the respondents in the local social context, as they do not mention dyadic and isolated relations. On the other hand, this information points towards a close and self reproducing network which risks of having a prevalence of bonding features. These are not exclusive of course. The friendship closure of the Milanese respondents emerged also in other research: Barbieri analysing a sample of young Milanese employees' social networks found similar results (1997). This is a key different with the Paris respondents, where the three best friends do not meet on their own, or only exceptionally so.

Next to no relations with neighbours

Does local embeddedness also include dense relations with neighbours? Our conclusion is similar in both cities: our respondents have very limited interactions with their neighbours. They do not invite them for dinner or for a drink and they hardly exchange a service. Minimum interaction (saying hello and asking for some salt) is the general rule. Relationships between neighbours are mostly at low ebb and there is no obvious difference between the two cities.

In the discourses of the Milanese respondents – and here there are no differences between the three groups of immobile, fixed-term mobile and nomads identified earlier – neighbours do not appear to have any important role in the sociability sphere. The Milanese respondents have few contacts with neighbours, the majority of them limiting these contacts to 'good morning-good evening' or 'exchange of information about the building matters'.

In both Paris and Milan, neighbours are not seen to provide support in the emergency situations (e.g. illness, problems in the flat …). Respondents prefer to solve their problems on their own or asking their relatives or friends who often live nearby. Indeed, if relations with neighbours are almost non existent, most respondents have in the same neighbourhood friends (in Paris) or living parents (in Milan) with whom contacts are regular, almost on a daily basis in Milan.

The weakness of neighbour relations appear to be independent both from the length of residence in the neighbourhood, and from the house property, so that interviewees living in the same building for very long time do not report strong contacts. It is not even the case of closure towards neighbours differing from respondents' socio-economic characteristics as respondents have the perception to be on economic average of all residents. In this sense, our findings highlight the selectivity of relations even within the local social context, bringing some elements in favour of the closure of these networks. What seems to emerge from our finding is a dense, close, homogeneous, rooted but selective network.

Transnational networks

Some authors have stressed the 'disembeddedness of relations' (Giddens, 1990), i.e the fact that social relations and friendship are more and more stretched over space and time. This does not seem applicable to the Milanese respondents and only partly so in Paris. Our research is too limited to entirely reject the disembeddedness hypotheses. We find similar elements in the relations Milanese interviewees have with people living abroad. Milanese respondents mention few of these nodes. Some of them (twelve of the respondents) could not even mention any friend living in a foreign country. Contacts with these people are not based on a regular frequency, and visits are quite rare (sometimes every three years or even less). However, the respondents think they can easily mobilize these 'silent' relations, abstracting the relation from time.

By contrast, most Parisians mention two or three foreign friends with whom they have regular exchanges, and contacts, they are completely part of their social life. In the Paris case, this element is very striking. Most interviewees have no difficulty in naming two or three 'good friends' and point to other people with whom they interact with on a regular basis, but without being 'real friends'. Regular exchange and visits to foreign friends (at least once a year) or to friends living elsewhere is an important part of Parisian middle classes way of life and networks.

It is quite interesting to note, given the discourse on globalization and transnational networks, that the people mentioned by our respondents who live abroad are settled in the Western part of the world, and mainly in Western Europe with the cities of Paris and London most importantly. Those two cities are very close for many Milanese respondents but some other cities are also mentioned in interviews such as Barcelona, Madrid, New York. In the Paris case, more cities are mentioned by the respondents. Many Parisians are very familiar with many European cities that they visit over week ends – Italian cities certainly, but also Brussels, Prague, London, Barcelona. They also name American cities and cities in Asia, South America or more commonly Northern Africa.

Secession or Participation in the Urban Fabric?

Apart from social networks, rootedness in the local social context and the hypothesis of the partial exit have been further investigated through examining effective participation in local initiatives and associations, and the use of public local services. The literature on civic culture on the one hand, and on social capital on the other, highlights that those more likely to join associations tend to be middle aged, well educated, employed men in the labour market. We therefore expect our respondents to be relatively involved in associations. However, in both Milan and Paris, our managers and engineers are not involved in a neighbourhood association or organization (none in Milan, less than 10 per cent in Paris) and only seven out of the 31 respondents from Milan belong to other kinds of associations. Yet, these are professional associations entailing a national and not transnational dimension and do not require an active participation but mainly perform information and fiscal duties.

These findings can be interpreted in two contrasting ways: on the one hand this points towards civic disengagement, an evidence of urban 'partial exit strategy'; on the other hand it can be just the result of the fact that these people simply do not have time to join associations as they tend to work ten or more hours per day and to travel. The first hypothesis would appear more robust if the respondents' practices in terms of use of services and participation to the city life demonstrated retrenchment from the public sphere. However, in Milan past researches on the Milanese managers report a low participation in associative life compared to the local average (Cesareo, Bovone, Rovati, 1979; Rovati, 1991). This does not seem to go in the direction of the retrenchment, rather it would show a persistence of the 'non engaging' strategy. As far as the other actions are concerned, our findings do not go in the direction of the complete disinvestment from politics as well. All Milanese respondents declare that they are rather interested in politics, have voted in the last elections, have discussed of policy matters in the last month, and think that the Italian society would need to be reformed in several points but not in its essential features. In this sense, our respondents show an interest in national politics, and do not seem to reject *in toto* the society where they are living in. In Paris, respondents emphasise their participation in city life, in social events in the neighbourhoods and the vast majority is using local facilities, schools, public transports, public services on a very regular basis. They are also very aware and participative in political terms, critical of the French society and of the government.

Conclusion

In this chapter we empirically explored the idea that the upper middle classes may be engaging in 'partial exit strategies' both from the national society and from their cities of residence. We have identified the sociability sphere – friends, neighbours and family relations – as a good proxy to understand how and to which extent these individuals put into practise partial exit strategies and to which extent they are locally rooted or they resemble to the *New Barbarians* or the Nomads interacting at a global level, disregarding the local one – the city and the neighbourhood. Our empirical findings do not support the partial exit hypothesis and the spread of the *New Barbarians* profile.

Our findings suggest that these managers are mostly very mobile; they travel a lot but mainly for fixed-term periods, and they come home for the week ends even when they work for the whole week abroad or in another city. For these reasons, they cannot be considered Nomads, as they keep a strong attachment to their residential place where the family and friends live. Our managers and engineers, both in the city of Milan and Paris, all have indeed a lively social life in the city, and use the collective services. In both cities respondents declared they have several friends who they visit regularly and their relations are quite long lasting, though they do not have contacts with neighbours. Not surprisingly, in both cities respondents have a quite homogeneous social network with friends having the same educational and professional degree.

These features are extremely clear for the case of Milan: respondents' social networks exhibit high density, long lasting relations which date back to childhood and a strong rootedness in the social and territorial local context. In the Paris case, respondents' social networks are more varied, and open. Our results on this point differ substantially from the ones of Savage, Bagnall and Longhurst (2005) for Manchester and Butler for London (2003) where relations with friends remain more abstract than real.

The major difference between Milan and Paris is in their transnational sociability. While in Paris respondents mention several friends or acquaintances living abroad who are actively part of their social life, in Milan this is not the case. Respondents in Milan mention few people, when they do, the frequency of contacts is very weak and these relations are often 'silent' or abstract – that means that respondents do not have recent contacts but they think they can activate the relation.

The profiles of managers emerging from our empirical findings fit only one part of the diagram we proposed at the beginning of the chapter. In that diagram four ideal-type profiles were proposed stemming from the crossing of two dimensions – transnational exit and urban exit/secession –: 1) the nomads retreating from the city;

2) the immobile retreating from the city; 3) the mobile well rooted in the city; 3) the immobile well rooted in the city. The first two profiles, both in Paris and Milan, do not fit to our managers and engineers. The third profile is the most widespread with respondents very mobile, involved in the city life and using the resources proposed by the local context, investing in local relations. This investment is however very selective, as they do not have contact with neighbours and they are not involved in neighbourhood associations or activities. The fourth profile fits a very small group of our interviewees, almost all located in the city of Milan.

Despite the importance of transnational mobility, the situation of managers and engineers in Milan does remind us of the classic urban bourgeoisie profoundly rooted in terms of capital and social capital within the central area with transnational networks. The degree of local sociability with friends that our respondents exemplify lead us to question more extreme arguments about the 'end of urbanism', or the significance of hyper segregation. However, one important finding which relates to the social capital debate is the extent to which the networks of the upper middle class are characterised by strong homophily. There is little evidence that our respondents socialise with diverse groups within their city, and instead, they predominantly associate with 'people like us', in Butler's formulation. The social capital which they generate, whilst clearly locally rooted, is of a socially specific kind. The lack of involvement in voluntary associations further indicates their separation from more public activities within the city. In general, what we see, therefore, is an urban middle class which is still rooted in the city, but one which is nevertheless exclusive. Place and locality, rather than mobility, remains an important feature of class formation.

The main factor of change that we plan to explore in further publications is whether the changing scale and density of transnational mobility and connections provides some ground for partial exit (in practices, representation of values) from the national society. Social networks of our Paris interviewees are based on three pillars: Parisian, provincial and international. The density of social interactions among friends and family is also very high, on top of this, many foreign friends come to visit them in Paris. The importance of mobility and transnational interaction is more central, more regular, more structuring but the logic of *entre soi* in social terms remains as powerful as ever.

References

Angel, R. (2000), *New Barbarian Manifesto* (London: Logan).

Barbieri, P. (1997), 'Il tesoro nascosto. La mappa del capitale sociale in un'area metropolitana', *in Rassegna Italiana di Sociologia, n. 3*; pp. 343–370.

Boltanski L. (1982), *Les cadres* (Paris: Minuit).

Bouffartigues, P. (2001), *Les cadres* (Paris: La découverte).

Bourdieu P. (1979), *La distinction. Critique sociale du jugement* (Paris: Minuit).

Bourdieu, P. (1980), 'Le capital social', *Actes de la Recherche Sociale*, 3, pp. 3–7.

Butler, T. and Savage, M., (eds) (1995), *Social Change and the Middle Classes* (London: UCL Press).

Derosières, A., Thévenot, L. (1988), *Les catégories socio-professionnelles* (Paris: La Découverte).

Cesareo, V., Bovone, L. and Rovati, G. (1979), *Professione Dirigente* (Turin, Edizioni della Fondazione Giovanni Agnelli).

Esping-Andersen, G. (ed.) (1993) *Changing Classes: Stratification and Mobilities in Post-industrial Societies* (London: Sage).

Favell, A. (2008) *Eurostars in Eurocities* (Oxford: Blackwell).

Fischer, C. (1982), *To Dwell Among Friends* (Chicago: The University of Chicago Press).

Giddens, A. (1994), 'Living in a post-traditional society', in Beck, U., Giddens, A. and Lash, S., *Reflexive Modernization: Politics, Tradition and Aesthetics in the Modern Social Order* (Cambridge: Polity Press).

—— (1990), *The Consequences of Modernity* (Cambridge: Polity Press).

Giddens, A. and Mackenzie, G. (eds) (1982), *Social Class and the Division of Labour* (Cambridge: Cambridge University Press).

Golthorpe, J. (1982), 'On the service class, its formation and future', in Giddens, A. and Mackenzie, G. (eds), *Social Class and the Division of Labour* (Cambridge: Cambridge University Press).

—— (1995), 'The service class revisited', in Butler T. and Savage, M., *Social Change and the Middle Classes* (London: UCL Press).

Groux, G. (1982*)*, *Les cadres* (Paris: La découverte).

Kadushin C. (1995), 'Friendship Among the French Financial Elite', *American Sociological Review*, 60 (April), pp. 202–221.

Le Galès, P. (2002), *European Cities, Social Conflicts and Governance* (Oxford: Oxford University Press).

Lin, N. (2001), *Social Capital Theory and Research* (NY: Aldine De Gruyter).

Martin, B. (1998), 'Knowledge, identity and the middle class: from collective to individualised class formation?', *The Sociological Review*, n. 4, pp. 653–686.

Oecd (2006), 'Background for the Territorial Review on the Milan Metropolitan Area', <http://www.mi.camcom.it/show.jsp?page=416910>.

Piketty, T. (2001), *Les Hauts revenus en France au XXème siècle, Inégalités et redistributions* (Paris: Grasset).

Pinçon, M. and Pinçon-Charlot, M. (2000), *Sociologie de la bourgeoisie* (Paris: La Découverte, Repères).

Préteceille E. (2003), *La division sociale de l'espace francilien. Typologie socioprofessionnelle 1999 et transformations de l'espace résidentiel 1990–99* (Paris: OSC).

Préteceille, E. (2006), La ségrétation contre la cohésion sociale, le cas de la métropole parisienne, in Lagrange, H. (ed.), *L'épreuve des inégalités* (Paris: PUF).

Putnam, R. (2000), *Bowling Alone: The Collapse and Revival of the American Economy* (New York: Simon & Schuster).

Ricciardi, F. (2004), Entre quadri et dirigenti: les cadres en Italie, in P. Bouffartigue, A. Grelon, *Les cadres d'Europe du sud et du monde méditerranéen*, Cahier du GDR Cadres, n. 8, pp. 123–137.

Rovati, G. (1991), *Un ritratto dei dirigenti italiani* (Turin, Edizioni della Fondazione Giovanni Agnelli).

Savage, M., Bagnall, G. and Longhurst, B. (2005), *Globalisation and Belonging*, (London: Sage).

Sklair L. (1991), *Sociology of the Global System* (New York: Harvester Wheatsheaf).

—— (2001), *The Transnational Capitalist Class* (Oxford: Blackwell).

Therborn, G. (1985), *European Modernity and Beyond* (London: Sage).

—— (2000), 'Globalizations: dimensions, historical waves, regional effects, normative governance', *International Sociology*, vol. 15, 3, pp. 151–179.

Van der Gaat, M. and Snijders, T. (2004), The Resource Generator: Social Capital quantification with concrete items, paper.

Urry, J. (2000), *Sociology Beyond Societies* (London: Routledge).

PART 3
Urban Associations
and Social Capital

Chapter 8

Gardening with a Little Help from Your (Middle Class) Friends: Bridging Social Capital Across Race and Class in a Mixed Neighbourhood

Talja Blokland[1]

Introduction

Public policies to generate more community participation take up different forms in various places, but often share three elements linked to popularized versions of social capital theory.

Firstly, high poverty neighbourhoods tend to be viewed as having social capital that is supportive, but not of the 'bridging type' and not providing the 'right' type of role-models. The point of departure then is that the spatial arrangements of bonding ties determine the workings of this social capital, with negative outcomes for both society and the individuals involved. Indeed, as Curley shows in her chapter, the close proximity of people in difficult circumstances may keep other people down. Whereas Curley approaches the spatiality of social capital through looking at poor people after relocating, this chapter looks at the workings of social capital for poor women in a deprived part of a mixed neighbourhood, and zooms in on bridging ties across race and class.

Secondly, economically and racially diverse neighbourhoods are expected to facilitate the development of diverse and productive networks (see Blokland and Van Eijk 2008; Field 2003: 11-2) and networks to be profitable (see Field 2003: 12-3). Spatial diversity instead of segregation should provide roads to resources for individual residents, roads that geographical segregation is blocking (see Kleinhans 2005 and Galster 2007 for overviews).

Thirdly, spatially organized social capital is expected to enhance the liveability of neighbourhoods. After all, social capital can improve cooperation in a group and

1 I am grateful to Beth, Ms Magnolia and all others who have helped me with this research, and to Mike Savage, Tim Butler and Sara Ohly for comments on earlier drafts. The ethnography presented here is part of my larger research project 'Does the urban gentry help?', funded by the Royal Netherlands Academy of Arts and Sciences, the National Scientific Organization (NWO), the Wenner Gren Foundation, and the Amsterdam School for Social Science Research. Thanks to Jolien Veensma and Petra Nijhove for their help with preparing this manuscript.

make their collective actions more efficient (see for example Putnam 1993, 167 *ff*). A diverse neighbourhood as a site of resourceful networks might thus contain localized forms of trust and cooperation that contribute to the collective efficacy needed for a liveable neighbourhood (Sampson and Raudenbusch 2004).

In all such ideas bridging, not bonding, arouses the highest expectations (see also, Blokland and Nordhoff in this volume). After all, those forms of social capital that 'tend to reinforce exclusive identities and homogeneous groups', and serve especially specific reciprocity (tit for tat) and mobilize solidarity (Putnam 2000, 22; see also Gittall and Vidal 1998) are bonding. Bridging are the forms of social capital that look outward and encompass people over the borders of social cleavages.

Bridging social capital has also acquired a very positive connotation in academic debates. Lin, for example, states that weaker ties provide better access to social capital for instrumental action (Lin 2001, 67). Burt's theory of structural holes is an extension of the positive feature of bridges connecting groups that are otherwise not related (Burt 1992, 2001; Lin 2001, 70–1). We exchange something for something else, if not now then somewhere down the road, and may be receiving from a third party, based on a shared understanding of generalized reciprocity or trust. Rational choice theory explains that bridges work because it is rational for people to make them work. This is how they build credit, create reputations that can later pay off, and cash in on earlier investments (Coleman 1988, S102–3). While there is a need for trust, such trust is an estimation of risks, not a substantial rational consideration (see also H. Blokland 2006).

This chapter challenges the notion of bridging social capital as consisting of morally neutral transfers of resources for which all that is needed is the existence of a tie. Using ethnographic data from research in an economically and racially mixed neighbourhood in New Haven, Connecticut, I explore bridging social capital at two different analytical levels.

At one level, the first half of the chapter discusses whether a concrete program, e.g. a program for a community garden in a low income housing development, created the community social capital and strengthened the bridging social capital that it set out to achieve. Wellman and Frank (2001, 235–6) have noted that 'there is more to interpersonal life than just individuals and ties' and that people are immersed in milieus filled with dynamics that go beyond the individual. But they have limited their exploration of this statement still to characteristics of networks, ties, network capital and, to some extent, social characteristics of network members (2001, 234–5). What, then, are those dynamics? This chapter aims to shed light on the remarkable *workings* of social capital, especially where some people invest more resources than they may ever receive, and there is no sanctioning if they would *not* do so. Why do they use their access to resources for the sake of others? It seems unlikely that they are simply 'irrational' exceptions to the rules of the rational choice, or saint-like altruists. Neither is bringing rational choice back in by claiming that such people 'really' do such things for a sense of self-gratification convincing. Instead, I suggest that there is substantial rationality to bridge-building work across boundaries of race and class that finds its explanation not in individual attitudes or characteristics but in a set of beliefs or a milieu (cf. Eade *et al.* 1997) of a loosely defined group or movement.

At a second level, the second half of the chapter discusses the discursive construction of 'community' in the actual workings of bridging social capital. It shows how this construction changed over time. It argues that the dominant discourse on deserving and undeserving poor that penetrates America on many levels also informed the micro-level social ties between the white middle class volunteers in the gardening project and the black poor residents of the housing development. As such, the transfer of resources over bridges is as moral or as value-laden as any other social interactions. The existence of a tie may thus not be enough for traffic over the bridge and may nurture acceptance of the status quo discursively – ironically so, as the aims of the progressive white middle class residents involved in this study were the exact opposite.

A Mixed Neighbourhood as a Research Site

This chapter draws on an ethnographic study of social capital in a 'mixed neighbourhood' in New Haven, Connecticut, USA, conducted from December 1999 to December 2000, January 2002 to July 2002, and January 2004 to May 2004. During these periods, I first lived in the northern corner, then in the historic district. The last return to the field was exclusively focussed on data collection in the low income housing development, and I lived on the other side adjacent to the light industrial area surrounding it.

The fieldwork included participant observation, observation and participation.[2] I attended meetings of neighbourhood groups and political organizations, including the Good Government Committee (GGC), social clubs and churches, and volunteered in a homeless shelter, in a youth program and in the gardening project discussed here. In-depth interviewing with key persons in these groups as well as casual conversations complemented this material, as did research on secondary sources and archives.[3] The people in this study knew that I was writing 'a book on their neighbourhood' with a focus on how they got together to get things done. Most research notes were written immediately after returning to my apartment. Where feasible, I took notes on site. In the last research period, I taped extensive conversations and conducted life history interviews with low income residents. I generally received very supportive reactions to requests for interviews. Two affluent, politically active residents welcomed me at political neighbourhood gatherings at their homes and allowed me to attend social events, but first postponed and upon my return for the second phase of fieldwork refused to be interviewed.

The ethnographic part of this project does not test pre-existing hypotheses about the relationship between geographical proximity of a middle class and the social capital of poorer residents. It explores mechanisms and patterns within such a context that may contribute to further theoretical insights into how access to individual assets, interactions and collective action relate. It thus is an abductive, rather than an inductive or deductive type of research (cf. Schuyt 1986).

---

2 See for these distinctions Gans 1962, 336–8.

3 A survey on social support and social networks among 250 residents is part of the larger research project, but has not been used as basis for this chapter.

As a fieldwork site, I chose this neighbourhood with circa 3060 residents and its distinct boundary of the railroad that separates it from downtown for its history of gentrification since the late 1960s.[4] This gentrification had brought about a make-up of residents different in race and class. The most affluent, generally white residents lived in the mansions around 'the Square'. Merchants and wealthy descendants of colonial families had ringed the Square with exclusive mansions in the first half of the 19th century. As the town developed its manufacturing industry and railroad, reaching the heydays of urbanism described in Chapter 2, the neighbourhood became an Irish, then later an Italian immigrant working class area. Much of the housing stock was of low quality. Two streets were replaced by public housing in 1942 as their condition was considered too severe. This became the home of the most deprived, black and Hispanic residents who nicknamed this housing complex 'the Ghetto'. When the city began to loose its industrial base, suburbanization accelerated, and migration of blacks from the South increased, the neighbourhood decayed. Redevelopment in the early sixties gave the final blow to what is now remembered as an urban village or 'Little Italy'. The urban regeneration, as also noted in chapter two, was both praised and despised. The highway built right across the area meant relocation to many families, and cut off the increasingly black low-income housing complex from the other residences. Zoning redefined the rest of this side of the neighbourhood as light industrial. The Square side of the highway remained mainly residential. Thanks to the efforts of, among others, active residents and the city's Preservation Trust, the Square was saved, and piecemeal regeneration revived its architectural exclusiveness.

Two census tracts make up the neighbourhood: one tract (1422) including the Square gentrified, the other tract (1421), including the Ghetto, remained relatively poor.[5] By 1960, the percentage of blacks had increased from virtually none in the 1940s to around 20 per cent. While more whites then again moved into the Square's tract, whites became a numeric minority in and around the Ghetto. In both tracts in the 1940s, over half of the population consisted of unskilled or semi-skilled workers. The Square's tract gradually showed a shift to managerial and professional jobs. At the other side, low paid service work replaced manufacturing. In both tracts, the number of residents older than 25 with four years or more of high school went up, but far more so around the Square than around the Ghetto. The gaps between median incomes of the tracts showed a widening gap over the years, as did the percentage of families living in poverty: 28.8 per cent in the Ghetto and 5.1 per cent around the Square in 1990.[6]

At the time of my research, most of the 532 official residents of the low-income housing complex were black single mothers with their children, and a dozen or so

---

4 For an overview of definitions and perspectives on gentrification, see Van Weesep 1994.

5 Based on US Census 1940, 1950, 1960, 1970, 1980 and 1990.

6 The growing differences between the two tracts are further reflected in the built environment, as shown in widening gaps in property values, median rents, and the number of owner-occupiers as a proportion of the number of units. See Blokland, 2002 for more details.

Hispanic families.[7] The gardening project, or 'Greenspace', that forms the core of this chapter was an effort of residents from the gentrified part to help beautify 'the Ghetto', as a means to community development.

Part 1: Bridging Social Capital and the Greenspace Initiative

'Wouldn't it be nice if we/they had a garden like this': the start

The Community Greenspace Program, a program of grants for residents who wanted to beautify their neighbourhoods together through gardening and planting shrubs and trees, was a collaborative partnership of a non-profit Community Foundation, the City and the Urban Resource Initiative (URI), connected to the university's Forestry School. Community building was the general idea behind the program. People needed to get together to get things done. Neighbourhood groups, not individual residents, were eligible to apply, and aims were high, as reveals the website: 'Community Garden projects are designed to encourage (…) community building and empowerment, environment/neighbourhood restoration and stewardship.' As said the Chair of the Board of Directors of URI in one of the newsletters:

> What people see in the environment around them affects both the way they feel and act. Order and beauty reassure, engage and inspire … Visions of crippled trees on crumbling streets have more than just negative visual impacts on viewers. They end up depressing the overall well-being of the neighbourhood.

Ideas about community building were hence linked to views on urban forestry and new urbanism, making gardening both a method and a goal. The program had had a few successful years in a number of neighbourhoods, but in public housing developments it had not achieved much. In the Ghetto, nobody seemed to have heard of the program prior to the initiatives of Beth and some other residents from around the Square nearby. Right from the start, a bridge between separate networks through a tie between two women, Beth from the Square and Ms Magnolia from the Ghetto, brought resources to the Ghetto residents.

Beth, a grey-haired woman with a very expressive face of the type that one remembers for its smile, was the mother of two sons and wife of a renowned architect. They had moved into a mansion at the Square in the 1960s. When Beth's sons were older, she had taken up her PhD studies in anthropology, and now sought to be a writer. She had been an activist in many ways for many years, after a very formative period in the American Peace Corps, but not so much in her neighbourhood. When her anger about the closure of a historic railroad bridge had finally brought her to become a member of the neighbourhood's Historic Association, she soon got involved in the much broader GGC.

This group of residents originally got together to advocate for a new alderman, as they felt that the alderman at the time was not the best for the neighbourhood. It then became a neighbourhood organization mobilizing residents around issues of

---

7 See Blokland, 2004 for statistical details.

neighbourhood assets and quality of life. Participants came from all over the area, including the Italian section, the section-8 housing, the privately rented apartments and the public housing project, but the initiative and leadership was in the hands of a group of white middle class professionals and one affluent black couple who, like Beth, all had lived in the area for a long time and knew each other quite well. Participation in such a group hence brought about the potential for bridging social capital.

The case is an example of how Beth's resources and network became available to residents of the Ghetto through her tie with Ms Magnolia. The initial stage of the project shows how, firstly, Beth's approach of the community garden built on other norms than the norm of reciprocity within the exchange model that dominates social capital literature. Secondly, we will see that her approach was quite different from the perspective of the Ghetto residents. They were much more likely to frame the gardening in a cost/benefit model of exchange.

The idea of a Greenspace in the Ghetto first came to her mind, Beth recalled, when the GGC, then in its early stage, held a couple of meetings at her house. Beth could not remember who had invited Ms Magnolia to that meeting: a fifty-something black woman, mother to a large family, who had lived in the Ghetto for over 20 years. She now lived there with her partner and two youngest teenage children, and, on and off, several grandchildren, in a three-bedroom duplex apartment. She was the elected president of the Ghetto's Tenants Representative Council (TRC), an official residents organization required for each Housing Authority (HA) project by federal law.

Ms Magnolia had expressed her admiration for Beth's garden. She had talked about how her mother used to have a garden when she was 'coming up down south'. Beth found it hard to recall how the Greenspace came about but said she must probably have known about the Greenspace program, as she knew students and scholars from the Forestry School. As an affiliate to the university and with an interest in ecology, she was generally well-informed about many programs. She was not sure: had Ms Magnolia said it would be so nice if they could have a garden where her 'community' could enjoy nature and socialize together, or had she herself thought about this while she saw how 'intensely' Ms Magnolia enjoyed her backyard? Beth believed that especially the older women, the grandmothers, could share their histories and memories through a community garden, and grow vegetables there like they used to do down south, before they ended up in a brick and concrete environment. She had started to talk to Ms Magnolia about it, and gathered information for a grant application for a quite large community garden on an empty lot adjacent to the housing development. Beth wrote the application, Ms Magnolia was to organize the residents, inform them about training sessions (an obligatory part of the program for new neighbourhood groups) and get them to participate in the gardening.

The application reflected their initial ambitions. They would start out with some perennials and shrubs, but work towards a true community garden with flowers, benches and even fruits and vegetables. The application spoke of community building ideals of bringing residents together, of stewardship in its hope that residents would develop a stronger sense that their community was theirs, of how a more liveable community would be created with plants and trees, and of how it would inspire people to turn their front yards, now often muddy dirty strips of badly maintained grass, into gardens. Taking *back* the public space from all the negativity that threatened 'the community' could, in this view, be achieved through programs like the Greenspace. The application reflected Beth's access to information. It tuned in to exactly the goals of the program as described in its brochure and used similar language of a community and ecology ideal as did the Foundation.

And Beth believed in similar goals and values as those behind such projects, based on the notion that a sense of a warm, positive community flourishes through contact, communication and working together, in every location, independent of structural inequalities. Especially after a bus trip to community gardens in Hispanic neighbourhoods in New York City, that URI had organized, Beth talked energetically about the spirit and positive energy of such grassroots community building.

She had such ideas in common with Kevin and Georgina, owners of a brownstone adjacent to the Square, and with Michelle, wife of one of the most active white affluent condo owners. Michelle, now in her late seventies, had worked as a social worker in the Ghetto about thirty years ago. At several occasions she recalled how simple things had given the then racially mixed, but generally poor residents, a sense of pride, and how the cutbacks on funding for such 'communities' had devastated them. Kevin, a counsellor at a drug-treatment centre in another town, and his wife Georgina became part of the GGC and the Greenspace a little later, shortly after they had moved into the neighbourhood. For a long time they had lived in a remote village, but they had come to live in the city because their village was too 'isolated', too 'affluent' and did not have enough 'diversity'. Their wish to bring their progressive ideas into practice had brought them to the city, and they were soon emerged in neighbourhood- and city-wide forms of activism. Occasionally, when they had been to the Ghetto, they would share thoughts about how badly maintained the place looked, how the community had to put up there with people from the shelter and how 'the guys' hanging around in the streets and the small park made the place unsafe.[8]

So Beth was part of a network with a progressive agenda of 'getting involved' with the poor black 'community' in their neighbourhood, with shared ideas about the value of diversity and social mix in an integrated society, the value of community spirit and mutual support attached to place, and ideas about community development that strongly reflected, for example, images they held of such empowered activist communities in Africa and Latin America (incidentally, a female activist from Africa had spoken to a group of URI and Forestry School people and one of Beth's sons had moved to Latin America temporarily).

The first year: getting people to participate

They got the grant indeed. In its stage of preparation, Beth invested a lot in getting people to participate. But she had not been to the projects much, and did not know many other residents besides Ms Magnolia, her 15-year-old daughter Princess, and the vice-president of the TRC, Ms Brown, whom she had met through Ms Magnolia. As Ms Magnolia was the president, Beth assumed her to be a community leader and spokesperson for 'the community'.

---

8 There was a homeless shelter located right next to the Ghetto.

So, she would make flyers in English and have them translated by someone at URI into Spanish, photocopied them and delivered them to Ms. Magnolia, well in time before the first planting session. But they did not get distributed (I return later to the reasons why). Beth would come to Ms Brown's apartment to pick her up for a training session at an agreed time on a Saturday morning, and Ms Brown would let her wait outside for quite some time as she was not dressed yet, an experience in the very beginning that Beth did not enjoy much. She described the emptiness of the projects so early in the morning, with the door only half-opened after she had been explaining who she was through a closed door, and a completely dark room behind the door, where she waited outside until Ms Brown finally came out, as 'grim.' Beth went out of her way to make sure the requirements of the grant were met, talked the plans over with the URI intern, and did all the coordinating for the actual planting sessions. All along, she made her skills, social ties, emotional energy and resources like her car available to the Greenspace project – a greenspace that she would not enjoy in her own daily life, as she had, like all white middle class residents, otherwise no reason to go to the Ghetto, nor would she develop social ties that would provide her with more or better access to resources.

Beth's efforts to help stimulate participation did not help much. Ms Magnolia, meanwhile, limited herself to calling on Ms Brown, on Pat, the secretary of the TRC, and Ms Meryll, her next door downstairs neighbour – Ms Meryll because she always 'helped out', the other two because they had to come because they were the TRC. Pat never showed up, she had other appointments every planting session. Ms Brown went to the training sessions but did not participate in the plantings.

In her mid-forties now, she lived in a three bedroom apartment with her two teenage sons. Another son lived next door with his girlfriend and her daughter, a single mother of two, lived across the courtyard. She was proud that her son had finished high school, although he had a lot of trouble finding work. She kept 'running back and forth' to the school to ensure that her other sons would also stay in school. Ms Brown had held several jobs and usually had work, but none of these jobs provided her stable employment with benefits.

Ms Brown had once been married to a marine. When they divorced, she had ended up in the projects because she could no longer afford the house where she used to live, and her bills were piling up – but she believed she did not 'belong' there. She had a 'different mentality' than 'the people out here'. With her van she gave people rides to the evangelistic church that she attended. Other residents called her the 'church lady'. Ms Brown would talk about her life very much in terms of the test that God was putting her through, and derived a lot of strength from her religion. She was half-hearted involved with the Greenspace, as well as with other community events: she came when she had no other option, as when Beth came to pick her up, but disappeared from sight as much as she could. We talked about this while we spent the nightshift of her security guard job in the university's dormitory together. Ms Brown explained that she wanted the community to thrive but then again did not want to be part of it, as it was full of things that she disapproved of – and she had regular conflicts with Ms Magnolia. A year later, she looked back and said that she had stopped going to the GGC meetings, and dropped out of the Greenspace, because it had not brought her what she had hoped for. She had wanted to find help for her personal plans to start a catering business or even a restaurant, through 'getting to know the right people' – Beth, and her friends. Ms Brown had thus hoped for the strength of weak ties that she might have developed this way, but her hopes did not materialize. She did speak to Beth and others about her plans, but the advices that she got remained, in her opinion, too general: 'they didn't, like, tell me really, like tell me what to do, they just went like, I had to write a business plan and all that.'

Ms Meryll, a slim, small woman whose wide eyes behind glasses looked at the world as if in constant amazement, had lived in the projects for roughly the same time as Ms Magnolia. In her early sixties, she was in bad health. She believed her sorrows affected her health, and she had a lot to worry about. Her only son, who lived with her, hussled in ways he did not care to tell her and she did not care to know. So when the Housing Authority officials threatened her with eviction because they *did* think she knew, she was honest when she said she did not know – and was met with entire disbelief by the HA employee, who nevertheless let her stay. She took care of her son's two sons over whom she had custody, because their mother was on drugs and disappeared from view. The boys were getting into more and more trouble now that they were in their early teens. She had basically lost all control over them. Ms Meryll did not like to talk about her life now, but enjoyed recalling her youth down South, where her family had had a beautiful garden with lots of vegetables. She participated in the program, she said, because Ms Magnolia was a friend: she therefore attended 'Ms Magnolia's meetings' when she was needed, and therefore participated in the Greenspace, but also because she 'loved gardens'. The Greenspace brought back memories that visibly comforted her.

By the time it was up and running the program was realistically slimmed down to planting in front of Ms Magnolia and Ms Meyll's apartments, and in the yards of some elderly in the neighbourhood and near the community centre. When the truck with soil and plants and gardening tools of the URI arrived, Ms Magnolia also got her youngest son to help out, and told Princess to go and get Spike and Jake, two men in their forties who usually stayed in the Ghetto with relatives, or slept in the shelter down the road. Spike, who had become 'quiet' after years of 'street' and now worked in construction, claimed that he had always been 'the type to give to the community' (indeed, in the heydays of his informal career in the late 1980s, when he was in charge of the scaling, cooking and bagging of drugs in one of the larger drug trade schemes that the Ghetto had had in its history he used to support community activities financially). Jake, who earned money at times as a day labourer and when he did not find work, spent his time finding other ways to 'get by or to get high', as his mother put it, was the son of a friend of Ms Magnolia much older than herself. He said he 'had nothing else to do.' Ms Magnolia rewarded Spike and Jake afterwards with a few cans of beer. Other participants were children, mostly boys sometimes as young as six, who were excited that something was happening that gave them a break from hanging around in the streets while their mothers were at work or were getting high, or too busy with other problems. Or because aunts and grandmothers with whom they were staying had sent them outside because they were too much trouble in the cramped apartments, where, as a rule, many more people stayed than were on the lease. Briana, a five-year-old girl who helped out vigorously, got a little flower planted at her front door across from Ms Magnolia's apartment. A few days later, police raided the apartment where Briana lived. Her mother was evicted and the HA boarded up the apartment. The flower died. Some trees and shrubs were also planted near the community centre, with the help of children in a summer program run by the only non-profit service organization with a steady presence over the years in the area, LEAP.

Other residents of the Ghetto did not participate, not even if they were aware of the program or learnt about it in passing. This had little to do with whether or not they liked the idea of a nice, well-kept garden. TC, 21, and looking for a job while on probation, did value nice gardens. When I drove him to hand in a job application in a wealthy neighbourhood with white, New England style houses sitting on perfectly mowed lawns, he explained that 'everybody' dreamt of having such a house with a beautiful garden and a white picketed fence (and TC was sure that if he would only get this maintenance job, it would give him a headstart to realize this dream for him and his girlfriend, who had five children, two of whom he had fathered). But few residents seemed able or willing to garden as an investment in community development. The community was not worth their precious scarce resources: time, energy, and long, carefully polished nails – even Ms Brown or Ms Meryll who did join would not see it that way. Nails, Timika, a 24-year-old single mother of two sons, explained, were important because they were *nice*. She did not agree that they might be a sign of not having to work with your hands, as their ancestors did in the fields, because as a dietary assistant in a home, she did work with her hands. But why would you 'mess up your nails' and get your hands dirty for gardening in a neighbourhood that you did not *want* to care about? All you wanted was to 'move up, move out':

> Ain't nobody living here because they like it, well, may be some people do, like the crackheads, you know, crazy people, but normal people, they don't wanna stay in the projects. If you don't wanna get out no more, the project mentality got you, you got to fight that. I want more for me and my kids. Just look outta the window. Just look at them guys. I don't want my kids to grow up like this. And trying to fix it up 'round here, like with them flowers, it's nice may be for the old people, they got their little garden or whatever, but ain't no use for, like, for me, I ain't got no time for that bullshit. I gotta work, I gotta provide for my kids, I gotta run back and forth to the school because my son's acting up. I ain't got no time, and anyways I'm getting outta here.

Yet Beth, Kevin and Georgina did not mind at all to get their hands dirty, and invest other resources, in a place geographically close but socially so remote from their daily life. This became even clearer when the shrubs and trees planted near the community centre were destroyed in the summer thereafter.

There had not been a design for this, but once planted, Ms Magnolia said the three trees commemorated the three victims of the latest drug-related shootings. She talked at several TRC meetings about plans for plaques and a dedication ceremony. Not everyone welcomed Ms Magnolia's idea of dedication. Giselle, 40, and herself struggling to keep her teenage son in school, argued that it was sad that these boys had died, but that it would not set a right example of something 'positive' for 'the community' to make them into heroes. Her friend Nikki agreed: 'They should dedicate them trees for the boys that graduated this year. They did something. You know what I'm saying, instead of just running the streets. But ain't even three boys that graduated this year. Guys out here, they don't care about finishing school, they don't get themselves no education.' The plaques never got placed – like many ideas launched at TRC meetings, they made it into the minutes but were not followed up. Still, the trees became informally known as one for each of the dead boys. Initially, Beth would come over to hook up a hose and water the plants and trees. The kids from LEAP then watered once in a while. But gradually nobody watered the trees. Kids broke off branches to horseplay with.

The HA then decided that they needed more storage space for their maintenance crew. They built a shed adjacent to the community centre, destroying the rather sad looking reminiscences of last year's gardening effort. Beth happened to see the damage done when she visited the community centre for an unrelated matter. Her actions then show the workings of social capital across a bridge of race and class. And we see how notions of a 'community', albeit not communicated by a community got constructed in the process, a relevant point for the discussion in the second half of this chapter.

Beth first wrote an email to the director of the HA. He was also a law professor at the university where Beth was affiliated and lived a block away from the Square where Beth lived. Beth addressed him by his informal first name 'Jim', not James, and emailed him from her university address to his university address, not to his work address. In her email, she described a meeting she had had with a local architect (whom she knew through another neighbourhood group of which she was part), the director of URI (whom she had got to know well through some fundraising events and other environmental movements in the city), the HA's asset manager of the Ghetto, the site coordinator of LEAP (who was also a friend of her son as they had been to the same high school), and Ms Brown as representative of the TRC – and hence 'the community' – describing this group in her email as a 'community coalition'. She noted that the asset manager had expressed his support for the gardening, and had worked with this 'community coalition' to develop further ideas for it. She was dismayed that next thing she knew, the HA simply destroyed 'all the work of the community last year.' An exchange of emails followed, in which another manager of the HA apologized, but also claimed that this was the only place for the storage 'available'. This evoked an outraged response from Beth, who pointed out that the location had not been available, and called the construction the equivalent of building a garage on the town's green. In doing so, she discursively constructed an image of a community space that expressed a shared identity – which Ghetto residents would rarely, if at all, do. The destruction was presented as the violation of a crucial community spirit reflected in the physical structure of the courtyard and its plantings.

This resonated with the views of URI and of the HA alike: they desired such community spirit and welcomed any positive effort in that direction. So her advocacy for 'the community' found willing ears. Knowing how to use the right access roads and fitting arguments, Beth and her friends from the GGC could thus quickly mobilize their resources. The local newspaper made the HA officials offer public apologies (with an article that referred to the dedication of the trees, stressing the community spirit of the gardening, and the HA director calling it a 'total screw-up on our part' and the asset manager saying it was a 'tragic mistake'). The director of URI called and then wrote to the HA director and the architect was ready to speak about the value of community space for community building in a meeting with the asset manager.

Beth went with him to a meeting with the manager, on site in the Ghetto, taking me along. None of the residents attended this meeting. In an email to her friend and co-chair of the GGC, Beth described this as a 'constructive' meeting, but one in which they also acknowledged the difficulties of the gardening program, including its low participation rate. She believed that access to water was why residents did not water the plants: '[the asset manager] will get access to water for the Greenspace and work with us – the neighbourhood, Greenspace program and residents – to expand it to new groups (…) It does seem that the Greenspace could bring other court yards together. As [Jim] says, it is a tough site; there are groups to build on, but they often move or avoid getting involved (…) I have been canvassing for more participants. Some people said earlier they wanted to do it, but did not come forward. Some said to me what happened in the community courtyard showed them there was no point. I said it would not happen again.'

At that meeting, the three of them also discussed what they saw as the main problems of the Ghetto, concluding that it was the absence of youth programs. Their consensus that they had to find ways to involve the youth in the gardening, reflected the shift of alliance that was already occurring in the Greenspace program from 'grandmothers' to 'kids'. We will continue this story in the second half of the chapter. For now, let us see what the development of the Greenspace teaches us about social capital.

Balance: Traffic over the Bridge

As we have seen above, there was quite a distance between the efforts of Beth to get the Greenspace off the ground and the involvement of Ghetto residents who were to benefit from it. I will make up the balance here through two related points. Firstly, I use the description so far to assess the social capital argument that social capital comes into being by virtue of the mechanisms of specific or generalized reciprocity. Secondly, I zoom in on the argument that doing something together strengthens a community's social capital, as was the rationale behind the Greenspace program, I offer some interpretations why this did not happen in this specific case, thereby critically assessing some taken-for-granted ideas about community development. This raises some questions regarding the bridging nature of ties between networks, including the gatekeeping that may occur.

Building credit or doing politics: rationalities

As we have seen above, Ms Brown came when she really had to, Ms Meryll, Spike and Jake all came out of friendship or because they owed Ms Magnolia something or got something from her, and children came because they liked it. But generally, participation in the Greenspace was very low.

Striking is first, that the dropping out of Ms Brown fits the rational choice models of social capital perfectly. In participation Ms Brown saw options to enlarge her network and build weak ties, which she hoped to use for other purposes, so she was clearly instrumental about it. However, she felt she was doing a favour to Ms Magnolia and Beth by her participation. Certainly Beth would not see anyone's participation as an investment in a dyad, or not even as an investment in a personal network to be cashed in individually later. Participation was an investment in the community that would benefit all, and make the Ghetto a better place to live for everybody. Beth completely missed the point that Ms Brown felt that Beth owed her something. But the idea that substantial rational motives about greater things than personal favours would guide behaviour was not quite how Ms Brown saw things, nor was it the perspective of Jake or Ms Meryll – Spike got closest to it, but even his giving to the community was something that he would phrase in other settings as 'giving *back*' in relation to the burdens that drug trade imposed on the residents. In line with such instrumentality, if social ties in the networks of the Ghetto residents had one shared characteristic, it was the mutual reciprocity: I do this for you now, and when I need something, I will be looking for you. They framed, in other words, such ties pretty much within a rational choice model. This, as we will see below, affected the potential for community social capital.

And it contrasted with the ideas of Beth, Kevin and Georgina. The dominant rational choice idea of return on investment raises the question: where was *their* expected return? Social capital theories alone are not enough to analyze such bridge-building forms of collective action, or not in the current forms. Social capital theories either assume that individuals eventually benefit from their investments in ties with others, or that 'the community' is strengthened and that then, by default, that benefits individual community members – including those who went out of their way to get something done. But Beth went out of her way to get something done and never got repaid down the line, built no reputation among people relevant to her, nor was she part of the community that was to be strengthened through participation in the gardening. So *not all* parties involved in webs or relationships derive benefits from the workings of social capital, and the traffic over bridges is *not* an equal exchange by definition. In this case here, the imbalance in access to resources of Beth and other white middle class residents in the GGC compared to the disadvantaged position of the residents of the Ghetto made the social ties highly unequal, and thus inherently power-loaded. As Simmel (1964, 379) and Gouldner (1973) have pointed out, reciprocity does not always characterize social exchanges. Instead of a norm of reciprocity social ties can reflect a norm of beneficence (Gouldner 1973, 283, 291). Social capital resulting from such a normatively embedded practice is hence less balanced (see Gouldner 1973, 287–8).

Adherents of rational choice theory may argue that Beth and others who became involved, gained self-esteem through their volunteering. Their activism might give them a sense of being 'needed' or the nice feeling of doing 'good' of good old philanthropy. However, they could have opted for many good deeds to achieve a similar sense of self gratification trough far lesser efforts. Moreover, such a rational choice perspective shares with psychological explanations of altruism its individualistic approach that incorrectly assumes that mental events in aggregated form cause social processes and structures (Tilly 1984, 26 *ff*). Beth and her friends did (and do) not just act as individuals with given private motives and preferences.

The Greenspace can be seen as an expression of the 'ideology' (Allen 1980, 409; cf. Cole 1985) or, as I would prefer to call it, substantial rationality of progressive gentrifiers as a group – especially of those who are or have been part of groups of renovators in early days of gentrification (not necessarily of those middle classes who move into gentrified areas once they no longer form a challenge). Beth, Kevin, Georgina and other white middle class members of the GGC had made a deliberate choice for living in the city, as they wanted to be part of a 'diversity' and an 'urban feel', and *because* they wanted to bring their political views into practice. Following Weber and Mannheim, substantial rationality informs social actions when people do not just calculate means towards given ends, but when instead cultural, moral and political values, or the ends of actions themselves, guide their practices (Weber 1978, 24–6, Mannheim 1940, 50–8).[9] Such substantial rationality is not a matter of the individual. People do not invent moral and political ideas by themselves, but they are typical cultural products brought about by social relations. Such relations are ties to other people, but also to bodies of meaning as media and arts, that form a locally embedded, but not locally defined milieu (cf. Eade 1997). Allen (1980, 409) argued that gentrifiers' quest for diversity and originality makes them part of a wider 'movement' of utopian quests for a certain type of community. Berrey (2005) has also discussed how progressive, white activists in an ethnoracial and economic diverse Chicago neighbourhood frame activism in terms of a desire for a diverse community and identity personally with a place as basis for political commitments and entitlements to make political claims (Berrey 2005, 160–2). To gentrifiers, as Ley (1996, 6, see also Ley 1986) has pointed out, gentrification may thus be not just an investment in property that then needs to be defended and a position of a neighbourhood in a stratification of places (Logan and Molotch 1987) that then needs to be maintained. It can also be an expression of 'cultural politics': 'a rejection of the suburbs and their perceived cultural conformity in favour of the more cosmopolitan and permissive opportunities of the central city. If so, then an inner-city home is much more than a functional convenience; for a particular fragment of the middle class, it is an integral part of their identity.' Similarly, Filion (1991) has shown that the combination of values of gentrifiers with their advanced education, consumption of political information and general 'political culture' adds up to effective mobilization strategies of a peculiar kind. In this sense, the efforts of Beth and others like her to launch the Greenspace, and hence to build bridges with others unlike themselves and offer them roads to access resources that they otherwise would not have, can be seen as a form of cultural politics that goes beyond pure personal motives – let alone gains. Congruent with the findings of Berrey (2005), such cultural politics downplayed the white middle class residents' own racial identities and their class status, as in the GGC out of which the Greenspace initially emerged. They, like the progressive whites in Berrey's study, 'politicize(d) their personal identification with

---

9 Mannheim also made the far less known distinction between functional and substantial morality, which might be better applicable here. See for a discussion H. Blokland, 2005: chapter 3.

a geographical place and their preference for living around people of other racial, ethnic and class backgrounds.' Such substantial rationality of people of the same milieu may thus produce bridges to others and social capital, that does not imply trust and collective efficacy, nor personal favours, reputation and credit building. To ask how social ties and processes produce social capital hence means we have to ask: whose social capital, or social capital from whom?

Building a favour bank, not building community

This, then, relates to the second point that we can draw from the description above. It criticizes the idea that doing something together *is* community development, and will bring about social capital on a community's level in every case. Simply put, the internal existing workings of social capital in the Ghetto prevented this. There definitely was abundant social capital in the form of people having outstanding credit for favours done in the past, and expectations for such favours to be repaid. There certainly was a structure of gossip and reputations to be used to sanction violations of such expectations, usually referred to as the 'he say she say stuff' or 'being in someone's business'. In line with Williams (2005) findings, however, social support did not get exchanged through associations or organized collective actions, but through one-on-one exchanges in dyads. So the approach that participants took towards participating in the Greenspace was fully in line with the usual workings of social capital.

Ms Magnolia would not go around the neighbourhood and attempt to get everybody involved through a discourse of community, but left the flyers where Beth had put them, on the sofa in her living room, she called on her personal friends by phone, often right before a meeting or event, and told them she 'needed' them to come. Ms Magnolia was the elected president of the TRC, but she was a stronger community leader in the perspective of outsiders than in the eyes of Ghetto residents. She was, indeed, a strong leader to some groups of residents when it came to resolving conflicts, giving advice to young men and women, and attempting to keep the consequences of the informal economy in check, especially when it came to urging men not to take their conflicts to a level of violence. But she was not so strong in organizing events such as cook-outs or community parties, or in following up on all the plans that the TRC made for 'the community.' She had a tense relationship with a social service program that was trying to set up some activities, so there were different circles of residents drawing on different resources, often excluding those outside their circle. There was, put simply, not one community that could be mobilized, but there were several networks of people exchanging favours.

As a gatekeeper at the bridge linking, in theory, the Ghetto to the network of Beth, Ms Magnolia did not always transmit information and resources to others in the Ghetto. Sometimes she simply did not get to it, as she had other things in her life to worry about, or different priorities at a given moment. But in other instances, she controlled the resources in ways that were common among several women who had somewhat of a leadership position, due to their access to resources, within the divergent networks in the Ghetto. So Ms Magnolia would introduce those residents to Beth who had shown her respect – just like someone who was in charge of distributing

Thanksgiving turkeys donated to 'the community' gave them not to residents who needed it most, but to those who had paid respect, expressed support or of whom one could expect personal favours in the future. Similarly, a resident-employee of the social service agency in charge of coordinating a monthly food- and clothing bank brought in her own circle of women to sort out the clothes and fill the paper bags with food the night before. Volunteering paid off, as these volunteers got the first pick at the food and clothes. But you could not volunteer to volunteer: one had to be invited. When there was a set of yellow, brand-new winter coats for children among the clothes, the resident employee distributed the coats among women who were supportive of her ways to work 'for the community' and with whom she had personal connections. There were no winter coats left when the bank opened its doors the next day for children whose mothers were not 'connected'. There were none for children like Pearl, aged nine, daughter of a crack user who came with her mother's boyfriend to look for clothes for herself, her little sister and her baby brother, or Larry, a ten-year-old homeless boy with his mother in jail, staying on a rotating basis with family, who could not even get inside because there was no adult to accompany him.

Inside the Ghetto, this was one of the scarce ways to use resources to establish rewards and sanctions, reciprocity, and reputation – in other words, to build social capital. But the usage of exchange and credit/debit as a dominant frame for social interactions among the residents of the Ghetto resulted not in low participation rates. People calculated that the costs were higher than the benefits to them personally, and, in addition, evaluated the entire scheme through such a perspective. This points again to the gap between the substantial rationality informing Beth's and her friends' actions, and the rationalities informing actions of residents of the Ghetto. Broken promises of all sorts of activists who had been coming through the Ghetto over the years had created cynicism. More importantly as it shows how reasoning evolved out of stronger instrumental than substantial rationality, residents often said that the Ghetto was 'used' by all sorts of people and agencies 'to get grants.' Never did a Ghetto resident explain the presence of whatever program, now or in the past, no matter how much they might have liked these programs, in terms of commitment of the outsiders involved to a substantial rationality of values like justice, equality, empathy, democracy, fairness – at most, they would refer to someone 'enjoying to help poor people.' Residents seldom saw grants as the results of activists striving to improve their lives, let alone as aimed at a better society. In their eyes, the grants were money given to people to get jobs out of 'doing something for the people out here that we have never asked for.' Whereas people like Beth thus came to the neighbourhood embedded in a certain substantial rationality, and not for personal gain, residents I talked to assumed that either this was her job (paid for by a grant intended for *their* neighbourhood, naturally) or that there was some other rational choice explanation. So they would think twice to get involved in improving a place where they did not want to belong, putting in their scarce energy and time for a community they did not experience, and without the prospect of a return on their investment. Not participating made, thus, much more sense than becoming a participant.

Part 2: Participation and Shifting Alliances in the Greenspace

Such internal workings of social capital, strongly based on the mechanisms of credit and debit of a favours bank, remained invisible to outsiders. They had to remain unknown, because activists such as those in the Greenspace program, the GGC or charities would probably, coming from a position of commitment to and striving for equality, find such favouritism unacceptable. And because a program like the Greenspace relied heavily on one main bridge – between Beth and Ms Magnolia – to 'work with the community', the internal controversies, lack of cohesion and fragmentation also remained out of sight. So Beth and the others deduced as much as they could from the information they did have, and decided that rather than on all residents, they should aim to get the youth of the Ghetto involved in the Greenspace in its second year.

In the first year, the group had been seeking alliance with the grandmothers, who had become the discursive backbones of the Ghetto community throughout the first phases of the program. Ms Meryll's tale of the nurturing comfort of a garden in face of the everyday hardship of Ghetto life had become the dominant trope in how the plantings had become a spatial symbol for community spirit. Whereas Beth in her first application had still presented 'the community' as a whole, when she reported back on the program in the GGC meetings, she would attune to Ms Meryll's and Ms Magnolia's story about the love for gardens of the older generation: the Greenspace might not have a community-wide support, she argued, but it was of great importance to 'the grandmothers'.

When the grandmothers, often not much older than in their forties and born in the projects, did not become a strong basis for the program, a shift in alliance took place when Beth again applied for a Greenspace grant. With the experience of the enthusiastic children, Beth and the intern of URI now sought to engage the children even more. These children, after all, were growing up in an environment not beneficial to them, and they could be taught the community spirit and stewardship, so that they would care about their community and take pride in where they lived. With the LEAP-site coordinator and the URI intern, children were thus more systematically included in the second year. A group of boys around the age of 9 to 11 planted shrubs in one of their grandmother's front yards, and proudly posted a sign with their names next to it. Kevin and Georgina loved the boys efforts and came over on a Saturday morning to plant some extra shrubs and flowers. Grandmother Angie, however, could not be convinced to be in charge of helping watering them, so Kevin and Georgina called on another resident, Cheyenne, who lived across the courtyard. They knew Cheyenne because she had come to a couple of the GGC meetings. She wanted to find out some things about the magnet school program, a theme that had been scheduled for a few meetings in a row, but did not plan on becoming a permanent member of the group, nor did she want to be engaged in doing more for 'the community'. She, as she explained in an interview, did not belong in the projects. She only ended up there due to bad luck, and she was moving out as soon as she could, if she could only hold a job for a bit longer than she had managed to do so far and save enough money for the security deposit for a private apartment – as she had tried for a couple of years now. But Cheyenne did not tell Kevin and Georgina so – she instead said that yes, she would help the boys with their garden and talk to them about some more gardening activities for youth that URI had been setting up.

When Kevin and Georgina came to pick up the boys to take them there, Cheyenne was not home, and as Kevin and Georgina did not know where to find them, they ended up not going. Cheyenne, it turned out later, said she had told Ms Angie but she must have forgotten. Kevin and Georgina had hoped to stimulate the boys with their little garden so that they had something 'to be proud of' and 'something positive in their lives.' The boys definitely had a good time as long as the planting session lasted. But only a few days later the plants had died because nobody had watered them.

Some of the boys were known as 'bad' in the Ghetto by the time they were ten. As the stories went, they stripped a girl off all her clothes once and then went around boasting about it, functioned as look-outs and money holders for drug dealers and spent more time outside than inside their classroom because of suspensions. A year later, Tommy, the 'leader' of this little group pretended not to remember he ever did such a 'corny' thing as planting. By the time that Tommy was thirteen and taking the fast road to becoming even cooler in school and in the neighbourhood, people would say he looked like his father, a handsome man with a golden tooth that many of the young women fancied, and who was one of the more successful local drug- dealers. He was released from jail recently and back 'on the block' right away. Tommy's mother took little interest in him. Grandmother Angie had taken to the bottle even more than before, unable to solve her problems with the boy. Factors like ambivalence towards 'the neighbourhood', strong notions of what was and what was not 'corny' and peer pressure to adhere to these, large everyday problems of youngsters with very little stability in their lives, the absence of adults who could organize the involvement of the children, the inability of parents to get their children to places on times agreed and the project-based nature of the program (with a presence of only a few weeks in spring and summer) all contributed to the failure to make the children stewards of the Greenspace.

So in their definitely well-intended efforts to get 'the community involved' Beth and others had been disappointed somewhat. In these efforts, one can trace a gradual shift in who were crucially the deserving part of the Ghetto, as 'the community' juxtaposed against the evils from which or the devils from whom they had to 'take back' the public space: the drug dealers, the crazy junks, the bums from the shelter next door, or sometimes simply 'the guys'. The 'community' had to take back the symbolic definition of a 'community space' through collective action and eventually enhanced social control, an idea popular ever since the revival of Jane Jacobs arguments (Jacobs 1961). Defining ownership and struggles over ownership of public space in troubled neighbourhoods certainly is an important issue, and collective action with such aims at times has proven effective, including to some extent in American housing projects (Venkatesh 2000).

Given the popularity of such ideas in current debates in the milieu of Beth, Kevin, Georgina and gentrifiers like them, including for example the embracing of ideas of New Urbanism, it is not surprising that these well informed, well educated and substantial rationally motivated citizens brought ideas along these lines with them to the gardening effort. Members of resource-rich networks as they were, they meanwhile lacked access to roads that could provide them with a more in-depth understanding of every day life in ghettos, and of the peculiarities of the Ghetto. This is not to say that they were to blame for this. Residents of the Ghetto actively ensured that they would not acquire such an understanding. In doing so, these residents themselves helped to reinforce dominant images of ghettos as the habitats of juxtaposed groups of deserving versus undeserving poor.

After all, the effect of mechanisms of workings of social capital within the Ghetto was a low participation rate that confirmed the standard image of the low-income housing development as a site where people were passive and disinterested, if not threatened by evil around them. Giving little access to in-depth understandings of the Ghetto meant that residents did not directly challenge the prevalent idea that there was such a thing as one community. For lack of alternatives, the Greenspace, like other programs over the years, by and large worked from that prevalent idea. The main differentiation that they worked with was the juxtaposition of the deserving community versus the undeserving troublemakers.

The actual practices of the Greenspace then further reinforced this juxtaposition, moving it towards a broader notion of an underclass, hinting at a separate category from simply 'poor' (also Gans 1995, 43). Although many of the robust plants survived in some of the yards, the third year there was hardly a visibly outstanding garden-like front yard left. Ms Magnolia more or less dropped out, partly because of health problems and partly because of increasing communication difficulties between her and the GGC. The resident who had worked for the social service agency that ran the food- and clothing-bank was elected the new president of the TRC by a handful of voters. She now had a blossoming cherry tree in her front yard (of the apartment she then left for another unit). She had helped organizing the participation of the kids. This had not been a great success, with promises made but not kept and a few occasions where she had not shown up.

When in the third year then the intern was fluent in Spanish, he and Beth targeted the Hispanic population, a category increasing in numbers but not in the black dominated social life in the public spaces of the housing project. With some exceptions, Hispanic residents communicated little with blacks, their children played outside far less and they socialized less frequently outside than blacks. They consisted more often of families that included a male husband, they seemed to be working in the formal labour market more often, and they were not visibly involved in the street drug trade in the Ghetto, which was dominated by black men. Beth and the intern had picked up on the fact that some of them already had gardened a little in their front yard. They hoped to consolidate such efforts through supporting them and including them in the Greenspace program. For the sake of beautifying the neighbourhood through gardens in individual front yards, this was a very viable strategy. For the Greenspace as a community program of and for the residents it meant a move away from attempts to strengthen or build community and social capital through gardening together.

For the social distances of class and race and emulation of discourses of inequality that in effect contribute to their durability (cf. Tilly 1998), the fact that the Hispanics who participated did so with enthusiasm and kept taking care of the plantings meant another reinforcement of the idea of a Black underclass distinctively different from other poor people, including dysfunctional people who did not even have the self respect to take care of the fruits of their own labour.

Beth and her friends in the GGC, URI and so forth did of course not formulate such constructions of an underclass actively.[10] Michelle, Georgina and Kevin, all used their professional experiences with the black 'underclass' to interpret the Ghetto and its residents of which they had so little actual knowledge. In interviews, they all did so within a framework of an underclass with no self respect, who faced the challenges and bad influences of non-deserving deviants assumed to be unrelated outsiders to 'their community'. And once more, they could also hardly be 'blamed' for formulating such narratives. Theoretically, they could not be blamed because as Tilly (1998, 36) argued, we all learn early in life to tell stories 'in which self-motivating actors firmly located in space and time produce all significant changes through their efforts' and we could hardly expect people to apply relational analyses to their daily lives (see also Loseke 2007). And in our case, residents of the Ghetto who did have contacts with them actively contributed to such a reinforcement of the dominant imagery of ghettos, the underclass and The Ghetto, too. However much they would drink in the Ghetto, they would not touch an alcoholic beverage at a GGC-meeting that took place in a local restaurant, on invitation of the owner, where almost everybody else – white and middle class – was drinking anything from wine to straight bourbon. They would dig the dirt planting flowers to fight the decay and unsafety with their sons and friends playing cards waiting for customers for their drugs in eyesight. They would lament the 'hoodlums' in the small park at the front of the ghetto and agree at GGC and other neighbourhood meetings that 'something needs to be done about them' and go play cards with them the very next day. They would reject violence in conversations with outsiders and have men owning guns in their house. They would call boyfriends husbands or the other way around. They would deny the existence of boyfriends as it was 'better' in their views on what their white middle class new acquaintances would think to be a single mother than to be the girl of a convicted drug dealer. And through distancing themselves in all such ways from others labelled 'the people out here', they helped to perpetuate the imagery of this Ghetto as well as of the ghetto as a socially constructed type as a neighbourhood with a clear demarcation of a deserving 'community' threatened by those undeserving poor. Sadly, such principles of emulation and adaptation (Tilly 1998) also meant that they were blocking roads to access resources. They might help enhance their personal and community social capital, if they had educated the progressive white middle class more about what it was that concerned *them* most. However, they had limited information, too. All they had to draw on was a container of memories of prejudiced, difficult encounters with white middle class people, often social workers, teachers, police or judges and lawyers. Such experiences made them not very inclined to see substantial rationality and commitment on their behalf. Moreover the power-loaded bridges, safely guarded by gatekeepers in a system strongly relying on favours, reputation and building credit, and the huge distance in

---

10 But some class constitutive effects did indeed occur in the relations between the gentrifiers and others, and hence do lay inside just as well as outside the neighborhood, unlike Bridge (1995, 245) has argued.

rationalities that residents from the Ghetto and those from the Square brought to the table, created barriers that simply communicating better would not resolve.

Conclusions

This description brings me, then, to the following conclusions about the workings of social capital as bridges crossing *and* maintaining borders.

The ways in which the bridges that programs such as the Greenspace and neighbourhood organizations like the GGC reinforced rather than challenged categorical borders and the dominant meanings constructed about them, were not the result of anybody's intentions or rational choices. They were the result of complex dynamics of social relationships within the Ghetto, between residents of the Ghetto and those of the affluent Square, and between residents of the Square and third parties. Eventually, people at both sides of the bridge in their interactions crossed borders of race and class but at the very same time communicated understandings of their own and each other's social identity or, in Bourdieuian sense, positioning (Bourdieu 1984).

This, then, had results for the reproduction or accumulation of social capital on a more individual level. As bridges were built but understandings of distance and difference rather than commonality crossed over such bridges, such bridge buildings for individual residents rarely translated into the sort of social capital as defined by Portes (1995, 12), 'the capacity of individuals to command scarce resources by virtue of their membership in networks or broader social structures.' When Ghetto residents expected personal returns, they did not acquire them, and when they could have benefited from support and resources from gentrifiers in cases of specific problems, the mutual imageries prevented the development of ties in which they could ask for such support. Thus social capital of the bridging type available on a group or community level and possibly effective there, as in the case of the Greenspace discussed here, does not in itself suffice for effective social capital accumulation for the individuals involved.

Finally then, this feeds into three conclusions about social capital. Firstly, bridging social capital in weak ties is just as much normatively and morally value – loaded as any other interaction, and rational choice exchange models cannot address this. Yet to understand the mechanisms of social capital, the transfer of moral or normative understanding of the other is on the other side of a bridge is crucial. Secondly, the study of social capital should pay more attention to the apparently simple question: social capital for whom? Thirdly, we critically need to rethink the ideas of bonding and bridging, especially when they are easily coupled with weak and strong ties and, in turn, with intergroup versus intra-group relations.

It appears that, first, some bonding, in the sense of a more thorough understanding of mutual social positions, motives, substantial rationalities and contexts and, second, some sort of processes allowing for social identifications rather dis-identifications would be needed for bridging social capital to do the job many think it capable of. In other words: gardening clubs (and maybe even bowling leagues) might just as well be sites where categorical borders and inequalities are reinforced as they can be sites where they are challenged.

References

Allen, I. (1980), 'The ideology of dense neighbourhood development: cultural diversity and transcendent community experience', *Urban Affairs Quarterly*, 15: 409–428.

Berrey, E.C. (2005), 'Divided over diversity: political discourse in a Chicago neighbourhood', *City and Community*, 4 (2): 143–170.

Blokland, H. (2006), *Modernization and its Political Consequences: Weber, Mannheim and Schumpeter* (New Haven: Yale University Press).

Blokland, T.V. (2002), 'Neighbourhood social capital: Does an urban gentry help? Some stories of defining shared interests, collective action and mutual support', *Sociological Research Online*, <http://www.socresonline.org.uk/7/3/blokland.html>.

Blokland T.V. and van Eijk, G. (2008) (forthcoming), 'Do people who like diversity practice diversity in neighbourhood life?', *Journal of Ethnic and Migration Studies*.

Bourdieu, P. (1984), *Distinction* (Cambridge: Cambridge University Press).

Bridge, G. (1995), 'The space for class? On class analysis in the study of gentrification'. *Transactions of the Institute of British Geographers*, 20: 236–247.

Burt, R.S. (1992), *Structural Holes* (Cambridge. MA: Harvard University Press).

—— (2001), 'Structural holes versus network closure as social capital', in: Lin, N., Cook, K. and Burt, R.S. (eds) (2001), *Social Capital: Theory and Research* (Hawthorne, NY: Aldine de Gruyter), pp. 31–56.

Cole, D.B. (1985), 'Gentrification, Social Character and Personal Identity', *The Geographical Review*, 75 (2): 142–155.

Coleman, J.S. (1986), 'Social theory, social research and a theory of action', *American Journal of Sociology*, 91:1309–1335.

—— (1988), 'Social capital and the creation of human capital', *American Journal of Sociology*, 94: s95–s120.

Crothers, L. (2002), 'Building social capital on the street: Leadership in communities', in: McLean, S.L., Schutz, D.A. and Steger, M.B. (2002), *Social Capital: Critical Perspectives on Community and 'Bowling Alone'*, pp. 218–237 (New York: New York University Press).

Eade, J. (1997) (ed.), *Living the Global City* (London: Routledge).

Field, J. (2003), *Social Capital* (London: Routledge).

Filion, P. (1991), 'The gentrification – social structure dialectic: A Toronto case study', *International Journal of Urban and Regional Research*, 75 (4): 553–574.

Galster. G. (2007), 'Neighbourhood social mix as a goal of housing policy: A theoretical analysis', *European Journal of Housing Policy*, 7 (1): 19–43.

Gans, H. (1962), *The Urban Villagers* (New York: The Free Press).

—— (1995), *The War Against the Poor: The Underclass and Antipoverty Policy* (New York: Basic Books).

Geismar, L.L. and Krisberg, J. (1967), *The Forgotten Neighborhood: Site of an Early Skirmish in the War on Poverty* (Metuchen, N.J: The Scarecrow Press Inc).

Gittall, R. and Vidal, A. (1998), *Community Organizing: Building Social Capital as a Development Strategy* (Thousand Oaks, CA: Sage).

Gouldner, A.W. (1973), *For Sociology: Renewal and Critique in Sociology Today* (New York: Basic Books).

Jacobs, J. (1961), *The Life and Death of the Great American Cities* (London / New York: Penguin Books).

Ley, D. (1986), 'Alternative explanations for inner-city gentrification: A Canadian assessment', *Annals of the Association of American Geographers*, 76: 521–535.

—— (1996), *The New Middle Class and the Remaking of the Central City* (Oxford: Oxford University Press).

Lin, N. (2001), *Social Capital: A Theory of Social Structure and Action* (Cambridge: Cambridge University Press).

Logan, J.R. and Molotch, H.L. (1987), *Urban Fortunes: The Political Economy of Place* (Berkeley: California University Press).

Loseke, D.R. (2007), 'The Study of Identity as Cultural, Institutional and Personal Narratives: Theoretical and Empirical Integrations', *Sociological Quarterly*, 48: 661–688.

Mannheim, K. (1940), *Man and Society in an Age of Reconstruction* (London: Routledge).

Portes, A. (1995), 'Economic sociology and the sociology of immigration: a conceptual overview', in: Portes, A. (1995) (ed.), *The Economic Sociology of Immigration: Essays on Networks, Ethnicity and Entrepeneurship*, pp. 1–41 (New York: Russell Sage Foundation).

Putnam, R. (1993), *Making Democracy Work: Civic Traditions in Modern Italy*, (Princeton: Princeton University Press).

—— (2000), *Bowling Alone: The Collapse and Revival of American Community*, (New York: Simon & Schuster).

Sampson, R.J. and Raudenbusch, S.W. (2004), 'Seeing disorder: neighbourhood stigma and the social construction of "broken windows"', *Social Psychology Quarterly*, 67 (4): 319–342.

Schuyt, K. (1986), *Filosofie van de sociale wetenschappen* (Leiden: Martinus Nijhoff).

Simmel, G. (1964), 'Faithfulness and gratitude', in: Wolff, K.H. (1964) (ed.), *The Sociology of Georg Simmel*, pp. 379–393 (New York: The Free Press).

Tilly, Ch. (1984), *Big Structures, Large Processes, Huge Comparisons* (New York: Russell Sage Foundation).

—— (1998*)*, *Durable Inequality* (Berkeley, CA: University of California Press).

Venkatesh, S.A. (2000), *American Project: The Rise and Fall of a Modern Ghetto* (Cambridge, MA: Harvard University Press).

Weber, M. (1978), *Economy and Society: Outline of Interpretive Sociology* (Berkeley, CA: University of California Press).

Weesep, J. van (1994), 'Gentrification as a research agenda', *Progress in Human Geography*, 18: 74–83.

Wellman, B. and Frank, K. (2001), 'Network capital in a multilevel world: getting support from personal communities', in: Lin, N., Cook, K. and Burt, R.S. (eds) (2001) Social Capital: Theory and Research, pp. 233–274 (Hawthorne, NY: Aldine de Gruyter).

Williams, C. (2005), 'Cultivating Community Self-Help in Deprived Urban Neighborhoods', *City & Community*, 4 (2), 171–188.

Chapter 9

Political Participation, Social Networks and the City

Mike Savage, Gindo Tampubolon and Alan Warde

Introduction

Douglas Rae's (2003) emphasis on 'the end of urbanism', associated with the decentralization of economic activity, the rise of suburbia, and the eclipse of central public urban space, poses serious issues regarding the significance of voluntary associations for generating involvement and activism in contemporary urban conditions. Rae relates the golden age of voluntary associations to the emergence of the industrial city itself, so re-iterating the emphasis of urban sociologists from Max Weber to Richard Sennett (1977) who insist on the distinctive role of the urban public realm within modern urbanism. What, then, is the significance of voluntary associations in the contemporary city? Some urban theorists now see communication and association as organized in fundamentally different ways, through the elaboration of lifestyle enclaves (Fischer 1982; Bellah *et al.* 1984), virtual communication and digital coding (Graham and Marvin 2001; Amin and Thrift 2002), and forms of belonging which do not require local, face to face interaction (Savage *et al.* 2005). Such an account is consistent with much of the social capital literature which sees voluntary associations as thriving better in small town locations and challenged by the rise of urban sprawl (Putnam 2000, and see the discussion in Chapter 1).

Despite this sense of decline, we need to recognize that voluntary associations continue to exist, and in large numbers of cases, thrive, in urban environments. Here we explore in detail how the urban context facilitates involvement in two voluntary associations located in Greater Manchester. We deliberately take two contrasting associations, so that we can reflect on their different capacities for urban engagement. One is a local branch of the Labour Party, located in an affluent suburb, and the other is a conservation group which operates in Manchester as whole. The different histories, aims, and spatial reach of these two groups make them suitable case studies. Whereas the Labour Party harks back to the classic urban age and campaigns on local, national and international public issues, the conservation group is a newly formed social movement, oriented towards environmental politics, the scale of which has risen dramatically in recent years, and draws in enthusiasts from across Manchester. By examining their network structure, and distinguishing between core members, those who are more peripheral, and those who are isolates, we are able to examine the different capacities these two groups have to engage their members.

Our research methodology, which draws on social network analysis, is distinctive in examining in detail the internal networks of associational members. We are thereby able to (1) gain data on whole networks rather than on samples of individuals; (2) identify network connections around different intra-organizational functions; and (3) link network data to life histories.

We begin, in the next section, by exploring theoretical issues in the study of mobilization and engagement, before, in Section three, laying out our case studies and methods. Section four uses our social network analysis to show that the Labour Party is systematically better able to generate more activism and energy from its members, and Section five shows how this can be understood in terms of the different relationships the two groups have to their urban environment.

Social Capital and the City

Although there has been a concerted attempt in recent literature on social capital to broaden the emphasis from the study of formal voluntary associations to include informal ties, nonetheless the study of voluntary associations remains vital. This literature has increasingly questioned whether Putnam's account of a steady decline in associational membership in the US can be generalized (see e.g. Halpern 2005: chapter 7). Hall (1999) argues that membership in associations has remained relatively stable in the UK, and Li *et al.* (2003) show that any decline which can be detected is largely attributable to plummeting membership in trade unions and 'working men's social clubs' rather than across the board. It is possible to detect some areas in which voluntary membership is booming, notably amongst environmental associations and sports clubs (see e.g. Crossley 2006).

In considering these trends, it is increasingly clear that qualitative indicators of the kinds of participation associated with membership are more important than head counts of how many people are formal members or not. Some expanding associations are of the 'cheque-book' variety, where a formal subscription is all that is required of members, who then can expect a service to be provided by the organization: a kind of 'commodification of engagement' which is not conducive to social capital. On the other hand, some forms of sociation can still be generated by commercially provided social capital, as Crossley (2006) shows in his ethnographic study of members of private gymnasiums. We should not assume that forms of engagement and activism cannot be generated from these. This argument applies with particular force to various kinds of social movement which have prospered in most nations, and which offer an alternative to mobilization in political parties.

These considerations mean that we need to avoid the assumption that being a member of an association necessarily conveys 'social capital'. We need, instead, to explore the kinds of conditions under which membership is likely to lead to engagement amongst its members, through a closer scrutiny of the particular mechanisms which generate this. Here social network analysis can be of major importance, since it allows us to assess the extent of interaction amongst members of organizations. Social network analysis has been used within the social capital literature, but mainly to examine how individuals can use their contacts to increase their own resources (Lin 2002 and Burt 2000; 2002; 2005). We instead are more interested in exploring *how* the internal networks of associations work, how they are related to the mobilization of members, and how they affect generalized trust. There is remarkably little literature in this area. The most relevant arguments are derived from studies of social networks and social movement organizations (see generally Diani and McAdam, 2003). However, much of this literature is couched within a resource mobilization tradition which sees networks as resources allowing mobilization within the context of opportunities and constraints imposed by political environments. Attention has focused on how networks may explain whether an individual is available for participation (McAdam and Snow, 1997, 120–1; Snow *et al.*, 1980; McAdam, 1986; McAdam and Paulsen, 1993), and structural availability focused on the 'meso-level' of organizations, institutions and communication networks in the emergence of collective action, so that activism is seen as driven by 'demand' as well as 'supply' (see the overviews by Morris, 1997; Mueller, 1994; Rudig, 1990). Within this context, social networks tend to be seen as some kind of personal resource which allow people to gain knowledge, further contacts, or resources that they can use, such that networks can be seen as a measure of 'social capital' (see generally, Portes 1998).[1]

This literature has become increasingly sophisticated as it engages with more technical network literature (e.g. Gould, 1995; 2003), but continues to rely on more individualistic approaches to social capital, concerned with the factors which lead individuals to join associations and social movements, rather than how involvement itself generate trust and co-operation. Diani and McAdam (2003) seek to reconcile American approaches, which tend to be couched within a rational choice framework ultimately reliant on a structural, resources based perspective, and European approaches, more likely to emphasize culture and to be interested in the agency of social movements themselves (see the discussion in Crossley 2002). In the hands of some network researchers, notably Harrison White (1992), the relational properties of networks are seen as crucial to the formation of identities, with the resulting implication that network approaches offer the potential for reconciling structure and agency (see further Knox *et al.* 2005). Although it is clear that these pointers indicate the value of whole network approaches to social movements, these are not spelt out or elaborated. Network analysis within social movement studies has mainly been applied to looking at the ties between organizations, (e.g. Diani, 1995; 2003) rather than between the individual members or activists within any social movement organization. One exception is Passy (2003) who explores how network affects members' intensity and duration of involvement, but she only examines the role of social networks outside the organization. Another is Mische (2003) who points out the importance of examining the interplay between networks and communication structures in movement settings, and suggests possible mechanisms whereby certain

---

1 The classic demonstration remains Granovetter's (1973) argument that those whose networks are characterized by weak ties (lots of people they do not know well) have greater potential to find jobs compared to those with strong tie networks.

kinds of network might generate social capital as a result of the relationship between the internal connections of members and their communicative relationships.[2]

In this chapter, then, we break new ground by examining the whole network structure of members of two contrasting organizations to examine how they may be conducive to forms of engagement and interpersonal trust, and how such differences may be related to the urban context of these associations.

Methods

Most studies of political activism have used either detailed case studies of particular social movement organizations (e.g. Bagguley 1995; Diani 1995; Eckersley 1989; Mueller 1994), or survey analyses examining the characteristics of members or activists in general (e.g. Parry *et al.*, 1992; Hall 1999; Warde *et al.* 2003; Li *et al.* 2002; 2003).[3] We, however link the personal characteristics of members with their network ties, permitting systematic comparison of the structure and dynamics of activism in each organization. The two case studies are deliberately chosen from the Greater Manchester area (see also Devine *et al.* in this volume), which exemplifies many of the trends that Rae (2004) outlines.

Manchester was the first major industrial city, due to its role as capital of the cotton textile industry during British industrialization, and having developed a large inland docking facility and one of the world's first industrial estates, it retained a very strong industrial base down to the 1960s. However, from this period it was marked by intense de-industrialization, and the re-location of economic activity to the southern suburban fringes. Boosted by finance and service led development from the 1980s, it is now an excellent example of a decentralized urban agglomeration, with its population of six million dispersed through an urban environment connected by an orbital motorway network.

From this urban location we chose two different kinds of social movement organization to study. Firstly, we selected a local Labour Party branch, which has since 1918 been one of the two main political parties in Britain. This might be seen as an example of a 'traditional' organization, whose role is to campaign on public issues in its locality and contest local elections. It works in an old Victorian suburb which has a strong tradition of civic involvement and engagement, notably in adult education and church attendance. The case study branch is relatively active, and comprises a number of adjacent wards (neighborhoods), which operate together

---

2 Mische (2003) identifies four 'conversational mechanisms' that facilitate different kinds of mobilization. The first are 'identity qualifying' statements where activists align themselves to particular movements by using a phrase like 'as a member of …'. 'Temporal cueing' links activists into the temporal projects of the movement itself. 'Generality shifting' allow activists to change the scope and specificity of the groups that they identify as part of the movement, whilst 'multiple targeting' avoids specificity and tries to appeal to different audiences.

3 The exceptions here include historical studies of social mobilization where it is possible to use archival data to glean information on the characteristics of political activists. See Gould (1995).

organizationally because of low membership levels in any one ward. The size of the branch membership at the time of the survey was 128.

Our other case study is an independent conservation group in metropolitan Manchester. This nature protection association engages in 'pressure politics', mainly by lobbying local and central government to protect wildlife and natural environments. It began as a group of local wildlife gardeners in the 1980s, and later broadened its concerns to the conservation of wildlife within the city as a whole. It is thus an example of an enthusiasm based group, able to draw members from across the entire conurbation, and work in a number of locations across the wider Manchester area. The group participates in a national network of similar groups, but operates structurally as an autonomous local group. Like many local environmental groups (see Lowe and Goyder, 1983), it seeks to influence the local authority in safeguarding particular sites, as well as influencing general policies on conservation and development. The conservation group was in a quieter phase of a 'protest cycle' (Tarrow, 1995) at the time of the research, but still had 121 members.[4]

By contrasting these two groups we are able, therefore, to assess the different kinds of mobilization possible in older and newer kinds of association. The Labour Party represents a traditional, civic, locally oriented organization, whereas the Conservation Group represents a contemporary, enthusiasm based metropolitan organization. The former exemplifies an older form of urban engagement, and the latter a newer kind of urban movement Through tracing the specific networks within each groups, we are thus able to tease out the potential of each to generate mobilization and trust.

Our research had three stages. Firstly, using the membership lists made available to us by the organizations, we sent a postal questionnaire to all members, asking for information on their socio-economic position, the means by which they were recruited, and the extent and nature of their participation and commitment. We also asked people to name anyone in the organization with whom they 'discuss things to do with the organization (for example, activities, issues, strategy)'. We sent up to three reminders, and obtained a very high response rate of 79 per cent for the Conservation Group and 80 per cent for the Labour Party.

At the end of this postal questionnaire, respondents were asked if we could interview them face-to-face to elicit fuller network information. 108 members agreed. This amounts to a response rate for the Conservation group of 46 per cent of all members (58 per cent of those who had returned postal questionnaires), and for the Labour Party 41 per cent (52 per cent). In these interviews we asked respondents to identify, from a roster of all the members of their branch, who they met socially outside the organization; who they got information from, and with whom they discussed organizational matters. In this way, we were able to assess whether social networks were specific to one of these contexts or whether they spanned them. We also asked about people's networks outside the organization, though we do not analyze this data

---

4 We also had a third case study, an environmental group. Because it was much smaller with the other two organizations (it had only 31 members), we have omitted it from most of our analysis so that we can focus on the pair-wise comparison between the two larger organizations.

in this chapter since it goes beyond our interest in intra-organizational networks. Because respondents chose people with whom they had ties from a roster of names, all members of the organization could potentially be included as members of their network, even if they were not themselves interviewed. However, we are not able to determine systematically whether ties are reciprocal (since some of those named by a respondent will not have been interviewed and we therefore cannot check whether they would have in turn named the respondent as a tie).

Thirdly, we conducted life history interviews with ten members from each organization. These were sampled from those who participated in the second phase to obtain similar numbers who were very active, semi-active and relatively inactive. The interviews were usually conducted in the respondents' home but sometimes in a public space (according to the wishes of the respondent) and lasted between 45 minutes and three hours. A semi-structured interview schedule was used with open ended questions clustered around eight themes: activist trajectory, early home life, education, employment history, voluntary and community involvements, neighborhood, friendship networks and leisure activities. These interviews provided information on people's own activist identities and the relationship between their personal circumstances and their social networks. These three phases of fieldwork were conducted between 1999 and 2001.

Our data allows us to map the internal social networks of our case study associations, along several dimensions in unprecedented detail. We can distinguish the position of individual members within the organization, measured here as core, periphery or isolate; we can distinguish the different kinds of networks across four types of activity; examine their levels of trust in other people and in particular institutions with a social and political relevance; and members' propensity to play an active role in its formal activities.

Network Structures and Engagement

Figures 9.1 and 9.2 reveal the people with whom the members reported (during phase one of the study) discussing organizational matters. Figure 9.1 reveals that two-thirds of Labour Party members did not discuss organizational matters with anyone else. The core of the Labour Party network, defined as those who discussed issues with five or more other members, consists of nine people (9 per cent of the total membership). Ties between these core members are well developed, as are their links to more peripheral members who have between one and four ties to other members. Figure 9.2 shows that just over half of the members of the Conservation group are isolates. The core of the group, however, is much smaller, containing only five members (5 per cent of the total membership), with members of the periphery communicating primarily with only two members of the core. Beyond their ties to these two dominant individuals, there are very few other ties between members of the periphery. This is a very sparse network with a small core.

We might characterize the Labour Party as comprising an 'inner circle', with a significant body of 'networked' members, and a dense structure of ties with other core members, then stretching out to peripheral members, but also detached

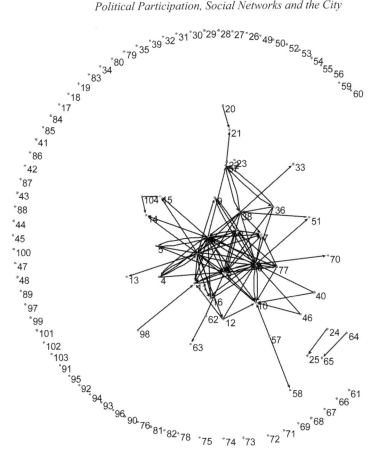

Figure 9.1 Communication networks within the Labour Party

Note: Respondents were asked 'with whom do you discuss things to do with the organization (for example, activities, issues, strategy)'.

completely from a large proportion of the membership. In the conservation group, by contrast, there is more of a bicycle wheel, 'hub and spoke', structure with a small central group communicating with a larger number of peripheral members, but fewer crosscutting ties between other members.

Let us cut to the chase by immediately examining whether these core, peripheral, and isolate members differ significantly in their activism and trust. Table 9.1 uses information from the first phase postal questionnaire to show that nearly all members were active somehow, but that this took very different forms. Nearly everyone read the newsletters, but less than half went to meetings, donated money, or attended social events. It is also apparent that there is a significant difference between the Labour Party and the Conservation Group. Activism in the latter was lower overall and involved less effort. Only one activity, reading the newsletter, was reported by more than a quarter of its members, and it is striking that this is largely a passive and

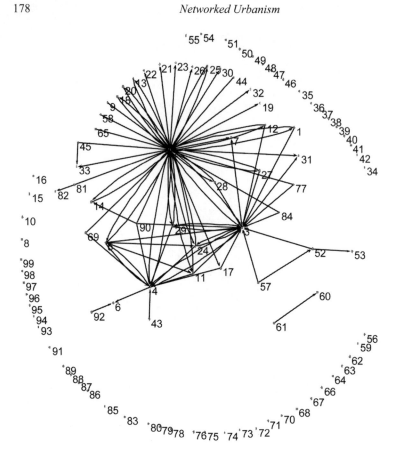

Figure 9.2   Communication networks within the Conservation Group

Note: Respondents were asked 'with whom do you discuss things to do with the organization (for example, activities, issues, strategy)'.

private activity. Less than a quarter of the membership attended meetings or wrote letters of protest. By contrast, Labour Party members were more likely to attend meetings, donate money, sign petitions, and get involved in fund raising. They were also considerably more sociable with each other.

Table 9.1 **Members engaging in particular activities at least once a year (percentage)**

Activity	Labour Party	Conservation
Reading newsletter	83	98
Donating money	42	11
Writing letter of protest	19	23
Signing petition	33	11
Purchasing merchandise	4	4
Attending meetings	40	23
Attending demonstrations	8	5
Awareness or fund raising	23	9
Organizing social event	6	0
Attending social event	28	2
Administrative work	17	9
Research or writing	8	11
Presentations to outside organization	4	4
Liaising with media	6	7
Consultation	7	11
Representation on committees	12	7
Direct action	0	4
N =	102	96

Table 9.2 examines the variables which correlate with levels of activism in the two organizations – defined here as the amount of time spent on organizational activities.[5] Table 9.2 shows that that network position is the only significant variable which accounts for different levels of activism amongst members. Core members (especially) and peripheral members are significantly more likely than isolates to be active. This is not surprising: we would normally expect that those in core positions are most active simply by virtue of their being in such positions, but it is striking that no other factor, including the individual social class position, age and gender of the members, makes any difference. It is important to note that there are no differences between the two organizations, apart from the network structures that we have elaborated above. The greater activism of Labour Party members is attributable to its 'inner circle' network structure with a larger core tends to generate higher levels of involvement.

---

5 The dependent variable here is the total number of hours per month spent active in the organization, using zero inflated Poisson, because In addition, we have used factor analysis to reveal three different forms of activism, one linking those who were collectively active, another linking those who were financially active, and a third linking those who were active in individual activities. However, since there are no obvious differences in the factors predisposing individuals to these three types of activism, we focus here on an aggregate measure of total time active.

Table 9.2   Correlates of activism

Dependent variable: number of hours spent active on organizational activity per month

Zero-inflated Poisson regression   Number of obs   = 169
                                                    Nonzero obs   = 28
                                                    Zero obs   = 141

Inflation model = logit   LR chi2(9)   = 60.99
Log likelihood = -87.94012   Prob > chi2   = 0.0000

	Coef.	Std. Err.	z	P>
Conservation group*	1.034998	.4213122	2.46	0.014
Network position+				
Periphery	2.444755	.5226387	4.68	0.000
Core	3.884796	.5829913	6.66	0.000
Female<	.246866	.3655539	0.68	0.499
Personal income	.1297753	.0767649	1.69	0.091
Class >				
Petty bourgeoisie	-37.40755	1.70e+08	-0.00	1.000
Small holders	.2938257	.5454603	0.54	0.590
Skilled workers	2.561105	.7123353	3.60	0.000
Non-skilled work	-39.98986	4.44e+08	-0.00	1.000
Constant	-3.733957	.8303775	-4.50	0.000

Reference categories are:
* Labour Party
+ Isolate
< male
> Service class

The reason why individual socio-demographic factors are not associated with levels of activism is largely due to the social homogeneity of the two organizations concerned (see Table 9.3). Both were predominantly white, middle class organizations, which is in keeping with the evidence that associational membership in the UK is becoming increasingly socially skewed towards highly educated, professional and managerial groups (Li *et al.* 2003; Warde *et al.* 2003). The conservation group members had somewhat lower incomes (in large part because they were more likely to be retired), were more often found in intermediate white-collar occupations and less often in professional positions, but had somewhat higher educational qualifications. In neither case were there significant numbers of non-white, working class, members.

Table 9.3   Socio-economic characteristics of the memberships

	Labour party (n=102)	Conservation group (n=94)
Personal gross annual income (pounds)		
<10000 (n = 57)	22.6	40.9
10000-14999 (n = 38)	16.1	26.1
15000-19999 (n = 21)	11.8	11.4
20000-24999 (n = 14)	9.7	5.7
25000-29999 (n = 10)	5.4	5.7
30000-34999 (n = 12)	6.5	6.8
35000-39999 (n = 5)	4.3	1.1
40000-44999 (n = 6)	5.4	1.1
45000-49999 (n = 2)	2.2	0.0
50000-59999 (n = 5)	5.4	0.0
+60000 (n = 11)	10.8	1.1
Highest educational qualification		
none (n = 12)	10.0	2.2
gcse (n = 17)	12.0	5.6
a-level (n = 26)	13.0	14.4
technical (n = 21)	7.0	15.6
nursing (n = 6)	3.0	3.3
degree (n = 44)	24.0	22.2
postgraduate (n = 64)	31.0	36.7
Total (n = 190)	100.0	100.0
Occupational group		
Managers and administrators (n = 49)	24.5	25.8
professionals (n = 71)	42.2	30.1
assoc profs and technicians (n = 33)	14.7	19.4
clerical and secretarial (n = 19)	4.9	15.1
craft and related (n = 8)	5.9	2.2
Personal and protective services (n = 5)	1.0	4.3
sales and related (n = 6)	2.9	3.2
plant and machine operatives (n = 1)	1.0	0.0
other (n = 3)	2.9	0.0

Table 9.4   Correlates of total trust

Linear regression		
Dependent variable		tottrst
Number of observations:		143
F statistic:		2,841
Model degrees of freedom:		13
Residual degrees of freedom:		129
R-squared:		0,223
Adjusted R-squared:		0,144
Root MSE		9,929
Prob:		0,001
Effect	Coeff	s.e.
org		
conservation	-7,967**	1,779
netpos		
periphery	-0,086	1,962
core	-6,244	3,398
gend		
female	0,018	1,715
age*		
25-34	-3,792	7,653
35-44	-5,737	7,603
45-54	-7,629	7,332
55-64	-5,427	7,435
+65	-3,299	7,399
Class		
Petty bourgeoisie	-13,126	10,345
Small holders	-5,312	10,629
Skilled workers	0,118	5,361
Non-skilled workers	-12,460*	5,176
cons	46,949**	7,411

* $p < .05$
** $p < .01$
Reference categories as for Table 9.2 except
* age 18-24

Although our main interest is in activism and engagement, evidence on inter-personal trust, which is widely used as a key measure of social capital, supports our argument (see Table 9.4). We measure trust here as a scale, the sum score obtained by individuals' responses to a questions on their degree of trust in a range of particular institutions (in central government, in the House of Commons, in the police, in local government, in the European Union, in banks, in major companies, and in the BBC), as well as in people in general. Members of the conservation group are much less trusting than the Labour Party. There is no significant difference between core, periphery and isolates (though it is interesting that the coefficients suggest that the cores may actually be less trusting than isolates, though these are not statistically significant), and nor do individual attributes make any difference (with the exception that unskilled workers are less trusting, but we need to note that there were only four such individuals in the two organizations). The findings are identical when trust is measured separately for each of the dimensions listed above. Our case studies thereby endorse the observation which has been made on the basis of aggregate national surveys, that there is no clear link between activism and involvement on the one hand, and generalized trust on the other (see Hall 1999, and Li *et al.* 2005 on the British case, and Paxton 2002 on the US). It is striking that these different attitudes towards trust are present even though the members of both groups otherwise share 'leftist' political attitudes, and overlap in their political culture (with evidence from our in depth interviews showing that most Conservation group members were Labour supporters, and most Labour Party members reported environmental concerns).

We do, then, have an interesting and robust contrast between the Labour Party, which generates greater activism and involvement, and a Conservation Group, which although having a similar size and composition of membership scores lower on all the relevant indices we have been able to measure. In the next section of this chapter we explore how far these differences may be attributable to the different relationships the two groups have to urban space, contrasting the local, civic, character of the Labour Party, with the city-wide, enthusiasm based form of the Conservation Group. Here, evidence from the in-depth interviews proves highly revealing.

The Urban Dimension of Engagement

It is clear from the in-depth interviews that although both organizations are involved in political campaigning, they have a different relationship to the urban public realm. The conservation group came into existence in the 1980s to protest at plans for urban development in central Manchester, and since this time has waged various campaigns to preserve wildlife habitats in the city. The venue for these protests has varied throughout the conurbation, and the methods mainly rely on lobbying the local council. These activities extend to 'consciousness-raising' strategies, through holding urban wildlife walks, becoming involved in voluntary urban clearance, and general publicizing of the need to preserve wildlife habitats. All these activities are organized in intense bursts and depend entirely on pro-active mobilization by members of the organization itself, which has no formal role within other organizations in the city.

The local Labour Party, by contrast, is characterized by its insertion into numerous decision making bodies, both within the Labour movement itself (in terms of its regional and national structures), but also within wider structures of urban governance. The important difference here is the way that this requires members to be selected to play various formal roles. Four of the eight Labour Party members who we interviewed in-depth, including those who were not active, had become Labour nominated school governors. Others had been candidates or agents at local elections, and still others had served on Labour Party committees at District or national level. Willy-nilly, Labour Party members were hence incorporated into 'vacancy chain' recruitment which was entirely absent for the Conservation group. This might lead even unwilling members into formal responsibilities. Member 486 put it in these terms:

So since you've joined, you wouldn't describe yourself as active, what sorts of things have you done, or have you been doing things in the Labour Party?

Oh yeah, I went to meetings for a while when I first joined, erm, I thought you know, I'd go and see what was going on and I helped at a couple of things, it's a very small group here as you can imagine, and, err, I did go to quite a few to start with, erm, and I did do some leafleting around, err, for the election and, erm, I also became a governor of a primary school. ... because they were very short of Labour Party governors in the area, (laughs), so that was something I felt that I could, erm, do, you know, because that's in my remit, I used to be a primary school teacher. (interview number 486)

This kind of institutional demand on the Labour Party members helps explain their greater internal network structures. Whereas Conservation group members largely explained their activities in terms of the personalities of themselves and their leaders and their own personal enthusiasms, Labour Party members talked in terms of the social groups and 'roles' who were mobilized in the Party. Consider the rather solipsistic accounts of the conservation group members:

Through one thing and another I ended up Conservation Group, though one thing and another, through leaving groups, joining groups, I read their newsletter, their magazine and thought, mmm, I like that, I like the way it's very localised, it's special, you know, it homes in on local, what's happening in Manchester, and I thought they were an organization I'd get on with, I went to one of their meetings and I'd never seen anything like it in my life, there were three people who could, I mean I can talk, and these three people all of them could out talk me, and it was a nightmare, it was awful and I decided at the end of the night I never want to see these three people again! ... I just thought I never want to see them ever again, they absolutely drive me crazy, but I thought ... right, on the other hand, what they are doing is fantastic and nobody else is doing it, and I'd like to be part of it. (1)

I'm only interested in people who are interested in what I'm interested in. And I only ever want to mix with people who care about the environment, err, broadly that's all I do ... (9)

Labour Party members, by contrast, were more likely to evoke social groups when talking about members, identifying what Tilly calls 'catnets':

So, erm, yeah I guess after 10, 10, 15 years probably, it, erm, began to wane a bit and as happens when we moved to, erm, to … there was some quite elderly people in the local Labour Party who kept it going, bless them, for years, and suddenly a new wave of people came and … so we sort of, not took over, exactly, but, you know, we became much more active and a whole group of people came in at once, and I guess the same thing has happened now, because there's a wave of young people have come in, I'm not saying there aren't any older people involved, there are, but, you know, sort of take on the bread and butter things, erm. (400)

Erm, there's a lot little old ladies in Labour Party branch, people who felt very strongly about, maybe joined the Labour party after World War II, that aren't really very active and they aren't terribly well informed about what goes on at the moment. There are some, there's, there's quite a lot of middle ground, quite a lot of people who feel strongly but maybe don't play a very active role, 472 and 473 for instance, who have very solid socialist principles, you know, they feel very strongly, they're both from immigrant families, they, you know, erm, 473's a social worker, you know, she's a sort of very practical socialist from that point of view, so in many ways it's, you know, from that point of view she's a better socialist than I am, if you like, you know, she's, every day she is putting into principle, putting into, you know, and, err, almost with a religious fervour, I think there's, there's for some people for whom socialism is a direct replacement for organized religion, and I think, you know, maybe somebody like 472 and 473 would be that end of the party, erm, but yeah a lot of little old ladies and a lot of people are on the right of the party just cos it's a prosperous area and, you know. (427)

We've got some excellent members, we really do have some excellent members, we have some excellent people, you know, they are not just, you know, I mean we have got all sorts in there, we've doctors, all sorts, you know, people in business, there's everything, there's retired, there's everything, so there are some excellent, and really, very, very good people, very nice people, very good, mmm (483).

It is clear from these extracts in particular, that it was Labour Party members who were more likely to identify cliques and factions in their midst.

But around here it's … all points of order and going to this, and you can't do that because of this, and they go round on their own little agenda, and that's agenda in inverted commas, but if you are not sort of active and wanting to sort of be 'dyed-in-the-wool', then it's not, it's not terribly interesting really (486);

[the local party's] cautiously towards the right now I think, I mean we've had trouble, we had a lot of dissension it goes back a long time (445);

It's funny 'cos I mean we have some very left wing and very sort of, I mean [name] I mean he's quite a difficult person get on with, and I mean he is, (pause) very much on the fringes of the party in terms of much more, probably closer to the Socialist Worker's Party, I think he's now given up his membership completely, so it's very much on the, on, you know, the extreme left of the party almost to the point of, you know, disenfranchisement from the Labour party (427).

This is not a portrait of a consensual group of associational members. Five of the ten Labour Party members we spoke to identified cliques and factions, stretching back over a long period of time. However, as we have seen, this internal division does not seem to be a barrier to sustaining high levels of civic engagement and institutional trust. Rather, the greater intensity of organizational life is linked to a sense that there are stakes worth mobilizing around, and that higher levels of interpersonal trust can be generated by having experience of, and dealing with, internal factions. Indeed this also explains why amidst this more concentrated networks, there were also a higher proportion of isolates in the Labour Party, some of whom appear to have become disenchanted by faction fighting and therefore were largely, and unconnected, members.

> I just didn't find anything interesting or engaging or anything, I mean it used to be quite dominated by, I suppose it was a very extreme left group of people at one point … they just wanted to have an argument for an argument's sake … (477)

Counter-intuitively, greater levels of generalized trust are hence generated by internal faction-fighting. Even isolated Labour Party members are not disenchanted by their perception of tense internal organizational affairs so that they report low trust. By contrast, members of the conservation group report much less antagonism between members with a stronger consensus about who should run the organization. Only in one instance (of ten) during life history interviews did a conservation group member identify cliques and factions, compared to five (out of ten) Labour Party members. But this sense that the Conservation Group was instrumentally organized, so that it could pursue 'business as usual', was precisely why it could operate without high amounts of trust from its members. Participation is generated not out of an unthinking collective identification, or out of a sense of consensus and uniformity, but out of the recognition of divisions amidst their ranks.

We can here pursue this argument further by examining the network structure of the two organizations in more detail, using dimensions from the more intensive, second phase interview data, where we asked three separate questions: about the transfer of information about the organization, discussing organizational matters (again), and meeting members for social purposes.[6]

Figure 9.3 shows patterns of ties for two of those activities, obtaining information and meeting socially. Obtaining information networks are reported in Figure 9.3.1 and 9.3.3, and meeting socially in Figure 9.3.2 and 9.3.4. The ties reported under obtaining information are a measure of the formal ties, as the transfer of information is necessary to generate coordinated activity. Ties of sociability can be seen as a measure of the informal networks which characterize the organization.

---

6   The questions were: 'Which of the people [on the roster] would you get information about the activities of the group?', 'With whom [on the roster] have you discussed issues to do with the organization in the last year?', 'In the last year, who [on the roster] have you met outside of the activities of the [Group]?'. The exception being one member who reported that when she joined she lived only 400m from another member. The surprise with which she related this coincidence underscores the general point here.

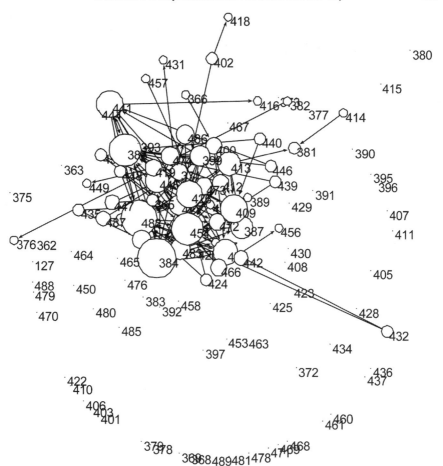

Figure 9.3.1 Obtaining information network in the Labour Party

Figures 9.3.1–4 shows that the two types of network overlap in different ways for the conservation group and the Labour Party. Figure 9.3.3 shows that in the conservation group only two people (17 and 83) are much involved in delivering information. They have many contacts (the size of the circle indicates volume of contacts) and few others have ties other than with them. This is a sparse and hierarchical structure, which we have characterized as 'hub and spoke', compatible with instrumental transactions and a business relationship. The pattern of sociability (Figure 9.3.4) is significantly different. Here, rather more members have several contacts, including the two delivering most information, and the network is no longer dominated by the latter. There are fewer isolates. This is more like the 'inner circle' model.

Figure 9.3.1 also shows differences in the Labour Party between the two network dimensions. Reinforcing the findings from Figure 9.1, there are a large number of people isolated from the information network (Figure 9.3.1), and a core of seven individuals involved in exchange of information, but with none apparently dominant.

The diagram showing sociability (Figure 9.3.2) indicates a greater degree of mutual engagement, with many individuals having several associates. By and large, however, it is the same individuals who are at the core of information distribution who are central to the network of sociable ties. The sociable connections are denser than those facilitating information transmissions. There is hence an overlap between the formal and informal networks within the Labour Party which is not characteristic of the Conservation group. This is in part attributable to the fact that the members of the local Party live closely together, all within their district boundaries. Several of our interviewees reported bumping into other members in the course of their daily lives, whereas this was hardly mentioned by Conservation group members, all of whom lived in different areas of Manchester and had no reason to run into each other.

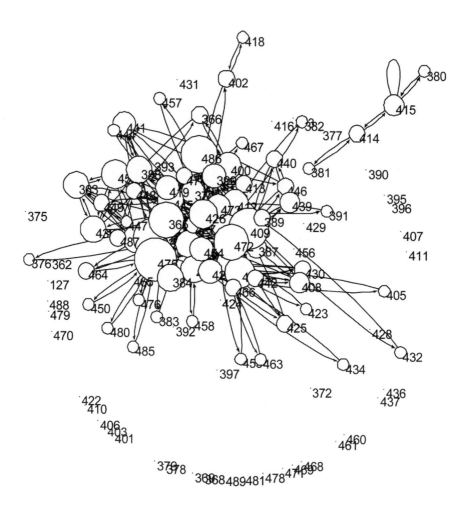

Figure 9.3.2 Meeting outside network in the Labour Party

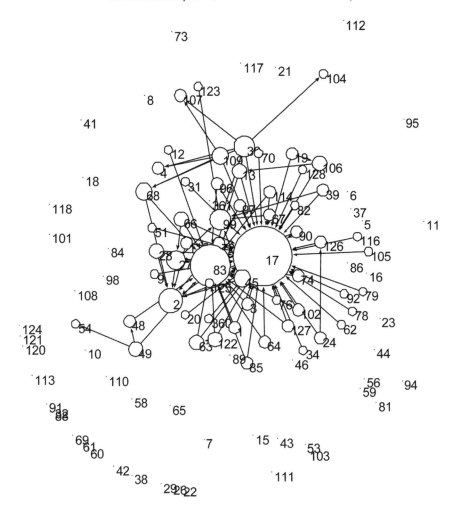

Figure 9.3.3 Obtaining information network in the Conservation Group

Examining the accounts of the members in more detail, it becomes clear that there are also telling differences in the way that members of the two organizations relate to and identify with the city. Six Labour Party members had been brought up in the conurbation (though none had been brought up in the locale itself), whereas seven out of ten conservation group workers had grown up outside the region and had migrated to Manchester at a later stage. Many members of the Conservation Group had a marked urban identity, in which defending wildlife sites was central to their sense of urbanism, and their involvement was linked to a personal enthusiasm for the conservation cause. One member had undertaken a three year adult education course on the history of Manchester. Conservation Group members mentioned Manchester (unprompted) an average of 15 times in their interviews, whereas Labour Party members mentioned it an average of seven times. Conservation group members had an enthusiasm-oriented sense of urban identity, and their activity was generally rendered in very personal terms:

> I think I was, I was always interested in, err, sort of nature and it's, mmm, it was a cross fertilization (laughs), if you can call it that, my youngest one when he, I remember he was quite small, he took a great interest in anything that was, flowers or, you know, sort of, it was really great, and so you got, I was getting more interest in it as well, and you sort of ... when we picked his brother up from school we always counted the different little flowers, daisies or whatever we saw on the road and then we checked it up in the library in books, and sort of, err, we sort of, what do you say, sort of got each other interested. (1)

Arrival in the city was often rendered aesthetically and emotionally (akin to the narratives discussed in Savage *et al.* 2005).

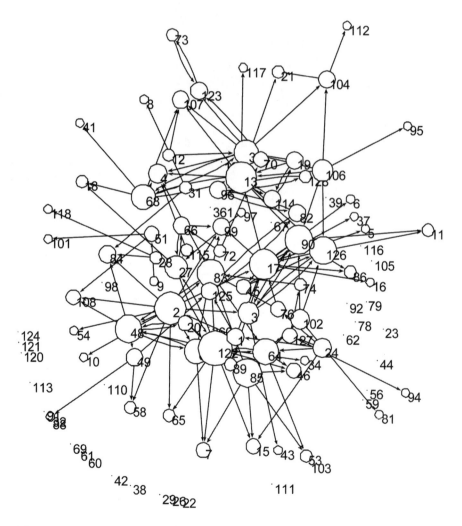

Figure 9.3.4 Meeting outside network in the Conservation Group

Manchester itself was horrible! (laughs) It was November, it was cold, drizzly and every, you know, erm, warehouses, they are not warehouses now, and it was black and sooty, you know, you couldn't see the buildings for soot, now they have been cleaned up and they look wonderful, but you couldn't see the buildings. (1)

The Labour Party members, by contrast, had a more pragmatic account of their local area and of the city itself. Several of those who had grown up in inner city Manchester stressed the relative affluence of their current residence, and their own sense of achievement in moving into a secure suburban location. In talking about their current area of residence, six reported an active neighbourhood life, including socializing and learning to deal with others who did not share their political views.

I might have thought that one day but I think, I find it hard, I find it hard to reconcile people who have the right values with voting Tory, personally, but I know that they do, and they have, some of the kindest people, I mean just, not somebody who's a friend, but like chairman of the school he's a Tory councillor, he's a lovely man, ... you know, so people, yeah, people can be OK whatever, and it's the sort of people they are that matters, not their political beliefs. (400)

We can see, then, a link between the relationship of the two groups to their local environment, and their network structure. The conservation group, with its personal identification to Manchester as a whole, exhibits a much more hierarchical and sparse set of links for passing on information than does the party, though information reaches a larger proportion of the membership. The Labour Party, with its more pragmatic orientation to its locale, has more decentralized channels of communication, as implied by the networks of discussion described in Figure 9.2. We can also see that the Labour Party has more isolates and a greater concentration of ties (there are more large circles on the diagram, indicating multiple connections). Part of the explanation of the difference is that members of the conservation group reported a substantial number of joint memberships with other conservation and environmental organizations and which were consistent with their enthusiasm based engagement and their attachment to a campaigning, activist identity. It is probably their engagement in these other associational activities which produce the dispersed pattern of sociable interaction mapped in Figure 9.3.4.

We have argued that whilst the Conservation group, with its hub and spoke structure, was well organized for administrative purposes, its lack of multiplex ties means that it these did not generate any wider ranging intensity that might generate inter-personal trust. In the Labour Party, by contrast, the picture is different. In part, the inner circle structure, where there are overlaps between informal and formal ties, generates more concentrated involvements. One result is that membership in the Labour Party was more intense and generated a higher level of internal faction fighting than was evident in the Conservation Group with its very clear hierarchical structure.

Conclusions

In case studies of the kind we have reported in this chapter, it is difficult to draw precise causal relationships between specific kinds of people, network structures, and forms of engagement, trust, and activism. All these are closely bound together in a way which makes it problematic to determine an exact cause of the differences we have delineated between the two organizations. In order to fully understand the dynamics of social capital, we need to do more than delineate the variables that appear to correlate with greater trust and engagement. We have shown instead that we need to carefully unpick the kinds of complex processes that generate different effects with respect to activism and trust, and that variable centered causal models are less useful than process oriented accounts which see causality as an emergent property of particular kinds of network structures (more generally, Abbott 2001; Emirbayer 1997; Emibayer and Goodwin 1994).

We are able to make four important conclusions for the analysis of social capital and the city. Firstly, just calling for participation is not enough, and being a member of an organization is a poor indicator of any significant form of engagement, and it would be dangerous to assume that membership results in 'contact with people who are not like us'. For the positive effects of social capital to be generated, it clearly matters not only that people are members of associations, but also that there are certain types of network structures and patterns of interaction within them. The compositional effects we found in the Labour Party of a more differentiated (in the sense of less overlapping) internal structure of ties are more conducive to the effects that Putnam considers positive for civic life. Engagement is actually helped by the existence of conflicts which create stakes and a sense of a project important enough to be disputed. In the Conservation Group, where membership was seen as related to individual interest, it proves more difficult to generate wider ranging involvement.

Secondly, in line with Skocpol's critique of social capital theory, we need to place organizations within their institutional environment. One reason why the Labour Party generated more energy was that it had more positions to fill and interfaced more extensively with various kinds of local institutions. Whereas the Conservation Group, as a campaigning movement, was left to its own devices to decide how to mobilize, and over what issues, the Labour Party routinely had to find candidates for elections, select school governors, and send delegates to Party Conference and other Party committees. This pattern was linked to the historical roots of the Party, which the Conservation group did not have. This history was, ultimately, a resource that allowed the Labour Party to continue to mobilize more effectively.

Thirdly, this different kind of institutional relationship is anchored in varying connections to the city itself. The urban environment cannot be abstracted from the workings of the two groups. This is true in several respects. The Labour Party, operating in a local ward, is better able to generate social engagements than is the Conservation group which works at the level of the conurbation. Conservation Group members are similar to Fischer's urbanites, people who chose to associate with like minded people in pursuit of a particular enthusiasm. The conservationists do this primarily through organizing walks and campaigns at particular named sites in the city, bringing together a scattered group for this purpose. For many members, their activity depended on a strong mobilization of the imagination, devoted to the idea of the 'wild' city, opposed to commercial development and environmental damage. The Labour Party, by contrast, performs much local routine business, and does not deploy a strong urban identity, but one more focused on social justice. It mobilizes people who are identified by others in the party not as enthusiasts of one kind or another, but as members of different social groups, and this ultimately allows more respect for difference.

Fourthly, in unraveling the differences between these two groups, blunt concepts of bridging and bonding social capital are not helpful. Both groups are concerned to 'bond', but the most effective in doing this, the Labour Party, also has to 'bridge' its internal divisions. The Conservationists, who do bridge the city as a whole are also ultimately concerned with mobilizing like minded enthusiasts. In some respects our arguments bear resemblances to Bellah *et al.*'s (1996) concerns about the abilities of 'lifestyle enclaves' – the Conservationists in our case – to engage in wider ranging ties and relationships. But the more important political lesson, we think, is that serious engagement will only happen when support for participation is accompanied by a serious devolution of power and responsibility. Ultimately, our more successful Labour Party case study indicates that it is when the 'stakes' are high, more intense engagement is more likely to occur.

References

Aguilera, M.B. and Massey, D. (2003), 'Social Capital and the Earnings of Mexican Migrants: New Hypotheses and Tests', *Social Forces*, 82: 2, 671–701.

Amin, A. and Thrift, N.J. (2002), *Cities: Reimagining the Urban* (Cambridge: Polity Press).

Anheier, H. and Kendall, J. (2002), 'Interpersonal Trust and Voluntary Associations: Examining Three Approaches', *British Journal of Sociology*, 53: 3, 343–362.

Bagguley, P. (1995a), 'Protest, Poverty and Power: A Case Study of the Anti-poll Tax Movement', *Sociological Review*, 43 :4, 693–719.

Bellah, R. (1985), *Habits of the Heart* (Berkeley: University of California Press).

Bourdieu, P. (1997), 'The Forms of Capital', in Halsey, A.H., Lauder, H., Brown, P. and Wells, A.S. (eds), *Education: Culture, Economy, Society* (Oxford: Oxford University Press).

Brown, R.K. and Brown, R.E. (2003), 'Faith and Works: Church Based Social Capital Resources and African American Political Activism', *Social Forces*, 82: 2, 617–641.

Burt, R. (1992), *Structural Holes: The Social Structure of Competition* (Cambridge: Harvard University Press).

—— (2000), 'The Network Structure of Social Capital', *Research in Organisational Behaviour*, 22, 345–423.

—— (2002), 'Bridge Decay', *Social Networks*, 24: 4, 333–363.

—— (2005), *Brokerage and Closure* (Cambridge: Harvard University Press).

Claibourn, M.P. and Martin, P.S. (2000), 'Trusting and Joining: An Empirical Test of the Reciprocal Nature of Social Capital', *Political Behaviour*, 22: 4, 267–291.

Crossley, N. (2002), *Making Sense of Social Movements* (Milton Keynes: Open University Press).

—— (2006), 'In the gym', *Body and Society*, 12, 3, 23–50.

Diani, M. (1995), *Green Networks: A Structural Analysis of the Italian Environmental Movement* (Edinburgh: Edinburgh University Press).

—— (2003), 'Introduction: Social Movements, Contentious Actions, and Social Networks: "From Metaphor to Substance"?', in Diani, M. and McAdam, D. (eds), 1–20.

Diani, M. and McAdam, D. (eds) (2003), *Social Movements and Networks: Relational Approaches to Collective Action* (Oxford: Oxford University Press).

Eckersley, R. (1989), 'Green Politics and the New Class: Selfishness or Virtue?', *Political Studies*, 37: 2, 205–223.

Emirbayer, M. (1997), 'A Manifesto for Relational Sociology', *American Journal of Sociology*, 103, 281–317.

Emirbayer, M. and Goodwin, J. (1994), 'Network Analysis, Culture and the Problem of Agency', *American Journal of Sociology*, 99, 1411–54.

Fischer, C.S. (1982), *To Dwell Amongst Friends* (Berkeley: University of California Press).

Frietag, M. (2003a), 'Social Capital in (dis)similar Democracies: The Development of Generalised Trust in Japan and Switzerland', *Comparative Political Studies*, 36: 8, 936–966.

—— (2003b), 'Beyond Tocqueville: The Origins of Social Capital in Switzerland', *European Sociological Review*, 19: 2, 217–232.

Fukuyama, F. (2000), *The Great Disruption: Human Nature and the Reconstitution of Social Order* (New York: Free Press).

Gould, R. (1995), *Insurgent Identities: Class, Community and Protest in Paris from 1848 to the Commune* (Chicago: University of Chicago Press).

—— (2003), 'Why Do Networks Matter: Structuralist and Rationalist Interpretations', in Diani, M. and McAdam, D. (eds) (2002), *Social Movements and Networks: Relational Approaches to Collective Action* (Oxford: Oxford University Press), pp. 233–258.

Graham, S. and Marvin, S. (2001), *Splintering Urbanism: Networked Infrastructures, Technological Mobilities and the Urban Condition* (London: Routledge).

Granovetter, M. (1973), 'The Strength of Weak Ties', *American Journal of Sociology*, 78, 1360–80.

Hall, P.A. (1999), 'Social Capital in Britain', *British Journal of Political Social Science*, 29, 417–61.

Halpern, D. (2005), *Social Capital* (Cambridge: Polity).

Inkeles, A. (2000), 'Measuring Social Capital and Its Consequences', *Policy Sciences* 33, 245–268.

Knox, H., Savage, M. and Harvey, P. (2005), 'Social Networks and Spatial Relations: Networks as Method, Metaphor and Form', *CRESC Working Paper No 1*.

Li, Y., Savage, M., Tampubolon, G., Warde, A. and Tomlinson, M. (2002), 'Dynamics of Social Capital: Trends and Turnover in Associational Membership in England and Wales: 1972–1999', *Sociological Research Online*, 7: 3.

Li, Y., Savage, M. and Pickles, A. (2003), 'Social Capital and Social Exclusion in England and Wales (1972–1999)', *British Journal of Sociology*, 54: 4, 497–526.

Li, Y., Pickles, A. and Savage, M. (2005), 'Social Capital and Social Trust in Britain', *European Sociological Review*, 21: 2, 105–123.

Lin, N. (2002), *Social Capital* (Oxford: Oxford University Press).

Lowe, P. and Goyder, J. (1983), *Environmental Groups in Politics* (London: Allen and Unwin).

McAdam, D. (1986), 'Recruitment to High Risk Activism: The Case of Freedom Summer', *American Journal of Sociology*, 92, 64–90.

McAdam, D. and Paulsen, R. (1993), 'Specifying the Relationship Between Social Ties and Activism', *American Journal of Sociology*, 99, 640–667.

McAdam, D. and Snow, D. (eds) (1997) *Social Movements: Readings on Their Emergence, Mobilisation and Dynamics* (California: Roxbury Publishing Company).

Mische, A., (2003), 'Cross Talk in Movements: Reconceiving the Culture-network Link', in Diani, M. and McAdam, D. (eds) (2003), *Social Movements and Networks: Relational Approaches to Collective Action* (Oxford: Oxford University Press).

Morris, A. (1997), 'Black Southern Student Sit-In Movement: An Analysis of Internal Organisation', in McAdam, D. and Snow, D. (eds) *Social Movements: Readings on Their Emergence, Mobilisation and Dynamics* (California: Roxbury Publishing Company).

Mueller, C.M. (1994), 'Conflict Networks and the Origins of Women's Liberation', in Larana, E., Johnston, H. and Gusfield, J.R. (eds), *New Social Movements: From Ideology to Identity* (Philadelphia, Temple University Press).

Newton, K. (1997), 'Social Capital and Democracy', *American Behavioural Scientist* 40, 575–586.

Padgett, J.F. and Ansell, C.K. (1993), 'Robust Action and the Medici, 1400–1434', *American Journal of Sociology*, 98, 1259–1319.

Parry, G., Moyser, G. and Day, N. (1992), *Political Participation and Democracy in Britain* (Cambridge: Cambridge University Press).

Passy, F. (2003), 'Social Networks Matter, But How?', in Diani, M. and McAdam, D. (eds) (2002), *Social Movements and Networks: Relational Approaches to Collective Action*, pp. 21–48 (Oxford: Oxford University Press).

Paxton, P. (1999), 'Is Social Capital Declining in the United States? A Multiple Indicator Assessment', *American Journal of Sociology*, 105, 88–127.

—— (2002), 'Social Capital and Democracy', *American Sociological Review*, 67, 254–277.

Portes, A. (1998), 'Social Capital: Its Origins and Applications in Modern Sociology', *Annual Review of Sociology*, 24, 1–24.

Putnam, R. (1993), *Making Democracy Work: Civic Traditions in Modern Italy* (Princeton, N.J.: Princeton University Press).

—— (1995), 'Bowling Alone: America's Declining Social Capital', *Journal of Democracy*, 6:1, 65–78.

—— (1996), 'The Strange Disappearance of Civic America', *American Prospect*, 24, 34–48.

—— (2000), *Bowling Alone: The Collapse and Revival of American Community* (New York: Simon & Schuster).

Rae, D.W. (2003), *City: Urbanism and its End* (New Haven, Yale University Press).

Robteutscher, S. (2002), 'Advocate or Reflection: Associations and Political Culture', *Political Studies*, 50, 514–528.

Rudig, W. (1990), *Antinuclear Movements* (London: Longman).

Savage, M., Bagnall, G. and Longhurst, B.J. (2005), *Globalisation and Belonging* (London: Sage).

Sennett, R. (1977), *The Fall of Public Man* (New York: Knopf).

Snow, D., Zurcher, L. and Ekland-Olson, S. (1980), 'Social Networks and Social Movements: A Microstructural Approach to Differential Recruitment', *American Sociological Review*, 45, 787–801.

Stolle, D. and Hooghe, M. (eds) (2003), *Generating Social Capital: Civil Society and Institutions in Comparative Perspective* (Basingstoke: Palgrave).

Szreter, S. (2002), 'The State of Social Capital: Bringing Back in Power, Politics and History', *Theory and Society*, 31, 573–621.

Tarrow, S. (1995), 'Cycles of Collective Action: Between Moments of Madness and the Repertoire of Contention', in Traugott, M. (ed.) *Repertoires and Cycles of Collective Action* (London: Duke University Press).

Warde, A., Tampubolon, G., Longhurst, B., Ray, K., Savage, M. and Tomlinson, M. (2003), 'Trends in Social Capital: Membership of Associations in Great Britain, 1991–1996', *British Journal of Political Science*, 30, 515–525.

White, H. (1992), *Identity and Control* (Princeton: Princeton University Press).

Chapter 10

Conserving the Past of a Quiet Suburb: Urban Politics, Association Networks and Speaking for 'the Community'

Fiona Devine, Peter Halfpenny, Nadia Joanne Britton
and Rosemary Mellor[1]

Introduction

In the 1980s and 1990s, scholars in urban studies focused much of their attention on the decline and then the resurgence of cities. In the UK, for example, London and cities like Glasgow, Edinburgh, Manchester, Liverpool and Bristol were studied in depth. This research, with its focus on the political economy of new forms of urban governance, prospered (Boddy and Parkinson 2004). Arguably, the social dimensions of urban change were largely neglected or considered rather narrowly with reference to the spatial concentration of disadvantage within inner cities. Social inequalities were acknowledged albeit with reference to the very poor occupying a particular space within cities. This situation has now started to change. Beyond urban studies, Robert Putnam's (2000) work on social capital has been influential in raising questions, once again, about social relations in urban settings. Within urban studies, there has been a more critical engagement with the effects of urban change on civil life as epitomized in the work of Douglas Rae (2003) and his 'end of urbanism' thesis. A growing interest in the spatial dimension of social inequalities beyond inner cities to a consideration of advantaged groups living in gentrified areas or gated communities (Butler with Robson 2003; Atkinson and Blandy 2005, Atkinson and Helms 2007) has contributed to this process too. Specially, the activities of middle-class residents, with high social capital, defending their privileged living spaces has provided new impetus to the analysis of social relations within urban spaces across the world (Davis 1999, 2006, 2007).

The aim of our chapter is to contribute to this new perspective by describing the activities of high-capital local 'influentials' seeking to defend the exclusivity

---

1 The arguments in this chapter have been greatly influenced by conversations with Rosemary Mellor before her untimely death in 2001. As a long-standing Didsbury resident, she was acutely aware of the generational conflict emerging in the suburb and its link to wider changes in family formation and household composition. As the urban sociologist in the team, Rosemary was the principal grant holder for the ESRC grant (L1302151046) which funded the research reported in this chapter (see also Mellor 1977, 1989).

of suburbs. The case of suburbs and suburban change is interesting because they have been largely neglected in urban studies. We focus on two exclusive suburbs in Manchester: Hale and Didsbury (which were part of a bigger project on the regeneration of Manchester city centre, see Hall, Halfpenny *et al.*, 2004). The city of Manchester has undergone a process of urban transformation as it moved away from the old economy of low-level manufacturing to the new economy of high-level services (Harding *et al.*, 2004, Peck and Ward 2002). Local entrepreneurs in the public and private sectors have sought to reinvent the city as a regional centre and an attractive place for high-level service industry professionals to work. Our research examined the restructuring of Manchester's business and financial centre by way of interviews with company employers and young professionals. It also considered the reformation of Manchester as an agreeable place to live. It was in this context that we considered whether the prestigious suburbs of Hale and Didsbury were assets in maintaining and enhancing Manchester by helping the city to attract and retain a highly-qualified professional workforce. Our attention focused on the development pressures that these suburbs have come under, as the city centre economy revitalized and the resistance offered by residents and others, and as they seek to preserve the exclusiveness of their neighbourhoods in the face or urban change.

The first section considers the growing literature on social relations and social inequalities in urban spaces and how they are recreated and perpetuated by those with high levels of social capital – in ways only fleetingly acknowledged by Putnam (e.g. 2000). The second section describes our research on Hale, a semi-rural suburb within Greater Manchester's boundaries, and Didsbury, a more urban suburb that is part of the city of Manchester itself. As will be seen, the main empirical findings derive from interviews with some 40 key activists and other local 'influentials' in the two suburbs. The third section outlines the development pressures on Hale and the considerable fears about the loss of its leafy semi-rural 'village' environment and low-density population and the consequences in terms of traffic congestion and crime as the 'urban' encroaches. The fourth section explores the development pressures on Didsbury and the perceived downsides of its popularity with young professionals as the proliferation of restaurants and pubs undermines its 'village' community feel. These two empirical sections illustrate the contested nature of urban change as developers and, to some extent, estate agents seek to break down exclusionary tendencies and 'open up' suburbs while activist residents and other local influentials seek to maintain the exclusivity of the suburbs. How the dynamics of this local urban politics plays out depends on the contestation between such local groups with different results for different suburbs as is shown in Hale and Didsbury. Our conclusion considers these empirical findings in the context of the literature on social capital, civil life in cities and the spatial dimension of social inequalities. It is argued that advantaged middle-class residents, high in social capital, try to protect the exclusivity of their own suburban way of life in ways that profoundly shape the urban dimension of social inequalities overall, although they enjoy different degrees of success. The description of how social capital works on the ground actually contributes to an explanation of how social inequalities are reproduced or not depending on local political dynamics in urban settings.

Social Capital and Urban Change

A renewed interest in social capital generated by the publication of Robert Putnam's *Bowling Alone* (2000) has not influenced urban studies as much as it has other social sciences disciplines, yet as the chapters in this book indicate, it has significant resonances. The decline of social capital – networks and norms – worried Putnam as he saw the effects of social capital as largely positive. He concedes that not all social capital is good and that bonding (inward looking and exclusive) can be distinguished from bridging (outward inclusive) social capital. Bonding social capital reinforces exclusive identities among homogenous groups while bridging social capital looks outward and embraces heterogeneity across social divisions (Putnam 2000, 22–23). Nevertheless, it is the positive effects of (bridging) social capital that he extols. Putnam argues that suburban sprawl has contributed to the decline of social capital in the US. The suburbs have fragmented into increasingly homogenous communities that do not sustain community life. Fragmentation has occurred along the familiar lines of race and class including, for example, the emergence of affluent 'gated communities' in the 1980s. Moreover, Putnam argues suburban lifestyles have changed with an increasing dependence on the car to travel to work and shop elsewhere, thereby reducing face-to-face interaction in the local community. Increasing social homogeneity and the rise of commuting, therefore, have disrupted the 'community bondedness' of the past (Putnam 2000, 214). This is why the decline of social capital is so regrettable to Putnam.

This thesis has resonances with Rae's (2003) influential book, *City: Urbanism and its End*, in which he noted the importance of social capital – in terms of a 'dense civic fauna' – from its golden age during what he refers to as the 'urban era'. In his study of New Haven, Connecticut, Rae tracks the development of capitalist and urban development. In the height of urbanism at the turn of the century to the end of the first World War, Rae argues that cities like New Haven were characterized by a concentration of economic activity, including a dense fabric of small-scale enterprises, close residential living facilitating a mixing of classes and 'civic density' with 'hundreds of organizations which provided vast opportunities for civic participation' which were all important, he argued, given the limitations of city government (Rae 2003, 18–19). By the 1920s, however, this process of urban centring was already in decline as capital reorganized itself outside cities, local enterprises declined; residential populations dispersed to the suburbs and civic disengagement in voluntary led organizations started to dwindle. By the 1960s, the end of urbanism was readily apparent. De-centring forces included, of course, the rise of mass car ownership facilitating mobility that opened up new spaces for living, including suburban tracks, gated communities and the like. The end of urbanism has promoted 'social homogeneity within municipalities, leading to the evolution of regional hierarchies in which purified municipalities' … bring likes together, safe from contact with others different from themselves. … The notion of urbanism provides a useful perspective for critical study of such hierarchies' (Rae 2003, 30–31).

Rae, therefore, also charts the demise of social capital in cities, although he is keener than Putnam to avoid the idea of a golden age and he does not proselytize for the return of a social capital of yesteryear. Critics of Putnam have argued that the decline of social capital is far less evident in the UK than in the US (Hall 1999, Warde *et al.,* 2003). The same could be said of Rae's end or urbanism thesis since, as Le Galès (Le Galès, 2002; Bognasco and Le Galès, 2000) has long argued, European cities are different in many respects to American ones. Crucially, the spatial nature of social inequalities in cities – including the extremes of poverty in central ghettos and gated affluence in quiet separate suburbs – is very different in the UK compared with the US. Be that as it may, the processes of gentrification and the rise of gated communities in the UK has not gone unnoticed and, contrary to Putnam, the activities of people – with high social capital – in preserving advantaged places have not been ignored either. Indeed, the role of social capital in reinforcing social inequalities – especially class – has been central to analysis of current urban and suburban change. Tim Butler (Butler with Robson, 2003; Butler, 2004; Butler and Watt, 2007), for example, has described the gentrification of parts of London like Hackney by an 'urban seeking' middle class who concentrate in areas where people with similar lifestyles also live. They are largely disengaged from other non middle-class groups – especially in relation to the children's education – and they are not involved in forms of urban governance. The effect of these everyday individual social practices is to recreate and reinforce pronounced levels of economic and social polarization in Britain's capital city (see also Massey, 2007).

While cities like London, San Francisco and Melbourne have been associated with rampant forms of gentrification, Atkinson and his colleagues (Atkinson and Blandy, 2005; Atkinson and Bridge, 2005) argue that gentrifying processes, including the rise of gated communities, can now be found everywhere (see his contribution to this volume). Long associated with North (and South) America, they are sweeping Europe and Asia and embracing regional cities from Leeds to Mumbai. There is evidence of more developments that are guarded and under surveillance and, by implication, a more defensive middle class. Atkinson and Blandy (2005, 2) argue these processes are creating new levels of segregation and amount to new forms of urban colonialism. Latterly, urban renaissance is increasingly associated with crime control and public disorder in the context of a heightened concern for security. Thus, an increasing feature of the urban landscape is (aggressively) defensive home ownership and urban fortification (Atkinson and Helms, 2007; Hancock, 2007). This somewhat scary vision of urban change is, of course, open to debate. Gated communities may be overwhelmingly middle class but most members of the middle classes do not live in them. Similarly, some sections of the middle class may be increasingly defensive and exclusive but other sections embrace the diversity and inclusiveness of urban living (albeit within the limits noted by Butler above). These issues aside, Atkinson and his colleagues rightly argue that the prevalence of such urban change demands that research is undertaken beyond the core of cities to describe and understand new forms of provincial gentrification.

The remainder of this chapter takes up that call. It considers how individuals and groups in two affluent suburbs, the 'outer suburb' of Hale in Great Manchester and the 'inner suburb' of Didsbury in Manchester, sought to protect the exclusivity of their areas of residence in the face of economic and social change – namely, the urban renaissance of Manchester – with varying degrees of success. It draws attention to the role of exclusive social capital in preserving privilege and elite space while noting there are forces working against it too.

Manchester and its Suburbs

The empirical work on the suburbs formed part of the ESRC's programme of research on 'Cities: Competitiveness and Cohesion'. The aims of the programme were to improve understanding of how cities develop and mobilize distinctive economic assets to secure competitive advantage and to examine the associated implications for cohesion. The specific purpose of our research was to consider the economic regeneration of Manchester and the implications for two 'exclusive' suburbs: Hale and Didsbury. (Halfpenny *et al.*, 2004) Accordingly, the research had two strands. The first examined the financial and business services sector located in Manchester city centre and focused on six areas of professional employment: commercial law, accountancy, corporate banking and venture capitalists, actuarial services, architecture and creative design and advertising. Semi-structured interviews were conducted with 34 city-firms and with ten key informants drawn from professional and other organizations. These were followed by interviews with 70 employees from the sample of these firms. These interviewees were mostly with young men and women in their 20s and early 30s. Some were at the beginning of their professional careers, while others were enjoying rapid promotion to senior positions (Devine *et al.*, 2000). The interviews covered the interviewees' career history, geographical and residential mobility and their leisure patterns in and around Manchester and its suburbs. The interviews, in other words, tapped in the lifestyles of young, affluent professionals with a particular focus on the spatial forms of their work and play.

The second strand involved research on two affluent suburbs: namely, Hale and Didsbury. The choice of suburbs was influenced by the view that having 'good' places to live for its middle-class professional employees is important if Manchester is to secure its status as a competitive city. In the past, it has been the city's long-established exclusive residential suburbs with large, good-quality houses at relatively low densities that have provided the homes for wealthy industrialists and professionals with well-paid careers. Hale, ten miles from the city centre is on the edge of the green belt and is part of Trafford Metropolitan Borough within Greater Manchester (see also Taylor *et al.*'s (1996) excellent study of Manchester and Sheffield). Didsbury is only five miles from the city centre, symbolically inside the M60 orbital motorway, and falls within the city of Manchester's local government boundaries[2] (see Figure 10.1). The two neighbourhoods are similar in that they originally grew as railway suburbs, with a mixture of workers' terraces, middle-

---

2 The political boundaries of Greater Manchester have long been the source of contention (Deas and Ward 2002). Ollerenshaw (1982) noted how few successful people lived in the city of Manchester itself and paid taxes to Manchester City Council. Only the non-commercial middle class, as she called them, lived in a Manchester suburb and, unsurprisingly, that was Didsbury. Arguably, the differences between Hale and Didsbury as places – and in terms of the people who prefer to live in each of them – are still there albeit with internal differentiation as well.

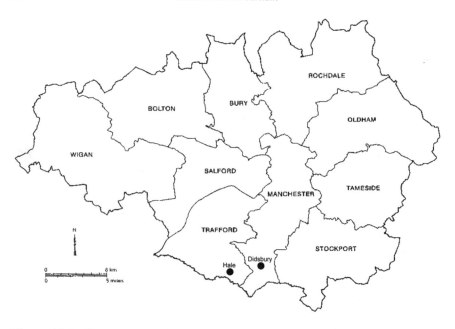

Figure 10.1   Hale and Didsbury within Greater Manchester local government boundaries

class villas and merchant-gentlemen's mansions. Today, they retain a core of large detached and semi-detached Victorian and Edwardian houses that attract high and (in the early 21st century) rapidly increasingly prices, especially if they are close to the shops in the 'village' centre. As an outer suburb, Hale has a more semi-rural residential feel to Didsbury which, as an inner suburb, has a more urban and mixed-use character. Hale's top-range prices well exceed those of Didsbury, reflecting these differences. Both have good access to the city centre and to open green spaces; they are close to the motorway network and the airport; and excellent state and public schools, NHS and private hospitals and leisure facilities are within easy reach.

The research on these two exclusive residential neighbourhoods focused specially on reactions to the development pressures that these suburbs had come under with the revitalization of Manchester's city centre economy. Property developers are constantly seeking sites, obtaining planning permission and building new developments in these two localities that, in the eyes of some locals, challenge the exclusive character of these areas, so leading to the commercialization of previously exclusive suburbs. Accordingly, interviews were conducted with some 40 key informants including property developers and estate agents, councillors and unsuccessful candidates in local elections drawn from all political parties active in the two areas, activists in civic societies, conservation schemes and residents associations, members of the Women's Institute, Soroptomists and Round Table, shopkeepers, religious leaders, community police officers, youth workers and key actors in the field of education. The interviewees were selected partly because of the key role of these organizations and partly through 'snowball sampling' among the local 'influentials'. These interviews focused on the informants' assessment of changes occurring in the two localities, the main issues that had exercised people living there recently, the property market, the quality of life and community involvement in the area, and the effects of Manchester's regeneration on the suburbs, as well as their reactions to contests over development proposals. A programme of secondary research, involving the analysis of local and citywide newspapers, documents from Manchester and Trafford Planning Departments and other relevant publications and websites on the city and the two suburbs was also undertaken.

The views of those seemingly fuelling development pressures in the exclusive suburbs, namely, the developers and the estate agents, are considered first, then reactions from activists in organizations resisting those pressures before considering a diverse range of opinions from other 'local influentials' in Hale and Didsbury. The highly contested politics of urban change will be readily apparent.

Conserving Hale

The developers that we spoke to certainly confirmed the popularity of Hale as a highly exclusive suburb. It was described as a prestigious location where people 'aspired to live as opposed to being a fashionable place'. It was a semi-rural location with 'some of the finest houses that were built in the Manchester area since the turn of the century' close to an extensive motorway network, the airport and well served with a Metro link into Manchester at nearby Altringham. That it was a leafy suburb of low density meant that property prices were extremely high and rising. Many houses were worth over £1 million pounds and, it was noted, many 'old Haleites' were happy with rising prices for it allowed them 'to live in peace and quiet and enjoy the lifestyle they have got'. Company directors and managers of large PLCs in Manchester were attracted to such areas. The developers were involved in the conversion of these detached properties into town houses and apartments to sell or rent. They were high-quality properties in small developments and, in effect, miniature 'gated communities' (Blakely and Snyder, 1997) with security gates and private parking facilities. Demand far outstripped supply and 'people are quite happy to pay a premium to live there'. The developers had a certain type of person in mind who would buy or rent: namely, young executives with high salaries who commuted from Manchester city centre. That said, they had found apartments for sale were quickly snapped by those buying for investment purposes (who would then rent out to young professionals) and people downsizing, either themselves or on behalf of their parents. The developers got 'their money back on the square footage' and more.

Development opportunities, however, were dwindling and there was increasing tension with the Trafford Metropolitan council planners as Hale was changing from a traditional quiet suburb to 'going a bit more glitzy'. Developers felt that 'if the planners don't move with the times, they are going to find that Hale becomes an even more boring place because ostensibly, there are a number of restaurants in the area, there is room for plenty more.' With the advent of big shopping complexes close by, one developer argued:

The suburban towns and villages, Altringham, Hale, Didsbury, Wilmslow, unless they adopt the attitudes that these are where people are going to live and therefore come out in the evening and do their entertaining and eating … there is no way that retailers are going to make a living in these areas.

Hale, it was stressed, is 'just getting left behind'. The estate agents shared some, though not all, of the developers' views. They also noted that Hale was 'one of most expensive areas in the region' and easily described the type of people – business people, professional people – who bought in and invariably stayed in the locality. In particular, they stressed the attraction of Trafford's selective grammar school system and the array of local private schools to aspiring residents (on school choices, see Gerwirtz *et al.*, 1995; Butler with Robson, 2003; Devine, 2004). The suburb, however, was under pressure. While restaurants might reflect changing lifestyles (Savage *et al.*, 1992; Warde and Martens, 2000) and compensate for the decline in local shopping amenities, too many restaurants made 'landlords a tad greedy' raising rents on shop premises and forcing traders to move. There was, it seemed, a 'tipping point' with such developments undermining small stores in the village.

The activists in the local civic societies, conservation groups and councillors discussed the development pressures on Hale with great passion. The pressures, it seemed, had taken and continued to take various forms from the development of the second runway at Manchester airport, changes to the motorway network nearby (Taylor, 1996), office developments and hotel extensions on the edge of the suburb, house conversions, apartment developments to the more prosaic infilling of large gardens and house extensions. All of these trends, it was argued, were increasing the population density of the suburb and reducing its leafy semi-rural feel. Increasing traffic and parking problems were eroding the greenbelt. What made Hale exclusive – a green area in which few people lived – was being destroyed. As a local activist explained:

> An attractive area to remain attractive and sought after needs its green spaces and one of the concerns is that you get to a point where you don't have your green spaces any more and eventually its not seen as such an attractive area.

The environmental pressures threatened property prices. Similarly, the increase in population density and the consequences flowing from it were noted. It was a case, one interviewee suggested, of 'cram in as much as you can into any available space without, in my opinion, really any kind of forethought as to what they are actually doing'. Such increases in population were undermining the 'semi-rural community' and the ideal that 'when you get a bit older and producing families then the ideal seem to be, you know, this ideal to be surrounded by countryside' (Champion and Fisher, 2004; Taylor *et al.*, 1996, 296–7).

The growth in the number of restaurants, wine bars and pubs also exercised local activists. The village, it was argued, now had too many of them and it had reached saturation point. The problem was they attracted too many 'outsiders' who were a nuisance late as night as they left premises, banged doors, shouted at the top of their voices and so forth (see also Taylor, 1996, 323–324). Most importantly, however, was the parking problem (as with the residential developments noted above). Outsiders, it was noted, come into the village to visit the restaurants and 'then park in the roads adjacent to the village and where people have their own parking and people are taking their parking spaces so that's an ongoing issue'. Local residents, it seems, were not pleased as drives were blocked, making parking a major preoccupation (on cars and cities see Sheller and Urry, 2000). Outsiders were problematic in other ways too. The rapid increase in the number of wine bars frequented by various celebrities attracted young people into the area who stood around on street corners, engaging in 'anti-social behaviour' and generally being 'intimidating'. These and other young outsiders were also the source of local crime including handbag snatches, car crime and vandalism against property. The view was that local youth from the council housing estates in nearby Wythenshawe and Parrington targeted the area. As one interviewee explained, 'I think it is well targeted this area because of what the area is' while another suggested, 'I think these youngsters just see all these old dears in Hale as fair game (…)I think these youngsters come in their cars and they do a sweep and off they're gone'. Outsiders were problematic in a number of respects, therefore, and the major source of Hale's crime problem (Taylor, 1996; Atkinson and Helms, 2007).

There was much anxiety about the village centre, especially the local shops, and the various threats to it. Living close to the village, it was argued, raised house prices by 30 percent and it was a case of 'location, location, location and it's the village that makes it'. The centre of the village was very highly valued. While a number of independent 'old-fashioned' shops, such as a ladies dress shop, had disappeared over the years, there were still plenty of shops for local use. Interviewees boasted about having the smallest Safeways Supermarket with the biggest takings in the country. Its popularity, it seems, stemmed from its ability to cater for the basics while have specialized lines which were 'geared to local need'. The importance of the 'local' was evident (Savage *et al.*, 2003: x). For these reasons, Hale had not suffered adversely with the opening of the Trafford Centre nearby. However, the fate of the village and its shops was under threat on two fronts. First, a number of activists were furious about the introduction of car parking charges in the village. As one interviewee suggested:

> It's a village. It is a small area and they've bought in car parking charges and it's a small area and its only 15p to park but the people don't want to park there because of the principle of the matter. It's a small area. Car parking is a problem for this area. People will say, "It's a very affluent area. Surely everyone can afford 15p?" but it's the principle. Yes, people can afford to pay. It's just the principle.

People were not popping in the local shop and trader's takings had dropped. Car parks were not being used and 'roadsides were clogged'. The effect would be 'to kill the village and local shopping'.

Trafford local authority came in for considerable criticism for the car parking charges and a local shop owner and member of the trade association said: 'We told the council it would happen. It happened because the council is not really interested. We told them this would happen and basically all they are after is a quick buck as they see it.' Charges, he argued, was tantamount to 'dropping a big lead weight on Hale traders toes'. Second, the introduction of a road development scheme to calm traffic as it passed through the village was seen as a disaster. It had involved widening the pavements and narrowing the road to slow traffic down. Leaving aside the aesthetics of pink pavements, it had caused serious bottlenecks in the village itself (compounding the problems of car parking of course) and further traffic congestion in the entrances to the village as queues built up to get into a small area. Again, the local council came in for much criticism. The authority was described at 'profoundly incompetent' and good at nothing but wasting money. Illustrating her disgust, a local councillor described a conversation with Trafford's Director of Engineering when she explained, 'I said "who was the idiot who designed the road layout in Hale village?" He said "it was me" and I said "you should be out of a job. You are a disgrace".' The village was under threat from major traffic congestion and the Trafford council, it seemed was not paying serious attention to the increasing 'busy-ness' of the area and the need for major investment in high-quality roads and pavements.

Criticism of the local authority was not confined to traffic issues, however even if it was the most contentious issue at the time of the interviews. Long-standing political grievances were voiced. An often-repeated view was that Trafford Council did not care about the south of the borough and places like Hale. As a councillor explained: 'We are lower down in their pecking order because we're supposed to be affluent'. Councillors talk about 'oh, you don't need spending money down there. You've got enough money. There are other trouble spots which need to be looked after.' Another said:

> We tend to pay the highest council tax and there is an awful lot of ill-feeling by people around here that we never see anything for it. There is millions being sucked into the north of the borough which we don't mind but please can we have our roads done?

Further to this, and irrespective of party politics, 'the balance of power is definitely in the north of the borough in Streford'. As a consequence, it was argued, nobody was concerned about development pressures in Hale. Again, as an interviewee explained:

> I think there has been too much building in the south. The remark that keeps getting thrown at us since I have been on the Council, people from the north say "well, you people in the south you have gardens which are as big as football pitches". There is a lot of jealousy.

The 'class struggle over housing' (Rex and Moore, 1967; see also Saunders, 1979) was apparent. Activists, including councillors, felt that they had no influence, they could not get things done and planning appeals were a one-way affair. Planning policies were not as stringently enforced as they should be. They could not turn to the Local Authority to protect Hale from development pressures and the consequences that flowed from them.

Of course, alternative views about change in Hale were expressed. Some of the interviewees were very happy to see increasingly numbers of very popular restaurants in the village. They generated a 'lively feel' (Williams, 1965) in the village in the evenings and made people feel safer. On the issue of crime, there were interviewees who readily acknowledged that crime was not a big issue in Hale. To be sure, there were car crime and house thefts and there was easy access into and out of the suburb. The local community policeman suggested that Hale residents were acutely security conscious however. As he suggested: 'The perception is far greater than the actuality, always. It's a fine line between awareness and fear.' Interestingly, he suggested that a preoccupation with crime derived from the lack of community in the area and furthermore, 'the richer the area, then the less community involvement they have'. Big houses, big drives and bar cars militated against casual contact with neighbours. Without this sense of community, people had turned to private security firms to 'give them piece of mind' (see also Taylor, 1996, 325; Atkinson and Helms, 2007). Another interviewee echoed this view. He said: 'You know, it's a wealthy area so it's a good area for chancing your arm so, you know, to some extent people feel slightly under threat and attack.' Noting the presence of private security vans, burglar alarms and so on, he went on to suggest:

> All these things are just little symptoms, I think, of a slight feeling of insecurity that exists in an area like this and the fact that people are well heeled actually makes them feel less secure, not more secure.

Again, it was noted that while many people formally belonged to specific community organizations, they did not contribute to the community in more informal ways.

Overall, the interviews with various types of activists and other local influentials in Hale revealed a strong sense of an exclusive suburb under threat from economic and social change. Development pressures were undermining the low density of the locality and its green semi-rural feel. Moreover, the consequences of these development pressures – namely, increased traffic and parking problems – were keenly felt. For many of the interviewees, the way in which Hale was changing was undermining the very reasons why they had moved into the area (Champion and Fischer, 2004, 121–125). The quiet semi-rural locality, populated by families (especially parents who placed a high premium on their children's education and were attracted to the local state grammar school system and array of local private schools (Butler with Robson, 2003; Devine, 2004) was being undermined. Its exclusivity was diminishing and they were fighting hard to retain it. In this respect, the regeneration of Manchester and the increasing popularity of Hale were viewed in a negative light. Indeed, many interviewees wanted to disassociate themselves from urban Manchester and Greater Manchester. As an interviewee suggested:

> We were taken up under the banner of Trafford which has never really gone very well because we have actually retained Cheshire in our address which we fought for. We did not actually want to be incorporated into Greater Manchester. I know a lot of people around here would love to go back to Cheshire. If they want to dump us, please do.

The struggle to escape the sprawling conurbation of Greater Manchester continued (Taylor *et al.*, 1996, 298). Thus, in contrast to Atkinson, the commercial preoccupations of developers were undermining exclusivity – rather than promoting it – and it was the local influentials who were struggling to keep their suburbs exclusive. The processes of urban and suburban change were highly contested in these ways.

Conserving Didsbury

The popularity of Didsbury was certainly confirmed by developers and estate agents operating in the suburb. Developers described how they were involved in converting old Victorian properties into self-contained apartments available for rent or sale. The conversions were of a high quality, with due attention to design and aesthetics, with secure on-site parking and electronic gates that were much valued. The demand for these apartments was considerable ensuring that rents, for example, were high. The demand came, as one developer put it, from well-paid 'young execs' looking for quality places to live who wanted the 'type of cosmopolitan atmosphere' to be found in the suburb (Meen and Andrew, 2004, 199–200; Robson *et al.*, 2000). As he explained:

> We find that Didsbury has been, and I think will be, very popular with people. It is very cosmopolitan, very lively. You can't drive through Didsbury at any hour of the day or night when the place is not packed with people so I think people will pay for convenience and we have offered them something there that is very convenient and suits modern life.

Thus, as in Hale, there were development pressures although they took a different form, giving Didsbury a different – youthful and fashionable – aura, to the more exclusive suburb with its older population. Developers' investment in restaurants and bars in response to demands had made it a 'vibrant' place while the increasing shortage of land for further development kept rents high. As a developer explained:

> … because it is expensive to live in, it tends to keep it in the main to where people are earning money and that is always an important thing. If you have village or town where people have to earn their money before they spend it, if it is expensive enough, it keeps its mark.

Despite its popularity, therefore, its exclusivity was not yet under threat.

The demand for housing in Didsbury was confirmed by estate agents. The suburb, it was explained, ranged from small cottages which commanded considerable prices to substantial properties although these hit a limit at half a million pounds. There were houses and apartments of all types to rent. Again, these interviewees explained the huge popularity of the suburb among young professional people. As an estate agent explained,

> The principal thing is obviously life-style. It's a very vibrant atmosphere in the village. It's quite bustling. There's a lot of activity here. You've got one or two traditional shops still here but that is rapidly being overtaken by the leisure industry with the opening of new bars, wine bars, food places and so on and so forth. It's attracting those people who like the hustle and bustle of Manchester but don't wish to live in the city centre. I also find a lot of people moving up from the south find it is very, very like many places in London, with its vibrant lifestyle and they like it.

Again, with more people eating out (Warde and Martens, 2000) the proliferation of cafes, restaurants and pubs in walking distance was commented upon favourably as was easy access to the same leisure facilities in Manchester city centre. The estate agents were aware, however, of over-development. Parking was problematic with inadequate car parking spaces. Traffic was always high. The bars and restaurants had become too popular and they were attracting the 'wrong element'. The loss of traditional shops in the village was seen as a disadvantage too in undermining a village feel and community spirit. The downside of popularity was evident.

It was these very problems that concerned the activists in the civic societies, conservation groups, local politicians and other 'influentials' that we spoke too. There was considerable concern that the suburb was in decline and the character of the area – its fine substantial houses, leafy roads and parks and village centre with local shops – were all being lost as a result of wider social trends. Some expressed anger and bitterness over the developments that were taking place in Didsbury. They described how much of their work involved advising on planning applications brought to them by residents (Parry *et al.*, 1992). They described their concern about the high level of development in the area and, most especially, the loss of or conversion of large houses into apartment complexes. Building of character, it was argued, were giving way to characterless blocks that were changing the environment of the area. They objected to apartment blocks that were four or more stories high in residential areas, lamented the loss of trees and gardens and the poor landscaping that replaced them and the increasing number of cars, lack of parking and general traffic congestion as the density of people in the area increased. While acknowledging the demand for such flats was high among young professional people, for such flats suited their lifestyles, developers and others were exploiting this demand with little regard for the area. As a member of a civic society suggested: 'If it's traditional housing, the developer doesn't get the same profit and the local authority doesn't get the same community charge do they? If they can penetrate it with as many units as they can get, obviously the income is greater.'

The proliferation of cafes, restaurants and pubs also exercised the local 'influentials' greatly. It had made Didsbury an 'evening and night-time centre'. Again, our interviewees saw these developments as part of wider social changes as young professional men and women spent less time cooking at home and more time eating out. The growth of the leisure industries in the suburb, however, was associated with rising crime. More pubs meant more people were getting drunk, engaging in acts of petty vandalism, damaging people's properties as they walked home, fighting for taxis and so forth. Indeed, some of the interviewees felt that Didsbury centre was a 'no-go' area at night as undesirable drinkers spilled out into the pavements and the atmosphere of the village felt less safe and more menacing. Fears about growing violence were expressed. In this context, some of the interviewees were upset that the local police station was about to close at a time when the 'visible presence' of the police was needed even more. As one civic society member put it:

> You get the youths come to where there is life and of course they will be happy if they have had a few drinks but then they do get rowdy. There has been a spate of young people walking down Wilmslow Road and pushing over walls, if they are a bit loose, and they have seen them and thought they would have some fun and push it over or taking gates off. It is all fun for them but it is not fun for people living here. There are other problems coming along but the police do need a higher profile. I do feel we are neglected.

The development of the leisure industries was associated with the loss of traditional shops in Didsbury village and nostalgically coupled with a sense of community (Blokland 2003). Great importance was attached to having local shops as a site where local people could meet other locals and stop and chat. It was this casual sociability that sustained a village feel – of knowing other local people as if in a small village – to Didsbury. While the village still had a bakery, greengrocers, and post office, interviewees lamented the loss of other miscellaneous stores. At the time of the interviews, there was much sadness about the closure of a local DIY store. As an interviewee explained:

> I think the closure of Griffiths felt like a deathblow really. Somehow it felt as though the community shops had managed to keep going with them. They were actually quite a strong symbol I think in the middle for the commerce in the village because they were thriving. It reinforced the fact that Didsbury is becoming almost a place for yuppies. I don't know what the right phase is, but you know what I mean.

The decision by the supermarket chain Tesco to close a small supermarket in the village and build a substantial site at the edge of the suburb, years before, was frequently referred to as well.[3] Such developments meant that the village was less of a service to the community and most notably the elderly and handicapped. Again, these developments reaffirmed the trend for people to get in their cars and shop elsewhere, exacerbating traffic problems and further eroding Didsbury as a place to shop locally (Sheller and Urry, 2000). Local traders commented on the decline of people walking and browsing in shops thereby reducing passing trade. The importance of 'local places' to people was evident again (Savage *et al*., 2003: 32).

The hostile attitude towards developers (and associated industries like building societies and estate agents taking over the high street) has been noted. Manchester City Council and its planning department also came in for considerable 'council bashing'. On local influential regarded the local authority as a 'pernicious influence' who were happy to see Didsbury go downhill. As she explained, in strong class terms:

> They don't take care of it, the council. You see, they've got their own places that they take care of in Manchester with their own constituents. They don't like Didsbury. They regard it as elitist and middle class. They will not do things. They do not reply to letters and they don't do things they should be doing and they always say the same thing. There's not money but they've got money for their projects. I really object to this because we pay very high council taxes and I don't think that we should pay a lot of money if they're not going to take care of this area. I think its classism.

Once again, it seemed, a class struggle was ongoing in the sphere of urban politics (Rex and Moore, 1967; Saunders, 1979). Others noted that increasing population

---

3 An Aldi Store had taken the place of Tesco not long afterwards but there was much disquiet about the fact that they had built of car park for only 75 spaces when it was expected to attract over 100 customers in any point in time. Since the research was completed, a small Marks and Spencer food hall has opened in the suburb catering, no doubt, for the income rich but time poor young professionals.

density was in the Council's interest for it meant that they could collect more council tax. The Council, it was argued, rarely took action against developers when they flouted planning laws so that 'the word goes around the developers, you can do what you want in Didsbury'. As one interviewee explained: 'The whole thing is weighed in favour of the developers. It's a very one-sided business.' The Council would eventually have to deal with pressures on schools and hospitals but they would only do so after the event. It led many to feel that the Council encouraged development and 'to hell with the consequences'.

It has to be said that some of the strong views expressed above, by those most active in the civic organizations and conservation societies, were not necessarily shared by other local influentials. It was noted, for example, that a number of the new developments were tastefully done and conversations of old properties were completed to a high standard. The Council and, indeed, the conservation groups, had been influential in changing planning applications and improving development plans so that they were in keeping with the character of the area. The development of more retirement complexes was wanted. Some of these interviewees were sympathetic to the position of the Council with regard to planning regulations, noting that planning laws were vague and difficult to work with. There were lots of legal loopholes in the law so that legal structures inhibited the Council as much as local people. Planning permission, for example, could not be refused on the basis of competition. The once left-wing Council that 'had had a down on any area that appeared to be affluent' had improved and even the Labour councillor, to people's surprise it seemed, had worked hard on behalf of Didsbury. With regard to local shopping facilities, a local councillor acknowledged that, 'you can't cause the clock to go back. People will always want to go into the larger shopper areas to get really important things. The question is if you need some food of something, you can still get that and you can still in Didsbury.' The 'village feel', with people strolling down to the local shops on a Saturday morning and casually meeting other locals – not unlike city *flaneurs* – had not disappeared altogether. A sense of community still prevailed.

Similarly, the increase in cafes, restaurants and pubs was not unwelcome by others. They attracted people into the village. The cafes attracted 'sophisticated professional women' and they were quite 'civilized' like those in France. The presence of lots of young people, especially students, contributed to a carnival atmosphere in the summer as people sat outside the cafes and pubs. Safety was not a problem. As a local influential stated categorically:

> I don't believe any of this garbage that it's not safe. All rubbish that. Complete rubbish. [My wife] and I walk everywhere and have never felt the remotest anxiety at any point ever. It's fantastically busier but that doesn't make it threatening. The only snag in on a summer Saturday if you happen to walk down to the village late at night you can't get across the pavement because it's so crowded, but that's hardly a safety issue. It's a nuisance.

Indeed, others rejected the link between the growth of restaurants and pubs and crime. Didsbury was not a high crime area. The local community police officer acknowledged that there was a great influx of young people attracted to the pubs and 'you've got a potential for public disorder'. That potential had never materialized into reality however. As he explained: 'We're quite on the ball down here with the licencees. We actually run a pub watch scheme in the village and if you get barred from one pub, you're barred from the lot. The licences have banned together from that point of view.' Incidents occurred, which were often 'blown out of all proportion' in local newspapers but there were few problems in comparison to other areas in Manchester.

Overall, what became apparent from these interviews was a generational conflict between older and younger members of the middle classes resident in Didsbury. Most notably, they had different family and household statuses (Heath and Cleaver, 2003; Savage *et al.*, 2003: 92) and these differences were being felt in the clash over 'urban cultures' in the suburb. The older residents, invariably the most active members of the civic and conservation organizations, sought to retain the exclusivity of the suburb including its low population density, fine substantial houses, leafy roads and parks and quiet and tranquil village centre with local shops whose use generated a sense of community. This exclusivity was increasingly under threat as a result of economic and social change of which the older residents were well aware. As one of the interviewees said: 'It is a centre for eating, drinking and financial services.' He went on to explain:

> People seem to want to come and live here but, of course, they're coming fresh to it and they accept it as it is, whereas a lot of the residents like me who've been here 50 odd years, compare it with how it used to be and I don't think the quality of life in the village is as good as it was, for example, 25 years ago.

The changing lifestyle of young professional men and women was a case in point (Meen and Andrew, 2004: 210). It was these activists who were the most resistant to change viewing the regeneration of Manchester and its suburbs from a negative perspective. Interviews with other local influentials, however, uncovered a more relaxed attitude towards the changes that Didsbury was undergoing. They were aware of the flipside of popularity – namely, over-development – and they shared similar concerns. They were not wholly resistant to change, however, embracing what they saw as some of advantages of change. The regeneration of Manchester and its suburbs was welcomed in this respect. In these ways, the development pressures and the responses to them were being played out in a somewhat different fashion in Didsbury to Hale. More local influentials were embracing change in the former than the latter.

Conclusion

This chapter has considered how exclusive suburbs are responding to urban change. The comparative focus on two such suburbs in Manchester illustrated the complexity of these responses in terms of the local political struggles over development pressures. Interestingly, the research showed that developers and estate agents are not necessarily at the forefront of creating exclusive gated communities. Rather, commercial pressures see developers want to break down exclusionary tendencies and open up the suburbs to more people – either to live there or to visit them in their leisure. It is actually middle-class residents – notably activists and other local 'influentials' with high social capital – who seek to preserve the exclusivity of where they live. The research uncovered their fears and anxieties about losing a certain 'quality of life' and how they tried to preserve it. In doing so, they sought to use their power to exclude others from enjoying their affluent lifestyles and, as a consequence, reproduce urban inequalities. The material also highlighted, however, that this result was not always a foregone conclusion since the outcome depended on the struggles between different groups. This is why Hale and Didsbury exhibited different types of exclusivity. Hale has retained its more old fashioned, more fearful exclusivity while Didsbury exudes a more vibrant openness despite being an affluent suburb.

These struggles have to be firmly located within the wider context of Manchester's regeneration and renaissance which has been accompanied by the polarization of social inequalities (Mellor 1997, 2000). They illustrate that, contrary to Putnam, the malign aspects of bonding social capital are far from a force for good. One final point needs to be made. Many of the preoccupations expressed in this chapter could be dismissed as the parochial 'bourgeois prejudices' of middle-class suburbanites. Preferences for homes in quiet semi-rural locations with little traffic, good schools and so on are not the preserve of certain sections of the population however. These aspirations are shared by a wider population (Champion and Fisher 2004: 122–124). Moreover, the development pressures are real as commercial developments of various kinds reshape the once exclusively residential suburbs into commercial centres for eating and drinking. The political responses to these capitalist developments are not unproblematic (Halfpenny *et al.* 2004: 264–267). Accordingly, we agree with Taylor's suggestion (1996: 318) that 'the utopias and dystopias of the suburban mind in England' have to be taken seriously in the study of urban social movements and, we would stress, research on the suburbs in a changing urban context.

References

Atkinson, R. and Blandy, S. (eds) (2005), *Gated Communities* (London: Routledge).

Atkinson, R. and Bridge, G. (eds) (2005), *Gentrification in a Global Context: The New Urban Colonialism* (London: Routledge).

Atkinson, R. and Helms, G. (eds) (2007), *Securing an Urban Renaissance: Crime, Community and British Urban Policy* (Bristol: The Policy Press).

Blakely, J. and Snyder, M.G. (1997), *Fortress America* (Washington, D.C: Brookings Institute).

Blokland, T. (2003), *Urban Bonds* (Cambridge: Polity).

Boddy, M. and Parkinson, M. (2004), *City Matters: Competitiveness, Cohesion and Urban Governance* (Bristol: The Policy Press).

Bognasco, A. and Le Galès, P. (2000), *Cities in Contemporary Europe* (Cambridge: Cambridge University Press).

Bourdieu, P. (1986), 'The Forms of Capital', in J.G. Richardson (eds) *Handbook of Theory and Research for the Sociology of Education* (Greenwood Press: New York).

Butler, T. (2004), 'The Middle Class and the Future of London' in Boddy, M. and Parkinson, M. (eds), *City Matters* (Bristol: Policy Press).

Butler, T. and Watt, P. (2007), *Understanding Social Inequality* (London: Sage).

Butler, T. with Robson, G. (2003), *London Calling* (Oxford: Berg).

Champion T. and Fisher, T. (2004), 'Migration, Residential Preferences and the Changing Environment of Cities', in Boddy, M. and Parkinson, M. (eds), *City Matters* (Bristol: Policy Press).

Davis, M. (1999), *Ecology of Fear* (New York: Vintage Books).

—— (2006), *City of Quartz* (London: Verso).

——(2007), *Planet of Slums* (London: Verso).

Deas, I. and Ward, K. (2002), 'Metropolitan manoeuvres: making Greater Manchester', in Peck, J. and Ward, K. (eds), *City of Revolution* (Manchester: Manchester University Press).

Devine, F. (2004), *Class Practices* (Cambridge: Cambridge University Press).

Devine, F., Britton, N.J. Mellor, R. and Halfpenny, P. (2003), 'Mobility and the Middle Classes: A Case Study of Manchester and the North West', *International Journal of Urban and Regional Research*, 27, 495–509.

—— (2000), 'Professional Work and Professional Careers in Manchester's Business and Financial Sector', *Work, Employment and Society*, 14, 521–540.

Gerwirtz, S., Ball, S.J. and Bowe, R. (1995), *Markets, Choice and Equity in Education* (Buckingham: Open University Press).

Hall, P. (1999), 'Social Capital in Britain', *British Journal of Political Science*, 29, 417–61.

Halfpenny, P., Britton, N.J., Devine, F. and Mellor, R. (2004), 'The "Good" Suburb as an Urban Asset in Enhancing a City's Competitiveness', in Boddy, M. and Parkinson, M. (eds), *City Matters* (Bristol: Policy Press).

Hancock, L. (2007), 'Is Urban Regeneration Criminogenic', in Atkinson, R. and Helms, G. (eds), *Securing an Urban Renaissance* (Bristol: Policy Press).

Harding, A., Deas, I., Evans. R. and Wilks-Heeg, S. (2004), 'Reinventing Cities in a Restructuring Region?: The Rhetoric and Reality of Renaissance in Liverpool and Manchester', in Boddy, M. and Parkinson, M. (eds), *City Matters* (Bristol: Policy Press).

Heath, S. and Cleaver, E. (2003), *Young, Free and Single* (Basingstoke: Palgrave).

Le Gales, P. (2002), *European Cities* (Oxford: Oxford University Press).

Massey, D. (2007), *World City* (Cambridge: Polity Press).

Mellor, R. (2000), 'Hypocritical City: Cycles of Urban Exclusion', in Peck, J. and Ward, K. (eds), *City of Revolution* (Manchester: Manchester University Press).

—— (1997), 'Cool Times in a Changing City', in Jewson, N. and MacGregor, S. (eds), *Transforming Cities, Contested Governance and Spatial Divisions* (London: Routledge).

—— (1989), 'Urban Sociology: A Trend Report', *Sociology*: 23, 241–60.

—— (1977), *Urban Sociology in an Urban Society* (London: Routledge).

Menn, G. and Andrew, M. (2004), 'The Role of Housing in City Economic Performance', in Boddy, M. and Parkinson, M. (eds), *City Matters* (Bristol: Policy Press).

Ollerenshaw, K. (1982), 'The Future of Our City', *Manchester Literary and Philosophical Society*, vol. 1, New Series, Manchester.

Peck, J. and Ward, K. (2002), *City of Revolution* (Manchester: Manchester University Press).

Putnam, R.D. (2000), *Bowling Alone: The Collapse and Revival of American Community* (New York: Simon & Schuster).

Rae, D.W. (2003), *City: Urbanism and its End* (New Haven, Yale University Press).

Rex, J. and Moore, R. (1967), *Race, Community and Conflict* (Oxford: Oxford University Press).

Robson, B. Parkinson, M., Boddy, M. and Maclennan, D. (2000), *The State of English Cities* (London: DETR).

Saunders, P. (1970), *Urban Politics* (Harmondsworth: Penguin).

Savage, M., Warde, A. and Ward, K. (2003), *Urban Sociology, Capitalism and Modernity*, 2nd Edition (Basingstoke: Palgrave).

Savage, M., Barlow, J., Dickens, P. and Fielding, T. (1992), *Property, Bureaucracy and Culture* (London: Routledge).

Sheller, M. and Urry, J. (2000), 'The city and the car', *International Journal of Urban and Regional Research*, 24, 7737–57.

Taylor, I. (1996), 'Fear of Crime, Urban Fortunes and Suburban Social Movements: Some Reflections from Manchester', *Sociology*, 30, 317–337.

Taylor, I., Evans, K. and Fraser, P. (1996), *A Tale of Two Cities* (London: Routledge).

Warde, A. and Martens, L. (2000), *Eating Out* (Cambridge: Cambridge University Press).

Warde, A., Tampubolon, G., Longhurst, B. Ray, K., Savage, M. and Tomlinson, M. 'Trends in Social Capital: Membership of Associations in Great Britain', *British Journal of Political Science*, 33, (2003), 515–525.

Williams, R. (1965), *The Long Revolution* (London: Penguin).

Chapter 11

Social Capital and the Formation of London's Middle Classes

Tim Butler

Introduction

In this chapter, I discuss the issue of social capital in the context of the spread of gentrification across inner London in recent decades drawing on recent empirical research (Butler with Robson 2003a).[1] In particular, I wish to show how space is actively used by middle class people – who are only relatively and not absolutely advantaged – to make new communities in the city. In different areas of the city, they create new 'habituses' through different strategies towards the area and its existing inhabitants. Thus, I show that social capital is not simply deployed to fill 'empty spaces' but rather to create new social spaces, by imposing new social boundaries with respect to the existing inhabitants of those areas. This is, I wish to suggest, a more satisfactory way – theoretically, methodologically and empirically – of looking at gentrification and its 'others' than its usual coupling with replacement or displacement (Atkinson 2001).

I utilise both Bourdieu and Putnam-type approaches to social capital, despite their different conceptual provenances, in recognition of the different components of this restructuring process. The Putnam perspective enables us to investigate the ways the bonding social capital of the disadvantaged communities – or individuals – has been replaced – fully or partly – by the bridging social capital of the incoming middle classes.[2] It is here that Bourdieu's treatment of social capital can be useful in understanding the ways in which the relatively advantaged are able to maintain their power and privilege (Butler and Robson 2001, 2145–6). However, the two usages can also be linked in the sense that inequality is a zero-sum game in which those

---

1 The research was undertaken as part of the ESRC's Cities Cohesion and Competitiveness Programme under the title of 'the middle classes and the future of London' (grant number L13025101). Dr Garry Robson who co-authored many of the earlier papers that have come out of this research undertook much of the research. His considerable influence on the ideas that came out of the research I gratefully acknowledge. I however, remain responsible for all the errors and omissions.

2 The extent to which this 'trickles down' to non middle-class residents remains to be investigated. The failure to encompass both sides of the gentrification process remains one of the great weaknesses of this work either leaving the reader with a somewhat triumphalist account of the onward march of the denizens of neo liberalism or with a sense solidarism with its victims and the loss of a working class past.

with power hold it at the expense of those without – the question being: at what spatial scale does this operate? Do the gentrifying middle classes need to maintain their relative advantage at the level of the neighbourhood or can they afford to share the advantages generated by their social and cultural capital for the benefit of both groups? In other words, can they afford to practise bridging capital locally without sacrificing inter generational social advantage?[3] Theorists of social reproduction tend to argue that an important reason for the middle classes choosing selective schooling in either the independent or state sector is to avoid precisely this kind of 'social contamination' (Power *et al.* 2003; Butler and Hamnett 2007). It therefore seems unlikely that we are going to see this form of social mixing and apparently altruistic deployment of middle-class cultural capital through their networks of social capital. There is also a danger that, when discussing social capital in relation to working and middle class groups, different concepts of social capital are being mobilised; this danger is minimized however if we look at these processes in their historical and spatial contexts.

Our findings demonstrate an interesting range of continuities and discontinuities. Taken as a whole, they are indicative of a generalised 'metropolitan habitus' which itself is sub-divided into a series of 'mini-habituses' (Butler 2002). The nature of the metropolitan habitus is not defined solely in terms of occupational affinities but a broader mix of socio-cultural attributes that distinguish between what Lockwood (1995) has defined as the 'urban-seeking' and 'urban-fleeing' middle classes.[4] Many of these attributes can be identified from experiences of higher education and the attractions offered not just by working in London's industries but by its cultural infrastructure and – crucially – the importance of living near similar people ('people like us') (Butler and Hamnett 1994; Butler 1997). However, what emerges is that there are also important nuanced differences *amongst* the cosmopolitan inner London middle classes which give rise to the different mini-habituses across gentrified inner London – and increasingly outer London (Butler *et al.*, 2008).

Warde (1991) notes a distinction between 'gentrification by collective social action' and 'gentrification by capital'. Most of the gentrification of inner London has been the former, undertaken by individual households or small developers whilst the main exemplar of the latter[5] has been restricted to the redevelopment of Docklands

---

3 Many of the points being made here about the middle classes were rehearsed in seminal studies of the middle class forty years ago by Ray Pahl (1965) and Colin Bell (1968); both drew attention to the national, as opposed to local, frame of reference of the middle class and also to the importance of extended kin and inter generational resource transfers.

4 This approach is perhaps analogous to the 'cosmopolitans' versus 'locals' distinction noted by Merton (1948) in his study of Rovere in the United States. Merton contrasted those with essentially localist attitudes to those whose reference point was the 'great society'. By analogy, the inner London middle classes, like the cosmopolitans in Rovere, see themselves as residing in a specific inner London location but living in the contemporary global society. By contrast the non metropolitan middle classes have concerns which are more rooted in their localities. Savage *et al.* (2005) argue against this approach in favour of their concept of 'elective belonging'.

5 There has been a relatively recent trend towards loft conversions in areas of the so-called 'city fringe' notably in Clerkenwell but also in Shoreditch – see (Hamnett and Whitelegg 2001, 2007).

by medium sized and large capital (Foster 1999). Thus whilst the distinction drawn by Warde has been a useful way of understanding both the process of gentrification and the explanations for it within social science (Hamnett 1991), it has tended to dichotomise what has become a much more generalised process of urban redevelopment. It is now generally accepted that there are distinctions and gradations within the gentrification process reflecting the deployment of various forms of capital by particular social groups. Préteceille's (2007) work on the gentrification of Paris, Butler and Lees' (2006) analysis of super gentrification in Islington in London and the argument about whether city centre developments are gentrification or re-urbanization (Davidson and Lees 2005; Boddy 2007) are recent examples of how the social base of gentrification processes has become increasingly differentiated. Nevertheless, the distinction drawn by Warde remains useful for understanding how the two forms of gentrification – by capital or by collective social action – can be mapped on to particular types of built environment and draw on different sources of capital and social relations.

These processes have resulted in different types of gentrification and social behaviour by their middle-class populations. The Docklands experience is much nearer to the process of 'revanchism' by which, according to Neil Smith (1996), the middle classes have retaken much of Manhattan block by block in a war against the lower classes. Elsewhere in London the process has generally been gentler if no less definitive. Whilst the overarching process has been one by which the middle classes resettled formerly working-class areas, the means by which this has taken place, the meanings which have been attached to it and the nature of the social boundaries that have been created are all different – and significant. Even where, as in Docklands, there is a formal eschewing of concerns with social capital, the process can be understood as one in which the relations (Bourdieu *and* stocks (Putnam) of social capital are transgressed and transformed from their old forms of associations into new ones. These new associations sometimes result in networks whilst elsewhere these remain non existent, nascent or latent; in these cases they are only likely to emerge in a time of serious external threat.

In the areas of 'collective social action', this has not been a uniform process; the process by which their largely working-class communities were disrupted by middle-class settlement has varied considerably. In addition, the deployment of cultural, economic and social capital amongst the middle classes between these areas has been complex and has varied according to the nature of the local habitus. I suggest that it is the variable geometry of the interaction between these forms of capital that accounts for the differences in commonly-held perceptions by local middle classes of their social habitus. Spatiality is central to the construction of these mini-habituses (Butler 2002).

Each of our case study areas is characterised by different modes and levels of social capital – both in terms of resources and deployment. In all our cases, formerly deprived 'undesirable' or simply 'uncool' areas have been – to a greater or lesser extent – transformed and made congenial to the requirements of middle-class life. This has invariably been a two stage process: firstly, the old associations of a working class community have been broken and second those of the new middle classes have been imposed and in so doing have, in some places, become embodied in distinctive social networks.

The remainder of the chapter is structured as follows. The next section discusses the level of social capital in terms of association found amongst its gentrifying respondents compared to that found in some national studies. In the following section of the chapter, I take up the issue of 'spatial naïveté' raised in the editors' introduction, in relation to what I see as the variable geometry of 'habitus construction'. There then follow some conclusions, in which I argue that the broad conception of social capital is helpful in understanding the process of class re-composition that is taking place in inner London. In other words, I start with associational social capital as described by Putnam and then seek to broaden this to examine wider social relations in order to assess whether this associational social capital is generating bridging or bonding social capital. I also suggest that the different relations of social capital found between gentrifying populations and their local 'others' may provide a more helpful way of understanding the dynamics of gentrification in a fast changing city such as London than a concern with the static and totalising concepts of replacement and displacement.

Gentrification and Stocks of Social Capital in Inner London

The research on which this chapter is based was carried out in inner London between 1998 and 2001 and involved in-depth interviews with 75 respondents in each of six fieldwork areas (see Figure 11.1) – full details of the research and the methodology adopted can be found in Butler with Robson (2003a). This research has generated a number of papers looking at some of the wider aspects of the gentrification process, notably the (non) relations with other social groups the structure of which we have termed 'social tectonics' (Robson and Butler 2001), how the deployment of social capital has varied in three south London gentrified neighbourhoods (Butler and Robson 2001), the interaction of education and housing markets (Butler and Robson 2003b), super gentrification amongst global elites in Islington (Butler and Lees 2006) and the nature of the gentrification process in Docklands (Butler 2007). All of these have focused on the narratives of the gentrifying populations and their perceptions of the ways in which their sense of space and place have informed not only their self identity but also their relations with their fellow gentrifiers and other local residents.

In the remainder of this section of the chapter, I discuss the levels of associational social capital that are exhibited in these six areas. Taken as a whole, the same low level of involvement in formal associations noted by Putnam characterises the life of respondents in all areas. Respondents were asked a series of questions which might indicate their level of activity in their neighbourhoods and with non-work-based associations – unfortunately none of these were directly comparable with the data analysed by Warde (2003), Li *et al.* (2003) or Hall (1999). The overwhelming impression from the responses was that there were three focuses for involvement: work, household and what might be termed 'play' – and much of the latter took place in the household. Eighty per cent of respondents 'went out' (i.e. for some social or

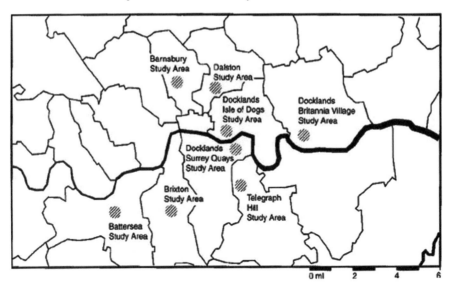

Figure 11.1   London, showing the study areas

cultural activity) at least once a week but the range of these activities demonstrated a low involvement in formal activities. For example, only 15 per cent were active in any neighbourhood association, 9 per cent in an amenity association (supporting for example the local park) and only 8 per cent in a neighbourhood watch association. This figure varied between areas but not significantly. However, whilst not directly comparable, these figures appear to show considerably more involvement than those quoted by Li *et al.* (2003, 2002) from the Oxford Mobility Survey and the British Household Panel Survey. These studies (for Britain in 1999) reveal that 9 per cent of women were involved in tenant/resident groups and 1.9 per cent in other community/ civic groups (2002: Table 3.1) – the figures for men are even lower (Li *et al.* 2002). However, these figures cover all social groups and we know that the most active groups in terms of associational social capital are middle class, so we would expect our figures to be higher than for the population as a whole. The gender issue is more complex and I return to this below.

When we compare our figures with the national ones for involvement in schooling, similar disparities occur. Fourteen per cent of the inner London respondents with school age children were active in the Parent Teacher Association (PTA) and 15 per cent took part in school activities; a similar percentage reported their partners were active which, given the quite strict division of labour some busy families operated, would probably boost the overall household involvement by up to 50 per cent. Of these, approximately a quarter held some position in the PTA and 42 per cent for the neighbourhood association. Compared to the national figures reported by Li *et al.* (2003) in which 6.5 per cent of respondents were involved in PTAs, these measures of involvement seem high but again there are caveats: firstly these figures reflect parents with school age children whereas the national figures represent all respondents and secondly, once again, we would expect a higher figure from middle-class parents. In similar research amongst affluent middle-class parents in Wilmslow, Cheshire reported by Bagnall *et al.* (2003), 80 per cent reported some involvement with the PTA and 63 per cent as having been involved on the committee or regularly attending meetings. In working class Cheadle the 'some involvement' figure fell to 35 per cent, indicating the steep class gradient that applies to these measures of social capital.

Given the general importance of education and neighbourhood amongst the London respondents and their anxieties about educational attainment (Butler and Robson 2003b), these appear to be remarkably low levels of involvement when compared to the very similar group in Cheshire. They may be indicative of different forms of involvement amongst the metropolitan middle classes in which nearly all adult household members were in full time paid employment. This compares to Wilmslow where many more women did not undertake paid employment outside the home and had followed their husbands to Manchester and appeared to use the relatively weak ties of PTA involvement to build a social life for the family. In London, the households were often quite long established in the neighbourhoods and the attitudes to schooling and education were perhaps more instrumental, favouring fewer but stronger ties. These often involved more informal and personal ways of supporting one's child through an increasingly competitive education market. Similar considerations applied in relation to how they identified with the neighbourhood. Joining formal associations fails to command such a premium as it used to, partly because this is not seen as effective and partly because of what was sometimes seen as an anti-collectivist ethos. Whilst the 'sense' of belonging to a locality was highly desirable, this did not extend to 'investing' in it ('putting something back') in any formal sense such as by being a local councillor or even school governor. To some extent, this finding is compatible with the work undertaken by Stephen Ball (2002) on 'schooling strategies' which he emphasises are individually constructed and crafted to the needs of the particular child. Following this, the household is then mobilised to insert the subject of these strategies into these yet-to-be-realized contexts. This requires less formal involvement in school governance and more in terms of individual support – which often takes the form of private tuition to supplement what is (or is not) being learned at school. More generally, it suggests that the real power of social capital does not lie with formal associations but rather with blending the considerable cultural capital of the gentrified household and carefully selected institutions of the public and private sphere. This is not to deny that such 'civic duty' is still undertaken, but it was very rare and usually involved the older retired, or early-retired, respondents. This might be something that is quite specific to the 'metropolitan habitus' but seems more likely to be a function of busy home/work lives (Jarvis 2005).

Of those that did belong to non work associations, the largest single category was some form of sporting association (19 per cent) followed by what I term 'campaigning' charitable organizations, such as Friends of the Earth or Greenpeace (13 per cent). The actual figures are given in Table 1 for the first mentioned activity that respondents gave. Care should be taken in interpreting these results because respondents often belonged to more than one such category and the order in which they cited them did not necessarily imply a rank order of importance. Overall 54 per cent of respondents were involved in some formal non work association which is comparable to the national pattern. Where applicable, figures from Li *et al.* (2002) are given to provide a context drawn from a national and pluri-social class sample.

Table 11.1   Membership of voluntary organizations

Type of Association	Example	Per cent	Valid per cent	National 1999[1] Fe/Male
'Do Good Charity'	St Martin's in the Field Crypt	2	4	
Campaigning Charity	Greenpeace	7	13	
Conservation Charity	National Trust	3	5	
Active Culture	Choir	4	8	
Passive Culture	Friends of the Tate	8	13	
Active Leisure	London Cycling Campaign	5	9	
Sport	Kickboxing Club	10	19	14.0/26.1
Religion	Church	5	8	11.1/7
Social Club	Army & Navy	2	3	7.0/17.9
Others		10	19	
None		46	0	48.6/40.6
Total (n=440)		100	10 0	

[1] Taken from Li, Savage *et al.* (2002) 3.1 Table 1.

Thirteen per cent of respondents belonged to a political party – this figure was four times greater than the national figures given by Li *et al.* (2002). Ninety four per cent claimed that they would vote if there were a general election tomorrow. Whilst these figures do not support the notion of growing political agnosticism, neither do they translate into political involvement because very few saw either belonging to a party or voting as demanding any involvement or commitment. Only three per cent saw their party membership as an active involvement, for the remainder it was a personal statement of position, and indicative of an 'expressive politics'.[6] This is borne out by the almost total lack of involvement in local (or national) politics by, for example, standing for public office or taking on a position in the political party.

What mattered were friends; friendship was what sustained their social networks. There were three main sources of friendship: those formed from childhood or, more usually, university; from work, and; from the locality or through their children. Although work was the single biggest source of friendship, in most cases, at least one of the friendships was originally made at university. In nearly half of the cases, the respondent's best friend lived either in the locality (i.e. the commonly accepted research area) or in the borough and in nearly 85 per cent of cases lived in London (see Figures 11.2 and 11.3). These friendships tended to be with people like themselves and it might be argued that their social networks were embodiments of their cultural capital. This appears to be something intrinsic to the 'metropolitan habitus':

> Friendship and friendship-based associations have become an increasingly important part of the urban social glue, many of whose pleasures lie simply in relating to others. Even though the forging of the bonds of friendship may be the result of the increasing emphasis on relationship as a value in itself, such bonds take us back to the very roots of cities as sites of association, and through this, political organization. Thus what may seem routine, even trivial, may have all manner of political resonances that we are only just beginning to understand – and mobilize (Amin and Thrift 2004) 235.

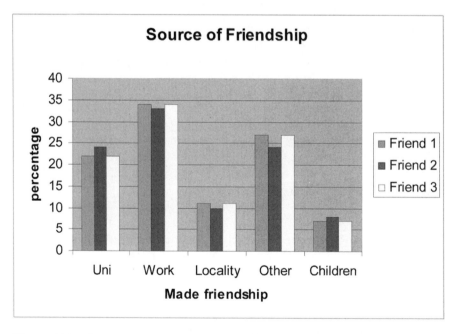

Figure 11.2   Origin of respondents' friendships

---

6 I am grateful to Mike Savage for this phrase which he applied to a similar group in Chorlton, Manchester.

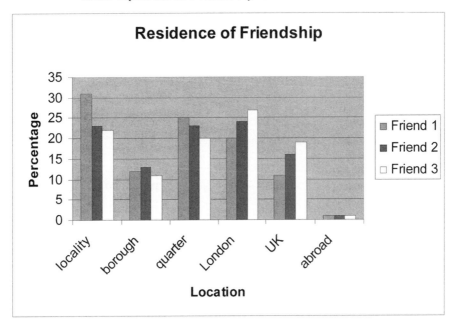

Figure 11.3   Where respondents' friends lived

If we take these measures together, it is clear that involvement tends to be personal and to be focused around the major activities of the household – work, education and the locality. The involvements are not collective in terms of the kinds of associations referred to by Putnam such as club membership, trade unions etc. Whilst 40 per cent belonged to a trade union, most said that this was for purely instrumental reasons such as employment protection, legal liability or insurance and not for any sense of social solidarism. In other words, the metropolitan middle classes do not appear to support a civic public realm but tend to have privatized, particularized friendship ties which are also more socially exclusive (Li *et al.* 2003).

My findings are similar to those of Andreotti and Le Galès (see Chapter 7), who also question the long standing sociological assumption that middle-class networks tend to be non-local (Bell 1968). The role of friendship has been subject to recent sociological work by, for example, Pahl (2000) and Allen (1989; 1996); this work shows how, with the decline of family and kinship, friendship has become increasingly salient and important and drawn from similar age, gender, class and ethnic groups – see also Li *et al.* (2003) and Spencer and Pahl (2006). Pahl (2000) shows that these notions of friendship nurture the notion of 'moral excellence' and are thus consonant at least with the normative associations made with social capital referred to in the editors' introduction of this volume. As Allan argued (1996: 7) the home is a crucial element in middle class notions of friendship and asking people into it for dinner is probably the best single indicator of 'becoming friends' which is also a crucial means of belonging in a middle-class community – we found that 40 per cent of respondents had had friends around for dinner in the last fortnight and 70 per cent in the previous month. In both inner London and the more affluent parts of the North West, these personal networks were rooted in their neighbourhoods and sense of place and overlapped often with key stages in respondents' personal and professional formation (Butler with Robson 2003a; Savage *et al.* 2005). This will be demonstrated in the next section where, despite the different strategies towards social capital which characterised the different areas, there nevertheless emerges a sense that 'social clustering' is made up by 'people like us'.

Social Capital in Inner London: The Difference Space Makes

In this section, I examine the role played by social capital in making the research areas into middle-class gentrified spaces. Whereas in the first part of the chapter, the focus was on the stocks of social capital associated with these middle class communities in the broad Putnam sense of the term, in this part I look at the term in the more dynamic sense used by Bourdieu. In the first part, I took inner London as a container for the 'metropolitan habitus' and did not look at differences between the various areas; here, I am concerned with the way in which spatial differentiation occurs and is at the centre of ways in which social capital, as part of Bourdieu's trinity of capitals, is deployed. In what follows I argue that social capital, in the Bourdieuvian sense, is at the heart of the different strategies to make the areas middle-class although how this happens shows considerable variation.

In Bourdieu's (1986: 246–50) model *Economic capital* refers to monetary income and other financial resources and assets, finding its institutional expression in property rights. *Cultural capital* exists in various forms, expressing the embodied dispositions and resources of the *habitus*. This form of capital has two analytically distinguishable strains, *incorporated*, in the form of education and knowledge, and *symbolic,* being the capacity to define and legitimise cultural, moral and aesthetic values, standards and styles. *Social capital* refers to the sum of actual and potential resources that can be mobilised through membership in social networks of actors and organizations. Critically, this involves 'transforming contingent relations, such as those of neighbourhood, the workplace, or even kinship, into relationships that are at once necessary and elective, implying durable obligations subjectively felt (feelings of gratitude, respect, friendship, etc.)' (Bourdieu 1986: pp. 249–50). This makes this form of capital more of a relational phenomenon than a tangible, or easily quantifiable, resource. There are three key aspects to understanding the mobilization of resources by the gentrifiers in the different research areas. Firstly, as has already been argued in Chapter 1, social capital differs from economic and cultural capital in that it is a relationship and not a stock. In this sense, it is often latent and – hypothetically – social capital becomes more manifest in a 'spatially delimited area' when the stocks of economic and/or cultural capital are relatively marginal. Secondly, I suggest that, in making these places into middle class communities, the 'idea' of the area and of how it 'might be' is of critical importance. This is what Pahl (1965) termed, in an earlier piece of research on the settlement of the countryside by middle class incomers, a 'village in the mind'. The achievement of these ideals of place-making requires the differential deployment of all three forms of capital in a process that might be termed 'imagineering' (Rutheiser 1996). In the case of

Docklands, this was undertaken by specialists in marketing, elsewhere it was the outcome of 'collective social action' (Warde 1991). Finally, I argue that friendship plays an important role in the spatialization of social capital in inner London. We saw in the previous section how embedded the concept of friendship was in respondents' personal formation with usually at least one of their three 'best friends' not just going back to university days but often living in the same area of London.

In each area, we can describe the 'idea' of the area held in the minds of most of those who have gone to live there; this in turn can be related to the way in which social capital is deployed in terms of associations or, in some cases, clearly identifiable social networks. Docklands, stands apart from these generalizations in two respects: firstly, that its main attraction is that there is a formal eschewal of the obligations of social capital (partly because these networks exist elsewhere) and secondly because the 'idea' of the area is the outcome of a sophisticated programme of place marketing as opposed to collective social action (Butler 2007). People who are attracted to living in Docklands want a 'low maintenance' existence both physically (new build with uPVC windows) and socially (no obligation to interact with fellow residents) in an environment where taste and distinction (old waterside cranes and other manifestations of gentrification kitsch) are carefully crafted and restored.

Elsewhere in inner London these aspects of gentrified living were indicative of high levels of cultural capital which enabled them to 'appreciate' the significance of the past and to craft the important signifiers of them out of several generations of remodelling of what were essentially Victorian lower middle-class dwellings (Jager 1986).

Whilst all areas had high levels of cultural capital, what did vary was the amount of economic capital and the ways in which social capital was deployed – to some extent, the two appeared to be linked. In Barnsbury and Battersea, which were both sites of relatively longstanding gentrification (Power 1973; Munt 1987; Carpenter and Lees 1995), stocks of economic capital were high with household incomes predominantly in the six-figure range.[7] In both cases, stocks of cultural capital were also high, but particularly so in Barnsbury where they had mostly been educated at the elite colleges of Oxford and Cambridge Universities ('Oxbridge'). Where they differed was in their notion of the imagined community and how they managed their deployment of social capital.

In Barnsbury, the attraction of the area was precisely its reputation as a gentrified area with a 'social capital rich' past, laid down as it were by previous generations of gentrifiers, typified by the 'Stringalongs' in the Mark Boxer cartoon 'Life and Times in N1' that appeared for many years in *The Times*. This is an urban middle class which practises, as the journalist Nicholas Tomalin (the original model for the Mark Boxer cartoon) put it, 'conspicuous thrift' (Carpenter and Lees 1995: 298). Islington's attraction was rooted in the image of an earlier age of socially inclusive gentrification – despite the reality of its highly priced and specialized kitchen shops, delicatessens and restaurants as well as its increasingly disenchanted 'others': ' ... the place does somehow manage to maintain a balance of extremes: even the rich

---

7 In many ways, these people were comparable to the middle class folks living in Wilmslow in Savage *et al.*'s study (Savage *et al.* 2001; Savage *et al.* 2005).

lawyers have been of the "right sort".' (BY54) – see Butler and Lees (2006) for a discussion of how this has transmuted into super gentrification.

They themselves however, have insufficient time or inclination to service the requirements of the social capital rich heritage into which they have bought and their social networks are increasingly mediated through the market – for example, not one respondent had a child at state secondary school in the borough (Butler and Robson 2003b). There is then a 'lack of fit' between the economic reality and social rhetoric; this enables the middle classes to forgo deploying their social capital into local institutions but cluster amongst people like themselves – largely because of the lack of any form of corresponding cultural capital amongst 'the locals'.

> I was amazed at how polarized it was when we first came. There's people like us and then the people on the council estates – they are very different from us, they don't seem to have resources, personal resources … I went to a children's fancy dress partly last week with my daughter. I made her a fairy costume, but most of the other kids had things that had just been bought from the shops – they only seem to have what's beamed into them or what they can buy. As my husband says, they seem inert, there's no leaven in the mix, nothing to help them improve, there seems to be nothing to draw on – these are the ones who have been left behind while others – like our builder – have moved out. They won't mix with us, not because of our money, but because they live in their own world, which is very different from ours. (BY43)

In Battersea, the manifest interest is based explicitly around the possession and deployment of economic capital; in purchasing education for example. To some extent, consumption relations form the basis of social networks – 'eating out versus joining in'. This is the attraction of the place and why people want to live there: all the good things of life are available in 'Nappy Valley' – the name afforded to Northcote Road with its well-known infrastructure of consumption. Nevertheless, despite a discourse about the primacy of economic relations, there are active intra middle-class social networks built around the institutions of private consumption – schools, health clubs and bars. In effect, the discourses of cultural, economic and social capital co-exist albeit dominated largely by the possession of large stocks of economic capital which have – for the most part – determined the ethos of the area. This is not a place to live if you feel unhappy about SUV's or want to express a degree of ambivalence about the nature of gentrification, as one more sensitive soul observed:

> The life has been sucked out of it [the area] … the old street market, the vibrancy, are gone … and this was one of my main reasons for moving here originally … There seems to be no daytime provision now, nothing for the local people … But Northcote Road is more anonymous, and anonymity is a poor side effect of gentrification. (BA13)

In economic terms, Barnsbury and Battersea are very similar, with house prices and stocks of cultural capital in Barnsbury even higher than those in Battersea. In both areas, there is a highly symbolic infrastructure of consumption based around its main street (Upper Street and Northcote Road respectively) which is the main meeting ground for its residents. However, the discourses of social capital could not be more different: Wandsworth was the 'wunderkind' of the Thatcher years with its privatized services and supply of selective state and private schools, whereas

Islington is the home of the Blair project (the Blair-Brown succession pact being allegedly negotiated over dinner at the Granita restaurant). Barnsbury and Battersea provide two very different discourses of social capital for the relatively advantaged in the inner city – those of social inclusion versus 'revanchism' (Smith 1996) – and, in terms of social capital, it is the perception that matters rather than the fact that the social practices on the ground may be remarkably similar.

The remaining three non-Dockland areas were less economically advantaged than Barnsbury and Battersea and had all been more recently gentrified which was manifested in part at least by the lack of similarly gentrified infrastructures of consumption. They all however offered distinctive different approaches to the conundrum of gentrification – how to maintain social dominance in the absence of the overwhelming economic dominance evidenced in Upper Street and Northcote Road. It is worth returning to the definition given above by Bourdieu of the various forms of capital. He defined two sub species of cultural capital – 'incorporated' which basically referred to higher education qualifications and 'symbolic', as 'being the capacity to define and legitimise cultural, moral and aesthetic values, standards and styles'. In each of these three areas (Brixton, London Fields and Telegraph Hill) there were very different 'takes' on this which had to with 'idea' of the area and the nature of the social networks, all of which achieved – in their different ways – the cultural, moral and aesthetic values, standards and styles of the individual areas in ways that could be seen to be constitutive of their respective and distinctive habituses. The middle classes in all three areas had adopted different 'place making strategies'. Only in Telegraph Hill was there an explicit deployment of social capital, in the other two the area was made distinctive by what could be seen as a self-denying ordinance arising from being white and middle and class but which, of course, like the earlier notion of 'conspicuous thrift' in Islington is highly distinctive.

The key feature of Telegraph Hill is that of the 'urban village' (Gans 1982) and it was this 'village in the mind' ethos, discussed first forty years ago by Ray Pahl (1965) that distinguished it from other areas of inner London in the minds of its middle-class inhabitants. 'It's a very attractive area, with a lovely view. It's like a haven, with tree-lined streets and an almost country feel' (TH42). These people are drawn mainly from the public and welfare sectors of employment and correspond to Savage *et al.*'s (1992) concept of *ascetics:*

> … We're into architecture and keeping the original features. The trees and mix of people mean a lot to us, the social mix, actors, artists, people from all sorts of backgrounds. There's a lack of stereotyping, they're not all working in the city, or as solicitors. It's an intelligent group of people, on the whole. So the environmental and the social go together. (TH12)

In reality of course, these differences arise out of a very restricted range of the liberal middle classes but the idea of the 'environmental and the social go[ing] together' is a key element to the formation of their social networks in which like-minded souls are able to support each other. In Telegraph Hill, more than anywhere else in the study, the sense of place is wrapped up in social networks which, to some extent at least, compensate for the relatively low level of economic capital (Butler and

Robson 2001; Robson and Butler 2001). This is deployed particularly in relation to social reproduction by constructing educational strategies for their children (Ball *et al.* 1995; Butler and Robson 2003b); the local primary school is the focus for the middle-class community.

> Telegraph Hill is a small community, near to the school, a close knit area. We socialize with people from school who live in the area as well … (TH44).

Although middle-class children are in a minority in the school, their parents have been able to transform the ethos of the school into one that is middle class and the relationships formed at the primary school then dominate the area and last long after the children have moved onto secondary education (Butler and Robson 2003b). This social capital enables them to identify suitable tracks into and through secondary education, even when lack of means rules out private education. Telegraph Hill respondents assiduously cultivated social capital, particularly in the sense defined above by Bourdieu (1986: 249) ('… transforming contingent relationships, such as those of neighbourhood …') to make Telegraph Hill a refuge from the global city and the to mitigate the downsides of the professional role as proposed by Sennett (1998).

London Fields is a similar area to Telegraph Hill – in terms of respondents' occupations and their outlooks – but there is nothing like the same explicit level of deployment of social capital within the group of middle-class respondents. The similarly high levels of cultural capital are deployed more individually by households. Both areas have a park but, whereas in Telegraph Hill this is clearly middle-class territory in which children play with relatively low levels of parental supervision, in London Fields the park is largely dominated by local black youth and is off-limits for unsupervised middle-class children: 'we don't really want them to become part of the local black gang culture, becoming the kind of kids you see patrolling London Fields' (LF41).

If Telegraph Hill was an (urban) 'village in the mind', in London Fields, by contrast, part of the attraction was its identification with the local borough (Hackney) and its radical (or so it was assumed)[8] working-class *urban* past. This fitted with the class background of respondents who tended to be more upwardly (or downwardly) mobile than in other areas. Identity derived from an identification with the 'idea' of Hackney, despite the fact that most of their non middle-class neighbours are no longer working class:

> London is losing its middle: you've either got people like us or refugee families in the local primary school … . School is where you really see it. (LF25)

---

8 London Fields is located in the London Borough of Hackney which is one of the poorest and worst performing boroughs in London. Whilst it is always associated in the public mind with being working class, it was never particularly radical. Whilst during the interwar years boroughs like West Ham and Battersea were associated with radical challenges to the existing authority of central government, Hackney was a model of moderation under Peter Mandelson's grandfather Herbert Morrison.

So, it is a kind of oppositional notion of social capital that loosely holds this middle class community together in a close identification with place quite unlike that in Telegraph Hill, Barnsbury or Battersea. In addition, there are few attempts to control the local institutions, be it the park or the school. Unlike Telegraph Hill, where cultural capital is distributed into carefully nurtured social networks for collective advantage, in London Fields it is invested in far more individual ways – 'it's difficult to know what to do. All we can do is try and equip them with a strong sense of personal identity and self-worth.' (LF41)

Brixton represents a yet different 'take' on urban gentrification from either of the two models just discussed in which there is an almost wilful disavowal of middle-class social capital. Whereas the other fieldwork areas were previously remembered for their largely working class antecedents, in the case of Brixton it was, until recently, *the* centre of African Caribbean settlement. In contrast to the idea of working class radicalism in the case of London Fields or the inclusive urban village in Telegraph Hill, it was the idea of multiculturalism that attracted people to Brixton – 'I like the cultural diversity, the weird and wonderful vegetables and so on. ... The Afro-Caribbean flavour is great.' (BN21) In practice, as elsewhere, the middle classes led entirely separate and parallel lives to their non white, non middle-class neighbours – a situation we have described elsewhere as 'tectonic' (Robson and Butler 2001). Like London Fields, but more so, what characterises the gentrification of Brixton is the rampant individualism and the flight from social obligation. This is perhaps best illustrated by contrasting it to the process of middle-class community building that we noted in Telegraph Hill. In Brixton, respondents were actively escaping the desire to build middle class communities and celebrating the difference of the area whilst, as we have noted, not actually interacting with other social groups. What becomes apparent, is that this appears to be unable to sustain a stable middle class community. For example, those living in Brixton were least able to manage the problems of the London schooling system and appeared to be the most likely to leave London altogether particularly when the children reached secondary school age (Butler and Robson 2003b). They had neither the economic nor the social capital resources to deal with the problem unlike in Barnsbury, Battersea and Telegraph Hill nor did they appear able or willing to create the individual solutions adopted by respondents in London Fields. This may also be indicative of lower stocks of cultural capital together with an unwillingness to deploy them either individually (as in London Fields) or collectively (as in Telegraph Hill). Their attempts to colonise a primary school and transform its ethos to a middle class one was in stark contrast to that practised in Telegraph Hill.

> It's difficult to know what to do. Sudbourne is our nearest school, but I couldn't get my daughter in there. A few of us in this street had the same problem, so we decided together to send our kids to 'Finniston' [not its real name], try to bring it up that way ... it hasn't really worked, that group of kids have just sort of become an isolated clique in the school in general. It's not ideal ... (BN21)

Just as in London Fields, the area's immediate past and the social capital that arose from it – in this case the bonds of ethnicity – have been disrupted but in sedimented form they constitute an 'idea' of the place that very powerfully informs its current middle-class settlement.

These nuances of difference in social capital are tied up with the spatially specific notions of the habitus in each area; respondents both sought out such areas and then became – to an extent – socialised by them. It was this which both distinguished them from other social groups (mainly the largely economically inactive working class) and from other groups of gentrifiers elsewhere in inner London. In other words, their identity was tied up in 'the city' (i.e. inner London) but also their particular part of the city (e.g. Barnsbury, Brixton or Telegraph Hill). This contrasts strongly with respondents in Docklands in which notions of urban living were entirely different. Crudely, for its middle-class residents, Docklands was 'in the city' but not 'of the city' (Butler 2007). It was an adjunct to work and its attraction was Docklands' accessibility to the city yet its disassociation from urban life.

Docklands represented the creation of a marketed 'community' through the destruction of a prior working class way of life, iconic of working class culture (Young and Willmott 1962); yet for many, the attraction of its gentrification was symbolised by the retention of the dockworking cranes in front of the waterside homes. However, the shadow of a previous working class community hung heavily over the area, which somewhat perversely accounted for its attraction to a middle class who were averse to forming relationships in the area. This was entirely unlike the somewhat wilful disavowal of social capital in Battersea, London Fields and particularly Brixton in which it nevertheless remained a powerfully latent force. The difference in Brixton was that when respondents came up against the perceived inadequacies of the education system, they tended to throw up their hands in horror and, in many cases, leave London altogether for the shires.

In Docklands our respondents had only minimal social contact with the area in which they lived, other than as somewhere they left early in the morning and often returned to late at night.

> … I like it because it's not congested – we don't need the services so the quality of the provision doesn't bother us. We like the anonymity – I don't know whether the people I see around the place are my neighbours or not. I can't tell. (BV7)

The environment was one in which respondents' descriptions of the area matched those of the marketing brochures, with their emphasis on 'ease of living' and security. This was not minimalist loft living in the twenty-four hour city (Hamnett and Whitelegg 2007), it was rather a much tamer, suburban view of living without social contact, social context or social conflict (Butler 2007). The Dockland respondents had very low levels of associational social capital – mainly out of choice, often because their social existence was elsewhere and they treated their flat or town house simply as a pied-à-terre during the week. The result was that they took no trouble to justify their displacement of the previous residents, here they crossed the boundary with no sensitivity or interest in maintaining or creating new boundaries with other social groups. This represented the naked power of economic capital, untamed by conscience or indeed the self interest that elsewhere required some genuflection in the direction of social inclusion.

Conclusions

We were working with two notions of social capital – that originating from the work of Robert Putnam and that from the work of Pierre Bourdieu. The former is concerned, for the most part, with social connectedness and its implications – getting by and getting on. Putnam's social capital is largely vested in communities through voluntary associations and other such groups. In many ways, these were largely working class institutions the high water mark of whose existence was probably in the 1960s. Bourdieu is more concerned about understanding the relation between capitalism and social behaviour and this analysis co-locates social capital with that of cultural and economic capitals. For Bourdieu, as we have noted, social capital flows through social networks and is a relational concept.[9]

We found evidence of both but at different times and in different contexts. Gentrification – in whatever form – represents a destruction of the Putnam kind of social capital (largely of the white working class but to a lesser extent and in a different way also in the bonds of oppressed ethnic groups). It is epitomised by dockworking communities in East London living in what Lockwood (1966) termed 'occupational communities'. Generally this has not been replaced either on a cross class or intra class basis: we found very little evidence for social capital of the bridging or bonding variety – even in Telegraph Hill; middle class life is simply not like that. In some areas, notably Brixton, there was evidence of a conscious avoidance of what might be termed the obligations of social capital but this was not the same as the avoidance of social interaction and was something for which they paid a price if and when they had school age children. Only in gentrified new-build Docklands was there a studied absence of both. However, with this major and important exception, each area had a different form of 'bonding/bridging' mechanism which involved a complex interaction between cultural, economic and social capital in delineating emerging social boundaries. The deployment of social capital tended to rely on the possession of high amounts of cultural capital – that, in a sense, is what gentrification is about and it points out a very clearly delineated social boundary. Bourdieu, quoted at the beginning of this chapter, defines cultural capital as having two forms which express the 'embodied dispositions and resources of the habitus' namely *incorporated* and *symbolic*. The latter he sees as the ability to define and legitimise cultural, moral and aesthetic values, standards and styles. This is what gentrification entails; it transforms an area, in which the middle-class incomers are nearly always in a numerical minority, into the image of those who are able to define its 'shape and feel'. This, as we have seen in this chapter, takes many forms whether it is in the small shops and restaurants of Barnsbury or Battersea, the funky multiculturalism of Brixton or the enclaves of London Fields or Telegraph Hill. In Docklands this is something that is constructed by the marketing departments of the developers with the icons of water and historical relics of its previous incarnation. In all of these areas, these symbols exist 'in the mind' and it is this realization of

---

9 Whilst not wishing to underplay the significance of Bourdieu's work, it should of course not be forgotten that, for many Marxists, capitalism is above all defined by reference to the social relations of production – eg. (London Edinburgh Weekend Return Group 1980).

cultural capital into social networks that help constitute the mini-habituses in each area and demarcate the boundaries around them. The fact that the socially inclusive rhetorics here are not lived out and result in social distance (social tectonics) is not important; these images matter to the residents and it is only those with the appropriate levels of incorporated cultural capital that are able to capture the nuances of the symbolic messages.

References

Allan, G. (1989), *Friendship: Developing a Sociological Perspective* (New York: Harvester Wheatsheaf.)

Allan, G. (1996), *Kinship and Friendship in Modern Britain* (Oxford: Oxford University Press.)

Amin, A. and Thrift, N. (2004), 'The Emancipatory City', in Lees, L. (ed.), *The Emancipatory City? Paradoxes and Possibilities* (London: Sage) pp. 231–235.

Atkinson, R. (2001), 'The hidden costs of gentrification displacement in central London', *Journal of Housing and the Built Environment*, 15: 307–326.

Ball, S., Bowe, R. and Gewirtz, S. (1995), 'Circuits of schooling a sociological exploration of parental choice of school in social class contexts', *Sociological Review*, 43: 52–78.

Bell, C. (1968), *Middle Class Families: Social and Geographical Mobility* (London, Routledge & Kegan Paul).

Boddy, M. (2007), 'Designer neighbourhoods: new-build residential development in non metropolitan UK cities – the case of Bristol', *Environment and Planning A* 39(1): 86–105.

Bourdieu, P. (1986), 'The forms of capital', in J. Richardson (ed.), *Handbook of Theory and Research for the Sociology of Education*, pp. 241–258, (New York: Greenwood Press).

Butler, T. (1997), *Gentrification and the Middle Classes* (Aldershot: Ashgate).

—— (2002), 'Thinking global but acting local: the middle classes in the city', *Sociological Research Online*, 7(3): www.socresonline.org.uk/7/3/butler.html.

—— (2007), 'Re-urbanising Docklands: neither gentrification nor suburbanisation?' *International Journal of Urban and Regional Research*, 31(4) 759–81.

Butler, T. and Hamnett, C. (1994), 'Gentrification, class and gender: Some comments on Warde's "gentrification of consumption"', *Environment and Planning D Society and Space*, 12: 477–493.

—— (2007), 'The Geography of Education', *Urban Studies*, 44(7): 1161–74.

Butler, T., Hamnett, C. and Ramsden, M. (2008), 'Inward and upward? Marking out social class change in London 1981–2001', *Urban Studies*, 45(1) 67–88.

Butler, T. and Lees, L. (2006), 'Super-gentrification in Barnsbury, London: globalisation and gentrifying elites at the neighbourhood level', *Transactions of the Institute of British Geographers*, NS31: 467–87.

Butler, T. and Robson, G. (2001), 'Social capital, gentrification and neighbourhood change in London: a comparison of three South London neighbourhoods', *Urban Studies*, 38(12): 2145–2162.

—— (2003a), *London Calling: The Middle Classes and the Remaking of Inner London* (Oxford: Berg).

—— (2003b), 'Plotting the middle classes: gentrification and circuits of education', *Housing Studies*, 18(1): 5–28.

Carpenter, J. and Lees, L. (1995), 'Gentrification in New York, London and Paris: An International Comparison,' *International Journal of Urban and Regional Research*, 19: 286–303.

Davidson, M. and Lees, L. (2005), 'New build "gentrification"and London's riverside renaissance', *Environment and Planning, A* 37: 1165–90.

Foster, J. (1999), *Docklands: Cultures in Conflict, Worlds in Collision* (London: UCL Press).

Gans, H. (1982), *The Urban Villagers: Group and Class in the Life of Italian-Americans* (London: Collier Macmillan Publishers).

Hamnett, C. (1991), 'The blind man and the elephant: the explanation of gentrification', *Transactions of the Institute of British Geographers*, 16 (New Series): 173–189.

Hamnett, C. and Whitelegg, D. (2001), The Loft Conversion Market in Central London – the case of Clerkenwell, Final Report to the Economic and Social Research Council.

—— (2007), 'Loft Conversions and Gentrification: from Industrial to Post Industrial Land Use,' *Environment and Planning A* 39 (1): 106–24.

Jager, M. (1986), 'Class definition and the esthetics of gentrification: Victoriana in Melbourne', in Williams, P. and Smith, N. *Gentrification of the City* (London: Allen and Unwin): 78–91.

Jarvis, H. (2005), *Work/Life City Limits: Comparative Household Perspectives* (Basingstoke: Palgrave Macmillan).

Li, Y., Savage, M. and Pickles, A. (2003), 'Social Change, Friendship and Civic Participation', *Sociological Research Online* 8 (4): http://www.socresonline.org.uk/8/4/li.html.

Li, Y., Savage, M., Tampubolon, G. Warde, A. and Tomlinson, M. (2002), 'Dynamics of Social Capital: Trends and Turnover in Associational Membership in England and Wales, 1972–1999', *Sociological Research Online*, 7(3): http://www.socresonline.org.uk/7/3/li.html.

Lockwood, D. (1966), 'Sources of variation in working class images of society', *Sociological Review*, 14: 249–263.

—— (1995), 'Marking out the middle classes', *Social Change and the Middle Classes*, Butler, T. and Savage, M.: 1–12 (London: UCL Press).

London Edinburgh Weekend Return Group (1980), *In and Against the State* (London: Pluto).

Merton, R. (1948), 'Patterns of influence: a study of interpersonal influence and of communications behaviour in a local community', in Lazarsfeld, P. and Stanton, F. *Man in the City of the Future* (London: Collier-Macmillan).

Munt, I. (1987), 'Economic restructuring, culture and gentrification: a case study of Battersea, London', *Environment and Planning A : government and planning*, 19: 1175–1197.

Pahl, R. (1965), *Urbs in Rure: The Metropolitan Fringe in Hertfordshire* (London: The London School of Economics and Weidenfeld and Nicholson.)

Pahl, R. (2000), *On Friendship* (Cambridge: Polity).

Power, A. (1973), *David and Goliath* (London: Holloway Neighbourhood Law Centre).

Power, S., Edwards, T., Whitty, G. and Wigfall, V. (2003), *Education and the Middle Class* (Buckingham: Open University Press).

Préteceille, E. (2007), 'Is gentrification a useful paradigm to analyse social changes in the Paris metropolis?', *Environment and Planning A* 39(1): 10–31.

Robson, G. and Butler, T. (2001), 'Coming to terms with London: middle-class communities in a global city', *International Journal of Urban and Regional Research*, 25(1): 70–86.

Rutheiser, C. (1996), *Imagineering Atlanta: Making Place in the Non-Place Urban Realm* (London: Verso).

Savage, M., Bagnall, G. and Longhurst, B. (2001), 'Ordinary, ambivalent and defensive: class identities in the northwest of England', *Sociology*, 35(4): 875–892.

—— (2005), *Globalisation and Belonging* (London: Sage).

Sennett, R. (1998), *The Corrosion of Character: The Personal Consequences of Work in the New Capitalism* (London: Norton).

Smith, N. (1996), *The New Urban Frontier: Gentrification and the Revanchist City* (London: Routledge).

Spencer, L. and Pahl, R. (2006), *Rethinking Friendship: Hidden Solidarities Today* (Princeton: Princeton University Press).

Warde, A. (1991), 'Gentrification as consumption issues of class and gender', *Environment and Planning D Society and Space*, 6: 75–95.

Young, M. and Willmott, P. (1962), *Family and Kinship in East London* (Harmondsworth: Penguin).

Index

ABOUT SUPERSONIC

From how to handle a political crossfire, to mapping your brand character, to dealing with sex in the office, *Supersonic* offers advice that you won't find in any college curriculum or in any company training program. Whether you're looking for tips on how to move up the ladder, or are thinking about redefining yourself to have a more fulfilling career, this book offers straightforward learning and big picture thinking from a *real, working executive.*

Philip's experience includes over 25 years in advertising, marketing, product development and innovation. He has held senior positions at McCann-Erickson, Grey Advertising, Nike, Loews Corporation and The Walt Disney Company. Through his work he has also gleaned insights from a diverse array of companies like Coca-Cola, Nestlé, Black & Decker, Walmart, Burger King and Procter & Gamble.

Written with intelligence, humor, and real-life examples, *Supersonic* is destined to become a classic read for anyone who is looking for insightful and revealing advice on how to get the edge in business.

SUPERSONIC

27 Secret Lessons
On How To Make It In Business
Without Imploding Into
A Smoldering Fireball

By a real, working business journeyman
PHILIP A. SHAW

Cover design by Byron Lee

Published by Kamirak Press, Los Angeles, California.
Printed in the United States of America

ISBN-13: 978-1477413777
ISBN-10: 1477413774

CONTENTS

DEDICATION

This work is dedicated to my mother, Margaret Anderson Shaw, for her unconditional and unending love, her patience and her unstoppable, inspiring fortitude through life's trials and tribulations.

This book is also dedicated to my wonderful children – Tucker, Katie, and Jack.

ACKNOWLEDGEMENT

Every book rests on the shoulders of giants. The giants in my world who have helped enormously with this book are: Dr. Fred Milne – whose editing, guidance, and encouragement have helped make this book come together; Susan Shaw and Vonda Shannon – whose love and perspective helped me keep mine; Nathan Shaw – whose simple question about his job at Cisco, "so what should I do now?" helped inspire me to write this; my father, Stuart Shaw – whose business acumen and 'wisdom of our Scottish clan' helped me through some very challenging times; Bob Bobala, whose insight and positive energy helped me to carry on with this effort; Byron Lee for an intriguing cover design; my higher power for the inspiration and mystical help in this life journey; and finally to the incredible talent in the halls of business who I've had the privilege to meet and get to know along the way.

INTRODUCTION

It can happen to the best of us.

Things are just flying along. You've completely built up your little business from nothing to a super-sized Whopper megabrand, you've carved a few deals with sushi-chef precision, and you have gone after each promotion like a starving dog on a meat wagon. Life for you, my friend, is *very good.*

Then your synapses suddenly spark into warp-speed. Your mind is thinking, "Damn! I do have a shot at this! The big slot, the big chair!" That savory top position you've been craving down the hall that once seemed as close as Everest/Base Camp 4 now seems within reach. "Yes! It is…gasp…possible!" you sputter excitedly – you *could* have that corner office, or become some Divisional Deity. Hell, you might even have a shot at the REALLY BIG CHAIR: the CEO. And just for a minute you start thinking about the jets, the million plus in cash compensation, the zillions in stock, the jets…did I mention that already? But before you leave this momentary flight of ecstasy, the good news about this dream is that you *might be closer* to the top slot than you think.

The crazy thing is that even when you're just starting out in business, it is an immutable phenomenon that you are less than five org-chart boxes from the CEO position. Really. If you diagram out the direct reports you'll find you're amazingly close to the Mecca of Mercantilism. To illustrate:

- In my first job, I was entry level – the very….and I mean the *very, very slug-heap bottom* of the ladder. But I also counted and found I was only five positions away from being Chairman and CEO of the Big Old Ad Agency. Sure there were legions of people sporting preppier shirts, better golf clubs and fully automatic AK-47s who were vying for the spot. But that didn't stop me from thinking that by simple level counting I was five degrees of separation, not six, from being the Über-boss.

- As General Manager of Nike's Equipment Division, I was *one* position away from President & CEO of the entire company – albeit there were 12 VPs and 20 GMs, not to mention probably 30 'wild card' candidates and about 10,000 people who were all more qualified for the role. Nonetheless by clear report structures, the only thing between me and the President was the Vice President I reported to…and of course, the other 62 Power Players.

- In my job as Senior Vice President of Disney I was two positions away from Michael Eisner's role. "Just think," I said wistfully to myself one day, "I'm two small org- chart boxes away from the CEO of a $30 billion dollar empire that netted Michael somewhere north of $750 million." That's just scads of Disneyland tickets and yep, you guessed it…a full time G5 corporate jet at your disposal! There were probably thousands if not hundreds of thousands of people ahead of me in standing, political clout, experience, modern executive sabotage techniques, etc. But by level counting, I was just two boxes away from being the Don Correleone of Disney.

When you really 'take inventory' – a psychologically tortured, but perfectly apt phrase – you probably are in fact 'Five Degrees of Separation' from the Top Slot. So how do you get it? How do you beat the pack, run faster, jump higher, and outperform your way ahead of the hundreds (usually not thousands) of people who are all striving for the same thing?

I'll bet the chicken ranch that you've found what I found – that there are no textbook answers. No classes you can take. And you're damn certain that there's no Ph.D. with a book like "Dr. Wally's Seven Steps to Becoming A CEO, Shaolin Kung Fu Master, and Billionaire in 30 Days!" that is going to help. I'm sure you'll get a great business high colonic at Dr. Wally's Corporate Center in Aspen, but I really don't put a lot of stock in any Ph.D. or writer who has never held or managed any business at any major company. What you need is the closely held wisdom of a real business person who has lived in the trenches, run small and also mammoth businesses, and who has survived through it all. In my real world working life, I've been graced with what I consider to be the finest mentors, coaches, bosses and enemies that the best global companies in the world have to offer. These saints, sages and

Salieris have taught me invaluable secret lessons that can help you get ahead in business without crashing and burning.

So, you've finally found *The one book* that will help you avoid those personal business crack-ups and show you how to have more success, and meaningful success in business. Not that vacuous, ultra-materialistic, stinking-rich success is bad or anything. It's just that finding meaning in your business life is always a plus. Also know that this book has the secrets the Human Resources people want you to have and know, but can't tell you face-to-face because it involves too many taboo, dangerous subjects. The very taboos and subjects that, if you don't know them, can slowly and silently tip down the nose of that shiny plane called your career. This book is also built to give you these secret lessons in a compelling and hopefully engaging way. My hope is that these pages might save you from your own 'Career Kamikaze' and that you'll be able to go full throttle to supersonic speed in business. So buckle up, read on, and enjoy the flight.

WHAT IT TAKES TO MAKE IT: RADAR & RESILIENCE

Learning from winners is great. It's easy. And it's often laced with the unseen that you'll never know – the preparation, the perseverance, even the luck that befell certain business people as they ascended in stature and fortune. The bookshelves are littered with the triumphs of these Titans of the Modern Age, these Conquerers of Commerce…the lucky ones who made enough so they can sit back and write books in the August years of their overwrought careers.

You don't need that. Please God, not another Business Yoda that made a billion overnight, or some yahoo who led a behemoth company with glowing results *in 1980*. Nope. We don't need another history book or a theoretical treatise, but *how it really works*. The secret guidebook, the roadmap, the talisman, the oracle of business – the secret lessons written by those who were cut and beaten in the game and who came back like champion fighters to stand up again. That's real. That's no bullshit. That's this book.

So you want to know what it takes? OK…I probably shouldn't do this… because… gasp…you could just read this and leave the bookstore without popping for this treasure trove. It's pretty simple – you have to develop your psychosocial radar and you have to learn to be amazingly resilient. There. Boom! Said it. "Really?" you chortle (a great verb that needs to make a comeback), "just have radar and resilience?" Yep. That's it, smokie. OK, OK. There are 26 other lessons that you'll probably want to check out, but to make it in business, to really make it, you have to have radar and resilience. (And for you counters I included the 'five degrees' between you and the top dude or dudette as a lesson. Besides, let's face it, 27 is just a better number than 26!)

Psychosocial radar on the surface is simple: you want to have a heightened sense of 'social awareness' – knowing how the crowd thinks and how they react. To get this you have to have three things: 1) your mouth closed – so you can listen and observe; 2) your recorder on – noting people's reaction patterns to things, like good news, bad news, and personal interactions; and

3) tape delay – learning to hear what you are about to say in a meeting/business social interaction, repeating it to yourself with the filter of 'does this advance the ball? Does it add to the meeting? Does it help me?' By doing these three things you'll develop strong 'social awareness' or social radar.

The 'psycho' part of psychosocial radar is more interesting (thought I forgot about that, didn't you?). Nope. This kind of radar is *internal radar*. It's about knowing *who the hell you are inside*, and *why* you react to certain stimuli the way you do. It's like finally being an adult and knowing that feeling when your 'blood boils' and you start getting hot and flushed – and then you know to take a deep breath, to calm down the raging gorgon beast that is twisting your intestines like a pretzel. Your personal psychological radar gets into some heavy stuff and since everyone is a Bucket 'O' Strange Stuff in there, I don't have any magic formulas or a big 'A-ha!' But if you're not constantly checking in with yourself, reading good books that help you 'know thyself,' then this is a big billboard to say "Better Start Now" – that is if you want to make it in *any business.*

Part two of this lesson is Resilience. You've all had the parent, teacher or coach say 'gotta get back up and get back in the game' countless times in your life. But I don't think you've grasped the full depth of this yet. Whether you're just starting out in some kind of business career or if you're mid-ladder and looking to escalate further, one thing is clear: you've underestimated the amount of resilience you'll need if you want to truly make it in business. The reason I say this isn't about you, it's about them. Beginning to sound like a psycho-thriller novel? Good! What I mean is that I am certain that you are a resilient creature on this planet – most human beings with the human genetic structure are. You are resilient and can fight back – when you see it coming. The problem with most warfare is when a surprise attack happens. Hitler marching through the 'uncrossable' Magineau Forrest to beat the shit out of the arrogant and unsuspecting French, the Japanese coming out of nowhere to attack Pearl Harbor and sink half our Pacific fleet, assassination at the theatre when you're just getting into the play…all were masterful surprise attacks. No matter how many little league games or even college level sports you've suffered through, you'll never accurately estimate the resilience needed to survive the attack.

How do I know that these two things are the most important lessons in business? Because I screwed up both. To use an aviation metaphor, I was blind to the radar, had a sidewinder missile hit my jet, went into a 5G vertical flat spin dive, and hit the pavement just above Mach 1. I completely imploded into a smoldering fireball. The twisted chards of burning metal stayed white hot for about two years – searing my career, my belief in mankind and scaring my very soul.

If you're saying about now..."Wow. Uplifting. Great book...can't wait to catch the sequel," I completely understand. You've learned and I'm grateful. But for those of you that are wondering how someone with a stellar career, who never missed a meeting, always delivered his budget, who was diplomatic and congenial...how THAT guy could crash and burn...then read on.

It's surprisingly easy. First I was seduced by my own ego. Even though I was on a monster track at Nike and had been promoted to run Global Running Footwear, I was waylaid by the siren's call of more money, a flashier title and the lure of a much bigger company – a 'global superpower of entertainment.' I knew the guy I would work for wasn't known for being Mr. Loyal to his troops, but I jumped. Car. Private jets. Fortune 500 company. Big-ass title. Godzilla-sized paycheck. And when I arrived the battle order was clear: we have a green light to change anything and everything and challenge the organization to get better.

So I diligently went in and pushed, pulled and prodded. And then the firefights ensued, the sidewinder missiles started coming in. Didn't matter. We were vocal, direct and pushed new agendas with resolve. Every single review I had was 18 karat gold. Every business I ran had double-digit growth. But I lost one too many dogfights with powerful people and found myself on the wrong side of a few well-entrenched politicos. And then the call came. The shut door...the statement that my boss couldn't expend more 'political capital' and that we should probably find an 'elegant solution' to my departure. Bada bing! Bada Boom!

Without air cover, the war was lost. I realized I was 'disavowed' by the same

general who issued my orders. I had great radar – to see what the politicos and Machiavellis were doing, but *didn't even have the radar turned on about the guy I reported to*. This Kafkaesque situation was compounded by major issues I was having with my wife at the time. I hadn't had the radar on about my boss – and came home to find it was clear I hadn't turned the radar on about my wife either. Double Whopper served cold.

After two decades of fighting every issue to the last bullet, tackling every issue head on, forging a life....I simply let go of the joystick. The plane went into a slow dive and crashed and burned, me strapped tightly inside. I had lost my radar systems, and wasn't sure of much – just that I didn't have it in me to fight or parachute out.

So how does this story end? I took some time off, thought a lot about my goals, the types of places I wanted to work, and my motivations. It took me a long time to walk again – to forgive not those who shot down my plane, but myself – for carelessly flying into uncharted territory. I settled my divorce and started rebuilding my personal life. I had job offers from multi-billion dollar companies – even as a CMO of a two billion dollar publicly traded company. But my much-improved radar told me they were more of the same as where I had been – and I passed. I ended up settling into a small start-up and found I truly loved it. More importantly, I found I loved working with the men and women who worked there – and that team chemistry was everything.

This is the first time I've written about the crash – and it's something an executive *NEVER* wants to admit to or dwell on. I tell it to you because of the critical lesson: what I lacked was better Radar and more Resilience to fight. I completely underestimated the slings and arrows and *the hyper level of resilience needed*. That's what it would have taken to emerge victorious. And that's what you'll need, too.

OK, if you're saying "loooo – whoooo – whoooo – ssser! Loser!" I'd have to fight you on that. Mostly, that the lesson isn't about winning or losing, but what it takes to win. During the 'Great Recession' of 2007-2010, so many great men and women lost their jobs - some of them were superstar pilots flying shining jet fighters. But 91% of the country stayed employed. It's not

that the fired were the bottom 10%. It's just that they needed a better radar system and more 'bounce back' in the job they had. There's a strong likelihood you know someone who got clipped, and there's a very high likelihood that at some point in your career your plane will get shot down too, or at least come under heavy fire that might force you to take that transfer to the Siberian office. Hey, if I can recover from a Machiavellian high-speed smash up like the one I described, and then go on to live a fulfilling life in great companies, you can too.

Make sure before you take off in that Supersonic Jet called your career that you carefully check your instruments – and tap the radar & resilience gauges a few times to make sure the needles are moving. Then throttle down…and Shut Up.

SHUT YOUR TRAP

A wise sage who was wildly successful in business once pulled me aside, and with a warm but direct approach said, "Really. Seriously. Shut up."

Do I really need to 'splain it?

This lesson simply means that you can't listen if your mouth is running. On the surface level this means you need to be an active and good listener. The secret lesson from the Sensei Masters here is that listening is like muscle mass – if you don't exercise it, it goes away. But like hearing itself, listening ability goes away silently – you don't even realize that you pontificate and have stopped listening until it's too late. On a deeper level, this means that you should stop talking, and stop your internal brain chatter so that you can read the energy from people and situations. You might blast into a conference room, overreact to bad news, marshal your edict, then leave. But you'll have missed the energy which was frightened, or maybe contemplative and close to a solution. Reading the energy of teams and interpersonal relationships is critical if you are to succeed. So practice every day just sitting down for a moment and not saying much. What's amazing is that you'll find that the words you do speak will have more *gravitas*.

One of the big benefits of Shutting Up is that you'll have a better understanding of what is happening in your business. Call it a 'heightened sense of intuition' or 'knowing,' but it is critical to get it and pay attention to the signals. The rules of business change constantly, but the basic human needs of the people running businesses do not. You may find yourself thinking you're on solid ground since your last proposal or sale went great – only to find that your division is now downsizing and that you may be one of the 'expendables.' You may think that the boss loves you, and then find that you just got passed over for a promotion. A couple of beers or a hot bath will take the sting out, but won't solve the situation. It's essential to understand that subconscious human needs drive almost every business interchange…just like they are driving you. Despite all the strategic planning and number crunching, business is run by human minds largely influenced

not by black and white numbers, but by instinct, feelings and judgments filtered by personal experience. This goes beyond the 'social awareness' skills that were discussed in Lesson 1; it's really getting into the genetic and learned behavioral DNA. If you understand this, then you have begun your Ph.D. in learning how to truly operate in a business environment.

While discussing this subject with a friend over dinner, he asked me, "How do you know this?" "Simple," I replied, "because business could be run with nothing more than a computer and an optimization formula. Every decision could, and theoretically should be made on its economic return. But it isn't." If Bill Gates, for example, had run a simple ROI on the potential of making it in the nascent computer industry versus finishing Harvard and becoming a lawyer, the machine would have clearly sputtered out a message saying 'stay in school.'

If Ted Turner had run an ROI on buying the expensive Metro Goldwyn Mayer film archives or investing his cash elsewhere, clearly the computer would have said to put the money in a savings account. Turner's decision to pay the highest price ever paid for a film library ($1.5 billion) was the cornerstone of Turner Broadcasting – and has proven to be a brilliant decision, filling endless hours of cable programming on his network. The bottom line is that human experiences effect the brain in non-linear ways, and these are what govern business decisions – and de facto all business.

During the course of this conversation, my friend told me that I think too much, and he's probably right. But I left dinner that night truly convinced that emotion, and some Maslovian hierarchy of needs was governing most of the business world, not clean, clear logic.

You're now wondering, "Great! What do I do with this?" Simple. The key to success in your job is to shut up long enough to find out two critical pieces of information: 1) who is calling the shots, and 2) what motivates them. For example, it is clear that at Disney, Michael Eisner was, by his own account, motivated first and foremost by creativity. His background as an English major was part of this. But he truly knew that stock price, earnings and all those logical measures are somewhat meaningless in an entertainment company. They are after-the-fact. In an entertainment company, value is

created by creativity and content, not by analysis.

Phil Knight, founder and chairman of Nike, used to barb and sometimes verbally lay into Wall Street analysts. Early on Phil would say to analysts, "you clearly don't have a clue what you're talking about." Phil was right – the analysts at the time were poorly informed, but would his heart-felt approach *increase* the stock price? Was that the behavior of a supercomputer that wants to optimize shareholder value? Nope. Phil did eventually change his tune with analysts, but open the hood and you'll find that what drives Phil Knight is only one thing: Goosebumps. Goosebumps caused by that magic moment in sports when an impossible goal is scored, or a broken down ex-champion returns to win again. It's not logical, but in a way it is the heart and soul of what being a great sports company is about. In my first presentation to Phil and the senior executive team, I knew that I had one thing to convey: the passion of sports. The numbers were important (and yep, Phil is a Stanford MBA and a CPA), and the rationale was important. After all, I was asking for almost $3 million dollars for a completely untried Nike Sport Timing product category. But I invoked the learning from my sages – and knew that to clinch the deal, I had to connect emotionally with him on a level that had nothing to do with ROI or any logical business reasoning. At the end of the pitch I remember looking at him eyeball-to-eyeball and saying. "Sure, we'll make money, but that's not why I'm here. I'm here because we can make a difference. We can make a difference in athletes' lives. We can make them better. And in the end, our judge and jury on this product won't be you, me, or anyone here – it'll be the athlete who tells us this product helped them win." I received the full appropriation to start the business two days later.

And if you're thinking, "Great, my boss is just some overeducated fashionista in the corner office, how do I get to understand her motivation?" Well, you've just said two things about her. But you're right – we can know the top dog leaders in the company since there is usually a lot of press about them, but it's harder to know the day-to-day leadership. There are a couple of ways to decipher them.........nah.... I can't. I really can't. You'll laugh. OK, what the hell. There are three ways and the first two are so easy you probably already do them. First, check them out on LinkedIn – and see who their network is. Between what they write and their network, you'll learn a lot about them. Second, check out their Facebook or other digital footprint. It's amazing the trail people are willing to leave for others to see. The third one

you'll laugh at, but it is truly the Oracle of Personality. Buy Linda Goodman's *Sun Signs*. It's perhaps the most insightful book ever written about the traits of people's astrological signs – and she has sections about the 'boss' and the 'employee' of each sign. Got a Taurus boss? He's patient, but highly judgmental. Got a Virgo boss? Better take that Excel course and keep your desk neat. It's truly a fascinating read.

So the second lesson starts with Shutting the Hell Up..... listening...and increasing your true understanding of human behavior. Always make your valid and insanely brilliant points, but err on the side of silence – you'll have more *gravitas*. Use any tool you can, but you *have to* figure out whose at the poker table with you and what motivates them, and you can't do that when you're monologuing. You're career is completely dependent on it.

Oh yeah, one thing I forgot to tell you...you can't fake it. You have to rid yourself of all BS, all hyperbole, all lies or 'white truths' as I've heard them now called. You gotta be THE ONE who people irrefutably know will always give them the straight story. You should also remember that most execs who have survived to a quality position can tell if people are faking it. I know I can. So the key is to find that thing that the power players are motivated by and try to find the chord that resonates *inside of you* and t*hem*.

BREAK THE RULES: OUTPERFORMING YOUR PEERS

In an old book on how to succeed in advertising, a sage profit once wrote a telling paragraph that stuck with me for years. To paraphrase it:

'If you are working on an Oil account, get to know everything about Oil. Go to the gas station and start talking with the attendant. What's good about the gas? What's bad? What do people like? What don't they like? Study how the pump works, then get a schematic from the pump manufacturer and study that. Get books on the refining process and know every step of the chain from ground to market. When you do this you'll have the confidence to talk intelligently about the business. When you do this, you'll outperform your peers.'

Here are a few pearls for you to consider:

- Marion Harper rises from office boy to CEO of McCann-Erickson, the third largest Ad Agency in the world, in less than 10 years. He then creates the first 'global' ad agency with IPG, the Interpublic Group of Companies.

- Bob Iger was an entry-level TV guy undoubtedly being told as a young pup to run and get coffee for 'the biggies.' Twenty years later he is CEO of The Walt Disney Company – a $30+ billion dollar company.
- Michael Ovitz was a gregarious fraternity brother who in less than 15 years became the single most powerful 'player' in Hollywood with his talent Agency, CAA.

- Martha Stewart writes a couple of home books and inside of 15 years takes Martha Stewart Living public and in one day had her net worth rise to almost half a billion dollars. And yes her story has some downturns…OK, serving time in the Big House was more than a downturn…but you can't re-write the history of her incredible success.

You will find them everywhere – men and women who completely go full out and outperform everyone to grab the brass ring. How?

First, ask yourself if you *want* it. Of all the people I've met or read about who have outperformed everyone, the biggest factor is that *they wanted it real bad.* A while back Barbara Walters interviewed Arnold Schwartzenegger and asked him how in the world a beefy body builder who barely spoke English, made it into the Hollywood elite. His answer was one word, delivered with his classic 'Arno' Austrian accent – he said, "DRIVE." He was simply driven to win – whether it was the Mr. Universe title (which he won 5 times) or making it to the top of the Hollywood acting pack. Interestingly, as reported in *USA Today*, most CEOs said that it isn't education but "drive" that got them to the top. Drive is just another way of saying you want it so bad it hurts.

There are immutable laws for outperforming your peers, which fall under three super simple headings; ideas that are all about how *you* are going to *be*: 1) Work Harder 2) Be Smarter, and 3) Sacrifice Short-term for Long-term. OK, you got it, but a little on each:

Work harder: The people I've seen who beat the game and outperformed others really *did* work harder. A *lot* harder. For example, their reports were done earlier than expected. They always did the 'plus projects' that went above and beyond the call. They got in earlier. They stayed later. They were always networking with someone. They became the 'go-to' people to get stuff done when others were going out to the Hamptons or dealing with some bovine home crisis like 'honey, the dishwasher broke.' Nope, if you want it, you work for it. I'd bark this like a Marine and tell you to drop and give me twenty right now if I was with you! You have to be GI Jane or Joe and just realize that if you want to make it in business, part of the equation is to just outwork the folks next to you.

At McCann-Erickson Advertising, I started on the Black & Decker account – considered to be a secondary piece of business with hard-to-win-over clients. OK, that was too politically correct. The truth is that at the time it was considered the real Dog account at the Agency – a wasteland of non-creativity dotted with broken account executives. Unlike the other Account Executives on the business, I completely threw myself at it. I pulled apart

their appliances on weekends to see how they were made. When I visited the client, I roamed the halls and talked with the Engineers, the Packaging people and Marketing people who were not working on the sexier 'advertised' products. I spent weekends writing computer programs that calculated our media spending and commercial rotation by each city by each daypart. I forced myself to write a recommendation on a new product idea every month. What happened? I got more raises, more promotions, and soundly beat the other Account Executives who couldn't keep up. As a result, I was put on the most prestigious account at the agency, Coca-Cola. It wasn't my Einstein-like mental powers (which I might add have been sadly dormant since before birth), it was just a lot of hard work, having a 'get it done' attitude, and getting out there in front of people with positive energy.

Be Smarter: You get this one too. "But wait a minute!" you ask, "How can I work smarter? Isn't my IQ what it is?" Yep. But you *can* work smarter. First, hire great people and delegate to them. Delegate as much of the routine junk as you can – to anyone you can. Second, read the papers and program your Yahoo! or Google homepage to comb for news on your business and start the day with this. More and more, the top dogs are 'info-brokers.' Getting the latest scoop and reacting to it is a foundation for what's needed for success. Be smarter by reading the occasional business book also, and force yourself to use it at some business event – weave it into an address or an internal speech. Most people who are working their brains out and working as smart as they can, do not have time for an advanced degree. But if you can somehow manage it, go for it. A master's degree and especially a Ph.D. is a ticket that will not only play well in the work place, it will keep your gray matter a little sharper and probably perkier with that enthusiasm that happens with learning.

Sacrifice short-term for long-term: The biggest thing every ladder-climber is confronted with is the inevitable 'outside' job offer that comes at about year 3, year 7, and year 12 in business. Someone in some other company wants you bad, and usually it's around the time when you're getting a little fed up in your own company. Most of the time the money is so tempting that people take it – and I'm constantly amazed that young 'stars' take these deals when the companies that are waving the cash are so much smaller. Take Gretta. She took a pay cut to come to Nike from some 'Ol Boy Investment House' –

because she wanted the sports lifestyle that Nike offered. For the first year she aced every assignment and was on the fast track. Then in year two she was up for a few jobs, but simply needed more seasoning – all the while she was given raises and told she was on the fast track. In year three, she wrote out her 'demands' which included paying her what she was making before she came to Nike (a 35% raise). She also requested a title jump and a few other unattainable perks, or the letter stated, she would seek employment elsewhere. Needless to say, I told her manager to tell her that she should take a flying leap at a rolling donut.

Sure enough, she proudly walked in and told us a month later that she had a manager job with a big apparel company in NYC. I said, 'But Gretta, you are already a manager…couldn't you get a promotion from them?" She stumbled, but said the money was good. I couldn't believe it. She had the brains, the work ethic, and all the raises and performance reviews that would have led to a stellar career at Nike, but she simply could not deal with short-term sacrifice for the long-term gain.

Which all brings me to another snappy point: you are crazy, certifiable, ready-for-da-nut-hut, if you choose to suffer in silence and live a life of 'short-term sacrifice' for any longer than 3 years, without some kind of reward. In other words, if you're busting your butt and you know you're outperforming your peers, but are not getting some kind of recognition over a good period of time trying – then you should think about dusting off the ol' résumé. Something isn't cooking. Don't blame them, don't blame you (remember to stay positive!). But if it isn't jelling, all your work is probably just being wasted. When you do jump, make sure it's the right thing. Who knows, maybe they'll have an epiphany and do everything to try to keep you.

If you want to avoid crashing your plane early in your career and go on to become a real Power Player in a Fortune 500 company, or any business, you'll have to pay your dues – and sometimes that means waiting…and banking on the long-term gain. You'll have to know when to adopt ELP (Extremely Low Profile) and when to charge forward recommending your newer, bigger role. There are no rules or guidelines on when to play your cards – that really comes down to trusting your gut instincts. Don't always hide when things go bad, and don't always charge forward when they're good. Patience is the true beacon of navigation. If you can stay cool and keep your head level, you'll find the kind of success where and when you want it.

YOUR BRAND CHARACTER

In the music business, the greatest successes are not necessarily the singers who have the best range, or who have perfect pitch. If you canvass the last 50 years in music, the greatest singers, the most successful and enduring singers, are the ones who have the most *unique* sound. Frank Sinatra had a resonance, a cool phrasing, and a confidence – almost a swagger – in his voice. Dave Grohl of the Foo Fighters has the quintessential rock 'n roll voice – gravel texture with a very piercing sense of reckless abandon. Sting has that minor-key choral sound to his voice – and sings in the higher octaves. There are plenty of people who make a living and make the charts, but it's the ones who are unique that go the farthest. So what in the bloody hell does this have to do with business? Simple. The greatest, most successful singers have a unique Brand Character, and like them, *your* Brand Character is a big determinant of how far you will go in business.

In classical marketing terms, Brand Character means the personality attributes that are ascribed to a brand. If you are Disney, your Brand Character is described as 'a safe haven for kids' or 'personable, fun, clean, and happy' or words to that effect. If you are Victoria's Secret, your Brand Character is simply 'sexy.' People are actually easier to peg – particularly actors. Clint Eastwood's Brand Character is 'tough guy.' Ben Affleck's Brand Character is 'vulnerable sexy guy.' Jim Carrey's would be 'bonkers.' Whether we are looking at actors or brands, it's clear that Brand Characters are often rooted in who the person really is. Figuring out *who* you are and *what* you stand for is critical if you want to grow in business. The Players at the top all have a very defined view of themselves and innately know their unique Brand Character.

Getting to the heart of your Brand Character is not a simple exercise and does take some time. Don't be all bummed out if you're reading this thinking that you are pretty much a bland, as-exciting-as-oatmeal type person. That's OK. But to advance you'll have to work on your definition – or if you don't, *you'll be given a Brand Character by others in your company*. Truly. Define yourself for others or you will be defined *by* others. So how do you begin to get at it? First, you gotta do that screwy-phrase: take stock. It starts with taking stock of your basic personality – which is shaped by the age of 7 and really doesn't change all that much. If you're shy and unassuming, it's probably not good to say "I'm going to be a LION in business!" It isn't you. And as much as you get coached to roar in the shower in the mornings and put up pictures of lions in your office, it really won't work long term since this isn't you. Start with the basics: Who are you? Shy? Aggressive? Forceful? Temperamental? Intellectual? What are your beliefs? Kill at all costs? Religious? Do unto others? Let's all be nice? Do what it takes?

A good place to start is a Myers-Briggs personality test, or talk with your closest friends about what they think of you. This is a toughie, but usually your mother or a close relative can give you pretty good insight.

Once you have some basics sketched out, then you want to think about how you *want* to be. This is critical since it helps you figure out your direction. Do you want to be dominant? Laid Back? Cool? Professorial? Joyous? Note that these are not so much business traits, but personality traits. Then the big crossover: match *who you are now* with *who you want to be.* An example might be that you are confident, but shy. Smart, but not aggressive. Instead of 'action driver' your Brand Character might be 'innovative leader,' or 'entrepreneurial supporter.' You really can't depart too far from your core personality. The big win is to play off of it. In my case, I've had two major Brand Characters. First, in my twenties, I was a pretty angst-ridden, hyperactive, funny, but crazy guy (a by-product of caffeine, being in New York City, and an intense need to succeed). My character was simple: Bold Energy. I wasn't afraid to hammer home points of view with Agency Presidents, or to call up the President of one of our big clients. My energy was non-stop, hard driving, take-no-prisoners type of energy and it worked in the 'formative years.' As my experience and the years tempered me over time, my tenacity (or impetuosity) has settled down. My character has since evolved and is best described as 'Innovative Driver.' For me, my big mantra is that to get ahead in business, we have to find ingenious solutions and then hammer them into tangible programs that work. It's about finding a new angle and then executing like crazy to get it right. This Brand Character projection of myself is what people will buy or not buy.

Over the years I've come to know a few power-hitters in business with rather unique personas. The millionaires and even a few billionaires that I've met and worked with seem to have a lock on their own Brand Character. Here are a few that might help illuminate this lesson:

Philip Knight: Chairman of Nike – Phil's brand character is simple: 'Reclusive Deity.' Think about it, you create a $24 billion company in 25 years, you are personally worth $10+ billion and considered to be the most powerful man in sports. It's gotta have an effect on you – and it did on Phil. Always shy, Phil dodged the limelight. But his behind-the-scenes brilliance, and desire for action, make him a father figure to the Nike-ites. The funny part is that compared to other hard-working CEOs, Phil really had it easy. He didn't spend time with accounts, didn't really ride with the troops, and is the founder of the new business concept called MBC, or Management by Cameos – showing up to give awards or to say something profound, then leaving. The funny part is that it *works*. I've found myself in tears at the profundity of his words – and I believe he truly understands his Brand Character and how he can single handedly get his 25,000 workers to have the same heartbeat.

Sergio Zyman: ex-Chief Marketing Officer of Coca-Cola. Sergio was the Cuban-born marketing chief at Coca-Cola who changed the formula in 1985 to 'New' Coke. Years later, I was with McCann-Erickson Advertising and was brought in to help clean up the New Coke mess, and worked closely with Sergio. His Brand Character is simple: In-your-face, nitro-burning Cuban Missile Crisis. Think about it: You blew the research and convinced yourself and the entire company that the 'new' Coke formula was better. You launch it. Consumers REVOLT! Your company then loses 1 billion a week till Coke Classic was invented to stop the bleeding (no, it was not pre-planned!). You get fired – and are given a surprisingly rich severance package. Then even more surprisingly you consult for Coke. Then later you get brought back to be CMO. Why? It's simple. Sergio was the only guy who could make things happen quickly at Coca-Cola. When he came back he launched a dozen new campaigns plus Fruitopia in less than a year. The stock went up 20 bucks. All the while, what I admired most about Sergio was that he was a maniac – and he LOVED the game. His Brand Character never changed. And most would agree it served him well in good times and bad.

Bob Iger is a consummate CEO – tall, dark, and handsome of course, but he has expressive brown eyes and a warm, endearing smile. If there is a brand character Bob adopted early it's this: 'Mr. Solid.' Yep, solid as a rock…or all that granite that ABC was built on in New York City. When Michael Eisner, the former CEO of The Walt Disney Company, started to tread shark-infested waters during his last five years, he increasingly turned to 'Mr. Solid' – and eventually made him president. The Board even conducted a broad search for Michael's replacement. Most top guys like Iger would be irate and would probably split….especially since he was a multi-millionaire before he took the job as President. But no, Bob is solid. Real oak. And during the stormy end of Eisner's nearly 3 decades at Mouseworks, it was Bob who was the calm voice. His Brand Character of 'Mr. Solid' paid off – and the search ended where? You got it – with the Board giving him the nod. And let's say a silent 'Amen!' since he made peace with the Disney family, made peace (and purchased) Pixar, and did a long-overdue house cleaning.

OK, enough of the juicy gossip. But if you take anything away from the stories of these Behemoths of Business, it is that they understood their personal Brand Character from the get-go and stuck with it. Call it inner-confidence, call it one-ness with their inner being, or call it just-plain-smarts – it's a fundamental requirement if you want to become a true Power Player.

A wirey old, leather-faced salesman once told me: "People don't buy pieces of paper, son. They buy people." He was so very right. You often hear that people seem 'fakey,' or 'slippery,' or 'insincere.' My guess is that those people are trying desperately to project a Brand Character that is completely out of alignment with their personality. So the rule of the road is to make sure you are anchored in yourself and that you really spend some time thinking about your image. Here's your homework:

What are three dominate personality traits you have?

What are the ethical standards that you subscribe to?

How would others describe you?

How would your family describe you?

Are you right brained or left brained?

What kind of car do you drive?

What is your clothing style?

Are you cerebral or physical?

Are you prone to think first, then act, or vice versa?

The list can be pretty endless, but just stop for an afternoon and really think about it. Are you a crazy, energetic, innovator? If so, why are you wearing that stuffy Brooks Brothers suit? Are you flashy, hip, and smart? Great, the Armani suit looks good on you, but the Chevy Tahoe you are driving doesn't cut it. These are intrinsic-extrinsic articulations of why it's right to have solid alignment of your personal style with your business Brand Character. Take time. Think about it. Be you – or at least be compatible with the Brand Character that you project. Write it down. And then check it 6 months later to see if it still fits. To be a heavy hitter, it's critical you take a hard and honest look at *who* you are, and then figure out the best way to create an inspiring, charismatic Brand Character that radiates your true self and that energizes your whole company.

A.Q. (AWARENESS QUOTIENT)

If somewhere along the way someone told you that your IQ was low, don't sweat it. If they told you it was high, forget about it. Intelligence Quotient tests are a solid indicator of how your brain processor works, but they have zero correlation to success in the workplace. It's not about IQ, it's all about AQ.

So what in the world is AQ? How do I get it? Can I bottle it and sell it to the craving masses? Well, here's the lowdown: developing your Awareness Quotient is one sure-fire way to stand out and be successful in business. A million years ago in the Pleistocene era, Procter & Gamble tested their 'star' executives to learn what made them stars (and undoubtedly they wanted to bottle it!). They found there were no consistent commonalities – just a little of a lot of things like verbal skills, logical reasoning, and on and on. No single factor popped up except for a heightened sense of awareness of the world around them. My father, Stuart Shaw, was the P&G exec who spearheaded the study, and later he coined the phrase 'AQ' to describe this trait.

Said differently, AQ is a unique mix of attributes that accelerates your understanding of the modern world and allows you to transfer learned knowledge from one field to another. Mapping out some of the components of AQ would look something like:

- Awareness of popular culture
- Understanding the fundamentals of industry business models
- Studying patterns of human tropisms
- Getting a beat on future trends that could affect your business
- And plain and simple: training your mind to wander – and skip through your hard drive, looking for insights and innovations

How do you get it? Is there an infomercial with some cheesy, tan geezer selling it? Ok, you weren't paying attention. You *already have* AQ – it's how to accelerate and improve it that matters. The key to improving AQ is throwing yourself into the unknown. And to do this often. The cornerstone of

AQ is expansion of thought and possibility, and to stimulate your brain to accept this. You have to constantly try new things and absorb new material. 'Oh sure,' you say, 'I do that already.' Funny thing is that most execs move from a very wide circle to ever-decreasing smaller circles of brain-input over the years. You get up, drive to work, read the Times, listen to NPR, watch a few TV shows and go to bed. Add a few kids and some house projects and the next thing you know you're taking the big dirt nap. But to harness the power of your AQ you have to push yourself to do different things – and then think about their potential relevance across a number of platforms, products, and industries. Here are a few examples:

Read different avant-garde magazines each month. In addition to your normal reading, pick up a copy of Sunset or Nylon or Airplane or Guitar Player. Study the ads, read a few of the articles, get the tone and timber of the writing style. Reverse engineer the audience they are going after. Clip the relevant articles/ads that you think make the difference. Go to a newsstand and study the covers of all the magazines – what are they focusing on? What are they missing? What's the new trend? And it doesn't matter if it's your interest or not – it's about new stimuli from popular culture.

Go to a Big Time Wrestling Match. Ridiculous? Ever notice that they are still selling out 60,000 seat arenas? Ever notice that it is a several billion-dollar industry? It's patently fake – so why, since we all know this – do people still want to see it? It's still a modern day phenomena for teen boys – and whether you are in Marketing or Information Technology, this phenomena has an impact on your business.

Visit an out-of-the way place on a vacation. I've been to the jungles of Ubud in Bali to the ancient streets of Ljubljana, Slovenia – and it's pretty clear to me now that I have been able to be a more global thinker as a result. Their customs, the way they think, the way the streets are laid out, the way people dress are stimuli that help drive trends and new ideas for my businesses. More important, it has given me a feeling for the breadth of the human experience – something that has had a profound effect on my business approach.

A couple of other off-the-wall, right brain, AQ-Building suggestions:

- Go to a dog-show. I didn't learn jack at the Westminster Dog Show in Madison Square Garden, but it was one of the funniest nights of my life
- Never pass up a county fair
- Definitely see any circus or Cirque de Soleil production
- Eat at out of the way, different ethnic restaurants
- Make a CD, write a book, or paint
- Dive in and work behind the counter at your company store
- Go to the X-Games
- Know and go to SEMA, CES, NAMM, and ComicCon
- Watch MTV's Spring Break for 12 straight hours.

The secret is simple: you'll accelerate your company, your career and your character if you pay attention and actively stimulate your AQ. It has been said that all the ideas in the universe are already invented and lurking somewhere on the planet. Your job is to find them and free-associate how these great ideas and inventions might have applicability to your business. And best of all, by improving your AQ, you'll become a more interesting, richer person in life – a great thing for yourself, your S.O. and your CEO.

POLITICS 101

Here's the bottom line on it: Politics happen when two people get into a room, sometimes less.

It's inevitable that politics will be a part of your life in business. Fortunately, politics has gotten a bad reputation. I say fortunately because politics is largely counterproductive and saps energy. At its best, politics is simply a means to an end – a way to rally support for your point of view. But most often it's a way to unseat peers and illuminate your brilliant plan by dimming the light of others.

So how political are companies? It really varies by company and often by division in those companies, but *all* companies have political hardwiring you'll need to know. The companies that I have worked in and around have run the gamut on the political spectrum – from Zip-City-No-Politics-Here to Mouthguard-Wearing-Uzi-Carrying-Yes-It's-OK-To-Firebomb-Your-Car politics. Bottom line is that the amount of politics in business is completely arbitrary and mostly depends on the boss you're working for and the chemistry of the group you're working in.

One thing is clear: It doesn't matter what size the company is, or what its location is for there to be an excessive amount of politics. Nike is a clear example of a multi-billion dollar company that has what I consider to be the lowest amount of BS of any company I've ever known. How? It's the mentality of the principle players that makes it work. Phil Knight, Charlie Denson, Mark Parker, Clare Hamill and the 'old school' Nike management really have a 'don't bullshit me' approach. For most of the troops the mantra is about innovation, and you'll simply lose if you start whining about people or politicking with some backroom BS. My guess is that it is rooted in the athlete culture. Think about it: If you've ever run track or played any kind of sport, you can politic all you want, but it doesn't mean a damn thing. In the end, you run fast and win or you don't. That's the athletic mindset that helps Nike transcend politics.

Politics happens to be worse in idea-driven companies, since the only 'product' is that intangible 'idea.' Advertising, Design and Fashion companies are usually rife with politics since what they 'sell' is nothing more than an idea - something conjured up in the mind. And what makes an idea better? An idea only becomes better when people convince other people it actually *is* better – and here starts the politicking. In 'idea companies,' like Disney, success has many fathers, and failure is....well...wasn't that last box office 'bomb' *your* idea? In product companies, that's harder to do since the product line you built is still selling $250 million a year – and it is impossible to take that 'track record' away from people.

So, you've settled in and you've found yourself in a hotbed political situation. What do you do? I can't say that I've really excelled at politics – since I despise it so much. But I have survived my share of gunfights and can give you a few rules of the road that might help. Here's a short list:

1. Be honest. Don't BS
2. Tell it like it is – lay out the whole story
3. Actively be the one who is not political
4. Try to be positive, even on the Titanic
5. If it's bad, it's bad. Get out of the hood while the getting's good
6. Don't react to rumors – at least overtly. They'll know you're easy to play
7. Don't spread rumors – don't get branded as a politico
8. Do play to power: know who makes the call and who doesn't. Don't negotiate with the wrong person
9. Keep Clean: follow the rules and regs – people tend to jabber about people who stretch the rules
10. Be the way you want others to be

You can spend your time reading all the modern-day gurus who spew out titles like *Survivin' and Thrivin' in the Modern Corporate World*. You can study Machiavelli or *The Art of War*, or the *How to Swim Naked with Big-Man-Eating-Fish* type books. But my counsel when it comes to politics is to simply skip all the black arts. Spend your very rare time not plotting how to unseat the winners or sabotage others, but on writing that great, top flight presentation on how to *grow* your business. Create a new recommendation on how to drive volume and build new markets. Keep making things happen in your company and you'll leave the politicos in the dust. Remember that you don't see flies on a horse that's running fast. Run fast, stay positive, and focus on bringing in business and ringing that corporate cash register.

POLITICS 501

The most sophisticated form of politics is invisible. You don't see it, hear it, or smell it. It is as still as air, but as fast and lethal as a venomous python. This may sound a bit dark, but it's something that I have to tell you about. Politics 501 is something you'll have to learn…and fully understand…if you want to truly succeed in modern business environments.

There are probably 500 golden rules to avoid the political sidewinder missiles you will encounter. But since my bet is that no one wants to read 500 rules, here are just a few:

1. Know that you'll never see or hear the *real* politics being played. At best, you'll feel it…usually after the fact
2. Remember the famous words Agrippa said to the Roman Emperor Claudius, "Trust No One"
3. You should never directly respond to politics being waged against you
4. Revenge is a black art and my advice is don't use it. Turn to the positive and beat them with momentum
5. Take stock of where you really are
6. Take no prisoners
7. Take as much turf as you can and hold it for dear life

Here's a little more detail to give each point some context:

1. Politics is invisible; you'll only feel it. There are no clear signals, or lights, or tests to know here. The best thing is to simply trust your intuition. If it feels bad, it is bad. Also ask yourself – do I fit in with them? Does it feel right? Close your eyes, turn down your brain and ask if it simply feels good or not. The other lesson here is to know who the power is and make sure you have a voice at their table.

2. Remember the famous words Agrippa said to the Roman Emperor Claudius, "Trust No One." Unless you have been with a business

comrade and shared more miles on the road with them than a Greyhound bus, or have literally known the person for most of your life, trust no one in business. OK, you can trust people…but you have to do the Nintendo Game-Boy system, where you give them little tests and little confidences….and see if they keep it to themselves. If they do, you progress to the next level. Then you give them a 'big' confidence or test (although not an irrecoverable one) and see if it works. I finally discovered while at Nike that most people do this in business…and in life…and that I was just the truant student who must have been absent the day that was covered. So learn the lesson and be sure to do tests to see who's in your camp.

3. You should never respond directly to Politics being waged against you. On more than one occasion in business I've decided to do the Clint Eastwood thing and have asked people if they have problems with my team or me directly. Invariably the response is "Uh….well….of course not, I just….." and they backpedal faster than a circus clown in reverse. I've never in my life had anyone say, "Well, now that we're putting cards on the table, I do have a major issue with you…" Never happens. And for God's sakes, don't ever directly respond to a 'rumor' or political move. If Ted is badmouthing you at the water cooler, the second you overtly or directly respond to Ted, he is controlling the game…and you. There is no gain in it. You'll just look like a weaker warrior. Instead, respond indirectly. Have drinks with one of Ted's favorite teammates – and don't talk about Ted at all. Instead, talk about a new growth initiative that they might be great for and possibly promoted into. When Ted finds out and grills his teamboy, it will become apparent that Ted is paranoid…and the teamboy will do the dismantling for you. No, you're not E-Vil, you're just playing the game. The trick is to do it smartly and always take the high ground, not the Revenge ground. That's such a perfect segue into the next point…

4. Revenge is a black art and my advice is don't use it. Turn to the positive and beat them with momentum. Yes, you could do NASTY things. Like getting Ted a subscription to some racy sex magazine and making sure his copy of Bodacious Unnatural Acts is sent to Ted

in the office. As tempting as this is, don't do it. Laugh about it, but
don't do it. It's simply not worth it. Revenge takes negative energy
and will suck you dry. Revenge is a short-term game, and usually is a
lethal one if you're not Einstein bright about it. I've done Revenge,
and yes it is a short-term feel good and a short-term advance on the
board, but in the long run it didn't win the game. Only positive, high
ground, 'momentum moves' win the game. And if it doesn't, then
you're in with a bunch of losers and you should move – not only for
your sanity, but also for your family, who clearly are seeing the worst
of you if you are in such a negative atmosphere. In the face of nasty
politics, stay classy – recommend things, speak only in positive
terms, find the good things to take stock of and hammer away at
them. You'll always win that way. Promise.

5. Take Stock of where you really are. What the hell does this mean?
   Well, you're not gonna like it. It means if you are in a downer-of-a-
   job, gonna-slit-my-wrists-if-I-gotta-do-one-more-day kind of place,
   then you must take stock of where you are and find a new gig. People
   manufacture politics. It doesn't exist in nature. Politics is allowed to
   fester in organizations because leaders are weak and afraid to take
   out the nay-saying politicos. We all know who they are and yet it
   happens. Remember, politics happens when you get two people in a
   room, sometimes less. But take stock. If it feels bad....you know by
   now it is bad, and it most likely won't get better anytime soon. The
   really bad part you're not gonna like is this: If your company
   environment is a political hothouse, then most likely people outside
   of your company know this. Headhunters, key execs at Sizzle Hot
   Corporation who you really want to work for, the business
   community – they most likely know that CatFarm Inc. is a terrible
   place to work where only the non-producing politicos survive. Take
   stock. Then take the challenge to rise above it...or get the hell outta
   Dodge.

6. Take no Prisoners. This is a simple one. Don't take anyone's hostages
   – or said differently, when other people try to get you to take their
   second-string players, or other assorted non-performers, complainers,
   dorks, or dweebs, just say no! Get rid of Ted's ex-water cooler

buddies and people who have allegiances to others. Don't take any 'freebee' transfers or hires – even if they are the President's 'he's a genius!' nephew. Take no Prisoners – it's hard enough keeping your own people tried and true.

7. Take as much Turf as you can and hold it for dear life. In Politics 501, this is the lesson that is above all lessons. Get Turf. Get P&L businesses under your control. Then get more. And when they ask you to let go of a few in a 'realignment' say 'Hell No!' and keep them. Get Turf. And keep it. And build it. He/She who has the most Turf: a) usually keeps their job in economic 'downdrafts'; b) usually is protected against Jhonnie Bhaadass, the new German CEO who doesn't like your power base; c) is on the path to the top slot when Jhonnie Bhaadass dies in a tragic and embarrassing ballet skiing accident.

Take my good friend and first boss I ever had, Steve (and being a very savvy, politically astute man, he asked me to use a different name…so we'll just call him Steve). He started in Advertising in New York a year before I did when he was about 23. He steadily moved up the ranks and then got to be one of a handful of EVPs at the company – at the age of 35. This was a huge and needless to say lucrative accomplishment since his company is a mega-Agency in the Fortune 500. But alas, Steve hit that ceiling and was restless. While others would have bolted, losing their track or their tenure, Steve pitched to the board to start a subsidiary consultancy. He already had pre-sold his clients on the idea, so it was hard for the board to refuse. Having long-term, good money clients is part of owning 'Turf,' since they spell income. Steve then grew the business to have offices in 15 countries. Next thing I know, he's telling me he pitched and got under his control two other plums: the Agency's Interactive Division and the Direct Division – small in the grand scheme of things, but important in getting….getting what? Getting TURF. Wouldn't surprise me if he were plotting to get as many of these satellite companies as possible – and ultimately position himself for the Top Slot. That's called Getting Turf.

Politics 501 is simply the reality of growing up in business. It's the unfortunate byproduct of human brainpower put towards non-productive personal power – and all at the expense of someone. Worse, it's at the expense of the company as a whole and its shareholders and worker bees that slave every day to try to make something. If more companies thought of Politics as 10% of the cost of every product, they'd find a way to reduce it. And at most Fortune 500s, particularly at the top, more than 10% of their executives' time is spent thinking about the Politics of Personal Power. You can't ignore it, or one day you'll notice the view out of your career cockpit is doing a Google Earth zoom-in...... Kamikaze style straight for the ground. You *can* be savvy and move around it and help convert the energy into something productive. Remember to be the positive light in your company. You'll either be rewarded handsomely or you'll find out quickly that you have to go somewhere else where your energy will catapult you to a higher orbit.

SEX IN THE OFFICE

Simple mathematics tells you that you'll find yourself in an awkward situation at the office at some point in your career. By all measures, you'll spend significantly more time in the office than at your home – and it is not uncommon that there could be that certain someone who comes across your path who just seems to answer all those needs that are simply being unmet in your life. To complicate matters more, good companies, especially Fortune 500 companies, are like cosmic magnets – attracting the very best and the brightest…and usually the most beautiful men and women in business. Don't fret. The interoffice romance and even the torrid adulterous affair have happened to the best of people. Like John F. Kennedy, Bill Clinton, Jack Welch, just about every celebrity ever born, and countless presidents of countries and corporations.

OK, so let's review a few ground rules and then go into realities. Ground rule numero uno that anyone with half a brain will tell you is…*Just Don't!* I've seen both sides and let me tell you from direct experience that having an affair in the office is almost always a no-win. I was single… yes…single, had an office romance, and ended up marrying the woman. You guessed it – a short time later we divorced. But it clearly took its toll on my career at the time. Worse, the sizzle of 'we shouldn't be doing this' *does*, in fact, make the bar-be-que-hot love and romance *just that much hotter*. Yes, it's *worse* because then you 'go legit' and the sizzle goes. So went my first marriage. Bottom line, you'll either compromise your position in the company, or worse, completely compromise and damage your career. One executive came up to me at Nike once and said about another colleague, "The guy is solid, but he's got a wife and young kids and he's openly having an affair with someone here. I mean how can you respect a guy like that?" That's what happens. It's plain and simple. For most companies, having an affair is off-limits…and an extramarital affair is a guaranteed-to-happen, supersonic Career Kamikaze.

In some companies, biting the company apple and dating (while single) is tolerated but usually it doesn't play well. Not to mention the 'ultimate living hell' – seeing him or her in the hallway after a bad breakup. Yeeesh! And then the rumor mill starts to really take over. So even though you just had a major business victory, or scored some major win, the rule of yellow journalism says that the negative stories will always win out. Shakespeare once wrote "the evil men do lives after them; the good is oft interred with their bones."

OK, OK. Now that I've hopefully shaken you a bit and warned you, there are some realities. It goes like this: You're working like a dog and your home life is either non-existent, or dulled-out by the same old year-in-year-out routine, or reduced to the all-too-common state of benign neglect. And then one day the woman from down the hall comes in and gently, gracefully sits down in the chair in front of you. You hadn't ever noticed before how glossy her hair is, or how her smile was so sincere and warming. And later you find yourself asking her out for that innocent lunch or quick glass of wine before heading home. She smiles warmly and genuinely listens to you. You tell her about your life and your woes, and she somehow knows and understands you. And then one day you find you're lost to her. You're consumed by her. You can't think of anyone else the same way. She is your sun, your moon, your stars. Drinks give way to dinner. Dinner gives way to that quiet evening where you touch her and she melts into you....OK, OK, stop the violin music!....you get it. Same old story. Bada-Bing, Bada-Boom, despite everything you just read in the paragraphs above, despite every warning, you are smack dab in the middle of a searing hot love affair. So, what to do? There are ten rules of the sexual road in the business world:

1. If you're reading this and you're already in a skin-deep affair, my suggestion is to love the hell out of it! Yep. You heard me. Eat it, live it, love it. Do it morning, noon, and night. Do it till you get arrested. Well, almost. A good friend of mine once helped me out tremendously. She said there is a Buddhist saying that in order to get over something, you must lose yourself to it. Do it over and over again until you don't want to do it anymore. In my life I've found it true. I wouldn't recommend that for toxic habits, but if you find yourself in love, then I fully subscribe and advise adopting the "Italian Rules of the Road" – which is simply to love madly, passionately, and completely. Life is short and there are no

guarantees that you'll live a long life. Tomorrow could be your last day on Earth. So live, Bello et Bellisima! Love Life, Love Well.

2. OK, OK, OK. Now that you've read #1, read this: *You're completely screwed.* If you're married, you're going to Hell – forget the strapped-to-a-burning-rock underworld Hell, it's the *LIVING HELL* that you're about to go through. If married, I'd recommend that you start looking for another job, since the news of the affair, no matter how careful you are, *will* surface. When it does, you'll be taken out. Somehow, someway, you can take it to the bank that you'll be terminated. Start looking amigo – and hope it was worth it. If you're single, you have two roads: 1) start looking since you'll need to get out of the environment where that bastard/that bitch is working down the hall after your breakup; or 2) marry them. Under NO circumstances should you marry to 'save' your career! But if it's really good, consider yourself lucky and ask that Flaxen-haired butterfly or beefcake to be your mate.

3. For those naughty souls who are getting some company action: My only other advice is to have some class and to be discrete. Set the rules of the game early and be sure you both know that any indiscretion will only speed up your imminent demise. Like many Fortune 500 companies, Nike had large convention-like Sales Meetings. At these mammoth, 1,000 person sales meetings, you could just feel the sex in the room. I learned from a Nike woman I was dating (yes…as a single man), that there were a few sales people who had multi-year affairs – but only seeing their love snack at the company sales meetings. And they would stay in the same hotel room together! That's not playin' with fire, that's juggling napalm bombs with lit fuses! Don't have lunch together in the cafeteria. Don't have drinks at company waterholes. Don't be caught behind closed doors. Don't socialize beyond a hello at company functions. If you're joined at the hip, the only thing for you to do is to prolong your life expectancy at the job until you find a new one. Notice I didn't preach any commandment at you – that's for you to figure out. We all have our own crosses to bear. But if your having an affair at the job, discretion is the better part of survival.

4. If you're single, it's OK to keep seeing her after you get your new job. But be careful. The transition from that 'secret' life to 'she's my open and above board significant other' is a tough one – and surprises most people. The only thing I can suggest is that you spend some quiet time talking to each other about what's going on. At the new company, you'll start clean and above board. And don't make jokes about how you 'fished off the company pier,' 'got your steak where you got your potatoes,' or loved 'doing the help' at your last job.

5. If you're married, *you're screwed.* Did I say that already? Oh…Oh… No…don't even try to do the 'but I'm in a bad marriage' rationale. If you're married, I strongly urge going to counseling. You stepped out for a reason. It wasn't just her or him. It was in you. Needless to say, being married and having an affair and then leaving to carry it with you to a new company is …well, you are in the same place amigo. The only benefit is that it's not with someone IN your new company. But if you're smoochin' at Café Swanky in the middle of town, you're just spiraling. If you can't resolve your marriage/affair, if you can't change your life to live clean and healthy, then for God's sakes, be discrete.

6. If someone tells you about an affair someone else is having, bury it. Don't talk about it. Period. Play mute. It's their Karma to deal with, not yours to disclose.

7. This is also covered under the "Travel" chapter, but another primal, if not cardinal, rule is "What Goes on the Road Stays on the Road." If you or any of your business colleagues get a little action on the road, you need to forget about it. Just erase the tapes. Men and women have been known to do stupid things away from home – funny, it always seems to happen a few margaritas later. It can happen to anyone and you have to take it on face value that this was a slip and not worthy of bringing the house down for it. Turn the other cheek and let it go. Forever.

8. Paid Romance: Under no circumstances can you expense strip clubs, or other X-rated habits. You laugh. Truly, I've seen it tried in two Fortune 500 companies and I just shake my head saying, 'What in the hell were they thinking?!' If you have to see that Chippendales show, or are

compelled to hit the Cottontail Ranch, you have to pony up your own coin. If you do expense it, then you should be fired for stupidity.

9. Skip the nuts: walk away from the superfreaks and wankers. True story – swear to God…. one time I walked into the restroom of the Super-Sized Ad Agency where I was working. It was early, around 7:00 am, and usually the place was empty. Just as I opened the door I saw Bill, pants down, washing Mr. Naughty in the sink. He was like a deer caught in headlights. Speechless, he quickly dried off his manliness and pulled up his trousers. I couldn't help myself. I said, "Uh….Bill, cleanliness is next to Godliness, but isn't this going a bit far?" He was so shocked to be caught, he just scurried out. I never said a word. So what's the rule? Never wash your private parts in a public restroom, no matter how comforting. There are some bizarre people in the world. Unless they're hurting someone or about to climb to the top of the building and pop off a few sniper rounds, my advice is to leave these people to themselves.

10. Learn the Law. Every person has the right to a harassment-free workplace. Take that seriously and defend it. It also means that if you are male, your traditional role of being the 'initiator' must be suspended. The unfortunate side effect of the few abusers of the legal system who have set the precedent is that neither men nor women can pay compliments of any kind to each other. You cannot and should not touch each other beyond a handshake. And if there are randy jokes or sexual barbs being bandied about, you must either stop it or excuse yourself. Because of the legal precedents, gone are the days when you could laugh and smile and maybe pay a compliment like "you look nice today." If you want that, or need that in your life (and I think this is only natural), the only place you'll find a great balance of protection that still preserves the fun dynamic between the sexes is in Europe. Meanwhile in the U.S. and for U.S. companies abroad, put it in your pocket, hold your tongue, keep your e-mails clean (and never forward dirty jokes or pictures – don't even accept them), and let's give a silent prayer that we'll actually stop the madness and reclaim some of the innocent fun that used to happen between men and women.

Do the right thing. We all can't marry our high school sweethearts. And most of us are working too hard to find time to actively socialize outside of work. If you do find yourself in love, then you know what it takes to do the right thing. Just do it. If you're in lust and it's a 'Sex and The City' thing, then pull up and get over it. And know that even though you're dashing around the world working all day and night and traveling like a banshee, good things happen to good people. After an interoffice affair turned south at one company I worked for, I swore that I simply would not date people from the office. Even though I was young and single, I just didn't like the idea of meeting people through work. At first it seemed impossible to meet people. But then it happened at the bagel shop, at the bank, and early one morning at an airport – I met the most wonderful women who were great friends and lovers and to this day I believe that you can find a life, you can find love, and you can find incredible sex *outside* the office.

ROCK STARS, BOBBLE HEAD
MANAGEMENT, & CORPORATE SIBERIA

So you're thinking, 'Interesting combo! And exactly how do these far-flung topics help me get ahead?' Well, you're asking the right question, but in reverse. Understanding the management styles in your company is not only essential to your success, but one of the single greatest ways to *avoid abject failure*.

The secret lesson here is to figure out when to stick and when to fold – when to hang in there and build your chips, and when you should find level ground, slow the plane down, and carefully hit the "eject" button.

So we start with some simple definitions about these ever-pervasive management styles. What they are not: They are not well-trained, disciplined, well-studied styles that you'll find in smart companies like Procter & Gamble, Nike, Nestlé, Dell, Apple, and a host of other top-flight places. Nope. The types I'm talking about are found in the 'wannabe' companies – the companies that may have hit $500 million or a billion or two, but never made it to the top-of-the-class. Why? Or better yet, how? How can companies like Skechers ($2 billion), Black & Decker ($6 billion), Swatch ($6 billion), or the Cheesecake Factory ($2 billion) – how can these great names be less than stellar places? Sure, some of them have posted decent stock gains, but few recruiters say, "Hey, let's raid the top guys from Skechers!" Nope. Never happens. Why? Because they know these companies are not among the 'best managed' – and the line management there is 'suffering in silence' every day that they trundle into the office.

Rock Stars: The type of management style in a company led by a single Rock Star or a group of Rock Stars is hard to deal with. Not because they are screamers like in the Garment industry. No, it's because they are *s-e-x-y*. Yep, they are seductive, cool, hip, and can always flash a smile and find the right line to get you to be a groupie. Richard Tait of Cranium fame was a Rock Star. Ooooh! Sex-eh! (said in a Scottish accent – since Richard was a

Scott). He's insanely bright, fantastically charismatic, and has incredible vision. What could be wrong, right? Richard was going to 'pioneer a whole new world of games and toys' and was off to a roaring start. He wanted to 'break the rules, do it differently, shake up the sleeping giants, and challenge every tenet of the industry.' And he was on his way…but when push came to shove, he hired a bunch of toy people, including the president. Why? Because the board & investors liked his talk, but wanted 'pedigree that was saleable.' And what happened – all his groupies found out that the dream to change the multi-billion-dollar toy industry was for sale….at a mere $70 million. Richard pulled out several million, and walked away – leaving his groupies, who undoubtedly have become typical toy zombies by now, behind. Rock Stars are also megalomaniacs – but they are fantastic at acting the part. You'll think you are in a progressive, change the world company – but you'll find it's their way or 'you're just the stupid idiot who isn't getting on board the bus.' Careful, Rock Stars tend to push vocal people under the tour bus just when you least expect it. So check out the tune before you buy into it.

Bobble head management: This is another style that is indicative of our entire U.S. (if not world) society. In a fear-based culture, no one is willing to step up and challenge the über-boss. What you see in a myriad of companies is a propensity for the surrounding management to 'yes' the leadership in charge. It's a perfected science though – it's not just 'yes,' it's usually couched with comparative thought. You'll hear the SVP talk about 'options' and the 'white elephant in the room that has to be addressed.' But it's not really the issues, or real options, and the white elephant is usually a white rabbit – small and edible. The big boss can then feel effective and smart – by jumping in and dismissing the options and elephants and pushing his or her agenda. Every last one of the suits bobbles their head up and down in tacit agreement. Yes! It's clear that Sardines Airlines needs to cram in more seats, offer less snacks and drinks, and implement the 'seat auction!' Want a center seat forward in the plane next to the thin people? Then pay for it! Brilliant! And yes, you're right! I, Mr. Best-CEO-Ever should actually talk to the lunch bucket losers who fly our airline and address them in the safety message! What a great idea! Meeee Me Me Me Meeeee! Glad you guys thought of it! It's funny to watch all the CEOs give the 'welcome aboard' message on airlines – it's an embarrassing reminder that Rock Stars and Bobble Head Management are so pervasive.

Corporate Siberia: OK, so you can't believe that you're in a company run by an aging Rock Star or that you're surrounded by Bobble Head Management. Here's what you do to avoid imploding into a smoldering fireball. *Split.* Yep. Eject. Get off the ship Ripley before that slimy beast munches your head! Why? Because if you're like most people, you're one of two kinds: the gut-it-out, grin-and-bear-it type, or the get-frustrated-and-tell-it-like-it-is type. The gut-it-outs will survive, but I ask you, if you're that type – what kind of life is that? Can't tell you how many zombies I've met in business. They just gave up and are hanging in for the paycheck. God love them – they're paying for kids, for schools, and marching one painful step at a time toward a little nest egg in retirement. Most will have a heart attack within 5 years of retirement, but no matter. It's just a waste of a life in my opinion. The tell-it-like-it-is types might get ahead for a while with their candor and fearlessness, but ultimately people in charge don't like these people – they cause trouble, challenge convention, and usually make the über-dudes look dumb. So what happens to both types? Corporate Siberia. Yep. Freeze-dried and put on ice.

Usually people in mid-level management or higher know enough to not say or do something so stupid that they would get fired. Nope, you learn how to operate, dodge, duck, and dive. But ultimately, you'll be cast out. The groupies, the yes-sayers, the young and the pretty (male or female), and the plain vanilla folks are the ones that often move forward and gut-it-outs and tell-it-like-it-is folks are put in Siberia – some place where the senior team doesn't have to interact with them, where they can't show any worth, and where they'll be till they retire, get downsized, or depart. A lot of big companies will put you in Siberia where you have no traction or ability to regain momentum – then once there, it's easier to fire or RIF you ("reduction in force") for non-performance and 'zero positive impact on the organization.' Think this is a bit dour? Never saw them, but I heard that Disney had a few buildings that were actually called 'Siberia' by the locals.

If you didn't read the interview tea leaves correctly, or if you were so desperate that you jumped into a company of Rock Stars, Bobble Head Management, and chilly Corporate Siberia corridors, then the lesson is simple: *strategize your exit.* Plan it, time it, make it work to your advantage, but you *have to get out.* What's important to note is that recruiters and other better companies *know these guys, know these companies,* and you'll be stained by staying too long. Nike almost never takes Skechers people. But Skechers frequently takes ex-Nike people. Ask yourself why. Then figure out when to level off that bullet riddled jet and set course for a new continent.

CAREER MAPPING

Career Mapping is simply this: charting out what you want to achieve or do in your working life. Sounds easy, right? If you look around at the people who are *not* making it, you come to a pretty fast conclusion that most execs have not mapped out a plan. Instead, most are like lone French Fries in search of the next Happy Meal, clinging onto any meal ticket they can. But Career Mapping is one of the top three things you have to do to be a Big Mac in today's business world.

There are two secrets that can help you become the fat cat with the most tabby treats:

1. *Stay in the same company*, or

2. *Stay in the same industry.*

You very rarely see wildly successful people who have switched careers *and* changed industries. You can still make millions in a hundred ways no matter what path you take, but the odds are slimmer that you will. In my own career, I've experienced this first hand – I went at it bass-ackwards and switched companies and industries. And even though I did well through it all, I paid a dear price in unrealized income, lower titles, less solidity and security and…well, let's just say it was a lot of moves and business cards to keep track of. I started in advertising, moved to client-side marketing in the watch and jewelry business, then moved to the sports industry, then moved to the entertainment industry, and then to the consumer technology industry. I definitely feel good about what I've achieved, and reaching the position of Senior Vice President at a $30+ billion dollar Fortune 500 company was no small feat. But I have definitely witnessed those who started at the same time I did achieve even greater success. Part of their meteoric rise is that they stayed put in the same company or in the same industry.

The problem with switching companies and industries is multi-fold. First, you don't vest in long-term shares or stock options. This is one of the main ways people become so ridiculously rich. Case in point: I left Nike with a boatload of stock options that were 'underwater' or worth nothing. Less than four years later the stock price had more than doubled and I would have been sitting on over $2 million in gains. Six years later that same option group was worth over $4 million. OK, pause....ready? OUCH! OK. I'm over it. The second big problem with switching companies is that you have to 're-learn' the players – and in the big league poker games of business, it is clear that knowing who your allies are and where the 'snake pits' are is a huge help.

If you follow the first pattern, and stay in the same company, you have the benefit of also having your 'wins' or accomplishments become *additive*. You could be a butt-ugly dog, but with a list of accomplishments at a company under your belt, you have what is known as a 'company pedigree.' You can hear the chatter in the hallway: "Harry has been a bit lackluster over the past two years, but he did start the wildly successful inflatable chair business and the bark-o-lounger for pets series...." Your past history does carry you in tough times and unless you've had some major losses, staying in the same company affords you the ability to have the wins, focus on the new ideas, and spend less time learning the ropes or navigating through the political minefields that you find in new companies.

If you follow the second pattern, then you are switching companies, but you're staying in the same industry. This affords you the ability to know the key players, the best suppliers, the retail connections for your industry, and the power-brokers who undoubtedly will be allies (or future bosses) if you play your cards right.

These truths hold for ANY industry. If you're a New York stage actor, you'll have the most success if you work the stage beat. You can move to TV and Movies and do well since it's all the same industry. But change and become a stockbroker and you're starting anew. Even if it's 'marketing,' you should stay close to a theme. If you market sports products, stay in sports, don't switch to jet engines. You'll lose traction and find you're losing years of a knowledge base.

Funny thing though. No one told me to stay in the same company or at least in the same industry. The titles and the money in my disparate far-flung jobs all sounded great. And the executive recruiters, or headhunters, all said 'do it.' But not one of those bright people ever offered the advice I'm now sharing with you.

Career Mapping also involves thinking about how you'll make yourself 'Global' and usually that means taking an international assignment. Two golden rules here. First, NEVER take a lateral move overseas. It should always be a promotion of some kind. The only exception is if you want to do the gig real, real, real bad. You know what I'm talking about... you're dying to write a book on the 'Borscht Curtain' in your off time while working in Prague. Otherwise, don't move laterally – it looks like your're being swept into the corporate backwater. The second rule is ALWAYS make sure you've got P&L responsibility in your new role. A staff function overseas is definitely a sign that things are stagnating in your career. A P&L role with a title increase says that you are being groomed for something bigger. And if nothing else, you can leverage that a lot more than a lateral move or staff assignment.

The third big thing to consider is what you want your quality of life to be. If you're single, going overseas could be a HUGE and wonderful experience. If you are married, it could be the same great time, or a real Freddy Krueger buzz saw through your marriage. So really take the time to read the literature and know if you really want to do the job and be away from friends, family, and home.

The final analysis on overseas assignments is that they season you, mature you, and make you a 'global' player, which is essential if you want to be a player in the big leagues. And usually the ex-pat packages are pretty healthy, so you'll pocket a few greenbacks along the way. More importantly, it's a great way to really see the world and experience life – in a way that most people could never afford. If your personal life can stand it, and if it's a step up, my advice is to take it – and have a great time for a few years. Then get back home close to the flame at corporate.

The last note here on Career Mapping is that you have to really do this with your significant other. You simply cannot do this in a vacuum if you want to stay involved. Single? Enjoy life to the fullest. But for the rest of the world that is married or wants to settle down, you really need to think about how both of your careers will map out. The deciding factors are just two: happiness and money. What will make you both happy and self-fulfilled, and what will yield you the most money for the time you spend. Simple as pie.

The main thing in Career Mapping is to just do it. And do it again. And again. You must constantly map what you think your next few moves are – and how you'll build wealth and stay mentally challenged. So get out that pen and start diagramming your life. And remember that with every map there is always a hidden treasure.

ACCELERATORS AND DECELERATORS TO YOUR CAREER

Here's a 'real life' analogy. To run a marathon you have to train. I mean really train hard. Every damn day, rain or shine, whether you're feeling good or not, you have to get up and run. To win a marathon, you have to do the same thing, but on a much, *much* higher and more intense level. Having run (not won….OK…just barely finished) the Boston Marathon, I can safely say that the only way to get through it is to relentlessly train – at the expense of all else. To win at a game, any game, you have to be incredibly focused. And for many who aren't in the game, or who never strive to win, you'll appear rather self-centered, selfish, or worse. The big question you have to ask is 'do I want to finish the marathon?' or 'win the game?' If you want to win, that self-centered focus is the only method I've ever seen that works.

Winning is glorious. But winning is painful, and there is a cost. It's worth it when you cross that finish line, but all who have gone before you know that to cross that line, you've had to pay the dues. Europeans have a saying for this: "the other side of the medal." You should just be aware that some people do not get this and if you're involved with one of them, don't ever expect them to.

This analogy is germane because it is identical to business. You've got to be tough, focused, and train – relentlessly – for years to stay ahead of the pack and make your way to the position you aspire to. And there are certain 'life' decisions you'll make that will either accelerate this or decelerate the speed of your ascent. A few to consider:

Baby! Having children is a gift from God and a life-positive move that brings a great deal of joy and happiness into the world and your life. I have three children and recommend it, *highly*. But having children decelerates your career – and you need to be prepared for that. Why? Because your spouse cannot do all the work by herself or himself. And when lil' Tabitha starts squealing in the middle of the night, you have to pitch in since it's your turn to console her – sometimes for hours. Then ask yourself how bright and mentally alert you'll be when you race to work for that 7:30 a.m. meeting. Bottom line is that you'll be tired. You'll split your focus – and you should. But it's split nonetheless. And you'll see those without children speed past you. The good news is that kids eventually get easier to deal with from about age five on. They start sleeping through the night and you'll actually have fewer emergencies. The other good news is that you'll be in the vast majority of execs who have kids and you'll have lots to talk about. Just know that for the first three years, you'll be pedaling harder just to keep up.

This is going to sound a bit rough, but Family is also a decelerator to your career. If you've ever cared for an elderly parent, had to bail out a 'misguided' family member, found yourself going to more weddings and funerals than you care to – you know how rough it can be. And it shows at work. You cannot do these superhuman feats and still expect to be performing your best at work. Just doesn't happen. Truly, if you ask the friends and families of the top guns in the Fortune 500, they would probably characterize these people as great business leaders…but probably not the warmest and most compassionate parents, friends, or family people. I don't think this is because they didn't want to be great fathers/mothers, friends or family people, but it's because they were just staying focused to win. And they knew that winning, though a personal sacrifice to them, would mean their family would be financially strong for a long time to come. Now, there are more psycho-kids as a result of this strategy than you can imagine, but the simple fact is that these people wanted to run a Marathon, and they simply made the call to focus on it. To some friends and family this sets a marvelous example. To others, it twists them up and apart.

One interesting note is that a strong family can also be an accelerator to your career. A sage parent who can help guide you and provide emotional support is invaluable. And for those of you who are parents to young people in their 'formative' years in business – the best thing in the world is to make sure they know there is a 'safe haven' for them if it all comes tumbling down. This will give them the courage to fight valiantly and without fear.

One big decelerator is your addictions. It could be sex, or gambling, or drinking, or hell, pick any of the vices. Most people have a vice or two – a real weakness that they just cannot help (shocked I say!). Just know that it's all an energy game. The more juice you put on say …topping your college tequila Jell-O shot record…the less juice you have to devote to your career. Be a great manager of the juice – your energy – and you'll find yourself on a rapid ascent.

By now you've surmised that a few of these decelerators can actually turn into accelerators – if you manage them carefully. The *biggest* accelerator and perhaps the biggest decelerator comes down to *one* thing – but first a little Jar Head wisdom:

Bob Weber was the hard-charging, Marine-trained VP of Operations at the Bulova Watch Company where I worked. He told me that he had been talking to his son about success. Bob had already achieved a great deal of success of his own at Bulova and was a 'Master of the Universe' at the stock market. He taught his son valuable life lessons – like focusing to win (both he and his son held wrestling titles at their high schools), and learning how to make oodles of money in the stock market. One day Bob's son asked him, "Dad, I've done everything you've suggested – got the Ivy League degree, got the job at a great Investment Bank, have a sizable portfolio, and I'm really happy. Your advice has been great – so what's the biggest advice you can give me from here?"

Bob said he thought for a while then said, "The single greatest thing that you can do now…that will either make you or break you…that will either significantly improve your wealth and happiness…or that will make you broke and miserable…is selecting the right spouse." His son was really taken aback. Bob explained that he's seen bad relationships wreck people – both mentally and financially. Marrying the right person when you are in your mid-term is the thing that will strengthen you and provide that solid foundation, or weaken you and break you. I think Bob is 100% correct.

In today's business world, you need to pay more attention than ever to your personal life. Really think through those decisions – from getting a dog to having a baby, from getting married, to how much time you plan to spend on family matters. And think of your life like a beaker filled with your 'Life Energy' – you need to figure where to conserve every drop and where you need to pour it on. Better yet, surround yourself with those activities and people that can really *add* to your Mojo. Every decelerator can be an accelerator and every defeat a victory, if you watch how you flow your Life Energy. Keep it positive and think through those life-altering decisions. The most heartwarming thing I can tell you after all these years that I've spent on the planet is that you'll just know it in your heart and mind when you make the right choice.

WHEN BAD THINGS HAPPEN

Story goes like this: Old, battered, fired executive is packing up to leave his office and accidentally bumps into the Mr. New Guy. The old guy says, "Oh, you'll want these three envelopes – the only thing I could think of that would be really useful to you." Mr. New Guy, full of piss and vinegar, shoved them in a drawer and forgot about them. And Mr. New Guy started on the quest to be the Jabba the Hut of Business at his job. Things went well for a while. Then, bad things started to happen. Inventories went up. Sales went down. Costs went up. Profits went down. And Mr. New Guy was under a lot of heat. He tried pulling this lever and that lever, but to no avail – all the stats were going the wrong way.

One day, while sitting with that morbid stare we sometimes see from numb executives, ba-boom! He remembers the envelopes and digs them out. The three envelopes are labeled "When Things Go Bad" and stamped "the first time," "the second time," and "the third time." So he tears open the first envelope and it says the following: "OK, you hit your first wall. You've tried a few things but nothing worked. So here's what you do. Fire 10% of the workforce. You'll have less workers, and your good workers will leave to find more secure jobs – but Wall Street will love you, and your balance sheet will look good for a while. Do this and prepare to win!" Mr. New Guy immediately called HR and implemented the plan. Like magic, Wall Street applauded this most excellent move – the stock went up, and the balance sheet was back on track.

And time went on. But things were not well in the Kingdom. Sure enough, having only the 'middle of the pack' managers meant less brilliance, no home runs, and harder-to-get base hits. Again, orders fell, profits shrank, and the wolves of Wall Street were very unhappy. Mr. New Guy, being a learning organism, immediately went to the desk drawer and pulled out the second envelope. He ripped it open and read the advice, "OK, you hit your second wall. Things went well for a while, but now you just don't see how to get it back on track. So here's what you do. First, axe 15% more of the workforce, and sell off a few divisions. Oh, don't forget to sell your headquarters and lease back the space. Your workers will be demoralized, and since you're selling divisions and your working 'home' they will not think there is a future. You'll drain your remaining talent, and if there are brilliant people left, they'll be in a coma – or hiding under a rock. Still, do this and your costs will go down, you'll free up capital, and Wall Street will love you. Do this, and prepare to win!" Mr. New Guy couldn't act fast enough. Pow! People were fired. Bam! Divisions were sold off. Boom! The Headquarters was sold. And it worked. Ahhh, relief.

And then one day, what do you know, it happened again. Competition was swamping the Widget factory with new and innovative products that Mr. New Guy's team couldn't even dream of. Competition seemed more nimble, more motivated, hungrier somehow. And Mr. New Guy couldn't think of what to do next – he had fired 25% of the people, sold almost everything, and cut every cost to the bone. Wearily, he held the last envelope in his hand, trembling a bit since he knew it was the last time he'd be able to pull on such sage advice. He opened it up and felt his jaw drop as he read "Prepare Three Envelopes."

Don't you love a good story!

Let's get a couple of facts on the table. First, all businesses have down cycles. Call it Keynesian economics, call it Darwinism, call it the Immutable Law of Business Physics, or just call it life. There are going to be ups and downs. The real key is how you handle them. The second fact is that you should know is not to take it personally. Sure, you may have caused it, but it's not about the world hating you. You are not the bad guy, and there isn't a flaw in your personality (well maybe there is, but we'll assume for now that there isn't). Third…not sure you're ready for this…is that all down cycles, all bad things, all crises in your life are *custom made* by the Great Cosmic Universe *just for you*, just for you to deal with and work through, just to teach you the lessons in life that you needed to have.

You attracted them into your life.

You didn't cause them, but you somehow, in some way attracted them to you. Take heart, for if you can attract problems into your life, you can attract solutions – and a better place too. OK, that's a bit heavy, so let's get to some concrete strategies and tactics for when things go bad. Here's what I've learned:

Don't just grit your teeth and bear it. Do something! And that something is to take responsibility for your share in it. Don't duck the bad stuff. Lean into it. When you do this you gain credibility with the team and superiors and you also gain power – power by recognizing it. Ducking it, shirking it, dodging it, or saying "Well, Dick's team was really the one that did that...." is whussy. Jump in and take control.

Wall Street Journal hard news style.
When things go bad, really – and I mean really – check your emotions and that natural human tendency to be negative, or sarcastic. Think 'Subject/Verb/Object.' Stick to using facts and make sure people are separating facts from fiction. Reserve judgments – make sure you are perceived as the one who is calm, levelheaded and dealing just with the facts. The only personality trait to show is a bit, underscore a little bit, of humor. Unless you're a surgeon and people are at risk of dying, most of what people do is not the cause of life and death – so be sure every once in a while to have a little humor.

Reflect.
When bad things happen, it is sometimes a good time to reflect upon what is going right in your life and what is going wrong. It's a good time to reflect where you're at and whether or not you want to be there. Take this seriously. Don't just hang on for the sake of hanging on. It may be just the opportunity you need to *reset*. That may involve short-term pain for long-term gain. But keep your eye on the big picture.

Don't hang onto a really bad situation.
It's better to resign. Once a long time ago I was in a job I couldn't stand. You know the feeling – when you open your eyes in the morning and the first thing you think of is "I just can't do this today. I'd rather sell hotdogs on the street than do this job one more day." And despite a "screamer" president, and despite an extremely negative environment where the three management tools were Ego, Blame and Contempt, I hung in there. For years. All the while I was thinking, this is a good résumé builder, a great

stepping-stone. You can imagine how odd I thought it that I had trouble finding another job. Hmmmm. Big title. Big Job. Great Guy. Blond. Cute. Makes a mean soufflé. No takers. What was up? Then I interviewed with an old company where I thought I would be a shoo-in to return. I didn't even get *that* job! Later I heard that it was down to me and another candidate – and that the President of the company said, 'I think he's a great guy and all, but he's been with that crap company too long. No real talent would want to work for those jerks for as long as he did unless something was wrong.'

Stunned. I was simply stunned. All that time, all that pain – when I was thinking I was gaining something by staying, the exact opposite was true. From that moment on, I vowed to abide by the cardinal rule: If the job feels like it sucks, then the job sucks – and other companies know it and will downgrade you for it. In the end, I didn't regret the experience (I don't regret many really), since I had some incredible times at that lousy old company and learned invaluable lessons like this one. So once again, sometimes bad things happen for a reason. But life is short and there's no reason to hang onto a bad thing. Trust that you are a good person who is talented and that there's a better job out there for you.

Watch your home life.
It's just a matter of fact that work influences our home life. If work sucks, chances are you're beating on the cat – or letting your Dr. Nasty Alter Ego surface at home. No big revelation here, only to say that you must try to leave your problems at the door. Or, at a minimum, set specific time limits (and no more) to discuss your troubles with your spouse. Updates are good. Whining is not. Communicating is great. Bitching is boring. When you get home, change and go for a run or a long walk with the dog and kids. And be sure you're getting time to meditate a little bit on what you want your work life to be and what you want your home life to be – and work like hell to keep them distinct.

The Power of Positive Thinking.
This is also a simple one: *Attitude is Everything*. You can elect to respond poorly to poor situations, or respond positively to them. The latter is harder, but you'll live longer and have more fun along the way. Once I

stenciled on the inside of my front door 'Think Positive.' In the next 24 months, I was promoted to Account Supervisor, and then to VP Management Supervisor. As I look back at the road behind, I can definitely tell you that I suddenly did not grow a second brain, or an extra set of hands – it was only because I became more positive about my work. Funny, it made me more positive about my home life, too. I said to myself: 'It's my job to walk into a room of people and charge up the place with positive energy.' It was very tough some days to keep this up. But I was not going to let myself get mentally down.

The real guiding light here is this: When things go bad, stay positive and be the 'voice of optimism.' And particularly for the team under you, be sure to compliment and 'juice' them. The law of karma says that you'll get more than that back in return.

WHEN GOOD THINGS HAPPEN

Here's the simple, two-word lesson: *Be Humble.*

A couple examples of good things (in case you have trouble recognizing them): a promotion; a big-fat raise; a little puny raise; a good note from your boss; winning a company award; being elected to an important committee; surviving a layoff; getting transferred to a better division; getting a lift in the corporate sled (the corporate jet); and winning the company football lottery. That's about it. Really. Won't lie to you – you're probably not going to find enlightenment or wake up in Shangri-La. Still, good things happen, and when they do, *be humble.*

What tends to happen to most worker bees and executives is that when good things happen, life becomes wonderful and we want to tell the world. Unfortunately, most people don't understand the basic human hierarchy of needs – including the famed Maslovian study on 'esteem' and getting the 'esteem of others.' What does this have to do with the price of tea in China? Simply this – the more you celebrate victory, the more some twisted, bent-out-of-shape slob down the hall will want to electrify your swimming pool. Seriously, people love an underdog, but will go out of their way to bomb the winner. It's more pronounced in America than in Europe or Asia, but it's a global human phenomenon. The worst part about bragging about your victories is that people will never come up to your face and say 'shut up Joe, you're not *that* brilliant.' Nope. They'll just talk behind your back about how arrogant you are. Then when the chips are down or you lose some major pitch or do poorly, you will be slammed by your personal Greek chorus of critics. It's truly best to be "Confidently Humble" about your winnings. Don't do the "aw shucks, it was just dumb luck" approach – I mean it's OK to take credit, but just don't bask in your self-appointed glory. So to recap, when good things happen:

- Be confidently humble. And yes, I'm gonna say that a few more times – it's really, really, really important.

- Use phrases like "yeah, it was a good win, the team should feel great," or "thanks, the promotion is great and I'm definitely celebrating – we have some big work ahead of us." Even as much as you want to say "Hah! Smoked all you lazy-ass bastards!," say that over a few margaritas with your best non-work friends - but never in the office.

- Realize that you're now under a greater microscope with your superiors. Whoever just rewarded you is, in effect, on the line for the praise/reward. So you need to really pound out the effort to make sure you keep the streak alive. And don't expect praise for the next big push – just do the job well and good things will happen.

- Share the wealth. If there are teammates involved, be sure to pass along the praise/reward. Don't overdo it, but a simple note to say 'thanks' goes miles. It's funny. If you ask managers what they want for their people, a lot of times 'simple recognition for a job well done' comes up. Then ask them when was the last time they actually gave praise to someone – and you'll see embarrassing looks since most people don't do it that often. Share the wealth.

Under all circumstances, avoid holding court. I've seen this with the most junior managers who have just one person to supervise, to SVPs who manage hundreds. Holding court is that nasty habit of *telling people all the good things that you do for them...or how smart you are.* This is a hyperextension of 'when good things happen' – since the good thing was that these folks found themselves in a position of power. Normally, you should focus on the obvious, which is becoming an effective coach of the team, not a dominating player.

The most incredible example of holding court I've seen is the case of a seasoned executive named Brent Willis (it's a public story, so I think it's OK to dish). Brent was the President of Coca-Cola Latin America and then became Chief Marketing Officer of K-Mart. At Disney, we had signed a several hundred million dollar deal with K-Mart, and we were in the throes of devising the advertising and in-store plans, when Brent and I were introduced.

Within a few meetings, Brent showed himself to be a smart, energetic, insightful leader – but there was one small glitch – he was reveling in his new roll of CMO of the third most powerful retailer in the country. Somewhere along the way, Brent just decided to hold court with *Brand Week* – you know, a 'day in the life of the new CMO' type of story. Mistake number one was that tootin' yer own horn in the mass media is a very dangerous proposition. Mistake two was that his boss, Chuck Conoway, was a total TEAM guy (actually played in the NBA with guys like Magic Johnson), and in his mind, to be a high-priced 'individual' player was probably not a good idea. Brent's a smart guy and my guess is he didn't get a fair shake in the article – but he succeeded in disenfranchising himself from the minimum wage worker bees at K-Mart, upset Jacqueline Smith who was one of their 'marquis' brands, and lost some serious altitude.

By now, you know my mantra: when good things happen, be confidently humble...and don't brag.

One last note about when good things happen: Celebrate early and often. When you have a victory no matter how small, be sure to go out to dinner with your S.O., or whomever, and give yourself a pat on the back. We tend to come home and report about the trials and tribulations of the day, but we don't usually find the time to celebrate. It doesn't have to be big, but when good things happen, share your joy and enthusiasm.

YOUR RÉSUMÉ: YOUR ENTIRE BUSINESS LIFE IN 2-D

Here's a mind-blowing fact: Over 80% of communication between human beings is non-verbal. Imagine this for a moment. That means 80% of all that great articulation from your Einstein-like brain is...well, it's just 'audio swill.' Only 20% makes it into the cerebral cortex of the listener. What else makes it through? A few things: how you appear, how you act, the body language you consciously or unconsciously present, and ultimately the persona you project.

So when we talk about presenting yourself in your résumé you better make sure you're also thinking about the *full* flight plan. Whether it's the reading you are doing, the business toys you are sporting, or a number of things you do or say, they all send out little signal beacons about you to everyone else. One of the big-as-the-Grand-Canyon findings that came to me late in the game is that from the moment you walk into the room, all eyes are *dissecting* you – every thread, every accessory, how you take notes, where you put your phone down on the table, the shoes you wear, and the persona you project through body language, facial expression and tone of voice. But it all starts with a little piece of paper.

Your résumé is the single greatest work you'll ever compose. It's your calling card, your executive history, your one-stop-'me-shop' that will mean the difference between getting you that interview...or becoming today's breakfast for Vinnie's Document Shredding company. It is the first thing that people usually 'see' of you – and more importantly, it's the first place you show your true values. Values in a résumé? Ha! You did miss the first day of class! Pencils up! Now read on....

Your résumé is your special aphrodisiac, meant to scintillate, cajole, bait, and lure your prospective employer. It's the potion that will intoxicate them and have them panting in ecstasy for this Titan or this Goddess, who has clearly moved mountains with 30% less resources and a 157% return on investment. What's so amazing to me is that so many people spend *so little time* on it. I think I've heard all the stories: "If they really want me, they'll want to see me." Or, better yet, "any company that judges people just on their résumé, well that's a company I don't want to work for." To this I say: Really now! You have to stop smoking crack! The headhunters may know you, but they can't get you past the gate if they don't have the magic key. Even if the best headhunter says something to a hiring company like, "Look Bob, you just have to see Maurie. He's a garmento, but he's the best, a real killer, the shark in the tank you need. Hell, I'd hire him today if it was my business," there is no way that Maurie is getting an interview if his paper looks like three day old cabbage.

Oh, and you young video turks or multi-media jockies who created a touch-enabled video interactive résumé hosted on your own server farm, then I applaud you for your killer creativity. Yes, it will break through. Yes, they will all nod with tacit excitement...but they still need your paper to make sure you're real. The videos, music demos, circus stunts will all get you noticed, but you'll never get in for the series of interviews at SexyJob Co. if you don't have clean, concise paper. And Yes! It's true, some companies are already all digital – and we all will be 100% paperless someday. But even for the digital submissions of résumés, you need the same thing: snappy content that keeps their eyeballs glued to you. So here's how it works best:

It has to be right. It has to be crisp. It has to show results. It has to be.....*HONEST.*

Let's talk about this for a minute. Raise your hands if you've ever been tempted to add in that extra 'exaggeration' bullet point on your résumé? Or how many of you have thought about using these obvious stretches?:

- Designed and Implemented Zee-Widgits new Zantac dispenser, yielding 950% market share gain in less than 4 months. Hard P&L responsibility.

- Invented the Wheel. Through innovative marketing, the wheel became the cornerstone of modern civilization. Drove sales personally to $47,000,000 trillion.

No one is going to believe that you had 950% market share gain. No one is going to believe that you invented and drove the wheel business to

$47,000,000 trillion (all of us seasoned execs would know it would be much, much larger than that!). I exaggerate of course, but the honesty I'm talking about is pretty clear to those with a conscience. It means that you really cannot state that you have a college degree when you don't. As much as you want to say "you're joking, no one would do that," I can tell you I've seen it twice in my career. Both people were excellent, upstanding, talented folks. They just felt they needed that extra 'oomph' on their paper to get ahead, and they just faked it. One was a dear friend, and when she got fired for lying on her résumé, I was in shock. Later, over a drink, I just asked, "What the hell did you do that for? I mean saying you won an award, or ran a business, or have a degree – when you don't, well that's just bald-faced lying." She told me that she had been on the street for a while and that a close friend had actually told her that she should just put down a degree. She said she thought it was a rare day in Hell when anyone checks. Well lesson #489: companies *DO* check – especially Fortune 500 companies. Especially today.

The key to honesty is knowing where the line is. And it's simple. *Don't make up anything.* If you didn't do that campaign, earn that degree, or get those results…then don't BS it. It's a Karmic Law that it will come back to bite you.

Now, that's not to say that you shouldn't make the most out of every experience that you've had. I was counseling a friend on her résumé and she had this big gap – big enough to drive a truck through – which read, "Took a year off to travel Australia." I started quizzing her. Why? What drove you to do it? Was it a sanctioned event? What did you do there? Turns out it was for a non-profit educational group, where she taught kids outdoor training skills. I rewrote the section, highlighting the aspect of working with kids in a non-profit company teaching them about sports. She later interviewed at Nike and they cited her volunteer work with kids and sports as real dedication. She was hired and is today a major player in their footwear business. It was real and she earned every minute of credit for what she did.

The key is to know the line. Deceit and lying are…yes…in case no one told you…*they are bad. Baaaad bad bad.* No, there are really no exceptions. And no, it's not too late to go back and edit your résumé to make sure that it's not deceitful or full of 'exaggerations.' But I do want you to think about making the most out of what you did.

If you are more senior, then the key is to fish out all the results possible and put them in the best light. For example, if you started a business, and then you left it when it hit $50MM, but now it's $700MM, it's OK to put "ideated, pitched, secured funding, and started Zee-Widgits, growing it to $50MM. The company is a $700MM company today." It's true, it's clean, and you've indicated (but not taken credit) that the business has since grown to be more successful – off of the foundation that you built.

On Extracurriculars. No matter whether you're new to the game or older, you want to put in some very cool extracurriculars to show depth of personality. They tend to fall into three categories:

1. **Professional.** If you're in marketing, you should join the American Marketing Association. If you're an English professor, you'll need to join the Modern Language Association. Join the tried and true associations of your industry.

2. **Charitable:** Make sure you have something that shows you give something back. Volunteer and put in the 'safe' charities, like Make-A-Wish Foundation. My advice is to avoid putting in religious or political charities – you never know how the reader might respond to your work with Baka Baka Jihadists of America. A short and safe charity affiliation in your résumé might actually be more important than your stated professional achievements. Some big dogs really feel that people who do this simply make better employees and are subsequently fast-tracked in their business career.

3. **Personal:** Home renovation, Gardening, Music…whatever. Put them in and show the future employer that you've got a life, that you are not one-dimensional. It also may end up being the talking point in your next interview.

The last point to cover is how to put it together. I'd advise that you *not* pay a résumé service. It's not a bad route, but you'll look the same as the next bub out there pedaling paper. My suggestion is that you can do this better yourself. Get on the web and look at sample résumés. Look at the layouts and how they deliver information. Always make your résumé look like the position you *want* to achieve...or even the one above that. Then spend time. A lot of time. If you are not spending at least 20 hours writing, editing, re-writing, re-editing your résumé, then something is wrong. It's absolutely, incredibly important. A few other 'bonehead' tips that surprisingly few people know:

- Use Times Roman, or a standard font. Don't put in any special graphics. Why? Because everyone e-mails résumés, and some machines may not have that Elvis watermark or Zee-Widgit typeface that your friend told you was 'the Shiz."

- Keep it under two pages if you're under 35 and under 3 pages if you're older.

- Be the reader: If you think about the number of pieces of 'crap' that come across the screens or desks of recruiting companies, then you'll know to keep it snappy.

- Don't be cute. No ☺ symbols or exclamation marks!! Keep out the humor, double-entendres, and the non-essential. Thx! BFF! XOXOXO!

- Have a friend read it. Flip it to someone you trust for a sanity check and a proofread for Pete's sake.

- Be real. It counts. It shows.

It is imperative in business that you are honest and real – but that you also take every point you've earned and highlight it. Armed with your new 'résumé heat,' you'll actually *attract* the job momentum towards you.

EXTRCURRICULARS FOR THE BIG DOGS

Your extracurricular activities are what most business people talk about when meeting for drinks after work, or during the office lunch. It is important that you choose them carefully – and if you really have to do semi-pro mud wrestling or you love getting more and more snake tattoos on your sizzling hot body – well, let's just not talk about those at the office.

Fitting In: Remember the profile of the people who are in the top slots and running the big companies. They are usually Protestant, Catholic, Jewish, or one of the 'big' religions. Layer on top of this that most subscribe to the Connecticut WASP culture that says 'have class at all times.' They probably went to better schools and have advanced degrees – or certainly are brighter and have more drive than your average bear. Most serious business execs read the *New York Times* and *Wall Street Journal* (no matter what remote part of the Earth they are conquering), and the media companies will tell you they read *GQ, W Magazine, Time, HBR, Runner's World, Pottery Barn Catalog* and…well… you get the picture. It's not *Hawg Tied Rodeo Times* or even *Chess Weekly*. It is, of course, good to drive up your Awareness Quotient and know that *Hawg Tied* is being merged with *Rodeo Roundup*. But the point is to add extracurriculars that help you build relationships with others by finding 'common ground.'

Some 'Approved' business extracurricular activities:

- Most professional sports. This means Baseball, Football, Basketball – not Curling, not Synchronized Swimming, not Biathlon. Nothing wrong with them, they just are not conversation sports. OK, I really don't mean it when I say there is nothing wrong with them. Biathlon? Come on?!…really?

- Golf. Say no more. It still remains the sport of Corporate MegaSaurs. Tennis is a close second. Again, if you love water ballet, you *gotta* do it, but it's good to at least know some of the basics of the bigger sports.

- Cycling, Running, Marathoning, Triathlon are all respected – you'll get admiration, but you won't get that true bonding conversation with a wide group of execs that you'll have with pro sports. Major exception #1) if you work for a company where the founder loves a certain sport. At Nike, I started getting big time into running – and even finished the Boston Marathon (and yes, it killed me. Seriously.) But then Phil Knight started the whole company based on running shoes. Major exception #2) certain sports like Yoga, Swimming, and the trendy Ping Pong are positive, conversational sports. But for now, you'll go further in the Fortune 500 or any business if you brush up on pro sports including Tennis and Golf. This is not an 'un-PC' comment, or 'confining,' or 'sexist' – it is simply today's reality. And for those of you who simply must raise your eyebrows, think of it this way: when you move to China, don't you think you should learn Chinese? Write us, OK?

- Reading. It's not so much an extracurricular as it is a prerequisite. Read a *New York Times* bestseller every once in a while – keep my publisher happy!

- Home renovation is also great. Doing that extension, dealing with contractors, doing the work yourself – are great conversation items.

- Playing a musical instrument or being a music aficionado is a safe haven extra curric in business. Music is pretty universal and most people have hacked away at some instrument in their past. It's a good executive conversation and playing music feeds the soul. OK....Skin Head Death Metal bands might be a bit much, but you know what I mean.

The Must Haves: There are a few extracurriculars that are 'Must Haves' if you want to succeed in the big leagues. First, you must have a spiritual affiliation – being part of a church, charity, or humanitarian organization and going regularly is critical not only for your personal and spiritual health, but also for your business life. Remember the profile of the top dogs – they are usually pretty anchored people and church/charity/humanitarian pursuits are a part of that. *It doesn't matter what denomination or flavor*, but dropping that you were doing the pro bono thing over the weekend is a real positive. Says you're solid (and best of all, *makes you solid!*).

The second 'must have' is family – directly *or by 'extension.'* You should spend time with family anyway – they're the only ones who will really tell it like it is. But being tight with Family is another real positive that says to business colleagues that you're solid. Having a family as we discussed earlier *can* drive you nuts and actually be a decelerator for a spell in your career. That's still true (it's good that I'm consistent!), but whether you have a family, or are an involved aunt, uncle, grandparent, or whatever gives you an edge over the lone wolf types that snarl whenever asked if they have family near by. Family and friends show that you're a real human being and not just another corporate cyborg.

The third must have is to be good at a sport. This doesn't mean that you have to be an Olympian – but being able to hold your own on a company golf or tennis outing is really important. Being on the sidelines is.....well...get back to me and let me know how *you* think you were perceived by being on the sidelines. And being good means you just know the rules and can hit the ball. No one really cares if you woof it – in fact it makes you one of us. But saying 'no, no, I never play' is just not good comradeship. Also remember it's better to *be a good sport*, than it is to *be good at sports*.

One last thought on the Must Haves – you can't fake these. You can't dabble and only learn half the game – 'what! 18 holes. No! I only play 17 at my club!' Commit. Play the game every once in a while. Hey, you never know, in the process you might actually get hooked on something new!

ETIQUETTE: A TOUCH OF CLASS IN THE MODERN WORLD

For all you Preppies out there, all Sons and Daughters of the American Revolution, all Oxford and Tokyo Academy trained students, and all Royalty – you don't need this. Someone probably put the Julie Andrews book on your head and made you learn the fine art of etiquette when you were growing up. For the rest of us garish low-landers, we need help.

The first role of etiquette is that if you suddenly feel awkward, *you are*. The most important thing you can learn is to humbly accept defeat and learn how to bow out of a bad situation. Take a cue from the Brits and say "Terribly sorry. Truly. Very sorry, Bad Show, So Sorry…" and move on.

Most of us know how to hold a fork and know not to chew with our mouths open. Forgive the 'remedial' nature of this section, but it just amazes me the number of so-called 'seasoned' executives who must have missed class the day these tips were given. So here are eleven essentials:

1. Men – Always open a door for a lady. No matter what is politically correct or not. It's the last vestige of civility and civilization must not let it go. If she opens the door for you, please say 'thank you.' Neither one of you are sexist pigs trodding on the backs of the other chromosome pool…you're just being nice.

2. Revolving door – Men, it is still customary to let the woman go first.

3. Women – Always let the men open the door or let you go first without making a crack about what a sexist pig he is (even if he is). Men have a role in this world: they take out the garbage, do all that car stuff, carry luggage, and open doors. It's simple, men understand it, and it works.

4. Please, wash your hands – especially in the bathroom. That goes double if there are other executives there with you. Sure, we know about the drug-resistant bacteria we are cultivating by over-washing, really we do. But you just wiped or touched your privates – and I'd personally feel

better about all the doors you open with those same hands if you wash them!

5. Yes, if you can see the underarm stains, everyone else can.

6. Get a haircut/see the hairdresser at least once a month.

7. Cologne, Perfume, Antiperspirant, moisturizing lotion and floss. Can't believe I'm saying it. Don't be a pioneer in changing societal norms on etiquette or grooming.

8. For Men and Women: Lose the piercings and the peroxide pink streaks in your hair. Want to play with the big boys and girls? Then don't make yourself into a carnival attraction – no matter how you think that *'says something'* about you. Unless…of course …you *work* for a Carnival and actually *are* the carnival attraction.

9. And just think twice, no….three times, about getting that Snake tattoo on your loin. So Harry, if you do decide to get the tattoo despite this sage advice, remember that if you 'do the horizontal mambo' with one of the people in the office, then everybody in the office will know about your 'trouser cobra' – and it will be like a thought bubble above your head every time you present anything to anyone. They won't hear your brilliant presentation on tax-loss carry forward. All they'll think about is that damn snake. And if this paragraph hit home, you'll want to read the chapter about sex in the office if you haven't already.

10. Men: In case you were never told, women look at shoes big time. Your shoes. And when your shoes are shabby, you are a "Cap L" loser. Plain and simple. Don't try to understand it, it just works that way. Have a woman boss? Buy nice shoes (several pairs, cowboy), and keep them nice. After all my years in business, I just learned this amazing fact recently. Ties are pretty important too, but shoes rule.

11. Read John T. Malloy's classic book, *Dress for Success*, or the newer *The New Dress for Success*. Be very mindful of your "image" – conveyed through dress, grooming, posture and language.

Speaking of which, cut down on the *fucking swearing* that you are doing! You talk like a goddamn sailor! Nope. It just doesn't fly as well. "Think Yiddish, Act British." Ask people to name the classiest movie stars – and you'll usually get Brits like Pierce Brosnan, Emma Thompson, Kate Beckinsale. The British way should be your role model for how to be classy.

Classy behavior and good etiquette will get your further in business. Period. Think about the last time you saw a guy who had pants too long, wearing a once-white shirt and a limp tie, who has poor posture and who is swearing with every other word. Then think of the President of the United States, or the CEO of General Electric, or the last interview you saw with George Clooney or Angelina Jolie. What do you see? Immaculate clothes (even when they are casual, they are usually very tastefully put together); well groomed; clean language. They didn't do that once they were at the top. They did it early on to *get* to the top.

You must also think about developing a unique sense of style. In business, my British father always wore a double-breasted suit and a matching bow tie and handkerchief in the suit pocket. I used to think it was pretty one dimensional, but he always looked well dressed. Later in life at a few social celebrations, I would talk to friends of my parents and they invariably would comment about how much they loved my father's sense of style – always with references to the double-breasted suits, the bow ties and handkerchiefs. It takes a while, and it's really got to be something inside of you that drives it, but you must develop your own sense of style – those accents that really define you from the rest of the pack. Yes, it does cost money to dress well for the office. But remember the Top Dogs – they didn't change once they got to the top, they got there because they had class, understood etiquette, were well groomed, and dressed with their own unique sense of style.

RULES OF THE ROAD: A TRAVEL PRIMER

Two options, pick one:

Option 1:
When on the road, drink like a fish, swear like a drunken pirate, spend $875 a night on the best hotel in town, watch several seriously questionable movies in your room while ordering a triple shrimp cocktail to go with the caviar and steak …or,

Option 2:
Ask yourself: "Do I like this job?" "Do I want to keep it…or maybe get promoted someday?"

If you've picked option 1, then forget about Option 2 and take a few days off to celebrate the fact that serious business isn't for you, and that your path is going to take you to all kinds of new and exciting low-budget places. If you've picked Option 2, then read on.

There is only ONE simple lesson on travel in business and in the Fortune 500: *travel smart.* Sometimes this gets expressed as 'spend the money as if it was your own.' I don't think anyone *really* subscribes to that. If they did, we'd all fly coach – even from New York to Singapore. If we did, we'd all be staying two to a room in Motel 6 like they did in early WalMart days, and we'd all be drinking domestic beers (oh, the horror!). Bottom line is that most people like to have a few comforts when away from home. For all the finance bean counters out there, repeat after me: this is a *Good Thing.* One of the biggest things that demoralized my troops for a while was when a policy moron wrote that personal calls on business trips could not exceed 10 minutes per day. I ranted and raved, but I'll be damned that on the very next expense report turned into me, one of my stars had a 65-minute call home – from Europe! OK, so there is excess and a lot of people get suckered in I guess. But the last thing to do is to punish the many for the sins of the few. The best way to ensure that you and your company will have the right travel policy is for everyone to travel smart – and not live life to excess. A few happy tips from a guy with several million miles:

Expense Reports

- Pretty simple rule: You *have to* do/organize the expense reports on the plane ride home. No excuses! No matter if you are the big-cheese EVP or the Assistant Project Manager. If you slip, it sits on your desk and you get this nasty reputation with Amex or your company card. Just get it done on the trip home.

- Don't put in for every damn nickel. Really, keep your karma clean and make sure your company always owes you a few bucks. I've never been audited, and my reputation for being 'cheap' on travel went a million miles in getting ahead. *Do* put in for everything legit and make sure that *you* pay the difference over the company limits – making sure it is highlighted for the company to see. So if your dinner max is $100 per head, and you spent $155, don't try to 'slip' it through – pony up the difference and only expense $100. Another rule on reports is to provide a good level of detail. The IRS really does want to know the purpose of the trip and saying, "to present films" really won't cut it. If you ever get involved in an audit, they will ask, and you'll be glad you put "to rollout three film properties to the New York Licensee network." It only takes a few seconds, but it really makes the system work.

- The last rule is to set up a company business bank account and your own non-company, personal business charge card. Put your expense check reimbursements into your company business account. If you take someone out to dinner and talk business all night – but don't feel it's a company expense – then put it on your personal business charge card. At year-end, Sal your accountant will be lovin' me since you'll have a clean record of every non-reimbursed business expense on your card.

Let's face it….business travel is tough enough without all this expense jazz. But until some bright CFO figures out the ultimate 'paperless' system, we are stuck with it. Some companies like Pepsi-Cola are way ahead of the pack where you simply charge on your corporate card and the bill gets paid. You review your bill and make notes and send it in. Voila! Millions of dollars spent on mindless tracking/shuffling of paper is saved. Meanwhile, dig in partner, and BE SMART.

Traveling Alone
Sorry that you have to travel alone, but traveling alone can be a great time to reflect, catch up on old correspondences, make lofty plans, or write a book on the how to make it in business! The big advice here is 'Stay Connected!' Don't be out of the loop back at the business ranch for long. Fly in, get it done, and fly the hell back home where your life is.

Traveling in Packs
God help you because there's always a troublemaker in the damn bunch! There are a couple of thoughts about packs:

• Never be the first one in the lobby in the morning.

• Never be the last to close the bar.

• Never be seen goo-goo eyeing anyone for any length of time – even if you're in the exact same hotel where the Victoria's Secret supermodels are staying, or the Hugh Jackman Look Alike casting call is being held.

• Never get 'wasted' at a business function. It's a bad deal in every way.

• Never use inappropriate humor or references...even when you are buddie-buddie-gee-those-five-margaritas-went-down-easy intimate with the group. Change the subject if someone is being racist or sexist – and if it's pointed and bad, and you feel awkward, then bow out. If you're a manager, it's your responsibility to cut that garbage off. Most of the time, though, people don't go there.....thankfully.

• Never be the one to drive the chock-full-of-execs company rental van, unless you plan not to drink. Take a cab – especially in a new city you don't know.

OK...enough of the 'nevers.' People do try to defy gravity all the damn time, though, so my advice is to just keep your mind alert to the pack mentality. When it's fun, it's great. When it's not, bolt.

One of the best things to do when traveling with a pack is to be the one who takes charge and tries to get folks organized for dinners, breakfasts, meetings, etc. It's a thankless job, but one that people do quietly appreciate – and you'll be seen as the de facto guy in control. Always jump at the chance to try to herd the traveling pack!

Restaurants

Three words: ZAGATS Restaurant Guide. In most cities, it is the definitive guide. Also, ask the cabbies for the hot restaurants – surprising what they know. And if you're a true pack rat, make reservations well in advance and then be the 'savior' when the group is floundering wondering where to go that evening. Can't tell you how I've impressed people with this. And it's not hard. Just use an app like OpenTable on your phone.

Hotels

Three words: ZAGATS City Guide. Live by the company policy – but always push travel to get the area you want. Can't tell you how many hotels I've added to the corporate list (including the W Hotel chain and the Soho Grand in New York). I think it's important to stay at hipper hotels (not costlier, just hipper), since you can learn more about what's happening in the world.

Also, when you find a good hotel in a good neighborhood in the cities you visit– stick with it. The concierge and the computer know you, and you'll get better service. Then, every once in a while, change it up to keep fresh. Stay out of 'theme' hotels – like the Dungeon and Dragon Motel or The Champagne Tub Palace. Ahhh…the memories! Just kidding. Really. OK, maybe a little.

"Dom Perignon for all my friends!" – What to Order (really, you need to know)

OK. No Spinach. It's just bound to stick in your teeth at the moment you can least afford it. OK, no garlic. It's gonna rebound on your breath like Shaq. And do *not* order the most expensive anything – entrees, wine, etc. It sets a really horrible example – or shows you are not a fiscally responsible sort. And yes, you can order champagne, but only for a huge-ass victory. I would not advise Dom. And for gawds sakes man, don't slurp the soup. Have British table manners – they never steer you wrong.

Bar Sluts and what to do with Floosies (male or female)

Sarah: 'Hey, Hal. I think you have a fan at the bar. The blond over there keeps looking at you.'

Hal: 'Wow. What eye contact! Let's have some fun…you go say something.'

Sarah: 'Not me Hal – she's your entertainment not mine. But go on, entertain the rest of us! Say something. Play a little! It's been a long sales meeting and anyway….what could happen?'

Hal: 'Common' Sarah, what would people say…especially if she really *did* like me. ?'

Sarah: 'Hal….no one but me…and everyone else here will know. Anyway, no one likes you anyway Hal, so what do you have to lose? (wink). Order another drink and I'll just watch you make your move!'

Hal: 'OK, but shhhhhhh…'

Hal will probably find himself in Business Hell after he gets done with Ms. Floosie. Not for being flirtatious, or rambunctious, or doing whatever. Nope. Hal is going to Hell because he is doing this at a *business* function. Now, it's OK for men and women to see a knockout and sigh a little or very discretely say "wow" under your breath while very coolly looking on. Everyone loves a super-duper model, whether male or female. But doing the pick-up thing on a bar bet is just not good form….and usually gets back to the office in the form of wicked gossip. Being social 'Italian Style' is one thing….but trying to pick up women or men is another. So what to do with Mr. or Ms. Bar Slut or Space Port Floozie? Smile about it, even crack a joke, and then move on. So one more time: *Do not hit on people during a business trip*. And yes, that even goes for you 'I'm-Married-So-I-Can-Play-Around-Free-Of-Charge' kind of people out there. There are so many other things to talk about: Cars, Travel, Movies, Gadgets – anything topical is good. But do not talk about your therapy session, your implant surgery, or how you're dealing with your depression with a cocktail of modern pharmaceuticals. No matter how much of a stud or studette you are, do not talk about your exploits with business colleagues, or business 'friends.' Unless they are die hard, been-through-hell-and-back, 'I'll-watch-your-back' business friends, you really can't expect people to keep their mouth shut. So keep topical and watch out for the Floozies!

"Oh live a little! A little Ecstasy chaser for that Yagermeister shot won't hurt!" – What to do when confronted with too much fun
OK, most folks who hold professional or white-collar exec jobs have one major drug of choice: liquor. Make no mistake about it, pounding those Tequila Jell-O Shots at the Banana Bar after the Sales Meeting is, in fact, a major drug binge. So here's a little test to see if you're in with the Hendrix crowd and in too deep:

1. Every once in a while, do you wake up not knowing where you are?
2. In the morning, does the room spin counter clockwise or clockwise?
3. Have you awoken in a nearby city with someone you don't know?
4. Do you say, "two is my limit" at business functions, and then have about half a dozen?
5. Are people commenting on your new little Snake tattoo? How did they know it was on your sexy butt? That was a secret!
6. Exactly how many tattoos do you actually remember getting?
7. Do co-workers come up to you the day after and say "Wow Bob, you're some kind of AN-I-MAL!"

OK, if you actually answered "yes" to *any* of the above, you are in fact a *party dawg* and should probably check into the ToughLux Dry-Boy Ranch for a while. I put this section in really to say only one thing: Don't do drugs or go on binges with co-workers. It's OK to share a few drinks and have a few belly laughs, but please watch the chugging contests. Funny thing is that most people do get wrecked with co-workers every once in a while – which is normal in the intense, pressure filled world of modern companies. The only advice if you do find yourself blotto in the House of Blues is to remember three things: 1) Don't talk politics (people really do remember through the haze, and most folks are pretty emotional on the subject); 2) Go ahead and dance the night away, but don't grab her or his butt (you may think they are coming on to you, but most likely they are just feelin' the love of the crowd). Stare and smile all you want, but don't be the instigator of an advance; 3) Have one big-honkin' glass of water and a couple aspirin before you go to bed and make that early morning meeting. If you do lose it the night before, get it back before daybreak.

Call Home

There's no magic formula here. Just call in every day. Call before you go out for the night or leave in the morning. Don't stay on the phone for a long time. Remember to laugh. It's hard enough being away for a while. Remember why you call home in the first place.

Tacking on Extra Time Before or After a Business Trip

Every company has different rules, but most are fine with you tagging on a couple of days before or after the trip. It's your vacation time of course, unless you have a cool boss who occasionally comps you days for the candles you are burning at both ends. Also, if you're starting out, and you're flying from NY to LA and want to stop in Cincinnati to see some old friends, just be sure the ticket doesn't cost a nickel more than the direct flight. If it does, you'll want to pay the difference. Clear it with the finance police and then book it. I'm a very big fan of telling folks to take a few extra days and chill out following a trip – especially when the destination is someplace like Milan or Paris. If you're jetting to Ibizia for a singles foam party on your own dime, you may want to say you are just 'spending a few days in Spain' after the Madrid business meeting. Bragging rights are for those very close souls who you can trust.

There's a lot to know about traveling in the business fast lane. Most of it is simply common sense, but hopefully you've gleaned a few pearls of wisdom here. The last thought on the subject is whether you *want* to travel for a living in the first place. When I was growing up in Cincinnati, I couldn't wait to leave. Don't know why, I just wanted to see the world. One of my best friends, Scott, stayed there and married his college sweetheart. Decades later, Scott is lovin' life – four kids and a big house in the beautiful gas lamp area called Clifton. I've been to places so remote I can't pronounce them and have been around the world no less than seven times. Scott's life is a rock. Mine has been fluid. Funny thing is that we both have had our shares of pleasures and pains. The big difference is that when you become a traveling exec and move around the country in search of a better job you give up some precious things: stability, sense of belonging to place, maintaining friendships, staying connected with a church – all these start to slip away. You get some other things in return: wealth and the wealth of seeing the world and experiences that cannot ever be had in your hometown.

For those just starting out, or for those in the 'formative years' on the road, take some time out every once in a while to think about whether or not you want to keep "goin' mob-ile and glob-ile." I've known several execs who have found themselves jumping off the jet-stream life to get back to the basics of a hometown. Whatever your choice, just remember to enjoy the hell out of what you do. If you're like my friend Scott, revel in the joys of little league, hometown parades, and the family barbeques. If you're like me, you'll love the incredible richness of life that the world has – from sipping coffee in Vienna with a wonderful friend, to understanding the cultural significance of shabu-shabu in the heart of Rappongi Tokyo. Decide what you want your business life to be, and whether you want to do the miles. If you do, travel smart, and truly enjoy the stories the road will bring you along the way.

LIVE THE POLICY, EAT THE POLICY

Who in their right mind wants to read a chapter on living the corporate policy? Well that would be pretty much *no one*. So this will be the fastest chapter in your extracurricular reading life. It's quite simple: be a Policy Czar! Be the corporate policy Love Slave!

You need to read your company's policy and be familiar with it from day one. Really. Saying 'gee I didn't know I couldn't expense that' after the report gets dinged by finance does not look good on your first week – or any week for that matter. Saying "Wow, doesn't Sally have the *perfect rack!?*" or "Mmmm, I bet Max studs like a well-hung Stallion!" just isn't the right thing to blurt out and there are policies (and laws) about that. And you may want to check into whether that upgrade to the Turbo Bentley at the airport is something your company really approves of or not.

Just live and eat that policy every day. The *last* thing you want is to be taken to task for some crappy little rule. Funny, I've seen some major players just snap, and I mean just go completely postal, over some little thing that the company said you couldn't do. One fine day at an un-named company, an astute political operator whispered to his boss 'Well, you know Joe does seem to get a little freaked about small things…like the time he…ha ha ha…you remember…ha ha…threw his telephone out the window because he couldn't order roller ball pens! Yeah…I really think Joe needs to relax a little and maybe not get burdened with the stress of the EVP position you were thinking about." Swear to God, this is a paraphrase of a conversation I was a part of about Joe's career. And the little political weasel who launched the attack won the day – not because we didn't see his move, but because Joe really did have a bad day where he 'lost' it. The big shining ray of light here to follow is this: *detachment*. You just have to accept the things you cannot change … at least until you become President. And the best way to get there is to pour some Detachment & Acceptance sauce over the Sacred Policy and eat every single word up like a fine meal. Told you it would be a short chapter!

NOW READ THIS!

This chapter should really be called "Read Every Damn Day" since one of big secrets is to be informed. It is a significant competitive edge.

I am constantly amazed at the breadth of knowledge of business executives, having had conversations on Tort Reform to travel to Tortolla, from the best metal to line your brake pistons with, to fast-break strategies in basketball. If you want to be on the fast track, you've got to increase your knowledge and be ahead of the curve. I asked some smart folks what they read, and here's what they came back with:

Magazines:
- Read the news weeklies – *every week*. And rotate them. *Newsweek* this week, *Time* next, *US News* the next etc. I know....Duh!....right?

- Read the magazines of your industry. It's OK to skim, but go deep on things you don't know about. For example, if there's an in-depth article on Kohl's stores and you are selling Target, you should probably read that. Double Duh....right?

- Read the magazines that can help you discern trends. Magazines are fast to print and the weeklies and monthlies are the ones where you'll start to see new trends emerge that could be germane to your business. This will also help you stay current with popular culture. Not only will it give you an edge, but you'll be able to be conversant with other executives. Here's a short list of a few titles that you should read and check off:

   In Style ~ for what's hot and what's not, it's the best read for what's In and what's Out
   Details ~ the fine points of being finely appointed
   W-Magazine ~ the "style bible," not to mention the most avant photos around
   Nylon ~ a mix of the "Cognoscenti" and the "Glitterati"
   Rolling Stone ~ get to know the charts – who's selling and who's up, who's down

PC (or Mac) Magazine ~ geek heaven – but the gear you need to
succeed

Discover or *Popular Mechanics* ~ quantum physics to 'Q' factors –
they'll give you a new dimension

Cosmopolitan ~ this is what both sexes are reading and thinking
about during that boring meeting

The New Yorker ~ good for the mind and with those cartoons it is
good for the soul

Sports Illustrated ~ gotta be able to trash talk your way through the
Final Four

People Magazine ~ it's just surprising what they cover –and how
many people talk about it!

The New York Times ~ especially the Style supplements and of
course the Business Page.

The Wall Street Journal ~ the daily oracle of business with some of
the best feature stories around

Any Music, Sports, Fashion, or Counter-Culture magazine!

Digitalis:

• Get Flipbook for iPad – the ultimate skimming tool

• Good.com is pretty hot

• Online versions of *Wired, New York Times,* and *The Wall Street Journal*

Books:

• OK, I'll say it now. Any 'Must Read' book list that you are told about is
just wrong. There is no such thing as an inclusive list or a list that's the
'perfect' list to leapfrog you up the corporate ladder.

• A philosophy that you should embrace is similar to the Magazine
philosophy: read a new business book every quarter. More frequently if
you can, but at least one per quarter. If you are in your 20s you should
rotate old 'classics' like *The Art of War* with new ones to build up your
library. Definitely be sure you're reading the new contemporary books
when they come out. When you are talking with your boss about your
new, ever-so-bright proposal, how will you respond when she turns to you
and asks, "Yes, it's similar to a case study in *The Tipping Point* – have
you read it?" Even if you say "no, not yet" in the smartest of tones, it
registers that you're not up on your reading. In fact, in the Fortune 500,
I've found there is a kind of subterranean sparring that goes on as senior

execs drop book names and ask if you've read it. What's really fun is to respond 'yes,' and then probe them on a salient point from another chapter. Sometimes you'll get the edge over the 'skimmers' in the pack.

• It is not recommended that you peacock your latest read. Bursting into the conference room every quarter with a new plan that is pulled from the pages of the latest business guru's book is worse than not reading at all. Be a sage leader and use your knowledge with reserve.

• When your arsenal of books has grown enough and you are current, *do* engage others in dialogues over what they are reading. Again, this is not to showboat your knowledge, but to really get a sense of 1) what is hot with people; 2) what is influencing *them*.

• Keep your (really good) books. Hey....keep this one!

• If you find a particularly great chapter or quote, flip down the page or underline it or write it down. You will use it. Promise!

A few *random* books that continue to stay on my shelf:
No book reports here, just some suggested reads that have survived on my bookshelf through the years and that have given me some pretty powerful insights in business and life:

• *The Art of War*, Sun Tzu
• *Zen and the Art of Motorcycle Maintenance*, M. Scott Peck
• *Business @ The Speed Of Thought*, Bill Gates
• *Straight from the Gut*, Jack Welch
• *Work in Progress*, Michael Eisner
• *Making a Life, Making a Living*, Mark Albion
• *Made in America*, Sam Walton
• *Confessions of an Adman*, David Ogilvy
• *Dress for Success*, John Malloy
• *The Seven Spiritual Laws of Success*, Depak Chopra
• *The Seven Habits of Highly Effective People*, Steven Covey
• *Guerilla Marketing*, Trout & Reis

- *Good to Great*, Jim Collins
- *Career Warfare*, David D'Alessandro
- *Power*, Robert Green

Know your stuff! If you're in a sports company – find the sport that turns you on and read a lot about it. Know the players and scores. I completely sucked at knowing pro sports, but when I was at Nike, I knew every downhill skier and world cup standing. And it helped that my then girlfriend was an ESPN SportCenter fanatic. On more than one occasion, I would excuse myself from a business dinner conversation about a sport, call her and say 'Quick! Tell me everything you know about hockey in five minutes!" At Bulova, I read every jewelry magazine available and books on the history of watches. But again, go beyond just the business periodicals, and read about the things that matter to the people who control your world – do they like boats? Hell, pick up a boating magazine or read *The Perfect Storm*. Do they like climbing? At one time Disney's largest shareholder was a brilliant businessman named Dick Bass. Dick is a hero of mine – not for the money he's made (which is enviably in the billions), but because he set out to climb the seven highest peaks in the world and did it. Naturally, I had to read Jon Krakauer's *Into Thin Air* and liked it so much I saw the Imax movie *"Everest."* I'm not a climber, but it was a fascinating side road. And now I understand the motivation just a wee bit better of the man who helped shaped Disney.

To most who are a few years out of college, your mental cannon is pretty solid. But watch how quickly you find yourself giving up that reading time to attend functions, to have a life, and to be the author of business documents, not the reader of them. Try to not let it slip away – and re-dedicate yourself to exploring new magazines, new books, and new learning of all kinds to enrich your life.

TOYS OF THE TRADE: LICENSE TO BUY THE COOL STUFF

The risk of a chapter like this is that as soon as the printing presses stop, POW! A new gadget or invention comes along that makes this seem horribly out of date. It's worth a fast review of a few things that can really help you get ahead of the pack and stay there. A few tips:

1. **Spend Money on the gear**
   When I first started in business, I remember seeing my first paycheck after taxes and thought, 'What the hell happened!?' We'll save the tax discussion for another book...but it is clear in the first years, then in the marriage years, then in the 'kids' years, that money is always tight. But you *must* spend a little dough on gear to get efficient. You must organize yourself and be able to put your hands on the gear that gives you every bit of information about your business. And best of all, it's tax deductible - Schedule A, Non-Reimbursed business expenses. So buy it and get strong!

2. **Get the Latest Gear**
   Buy the most up-to-date gear. Don't do this to be a fashionista or a Techpig, but do it because of a little known fact: billions and billions of brain cells go into every generation of software and electronic hardware that is created. They truly do improve with each generation – and significantly. Moore's law correctly states that computing power doubles every 18 months. Windows 98 contained 18 million lines of computer code. Windows XP had 45 million lines of code. Windows 7 was over 90 million lines of code. Big, and I mean *Real Big Brains* are working on this stuff – and by association and use, you'll be better. The latest gear really does give you the edge.

3. **Don't Brag**
   Don't go up and down the hallways saying, "Hey, look at my new Super Galactic Martini Maker Phone! Isn't the hologram s-i-c-k?!"

Be classy about it. Just use the damn thing. You'll find your Biz peers will engage you when they see you using it.

4. **Find the System That's Right**

   Over the years I've moved from personal daytimers to electronic formats to custom bound portfolios, back to electronic. The bottom line is that you'll eventually find the system that's right for you. If you do, stay with it. But don't be afraid to change it. After 10 years of using daytimers, I decided that my brain, my life, and my soul needed to explore new things. Hell, people were always copying my system and saying how life-saving it was. But every once in a while you need to step out and try something new.

5. **A few easy-piezy things to target:**

   • Two Watches. Yes, you'll need to buy two. One for dress, the other for the rest of the time. My advice is to buy something that will have some lasting value – a Tag Heuer, Michael Kors, or an Armani is good, but an IWC or a Panerai is better. I still wear my Bulova Accutron – a great, unique style in a watch with American heritage. Wear your 'good' watch to business 'power events,' and to all formal and black tie events. For the rest of the time, you'll need a cool digital with at least two time zones, alarms, and a chronograph for that morning run. Since I helped invent the business, I am a bit partial, but the best watch in the world for this was the Nike Triax Sport watch with its cool design and incredible functionality. So shell out and live right.

   • A Cool Car. Car?! In the Western world, you are what you drive. Pull up in a Daewoo or a Honda, and go home sister! You're not a player. Pull up in a Turbo GT Carrera, and you're a spendthrift and suck at handling money – not to mention that you're probably in that set that actually has thought about 'augmentation' surgery. Yeeesh! Now if you're the President or Chairman, the Porsche is cool, but only if you've got the top slot. No, *you* need something that shows your taste, your style, and something that is classy. Try a BMW, a Caddy, or a Lexus. Never a plain old Ford or Chevy, and never a Minivan. Truly nothing against those makes – they're all solid. But you need to convey an image of a serious professional and designed-by-the-people-who-brought-you-oatmeal type cars don't do that. You can make an 'eco-statement' and drive a Prius or an electric. Thankfully Hollywood celebs have made that cool. But do consider whether it really fits your image – like if you love to talk about your deer hunting weekends, a Prius just doesn't fit! And don't even think about a sub-sub-econ-o-box car (even though that is the smartest financial play). There are three types of cars in the world: Crap, Better and Best. So go for 'Better' and save your money for the Aston Martin DB9 when you become Chairman.

- Clothes. OK, clothes are not toys. But man or woman, low totem pole or high, you are very much defined by your clothes. My only advice here is to look as classy as you can with a sense of style. If you're a woman, don't try to look like the latest teen rock diva. If you're a man, don't succumb to the GQ look – you know, slicked back hair, tight 'show you my sexy butt" pants, with the iridescent Express dacron shirt that's so fitted your chest hairs peek out screaming for air. Not that there is anything wrong with the GQ look, and if you're a GQ kind of person by all means go for it. But in most business environments, the right dress for a man is a simple, classy suit and tie combo. The suit, shirt, tie and shoes should be conservative. The accessories (the cufflinks, the suspenders, the handkerchief, the watch) can show your colorful personality. For men or for women, keep it tasteful, classy, and as timeless as possible.

- If you are in the design or creative side of business, you may be saying 'no' to suits. You'd be right. Dress the part. If you are in Industrial Design, we'd expect a more casual look that is a little fashion forward.

- Perhaps the best play to make here is to dress for the position you want to be in, not the position you currently have. If you want to be the design boss, then dress like one. If you want to be the head of Marketing or the Chairman, then dress like him or her. In all cases keep it simple, tasteful, and classy.

- The last Toy is a good one. It's intangible. The last Toy is a simple and often trampled, overlooked thing: Fun. Yep, have fun with life. It's hard when you've got bills to pay, but in the end you'll probably always eat and there are plenty of places to live cheap. So have fun. People will enjoy you, and you'll enjoy life more. Live life. Love well.

The Toys of the Trade are, of course, too numerous to list. It's always a good idea to buy the 'gear guides' when you see them in popular magazines. Even if you can't bring yourself to buy them, you need to know about those great gadgets. Now the next chapter seems like a paradox – telling you to save your brains out – but hey, life is a paradox! Part of what you have to be smart about is spending within your limits. No, you probably don't need the latest iPad this year. Yes, you're probably OK skipping a phone generation – but maybe one, not three. The point of all this is that you do need to be efficient and the gear can not only help you do that, but also is reflective of your Brand Character discussed earlier. So don't go hog-wild, but do invest to keep current. Anyway, we all want to hear about that new ping-pong app you're sporting!

WHAT YOU EARN VS. WHAT YOU KEEP

A very close friend of mine had the illustrious career of college professor. You know the type – tweed jacket, drove a VW, loved a dry martini kind of guy. I remember when he bought a condo over 25 years ago and was flat broke. He was making $40K a year and didn't get much above that for the rest of his career. Over one of many martinis together years later, he leaned over and said, "Remember, it's not what you earn, it's what you keep. Pay yourself before you pay your bills." He's now approaching $2 million in the bank, is retired, and is enjoying a martini everyday at 4:00.

OK, so I won't put you in a coma over compounding theory or with the Sam Walton 'learn the value of a buck, son' kind of rhetoric, but it is true. Most millionaires clip coupons and keep their cars for 10 years. Most millionaires don't spend. How much you make has little correlation with wealth accumulation – it's all about how much you pocket.

Let's cover some of the principle rules in business about money:

- Always lose money on business trips. Whoa! Hold on there, smokie! You just said 'Don't Spend!' True. I didn't say how much to lose, but always make sure you don't put in for that last cup of coffee. We've covered this before, but it's important. So here's why: If you ever get called on the mat for an expense report, you absolutely, positively want to be able to look the auditors in the eye and tell them you're clean. Now, how much money? Hey, if it's $20 bucks a trip that adds up, but I've always figured it's the best insurance policy to have. It also teaches you to respect the company's money when you lose some of yours on the trip.

- Save like crazy. Don't buy stupid toys - the things that won't appreciate. Don't sell your house before you've owned it two years. Max your 401(k) match. Save on top of that (out of breath yet?). Do get a pre-nuptial agreement at all costs (the largest single depletion of wealth is from divorce and lawsuits). Do go on vacation. Don't go first class. Do tip at restaurants. Don't give to the homeless on the street. Do give at church and to charities. And above all, have a plan. OK! Enough!

- Don't even THINK about it. Every once in a while you see the headlines of some mid-level, or even high-level executive who gets nailed by taking a few bucks out o' the till. I can't understand these people. First, morally it's a major bad deal. Second, think about the math. Say you average a $75,000 salary per year over a career of 25 years. That's $1,875,000. Is it worth trying to pilfer $100,000? Just crazy. The best way is to keep karmically clean is to not even take a pencil or an envelope from the office. Buy them yourself at Staples. If you want to be a leader, or are a leader, you should completely drive yourself to be the most ethical person on earth. You'll live stress free. You'll avoid the hubbub at the water cooler. You'll be happier. So the next time your spouse says, 'Honey, can you bring home a few stamps from the office?" you should say, "Geez baby, what's next? A copier? Or how about some office furniture?" It's the same thing. So fly right the first time and you'll be a happier camper.

- A woman who worked at Nike came in wearing Adidas shoes. When asked about it, she matter-of-factly said, "Even considering the Nike Employee discount, I can get Adidas cheaper, so until Nike gives me a bigger discount, I'm wearing Adidas." Next thing you know she disappeared and was no longer seen again at Nike. People have the right to wear any brand within reason, but come on! Wear or use the stuff of your company. If you can't swallow that, at least don't wear the competition's product. "Duuuh," you say? You'd be surprised.

But there is one exception. Once a real running stud and business leader at Nike, Kirk Richardson, bought the entire Nike Running Footwear team New Balance shoes and told them they couldn't take them off for a week. That's powerful messaging – which led to a product that trounced New Balance's top running shoe at the time. But that's probably the ONLY exception. When I went to Nike, I threw out my Reeboks. When I went to Disney, I mothballed my

Bugs Bunny tie. Live, eat, and breathe your company's product. And yes, it's OK to spend a little on it.

And a few tips from the sages:

1. Start a business checking account used only for your business expenses. Do not intermingle business expense reimbursement with personal finances. It's a surefire road to hell. Also, if you do get audited, do you really want people looking at your personal checkbook records?

2. Automate: Get direct pay of business reimbursement to the Corporate Charge card. Get direct deposit for your checks.

3. Never use the Amex Travelers checks. You don't need them internationally since every place takes charge cards.

4. Stay out of Las Vegas.

5. Use your own cash on business trips and then put the reimbursed expense checks back into your business checking account. At the end of the day you should have a little savings account going.

6. Don't use all your vacation time. If you leave a job, you get paid for it, and it's a big ticket if you can roll the unused time forward and then cash it.

7. If you come from money, or are smart enough to have a lot of money, don't show it off. Don't drive the fanciest car in the company lot, or wear that 27-carat diamond ring that the Prince of Dubai gave you in Aspen last winter.

8. For God's sakes, you do not need to tell people what you make, or compare packages. Have some class.

9. Max and I mean MAX out your 401(k). There are few tax reliefs available anymore, but this is a surefire way to get tax relief and a matching program if your company offers it. Go the max and then adjust your lifestyle. Don't do it in reverse.

10. Do keep track of your unreimbursed business expenses – particularly meals out. If you have a friend at the office and you go out and talk about business, most likely you'll not be able to expense it at work, but you legally, and financially should itemize it as non-reimbursed business expenses on the 'ol Schedule A.

The last thought on money is this: *have a plan*. The only way to win at any game is not to SPAZ out and flail wildly in every direction. If you're human, you've probably tried this like most of us, but a few financial blows and you start getting it. The only way to win is to plan out how much you can save – so that one day you'll get that great summer vacation you remember as a kid…only this time it truly will be an endless summer in some villa you own in Italy. "Scuzzi, Vino Rosso por favore!"

THE CYCLES OF BUSINESS LIFE

The one and the only constant that we can count on in life is perpetual change. Economic laws about business cycles are truly no different than life cycles. Just when we think we've got it licked, and have life neatly tied up and in place – BOOM! You're fired, or have a family crisis that means you have to step off the fast track for a while. It's simply inevitable. The real question is *how are you going to handle it?* A key learning in life is that it's all a matter of how you *think* about it. It's all a matter of your attitude. A positive attitude will determine whether you fly through the storms successfully or get crushed in the ground by wicked wind shear. OK, right now you are saying, 'Yeah, and if I hear one more damn person yap about how I have to have a smiley, happy-faced attitude, I'm gonna hurl.' Well...hate to say it, but that positive attitude person will prevail over you. They'll get promoted more often and ascend to the better positions first. No question about it.

As a young turk Ad-Guy, I was feeling on top of the world. I was 27, had been promoted to Account Executive, and I made a very lucrative job switch to J. Walter Thompson Advertising on the Burger King account. And life was good. Had a good-looking fiancée. Got invited to all the great Ad parties with endless amounts of cocktail shrimp. Wore paper thin soled Italian loafers. You know: Livin' Large in Manhattan...Top O' The World... King of the Heap. Then the whip came down and came down hard. The account was in trouble. James Patterson (the now famed fiction writer) was the creative guru on the account and was quite distant from the business. His brainchild, the "Herb" campaign, had just broken and the awareness was huge, but the business was about as flat as a three day old flame-broiled burger. Then the in-fighting started. Camps developed. The Client was threatening to pull the business. At that moment in that great company's history, J.W.T. went from being a 'Gentlemen's Club' to a bunch of guys clubbing each other. I became wickedly negative. I thought everyone was a jerk. I thought Management was inane. The organization was contracting, downsizing, and the rats went at each other. And I fell for it. Every night I would go home and say, "My life is miserable. The place is the pits. There isn't enough vodka in the world to help this situation!" Funny thing, my home life became negative too. Everything about me became negative.

Then one day, my fiancée called and said she had just been fired by her madman-adman boss. I was devastated. She had been so miserable at her job, and to end in defeat was tough. I left the office and rescued her. Back at our apartment, I remember consoling her and said 'OK, relax a little. You'll get a job – no problem. And don't worry, I still have a job and I'll be able to cover our expenses." I went back to work, also feeling pretty beaten. Around 4:00 the Account Director walked into my office and said with dead eyes, "We're making some changes here Phil and I hate to say it, but we're letting you go. 170 people are being laid off today and unfortunately you didn't make the cut." I just shook my head. Three hours earlier my fiancée was fired from her job across town. What a world. I did everything right…but I didn't know how it really worked. That, my friends, was my first Career Kamikaze.

When a down cycle like this happens, it's easy to really get twisted into a negative pity mode. Worse, my fiancée got a job within two weeks. My search took eight weeks – fast in those days, but an eternity when you're home looking at the walls hoping the phone will ring. Every day is like a year to replay the things you said, or didn't say. One thing stuck out in my self-analysis: I had become this festering, Darth-Vader like negative person. I radiated negativity. And in one Satori moment I decided to change. I decided that no matter who was negative around me, no matter what gossip came my way, no matter how dire the situation, I would NOT allow myself to be dragged down in negativity. I was not going to let myself get sucked into the black hole ever again.

I got a job at McCann-Erickson on one of their dog accounts. I took it because I needed the work – but I also felt that it was a chance to put positivism to work. After one difficult client meeting, the Creative Director and I were driving back to the city and he was just bitch, bitch, bitching about the people and the meeting. At each barb, I would respond, "You know, the client is probably under a lot of pressure" or "Yeah, they really have trouble understanding ads, but we'll get them there. I think we'll get an award winning ad out of them yet…" He just stared at me and after a minute or two of silence said quite seriously, "Are you on drugs?" I laughed. "Seriously," he continued, "are you taking something? Because I've never seen you get down or be negative – it's just…well…it has to be Prozac or something, right?" I told him I was drug free and of my philosophy of positivism. Later, we did in fact get a Clio award for a TV commercial for that client.

Armed with my Positivism, I went from Account Executive on a very dodgy account to Vice President, Management Supervisor on their best account, Coca-Cola. All in three years. It was a meteoric rise and a very lucrative one and it was all about my attitude. I will say one thing: it's hard to do. And I haven't been successful at the 'Positive Attitude' thing every year, but I genuinely try to stay positive and look for the opportunities. It's simply a better way to live.

Everyone has setbacks. Everyone has bad days, even bad months and years. Every single person has run across a bad boss, or an untenable situation where life becomes miserable. The best course, the only course, is to be a little Zen about it and realize that good things will come after bad things. And don't get so 'hooked on the heroin' of good things, since tough times will also come again. The key in business is to stick with it. Don't give up the ship at the first sign of trouble. When you read about the big dogs at the top, you'll find that part of their winning was just 'sticking in there,' hanging in through the tough times. So stick with it and stay positive and ride those cycles up to the top of the tower. You'll not only be rewarded, you'll look back and see a personal history of great times and powerful positive moments.

HOW TO KNOW IF YOUR NEXT JOB REALLY BLOWS

You have to face a simple truth about life. People lie. Sometimes they don't mean to, sometimes they do. And in business it is the same. If you're shocked by this statement and can't believe that corporations can turn a 'white lie' into a darker shade of grey, then you have been living without TV or Newspapers. WorldCom, Enron, Global Crossing, and Tyco are examples from the modern era that prove that the top brass sometimes are corrupt and deceitful. Most of the time what is happening at the top of the company is also happening throughout the company. Let's be clear: Most corporations are populated with good people. But they sometimes lie a little or stretch the truth just a tad to get what they want…including *getting you.* Corporations sell. Period. And they plan to sell *you* on *them.* Your job is to figure out what is real and what isn't as you talk with your future employer. This chapter is a 'deep dive' into the subject, since choosing the wrong company can be a full-out Career Kamikaze, and finding the *right* one can be the single biggest factor in your long-term success.

The Company
There are two clues to any company's personality: one that is as large as a building and one that can be uncovered by a heightened perception of the smallest details.

Outside in: the first Physical Clue
The physical space that any organization occupies tells any job seeker almost all you need to know about the inner workings of the place. First, ask yourself where is it located? At my 'Bad Company Experience' company, I knew the address and knew that it was a bad location. But if one stood outside the building and really took a look at *where* it was located you would have seen that on one side of the building was a Freeway, and on the other a Cemetery. If you looked closer, you would have seen that you could not access the Freeway, and that the Cemetery and the whole building, was surrounded by concentration camp barbed-wire. As a big fan of symbols, one could say the

building was located in Purgatory – you could not access the 'Freeway of Life,' yet you were not quite six feet under in the Cemetery. And yet most people who came to the building looked at this typical borax-modern-techno-structure and said, "So what's so wrong?" It did look clean. The signs all had correct spelling and seemed to be in good repair. But starting with the location, it was clear there might be some issues inside.

OK. You've convinced yourself that symbols are for literature majors and after all you are a "Master of the Universe" (who will become stronger if you get this heavy-title job and make all that extra dough). Now you go inside. What's it like? Forget business and be a detective. What type of flooring does it have – linoleum (cheapskates), marble (could be an ego or budget problem), wood (could be creative, or could be cheap), or carpeting (no pile means cheap)? What kind of office decor is there? Steelcase carpeted partitions? Real walls? Metal or wood doors? Hanging lights or recessed lighting? Did they go cheap, or were they at least creative? Did they overspend for image sake?

The simple fact of life is that most people are worrying about what they'll say or whether they have dandruff on their best interview suit rather than focusing on the internal physical environment. Yet it is one of the most telling signs about a place.

At my 'Bad Company," the signs were easy to spot both outside and inside the building. But interestingly, other companies have grandiose headquarters, which are created by much more sophisticated architects that require a bit more sleuthing to uncover.

Take the 'Wow We're A Big Soft Drink Company.' It too is located in a rather unsavory part of the city, but one that sports businesses and universities. As the cab pulls up to the towering buildings, you have nothing but awe for the white granite structures, the beautiful landscaping, and the many fountains that plead a serene ignorance.

But take another look: The buildings have millions of shimmering windows, three multi-level parking garages, and two very, very large revolving doors at the front entrance. Most are struck by its presence and its ability to communicate dominance and power. You should be struck by the *sheer bureaucracy*. Exactly what do the people in those thousands of windows do? Ask GM. Ask IBM. Ask AT&T. Ask any big monster company that lost its competitive edge because it was a bloated bureaucratic behemoth in a tougher, faster world. Better yet, ask the people bounced out of those companies during downsizing. If you're a Chairman walking in, you know you have a problem before you hit the door. If you're a mid-level manager, make sure you're secure enough to survive the vacuum created when those chrome-plated automatic revolving doors start churning.

Inside the "Wow We're A Big Soft Drink Company," the bright light illuminates the domed marble rotunda. A very pleasant woman greets you at the registration desk. You get your security pass and move down the hall to the elevators. This time the carpeting is plush and seemingly triple-padded. The elevator bank has no less than six elevators – just for the west wing. The doors of the elevators and offices are solid mahogany, trimmed in brass....or is that solid gold?

On any floor you will see the Company's art hanging on the wall – original Wharhols, DeKoonings, Liebowitzes, and on and on. All told, the art collection alone is worth some $50 million. The halls are wide, expansive, and well lit, and the offices all have at least one of those thousand windows the complex has to offer. Add to this sunny picture a complete health spa, a cafeteria that seats 2,500 people, oh yes, and a bonus that traditionally pays 25% of your annual gross. Wow! All this and a high-profit, high-volume soft-drink business? I'll take it!

But wait.

The rotunda said it all. A tower. Albeit a beautiful tower made of white polished marble, trimmed with bronze and glass. And empty. All you could hear in the rotunda was the sound of footsteps from the various connected hallways. The sounds came from all directions, and like the company, you never knew whether you were coming or going, or who was in front or in back of you. A gilded cage and one that many people are happy with, and in fairness has a lot to offer. But any job seeker should know that no business on earth offers security, and the days of paying your dues at large marble-lined companies and being secure in your "danger years" are over. Big companies are a good résumé builder, a good paycheck, and a nice office, but don't over-leverage yourself – they have a nasty habit of periodically 'rightsizing' and 'realigning' to appease shareholders.

See the Light:
Lighting, and especially sunlight, is another physical clue that can uncover a corporation's alter ego. As a 'mature' executive with 'far-sighted' vision, I convinced myself before I took the job at the 'Bad Company' that fancy windows were only ornamentation for corporate egos – and something that one could live without. Remembering my first two visits to the company, I don't even think it registered that there were NO windows. After all, most of the time was spent in the president's office, which of course had floor to ceiling windows. But don't ever lose sight of sunlight – the absence of it can literally wreck your job and your life. Principal symptoms of long-term sunlight deprivation are shortness of temper, a heightened aggressiveness, depression, and lack of motivation. In fact, one study that placed rats in a dark cage with a slight overpopulation and adequate, but sparse food supply, found that the rats attacked and ate each other. In the sunlit cage, with the same variables, they did not. Think about all the rats you know in business, and then check out the glass...and the food supply.

After spending time at this old company, it finally dawned on me that there was a tremendous *mental* obstacle caused by the lack of windows. Then I stood in the center of the executive floor and looked around – all outside perimeter offices, windowless of course, faced *inward* and the general flow of the workstations was *inward.* In many offices, desks faced the side of the wall, but here every desk faced toward some invisible center, saying 'we spend our time looking inward at ourselves, not outward to the outside world.' Interestingly, the company paralleled this in almost every aspect of senior management – they cared more about the cost of business cards than of share loss, more about trimming expense report costs than the cost of a declining brand awareness in the marketplace.

Clearly a lack of windows is not the reason something does or doesn't happen, but it is absolutely crystalline clear that a workplace without sunlight is simply a much worse place to work.

The Gear:
The physical environment is defined not only by the building, the walls and the windows, but the "things" they have put inside the building. One of the most telling cues is the computer hardware a company sports.

The good news is that as an interviewee you can tell a lot about a company just by looking at the computer support in the offices. No, you don't need to have a mainframe dump EDI'd to your house so you can review the command sequence. But as you're being escorted around the building in the "once over," pay particular attention to the gear.

For those of you who really don't need to be involved with all the tech-gear, you simply need to look at the age and condition of the machines. Are they archaic, Jurassic-era machines that look worn and dirty? Or are they new, slim, and clean? If the gear is newer this is a sign that the company is dedicated to making sure its employees have the resources to win.

"We're Moving"
Here's the scenario: You drive up to the building and you notice that one of the letters has fallen off the sign. The building is a windowless barracks. Your walk around reveals that the company hasn't invested in anything in years. Just as you're about to write off this place the CEO says with eloquence "forgive our humble abode, but we decided not to spend any money over the last few years because we're moving." What follows is usually an understated description of the new place that baits you into thinking that it's really going to be the best corporate headquarters in the world. Now what? How do you read the physical environment now? Simple. You don't. Sure it's correct not to spend a lot of money on your headquarters if you're planning to move, but watch for the tell-tale signs: Is the paint old and disgusting? Is the carpet worn? Is there dirt on the air vents? There is simply no reason for this kind of disrepair, except sheer premeditated negligence – which means someone upstairs simply doesn't give a damn. At the McCann-Erickson Advertising Agency in New York, the old building had carpet that was plain shot and decor that was vintage 70s, but you could tell the place was neat and clean and that people kept their offices in good shape. More importantly, there was a great deal of plants, healthy and growing, scattered through the hallway. When I was told, "We're negotiating a move,

so forgive our headquarters," I flat out asked "When?" "Where?" and "Are you taking all this decor with you?" Just a few simple questions and the degree of detail of the responses clearly indicated that in fact they were very much negotiating a move and were serious about an upgrade. The new digs turned out to be world-class.

Offsite Interviews:
Just when you thought it was safe, just when you thought you knew how to read a company's environment, they spring a new one on you: the *Hotel* interview. Several years back, I was being considered for a position as President of a Giftware company. The call came and I was quite excited. The European man said quite eloquently that his chairman was flying in from the Fatha-land and that he would like to meet me. Nice, I thought. This must be serious. Then the phone began to melt as he said, "Meet us at the Intercontinental Hotel. Ask for Lars." A few things passed through my mind: first was "geez, these guys really know how to live. The Intercontinental in New York City is one of the finest, most elegant hotels around." Second thought was, "this must be an important company to be able to have this kind of meeting."

So off I go to meet the Das Fürer. The hotel lobby is of course splendid, with requisite amounts of power brokers and B-list celebrities. The number two man meets me in the lobby and escorts me upstairs. He mentions that they are having their sales meeting in the hotel and that when all was said and done, it was quite reasonable to interview at the hotel.

Stop. First of all, the Intercontinental is not reasonable. The Best Western in Hell's Kitchen is reasonable. Even the Marriott in Times Square is reasonable. But the Intercontinental was never considered a 'reasonable' venture. In fact, the room rates are among the highest in the city. What does this say? Either that they have defined 'reasonable' as a very high standard (which can be both good and bad), or they simply were laying it on thick. The other thing his statement told me was that the sales force was tiny. Just one peek around the hotel and you know that the structure simply isn't made for large sales meetings.

We get to the room and he knocks on the door. Of course, having lived many years in New York City, I'm beginning to think this is a giant con game and that any minute Lars is gonna shake me down for my wallet. But it was indeed legit. We sit down and begin to discuss the job. The first thing number two does is take about 30 minutes to go over almost every page of a product catalog.

Stop. Excuse me. If I wanted a lesson on your product line, I would have enrolled in the summer camp at 'Schloss Giftware' in Fürerberg. What does this say? How about "I have nothing better to say." How about "I'm so non-strategic that I will cover only the product in this catalog because it is the only thing I know how to do."

Then we begin to talk about their operation. If I tell you this gets worse, would you believe me? Well, it did. The chairman said that the company was located in Westchester, but they stay at the hotel because of the convention…

Stop. Westchester is about 30 minutes from the heart of New York – and the convention site. There would be no reason to stay at the hotel…unless the office is really a postal drop.

He continued by saying that they were looking for a President to help them get more volume by attacking the mid-priced segment of the market….

Stop. For a high-end producer of tabletop items, going down-market is a very bad thing. It says 1) they are losing their shirts at the high end and want quick bucks; 2) they don't understand the idea of a separate brand to gain mid-level market share without damaging their top-brand equity.

The day ends with the customary escort to the elevator. Alone in the elevator, I had that intuitive feeling. Something just wasn't playing right here. Why the hotel? Why the apparent inconsistencies?

Paying particular attention to a company's plans and strategies is the only way to uncover the true corporate culture in a 'Hotel Interview.' And, it almost goes without saying; you MUST spend time at their headquarters.

Right now several of you are saying, "Of course you need to see their headquarters, what are you crazy?" But, I actually know a woman who was interviewed and hired from a company's posh New York City headquarters, and who simply accepted the fact that the main facility was in the bowels of Queens. Needless to say, she was in for an incredible shock the first day she pulled up at Stalag Queens.

Take a last look. By now you're saying to yourself "I can't believe this guy! He's actually telling me to judge a company by their physical environment!" Simply said, Yes! Physical environments are just extensions of the collective corporate mind. After you leave the interview, close your eyes, say your mantra, and visualize the corporate mind that created that environment and built the house that could be your future home.

The Management

Bosses are a funny thing. How many of you can really say that you have had a boss who possesses all the traits of a great leader. In my career, I've had bosses who were great with people, but sucked with vision; I've had bosses who were great with vision, but sucked with people; I've had bosses with IQs that exceeded 200, but couldn't find the door; and I have had the incredible fortune to have worked for talented, smart, visionary, caring ones.

So, which kind of future boss are you looking at? How do you know? How will you cut through the facade that this person has spent years perfecting?

The first step is to take a little 'physical' inventory of the people you meet in your new perspective company. Are they all 'beat'… you know, looking like they had just a little too much Pink Gin at the Country Club last weekend? Or are they feeling and looking healthy? At Nike, you could see the health in people's faces and the wide-eyed gleam and vibrancy in the workers who wandered the campus. Be sure you take a long hard look at your future boss. Does he or she look in control, put together, and well…healthy? Of course you can't learn everything by the external look of the workforce, but pay attention. You can't ferret out the real nut jobs this way, but you can get a pretty good handle on how your boss will be and how the place will be just by taking a look at the faces and appearances of the people who work there.

Most people are good. I'm convinced of this and live my life believing this.

But in business, there is one type you'll have to watch out for in Management. The Great Deceiver.

Once a friend of mine and I were interviewing for the same job and we compared notes. Interestingly, we both thought Mr. New Boss (the poster boy for The Great Deceiver) was simply fabulous. He was young, full of life, had vision, had humor...had a great line. My friend ended up taking the job and later described the experience as "a cross between Attila the Hun and Adolph Hitler with a little Jack the Ripper thrown in." My friend was literally undergoing mental torture, until one day Mr. New Psycho Boss hauled off and fired her. Looking back, it was extremely difficult to read this person, since it was a fact that he really was pathological and lied to both our faces about what he wanted and what he could provide as an employer. Karma travels. Later I heard Hell-boy was decapitated by a corporate Jedi Master.

The most interesting thing about people is that we want to be with people like us – or people that we ourselves want to be. Rarely are we with people who are diametrically opposed to our views. This is great for the job seeker, because in most organizations the executive staff is usually cut from the same bolt of fabric – even though colors and weaves might vary. Simply said, a CEO won't keep an EVP who doesn't share his views. And an EVP won't stay under a CEO he cannot stand – at least not without obvious giveaways. The net effect is that as you interview up the line, look for similarities and uncover the hidden agendas that the senior management shares.

That's it. No real space age magic here. Just plain and simple detective work. Look for clues in their faces. Look for clues in their interactions. And if you can talk to your Stockbroker, or if you can find ex-employees who used to work at the company, you'll learn volumes about the management that you'll spend most of your waking hours with.

Ten Questions You Need To Ask:
You've already staked out the company and the type of mental and physical environment it offers. You've inventoried management and have determined how that psycho-social-animal behavior operates. During the interview two things will happen – they will ask you a whole bunch of questions and you will ask them the same. Both are part of a mating dance to see whether there

will be a union. All job seekers at every level have a few questions they believe are unique and insightful. Great! Here are a few telling questions for your perspective company that I've picked up from the sages along the way:

Question 1. The Vision Thing
Question: "Can you tell me your current positioning in the market and your vision for where you see this company long-term?"

You'll note it was a two-part question – one part dealing with the current status and one dealing with the future. A bright mind will separate out both parts of the question and answer them separately. If the future employer skips either one, or cannot address both, don't even ask a follow up question because the person is just fronting an answer.

For those bright enough to be able to split the question up, the correct answer lies in the specificity of the response. If the talking head says "we're positioned as a strong competitor in the mid-priced segment and we really see ourselves as the dominant force because of our branded unique product," then you know these are just middle-of-the-pack people who have the usual answer. Not very inspiring.

If the executive says "Our perfume is positioned to the consumer as 'monogamy in a bottle' – the safe perfume which gives us a distinct separation from what we call the 'sex pack.' Long term my vision is to extend this position along the core social values we have found that people are returning to. Products with our current position have grown over 15% a year in dollar volume and we think our new programs will exceed 25% in the next five to ten years." They gave a lot of specifics. Clearly they thought a lot about where they were headed based on something unique.

Watch out for the textbook generic answers that involve phrases like "growth oriented," "value," "price leader," "solid equity," and "profit focus" – all of these are just the normal non-illuminating babble. Look for the answer that makes an attempt to give something concrete. Even if the answer is rather simple, like "Hey man..Smut Magazine stands for Cheap and Sleazy. That's what we are. That's what we'll be." This answer is great, and you can believe it. It's a clearly defined vision for what the company sells. Just keep saying to yourself as you hear the answer begin to unfold 'does this guy really know where he is steering this ship? Does he really know where he wants to be?' It is simply shocking, shocking I say, how many Chairman's, CEOs and COOs have no real clue, no real vision for the company.

Question 2. The People Thing
Question: "I believe any company is only as good as the people who make it run – from the mail room to this office. How do you personally motivate your team and this company, particularly in a down cycle?" Right now the man or woman across the desk is saying "Holy geez...how do I get the hell out of this one!"

Press specifically on what the company does for its employees. Are the benefits for everyone? Are there Quality of Life programs like Daycare and a Fitness Center? Where was the last Christmas party held – at some interesting place, or in the company cafeteria? Everyone talks a good game, but actions are the only thing that counts. You cannot afford to leave the interview without a clear-cut understanding of how the company treats employees....after all, it's how they will treat you.

Question 3. Judgment: "Genius Is 80% Showing Up" (Woody Allen)
Question: "What are the key measures for success here?" The question is really very basic: "What are the rules of play?" Most people simply won't tell you. Sure, you'll get the standard fare of "Uhm…we like to see innovation and a sense of teamwork and the implementation of successful programs." Occasionally you might find a performance evaluation process that involves a lengthy, detailed report. Ask to see one somewhere along the way, but don't go crazy about it. I've seen too many executives who have brilliant write-ups get fired for simply being the wrong personality type for their boss or company. In many cases, there is no write-up, particularly the more senior you are. But somewhere along the way, somebody will evaluate you and you must get a handle on how they will process that information.

Question 4. The Background of Your Next Boss
Question: "Tell me about your career, your background?"
The critical point you are looking for is depth of experience. Does this person have a well-rounded background from different companies, or are they a

single-company person. Cases can be made for either track, but I think it's fair to say that single-company veterans can be the most dangerous. The "I've been with the same company for twenty three years" person only knows one way of doing business.

You may be pressured to do it his or her way, and your 'new way' simply may not fit there. The flip side is that this cat is well-trained in the art of survival. And he clearly knows the golden rule to 'stay in the same company or in the same industry' to build wealth. That's still true – but you have to just do a little extra digging when interviewing with a 'company' guy. Again, cases can be made for multi-company talent and for people who grow up in a single company – but you want to find out if they have kept learning and embrace new points of view from *outside* the berm. If they do, you're *quids in* – and you'll have a good run.

Question 5. Their View of the Principle Discipline
This area is about ascertaining the company's view on your specialty. To illustrate, let's assume you're in sales:
Question: "Tell me your view on Sales - what role does Sales have in this company?"

Now….sit back and get ready. The employer is looking across the desk and saying to himself, "Let's see. This guy has a sales background...so I'll tell him Sales is the most important force to drive business...he'll love it." Next thing you know this dude is making your heart race because he is saying all the things you believe in – how your discipline is the driving force behind a successful company. No matter whether you're in sales, marketing, operations, or any discipline, a lot of people will simply tell you what you want to hear.

The way to uncover their true intentions is first to know their background. If this is a finance boss, you can write off anything else. If this is a sales-grown boss, you can forget about true marketing. People always favor their own. If you grew up in a discipline, it is hard to change your biases – you should know and understand your area best. I've never met a salesperson that sees exactly eye-to-eye with Marketing, or vice versa.

The important thing to remember is that you need to be with your own. Don't try and be a rebel or 'the first guy who's gonna give this company a real sales focus.' Take it from me, it's a losing battle. Companies operate the way they do because they *want* to. The last thing you need to be is an outcast in a sea of contrarians. If you're Sales Management, stick with a company that has a strong sales group. If you're Marketing, be sure you're going to a marketing driven company.

Question 6. The Awareness Quotient
As covered in an earlier chapter, AQ is the ability to understand popular culture and how innovation in one industry might transfer to another. The only way to uncover this is to engage the person in a conversation that is about their industry. For example, if it's a fashion company, you might ask, "How is music helping to define the marketing program?" If you heard that Usher was being signed by one of their competitors, ask him or her about what they think? You'll know their AQ by whether or not they know Usher – and how he's positioned in the music world.

From the other side of the desk, I usually ask people a few AQ questions at the end of the interview. One is: "Music is a cornerstone of culture and has a profound effect on tweens and teens. Who do you think is the most influential music group today?" Another is: "Name the Rap group that is the hottest today?" Another is: "What Fashion designers are changing the face of fashion these days?" There is no correct answer, but I ask these to see how their mind works…and how they react to out-of-the-ordinary questions.

Question 7. Get them to peacock a little, and to tell you their biggest triumphs.
Question: "Tell me the things that you think the company has done right, what are you proud of, what do you look back on and say 'that worked!'"

The response will take one of two forms: negative or positive. If negative, the response will be something like "I really don't think we do a lot well…and that's why we need you…" OK, great. But consider that after your honeymoon is over, this person may have the same "just not happy" syndrome with you. Often, a CEO or President simply can't face the fact that they are lousy managers who simply can't get a winning team together – so they constantly want to blame others and are usually "unhappy" with results.

The second type of response is positive. You might hear, "I really think launching Monogamy Pour L'Homme was great for the company. It not only was financially successful, the company really rallied behind it..." So, you don't have to buy it lock, stock, and barrel, but at least this person focused on something positive. Keep your antennae up for the "I" syndrome. If the accomplishments list involves a lot of "I did this" and "I was able to do that," you might have a megalomaniac on your hands. Watch the All-Too-Humble game too. I also think it's overkill when you hear "It wasn't me, but my fantastic, lovely team who I constantly vacation with" kind of response.

Question 8. Understanding the Company Failures
Question: "What didn't work here? What really bombed and what did you do about it?"

I once asked that question to the then-President of Timex Watches and he answered very coyly. It went something like this, "Well...we've had our share of mistakes, but the secret is to plan for the downside. I don't mind mistakes as long as I feel the executive has really thought out the business plan from all angles. I say to my people, I think it's OK to make mistakes because that means you are really trying...but don't make a fatal mistake..."

I didn't need to ask a follow up question. The opening part of the response was solid – he was taking responsibility for the company's mistakes, but then the response graduated from a "We've" or "Our" response to an "I tell my people," and "I think." The shift is indicative of what's in his mind – he makes the motion that he's part of it, but by the end he distances himself from mistakes. The piece de resistance was "Don't make a fatal mistake." Read the subtitle: "You idiots didn't plan for this and therefore the blame, fault, and responsibility is solely on you! I'm saved with the board of directors, because my people failed...not me." Any CEO worth a damn usually blesses any major commitments of capital – and therefore has final and ultimate responsibility. CEOs are paid for their experience and should be able to spot obvious flaws in business plans. Unforeseen flaws or mistakes should be shouldered equally. When any future employer starts distancing himself from problems, stay away from that company.

Question 9. Find the hole
This question is about some inconsistency, or flaw in logic that you may have found during the interview. You *have* to ask. Here's an example, "You said you wanted to expand your audience and attract new viewers, but earlier you said that we pride ourselves on operating on a shoestring budget compared to the other networks. Without a real promotion budget, do you really think you'll be successful in reaching new viewers?"

Probe them on something that they were vague on. Example, "you mentioned that you feel the division's budgets were not optimized, and that I'd have free reign over redirecting funds. If I decided to take all of the promotional funds and convert them to advertising, would that cause a problem in the company or with accounts..." Hit them. Hit them hard. See how they react to you asking an insightful question that challenges them. If they don't like challenge, then get out. If they do, then you have a chance of growing in a vibrant company.

Question 10: The "Human" Touch: Barney Versus Bluebeard
Question: "Tell me a little about you, what kind of interests or hobbies do you have?"

I once interviewed for a position with a real tough-as-nails, type-A, person and asked this very question. In response, he had that Terminator 'I'm gonna kill you now' stare and with a droll, monotone voice said in disgust, "I really don't have time for games." Swear to God. I couldn't think of anything else to say as he glared at me except "... I strongly suggest you start. Thank you, it's been quite a revealing conversation." I got up and left. He just kept glaring. I thought the dude was gonna lunge over the table and kill me. One thousand hours of psychotherapy wouldn't make a dent on that boy. A simple question, particularly a 'human' question, can reveal so much.

Ten Simple Questions for your prospective company can save you from that one-way Kamikaze ride into the ground. Remember that you're probably wanting it *to work sooo badly* (which is why you are interviewing in the first place) – and this new-job-lust is distorting what you ask and what you hear. You must, underscore *must,* be direct and take the 'God-I-need-this-job" ear muffs off. The dance however, usually starts with what *they ask you*. The next section is a short primer on the mating dance questions you're likely to get.

Behind the Lines (what they ask you and what they *don't* ask you):
In almost every interview, the person across the desk begins by asking you questions. Note that we started with the questions you should ask first since *your* questions are more important than *their* questions. But 9 times out of 10, they'll go first and start jackhammering your brain with questions. The fun part is that their questions will tell you if they are serious about you and if you will be ultimately happy at that company.

Over the years, I've jotted a few down from the typical to the atypical:
- Tell me your strengths...and your weaknesses? (such a typical question, but be honest and real.)
- Let's talk positioning. How would you say Cadillac is positioned vis-à-vis BMW?
- What is the one thing that you are really proud of in your career?
- How did you lead a team to a successful completion of a task?
- We need someone who is very organized. Tell me how you have taken chaos and organized it?
- The company that you work for is considered parochial, how do you think you've overcome or worked around this?
- What makes you think you can make it here?
- Why do you think your experience would be a good fit here?
- How many people work for you now?
- Do you have any problem firing people? How many have you let go?
- Tell me about your ability to think strategically?
- What kind of P&L experience do you have?
- Name the last three books you have read?
- The team may feel demoted with you in the position. What will you do to compensate for that?
- Tell me about your career.... briefly.
- Give me an example of how you proved your leadership skills with a team?
- What's the smartest thing you've ever done?

All of these are real questions – some were for junior positions, some for very senior. But all are geared to put you on the spot, all saying 'prove to me you are worth it.' Half the battle is maintaining composure and showing grace under fire. This is particularly true in the case of stress interviews where the future employer believes that putting a person under attack is the real way to test the metal. It is an effective approach, but one that belies a much deeper pathology and a company fraught with problems. Keep composed. Remember that 'non-verbal' communication (or body language) is 80% of what people hear. Your words only account for 20% of what you communicate.

The best way to answer any question is to simply to be you. We all have a 'formal voice' and that's fine, but don't masquerade. If your style is a little looser, be that way. If you disguise it, you'll only put yourself at risk later as your bosses say you've adopted a laissez-faire attitude. Better to say outright in an interview "you should know I have a dry sense of humor and believe in laughter – I hope you share the same." Most interviewers won't disagree, and at least you've laid the pipe that you have more than a one-dimensional personality.

In most cases, what they *don't* ask you is as important as what they do. Psychologically, people tend to avoid areas they are uncomfortable with and therefore, you'll find they don't ask some obvious questions. For instance, when was the last time you heard "Tell me about the relationship you have with your present boss?" Most people don't want to know because they have a fair number of unpleasant relationships in their own organizations. How about, "Tell me about a personal hardship...how did it affect your work and how did it affect you?" We would be stunned, stunned I say, to hear this type of question because most people go out of their way to avoid these types of topics. It's not easy to walk out of an interview and say "Now what the Hell did this guy *not* ask me?" but you have to do it. The best approach is to start with the Human angle...did they ask any questions about me as an individual?

Ahh.... the magic questions! If the look of the place didn't give you a real clue, and if your research didn't turn up criminal activities, then you'll get the real story in the 10 magic questions. Actually, you can pull the "Optional 11th" by calling back one of the people you interviewed with and asking them a follow up question. This is usually a good idea because it tells you whether or not they will make time for you, or whether they act the same or are 'bothered.' The other great part about questions is the questions themselves. It's probably a good idea to jot them down somewhere – you never know when you're going to have to prepare answers in your head the next time you interview. It's also helpful when you're hiring people. Someone once asked me the "last three books you've read" question and I've posed it to every person that I've interviewed since. The responses are truly fascinating and give you an unobstructed view into the person's head.

So, in closing this chapter, how do you know if your next job really blows? The answer is that you need to calibrate your brain to think that it *might blow*, and *they* have to be able to prove to you that it doesn't. Any other mindset like "wow this unemployment thing is really getting old," or "I've just had it with my current job and I simply will take *anything*," or "clearly EVP titles at companies of this stature don't come along everyday" are all losing propositions. Recalibrate your thinking to have a "Missouri" attitude: *show me*. Adopting this mindset will clearly give you several advantages, the least of which is perceived confidence. Remember the dating game...the men and women who appear as though they don't need a date, and are incredibly confident, usually have a good-looking date on their arm.

Keep your antennae up throughout the process – your gut instincts are probably correct. Push the people in your prospective new company harder than you're comfortable with to make sure you know the real deal. And never forget that you're about to spend *more time in that company and with those people than you do with all your friends and family combined.* One of the greatest tips for success in business is this: Trust your intuitive powers, and you'll be able to close your eyes in a moment of silence and clearly see if that next move will be the right Life Move for you.

THE BIOGENESIS OCTAGON

Every self-respecting executive needs a theory. In fact, if you're really hot, you'll get a "law" named after you. Like "Moore's Law" – Gordon Moore was the Intel executive who stated that computing power doubles every 18 months. Turned out he was right and he's now a certified Techno-God of the Silicon Age. Having a law is good. You become famous. You get better tables at restaurants. You have endless hours of cocktail conversation about your 'discovery.' And just think of all the Marketing Association groupies that will come to your speaking engagements once you start playing the circuit.

Using your brain to try to advance the art and science of management is something that you are charged with when you don the robe of business. My strong belief is that this should not be confined to academics or those ex-Harvard profs who have never run businesses let alone Fortune 500 companies. The academic world is fantastic at reporting, analyzing, and coming up with the explanations of business phenomena. Six Sigma used by Jack Welch so effectively at GE was a great example of this. The Hedgehog principle by Jim Collins in *Good to Great* is another. But coming up with real-world laws or principles is a woefully neglected area for *real* business people.

I've always been impressed by modern day principles and systems, but for the most part they tackle the dimension of cause and effect. TQM and Six Sigma are ways to uncouple, analyze, and put back together the causes and resulting effects of business situations. Mostly these deal with the *process* of leadership, or the *process* of creating and marketing goods and services. Few deal with the people side of the equation.

What is so perplexing about the lack of popular principles about the human side of business is that *all* business *walks out the door at 5:00*. If every single person walked out the door at Apple and didn't come back tomorrow, the company would simply stop. How would a remaining Board of Directors hire over 25,000 employees fast enough to keep the place solvent and running? It couldn't. No one could. This leads to my theory…ready?….it's big…I hope! My theory is called: the Biogenesis Octagon.

Outside of sounding like a Robert Ludlum or Michael Crichton novel, the Biogenesis Octagon is simply this: a system of rethinking, retooling, and running business based on human engineering, rather than process, quality, or financial engineering. There is a large field of study in Industrial Relations and the Psychology of Social Systems in business, but these are not widely embraced by the senior management at large corporations. The Biogenesis Octagon seeks to advance this field of study by making it the starting point for corporate endeavors, not just an intersection point. OK, so by now your saying "what the f*&!*"! Yep, this *is* a little side excursion to get you thinking outside your daily routine, outside of the typical box. And I have to admit it: this stuff I'm about to tell you *is just a theory*, just a hunch really – and really is just about the people side of business…with a twist. My purpose is twofold: to stake out the snazzy soon-to-be-a-major-motion-picture theory name of 'Biogenesis Octagon' – which is just too much fun to drop at the aforementioned cocktail parties, but also to get you thinking about your own ideas, *your own theories* that can help you get ahead of the pack in business. So here's a bit more on what the hell this means:

The 'Biogenesis' part of the equation has its foundation in the universal law that says that the only way to define a living organism is not through movement (rivers move, lava moves), but through *growth*. It is *the one* biological factor that defines all living organisms. In business, we focus on 'Strategic Planning,' 'Annual Operating Plans,' and other process, marketing, M&A, or product planning methods to achieve growth targets. The Biogenesis Octagon seeks to dismiss this as mostly (not completely) wasted effort. The reason is that these other areas are *resultant,* not *systemic.* They are the result of something – the result of human beings coming up with them. By this logic, this result (and therefore your entire business) is not co-dependent, but completely dependent on the human machine that came up with those great Strat Plans, Operating Plans, etc. If we consider this fully, the focus on business growth should then shift away from the output of this human machine to the humans that make up the machine itself. Said simply, the Biogenesis part of the principle rests on the chemistry of human interaction as the fundamental driver of all business growth. Companies focus on HR and other Human Asset management – but they have not thought of/embraced this concept, which says that all growth plans should study the chemistry and makeup of the human element of the business unit teams – almost to the exclusion of all else.

One example of this was at Nike, during the time the Equipment Division was in its 3rd year of existence. It was clear to me and Clare Hamill, the brilliant and savvy VP running the Division, that several teams were failing. The Bag and Accessory team was in a shambles. The In-Line Skate business was hemorrhaging money. The Eyewear Category was barely in the black after three years of hard work. Yet my team, the Timing business, was on fire – with triple digit growth and year-after-year of breakthrough, award-winning products. I was asked, 'How are you successful when other businesses aren't?' My response was the beginning of the Biogenesis Octagon principle: "It's not that my business is successful and other businesses are not. The answer is in the human side of the equation. It's not just about skill set, competencies, or people with great business pedigrees…it's mostly *about the chemistry between people.*" In discussing it more, I conceded that a small part of this was just sheer dumb luck that our team simply clicked, but I also took credit for and shared the tools I learned and honed over the years to foster and build great chemistry in teams. If a company is to grow, toss the Strat Plan process and kill all the decks and presentations and focus on the 'Bio' part – the chemistry part – if you want to have 'genesis' or true and sustained growth.

OK, you're dying for the Octagon part right? In short, the Octagon is the multi-dimensional tool that I'm working on that will help drive team chemistry for growth. It is the eight inter-related, inter-laced factors and elements that must come together for chemistry to happen in the organization. If this chemistry is right, that team can conquer any task and achieve any target, almost to the indifference of other variables like R&D resources or marketing support. If my hunch (and future research) is correct, then by following the Octagon, the right team chemistry can be born to create killer success in any endeavor.

This chapter hopefully got you thinking – in your mind you either said 'yes, this makes empirical sense' or you said 'complete BS… my take on it is different…' In either case, you were *thinking beyond your daily routine* and well beyond your strategic planning routine. You were thinking about the 'Big…Really Big' picture. You have just started on the path of creating your own Law. Move beyond your current level (in both position and thinking), and fly to the higher elevations and get a real birds eye view of business. From there, you'll start thinking about the human power and team chemistry that drives every last success or failure – and then the real fun begins. So every once in a while, when you're trapped in the daily grind of business, think of the Biogenesis Octagon and let your mind rip. Come up with something new and write it down. I'll be the first in line to spread the word on your new Law.

LEADERSHIP PRINCIPLES (WITHOUT THE SNAZZY LINGO)

One thing about Business is that you get to go to a lot of leadership training courses. You know the ones where 'Tammy,' who is a surprise Ph.D. in Covalent Molecular Bonding, gets everyone to enact a human Rubik's Cube somewhere in the woods. Or where some retired ex-Green Beret Officer, who had the realization that killing people was really synonymous with leadership in business, tells you that that the Johari window is *'your freakin' window'* and that you have to jump through the broken glass in order to survive in the corporate world.

Come on now. Really?

Having studied a fair amount of Leadership philosophies, I can safely say that most "Leadership" writers don't know their ear from their elbow. This is for one simple reason: They never worked in a *real* business. It's easy being a critic; it's tough being the one on the front lines living it. Having lived it – and still living it – I think the principles of leadership are very straightforward and have stayed the same pretty much since the dawn of business itself. The difficult part is in the implementation. It's easy to say things, harder to live them. Here are the top seven in my own book:

1. Leadership Is Behavior
2. Leadership Is Power
3. Leadership Is Money
4. Leadership Is Tough
5. Leadership Is Vision
6. Leadership Is Compassion
7. True Leadership Is Separation and Ascension

Leadership Is Behavior:
The first principle is that leadership isn't a principle, it is a behavior. The elements of true leadership are learned. The great orators in companies, the

great minds, all have quirks and foibles that would seriously undermine them if they showed them to you. But they don't. They learned that to be effective they had to watch what they said. It's an interesting expression, since we don't normally 'watch' speech – but the real crux is that you should be able to think about what you are about to say and 'see' its potential impact on your audience. Great minds, great leaders do this. It's also interesting that the greatest leaders of humankind have been known not by their extemporaneous talks, but by their speeches – carefully meted out words that left no room for distracting thoughts.

Watching and carefully thinking about communication is only one aspect of leadership behavior. A second might be relationship building. If your behavior is very much introverted and you are a recluse, you'll have to change that behavior in order to succeed. One leadership program purported that 'it's *all* about relationships,' and that probably wasn't far from the truth. If you are a cynic or a misanthrope, you will have to modify your behavior (and most likely your beliefs) to be able to find ways to motivate and inspire.

Behavior seems like an easy one to change, but it isn't. "Shhhure" you say, "I can work on being better at relationship building instantly." But it's not so fast. Humans are nothing more than a bundle of nerves and synapses that operate in a similar way. The conditioning in our lives usually leads to behaviors that are like reflexes – we do them over and over again if the stimulus is the same. It's hard to break a reflex or a habit, but it can be done. It just takes time and perseverance.

Leadership Is Power:

It's clear that you need to have a power base in order to claim that you are a leader – or at least have one before you are in a true 'leadership' position. Power doesn't just mean down the ladder – owning a lot of people or turf; it means up the ladder – having the reins and the authority granted or won from senior leaders in the company. There are two ways to gain power: you take it or you win it. You never just 'get' it. And if you're hired in, you've essentially 'won' it, but you must be careful that it truly is there when you show up on day one. One key to effective leadership in business is knowing where the upper power base is and playing to it. Usually there are several factions – competing with each other – for control. Being able to read the shifts in power is essential to survival, and to having the power base to truly lead.

Leadership Is Money:

One of the key elements of leadership is that you are able to marshal resources. You have to have the money, sugar. If you don't, you're just another person with a plan – and no means to get it done. OK, you're thinking "yes, but Ghandi didn't have a big bankroll." OK, fine. Jesus Christ was in the same camp. In the more earthly bounds of business, having command of resources is power itself. Get the money. Get the resources. Or go…well…the cubicles are *that way*.

Leadership Is Tough:

It's ugly. It's brutal. It's heartless, and cold, and relentless. True leaders know that leadership sometimes requires these things of you. Not all the time. And you don't have to become a little Hitler or a Kim Jung Il of business…but you'll need to be the tough guy if you want to lead. What does this really mean? You'll have to fire your friend for underperforming – knowing that you'll never have the same friendship. You'll have to fire a 50-year-old man after 20 years of service, knowing he may never find another meaningful job. You'll have to lay off thousands of plant workers – upsetting countless lives. You'll have to choose between two good ideas…and two good people. You'll have to tell people there are no bonuses, or that there will be pay cuts, when they've been slaving away. Why? Dramatic Pause….because *someone has to be the heavy*. Someone has to make the tough decisions. No normal person likes to do it, but someone *has to* in order for the corporation (and the remaining jobs) to survive. That someone is you – if you're a leader. Having been the heavy – and probably not a good one – my only advice is that you do it with compassion. Do the tough acts in a way that are at least civil, humane, dignified, and respectful. Fight for the best package for your people, the best conditions, and for the basics that will make the tough act easier to swallow. And when conditions improve, fight for the increases and improvements for your team. Do that and balance out the uglies with the beauties. Balance being tough with being benevolent. Above all, have heart.

Leadership Is Vision:

Corporate Vision is simply this: *what you see*. If you can paint a picture of what you 'see' for the team, division, or company, you have shared a vision. It's as simple as that. And for God's sakes please erase from your vocabulary "best in class," "world class," "undisputed quality leaders," and "uncompromised blah blah blah." The world has heard it before and even though it may be true, no one can really figure out what to do with the words. So be bold. Be direct. Paint a picture of the place we want to live. Do it at every level in the company and watch the power grow from within. Lead with Vision.

Leadership Is Compassion:

I must admit that I've often been amused by the CEOs of monster-sized companies that talk the 'corporate giving' game – the "we care with our hearts" rhetoric that accompanies a gift tithing form. Yet they will lay off 5,000 workers, slash budgets, and then personally go on to pocket $15 million from the 'options' they received in that 'tough' year. It's incredible. And it's completely without compassion for people.

As a leader, I expect you to be compassionate to your workforce. These are the people who slave everyday for you. These are the people who will make or break you, who pay you your bonus, who ensure the 'pay' in your paid vacation keeps coming. Make sure you are treating them well. It is disgusting that in the Fortune 500, only a few dozen are ever picked as "the best companies to work for." It is a wonder that to this very day most companies don't offer daycare to their employees. Conversely, it warms my heart when Nike builds a second state-of-the-art gym with an Olympic size swimming pool. They could have opted not to and pocketed the money and given bigger bonuses – but quality of life for the employees is extremely important to them. One more time: Work hard to be a compassionate leader.

Leadership Is Separation And Ascension:

As you grow in an organization, as you lead bigger and bigger teams, you'll need to separate yourself *from yourself* and ascend to a higher plane. I promised no 'snazzy lingo,' so I'll keep this very straightforward. True leaders have the ability to keep their personal lives separate from their business lives – and from the leadership in their business lives. Further, real leaders are able to separate themselves from their own personal needs/wants/problems, and rise above them in their leadership. This 'ascension' is a critical trait of true leadership. We see this in American Presidents quite often. We have people who lead and then we have true leaders, like Abraham Lincoln, Franklin Delano Roosevelt, or Harry Truman. Unlike other Presidents, Lincoln, Roosevelt, and Truman rose above their normal lives when they took to the podium. They had conviction, depth, toughness, brilliance, and compassion – but derived from country not from their own self-consciousness. It's rare to see this in business. Phil Knight is one of the few in my nearly quarter of a century in business that I've witnessed who ascended to a true leadership position – above his personal sense of 'self.' It's a rare and unique thing to witness and we need more of it in our world.

To be successful in business you need to know that leadership all starts with a learned behavior – and ends with ascension into something that's much bigger, much more profound than us.

YOUR LIFE

As I write this final chapter, I'm flying to London on what is probably my 150th redeye flight. And for a moment I take pause from the computer and papers and gaze out the window at a brilliant-white full moon. Just past Bangor and St. Johns in the middle of a crystalline clear black night, the moon casts a sweeping beacon of light, illuminating the endless cascading waves moving east.

Right about now my son Tucker would say, "So....like... exactly what does that have to do with anything?" A good question, but I *did* actually take the time to look out the window and see a view of the moon over the water that I've never seen – after flying that same route too many times. This brings me to the last thought for you and for my children to whom I dedicated this book: When you're building your business career and going crazy trying to create a good life for yourself and your family...don't forget about a little thing called *Your Life.*

If you're like most trying to make it in any business, you know the amount of pain, sacrifice, and relentless compromising that takes place. If you think the Chairman in the corner office who is pulling down several million a year got there by lounging and lunching, well guess again. Most CEOs that I've met give 1,000% to their jobs. Bob and Larry Tisch of Loews worked 6 days a week (7 when they were starting out in the hotel business). Michael Eisner of Disney regularly had two dinners a night during the workweek – one at 6:00 and one at 9:00 – all to make time to meet, greet, and work deals with the Hollywood power players. No one who wants the brass ring is immune. If you heard of Conrad Hilton (founder of Hilton Hotels) telling his team, 'get the hell out of the office by 5:00 or I'll dock you,' then you have heard of the very rare exception. Most slave away for the big slots. Most compromise time with their daughters and sons; most give up those great, intimate discovery years with their spouses; most simply lose out on the wonderful, endearing, precious moments that happen with family and friends.

Why do they do this? Why would anyone sacrifice this? I know it's hard to understand, but deep inside, the motivation is really about two things. First, it's about the outward success and the security of money. Eisner is worth $750+ million. The Tisch family are billionaires. Philip Knight is over $12 billion. Most CEOs are multimillionaires through comp and stock packages. If you can get to the top slot at almost any mid to large company, you'll pull down a *minimum* of $500,000 per year, with a 20% bonus and probably 200,000 shares of stock options *each year*. And over time, if that stock moves $10, you just made $2 million. If it moves $30, you just made $6 million. Math got you going? Think about it. In 5 years at 200,000 shares a year (or 1,000,000 shares) you just made $10 million or $30 million at the same per-share price increases. We're talking Cristal Champagne flowing out of gold spigots and…you guessed it…your own private jet! Seriously though, that kind of loot is a lot of security and future protection for your family. That's the first reason people do this.

The second reason is more complex: It's usually because there is some driving desire either to have security, or some inner desire to have power over people or things. And after a while, if you get to SVP or EVP in a good company, the life gets a bit seductive and you see that glimmer of hope that *you can* achieve the top slot and really have security and power over people and things. The motivation may be a deep-seated psychological one or it may be the impact a person can have on the world in a positive way as a CEO of a company. But enough psychoanalysis. No matter why or how, the rewards are enough and the influence to do good works are high enough that the pursuit of making it big in a company makes it worth it for many. And then there are the perks – great meals at first class restaurants, the private jets, travel to cool places, the private jets – sorry, did I say that again? Real mental complex. I'm seeing someone for it – won't happen again. Remember, though…success comes with a price.

No matter what you choose to do, it is critical to not forgo, abandon, or postpone *Your Life*. It's easy to miss your son's first school play, or not be there for his birthday – hell, *they aren't going to change the sales meeting just for you, are they?* Sometimes we make sacrifices, but one thing I've learned the hard way is that you are not rewarded in life or in business by putting Your Life on the back burner. In fact, it's just the opposite, and very counter-intuitive. If you miss the meeting, or miss that essential off-site, you may lose ground...... correction...you *will* lose ground. But you'll gain something much more – you'll have the love, admiration, and respect of your family and friends for whom you sacrificed that meeting or off-site. You'll never hear your three-year-old baby daughter say, "No, Dad, I think for the security needs of this family you need to blow off my birthday and make the off-site. So stop moaning you damn sissy and get on that plane!" Yes, sometimes warriors need to be out on the hunt even during important family times, but *most* of the time, it is more important to be with your family or friends. You need it to survive. You need them to be strong and to be your foundation. You cannot compromise this.

And when you vote for Your Life and put Your Life first, then you have a much more intangible gain: You'll have this subterranean, unspoken respect from your whole company that your *Life Values* are in order. You may lose ground by not being at that essential meeting, but you'll actually gain points from the CEO on down by voting for Your Life first. And when you bounce back into work all positive and full of ideas that you picked up on the way to that school play, you'll outpace the Politicos in the pack and get ahead. See? Counterintuitive, but it works.

And now for the *BIG SECRET*. The secret in life, in relationships, and in business boils down *to one word*. Yes, you could have skipped this entire book and just read this one word and you'd have gained the Holy Grail of business wisdom, the Ark of Success in business.

The one word is this: *CONFIDENCE.*

Having confidence is the one attribute, the single most important attribute that acts as the Grand Filter. It filters out the weaker, entry level people; separates the middle managers from those that will go on; and is the biggest filter for selection of a CEO. Having Confidence in life is *everything*. If you feel 'light' on confidence, then I'd suggest that you get your act together and do those things in life that make you feel confident. Whether it's running five miles a day, dressing well, or getting a Ph.D., do those things that make you feel that you're smarter and better than the average bear.

Watch people. Watch how people gravitate to those people who are confident about themselves. Then check your own body language – and ask if you are projecting an image of total confidence. Trust me when I tell you it's not brains, it's not degrees, it's not athletic ability or schmoozability that gets people to the top of the pack. It's confidence. Plain and simple. So have belief in yourself and know that everyone is human. Every day, everyone puts shoes on the same way. Be confident in your God given abilities and watch success blossom.

In the end, Your Life boils down to a short line on a piece of rock called your tombstone. There are not many guarantees in life, but one we are certain of is that you will die. Yep. No getting around it. Dust, baby. Worm food. Dirt Nap. Curtains. The question is what do you want on that piece of rock? I've never read "Tell Mabel to cancel my meetings. Tell them I died" on a tombstone. I never read, "To my loving business colleagues, I already miss you." Nope. Your Life is more than business. If you miss that lesson you'll end up like Jack Welch, former CEO of General Electric, who obviously had a less 'anchored' life after he retired and got caught in a $500 million divorce. Say it slow. *Five-Hundred-Million.* Ouch Jack! And for such a savvy guy to actually sign a Pre-Nuptial agreement that had an *expiration* clause! *Double Ouch, baby!*

Your Life is what's really important here. All the success in business, all the chattels and bounty that you can accumulate, all the accolades are meaningless in the grand scheme of things. The real deal in life is to make a difference, and to look back and say, 'Wow, I'm proud of that.' For you, that might be running a Fortune 500 or perhaps some small company where you can look back and see how you helped people along the way and added some great invention or product to the world. But don't be bummed if you find yourself making choices that keep you from the 'Big Chair' – your reward is in the joys in life that you find and the positive energy and light that you radiate.

Above all, cherish the challenge, avoid the Career Kamikazes, savor the small victories, and celebrate the joys in life and in business early and often. No matter how much of a Top Gun Pilot you become in business, ultimate success is yours when you learn to really love those little precious moments with friends and family in this never predictable, always fascinating, incredible journey called Your Life.

May the flight of your life be inspiring, soaring, and full of wonderful times ahead.

Philip A. Shaw

ABOUT THE AUTHOR

Philip Shaw has served in entrepreneurial ventures and in Fortune 500 companies for over 25 years. He earned his stripes in top flight companies like Grey Advertising, J.Walter Thompson, McCann-Erickson, Loews Corporation, Nike, and The Walt Disney Company. A native of Ohio, Philip has lived for many years in New York City, Portland Oregon, and now resides in Los Angeles, California.